T0305197

Nonlinear Modelling of High Frequency Financial Time Series

WILEY

SERIES IN FINANCIAL ECONOMICS
AND QUANTITATIVE ANALYSIS

Series Editor: Stephen Hall, *London Business School, UK*

Editorial Board: Robert F. Engle, *University of California, USA*
John Flemming, *European Bank, UK*
Lawrence R. Klein, *University of Pennsylvania, USA*
Helmut Lütkepohl, *Humboldt University, Germany*

Further titles in preparation
Proposals will be welcomed by the Series Editor

Nonlinear Modelling of High Frequency Financial Time Series

Edited by

Christian Dunis
and
Bin Zhou

JOHN WILEY & SONS
Chichester • New York • Weinheim • Brisbane • Singapore • Toronto

Other Wiley Editorial Offices

John Wiley & Sons, Inc., 605 Third Avenue,
New York, NY 10158-0012, USA

WILEY-VCH Verlag GmbH, Pappelallee 3,
D-69469 Weinheim, Germany

Jacaranda Wiley Ltd, 33 Park Road, Milton,
Queensland 4064, Australia

John Wiley & Sons (Asia) Pte Ltd, 2 Clementi Loop #02-01,
Jin Xing Distripark, Singapore 129809

John Wiley & Sons (Canada) Ltd, 22 Worcester Road,
Rexdale, Ontario M9W 1L1, Canada

Library of Congress Cataloging-in-Publication Data

Non-linear modelling of high frequency financial time-series/edited
by Christian Dunis.
    p. cm. — (Series in financial economics and quantitative
analysis)
    Includes bibliographical references and index.
    ISBN 0-471-97464-1 (cloth : alk. paper)
    1. Finance — Econometric models. 2. Time-series analysis.
I. Dunis, Christian. II. Series.
HG173.N66 1998
332'.01'5195 — dc21   97–44713
                                             CIP

British Library Cataloguing in Publication Data

A catalogue record for this book is available from the British Library

ISBN 0-471-97464-1

Typeset in 10/12pt Times by Laser Words, Madras, India
Printed and bound by Antony Rowe Ltd, Eastbourne

This book is printed on acid-free paper responsibly manufactured from sustainable forestation,
for which at least two trees are planted for each one used

Contents

List of Contributors

HERVÉ ALEXANDRE
(CREGO-LATEC) Université de Bourgogne, France.

F.M. APARICIO ACOSTA
Universidad Carlos III de Madrid, Spain.

PETER J. BOLLAND
London Business School, England.

JEROME T. CONNOR
London Business School, England.

ROBERTO DACCO'
University of Cambridge, England.

MICHEL M. DACOROGNA
Olsen & Associates, Zurich, Switzerland.

JÉRÔME DRUNAT
IREFI, University of Paris XII, France.

GILLES DUFRÉNOT
ERUDITE, University of Paris XII, France.

CHRISTIAN L. DUNIS
Banque Nationale de Paris, London.

MICHAEL GAVRIDIS
Banque Nationale de Paris, London.

ERIC GHYSELS
Penn State University, USA.

ISABELLE GIRERD-POTIN
(CERAG) Université de Grenoble II, France.

CHRISTIAN GOURIÉROUX
CREST-INSEE.

DOMINIQUE GUÉGAN
ENSAE, Paris, France.

ANDREW HARRIS
Chase Manhattan Bank, London.

JOANNA JASIAK
University of York, England.

SWEE LEONG
Chase Manhattan Bank, London.

LAURENT MATHIEU
MODEM, University of Paris X, France.

LUDOVIC MERCIER
ENSAE, Paris, France.

JOHN MOODY
Non-linear Prediction Systems, Portland, USA.

ULRICH A. MÜLLER
Olsen & Associates, Zurich, Switzerland.

POOMJAI NACASKUL
Imperial College, London.

RICHARD B. OLSEN
Olsen & Associates, Zurich, Switzerland.

OLIVIER V. PICTET
Olsen & Associates, Zurich, Switzerland.

APOSTOLOS-PAUL REFENES
London Business School, England.

STEPHEN SATCHELL
University of Cambridge, England.

OLLIVIER TARAMASCO
(CERAG) Université de Grenoble II, France.

LIZHONG WU
Non-linear Prediction Systems, Portland, USA.

BIN ZHOU
BH Technology Inc, Cambridge, USA

About the Contributors

HERVÉ ALEXANDRE

Hervé Alexandre is currently Professor of Finance at the University of Besançon. He gained a DEA (Graduate Studies) in Econometrics in 1990 and a DEA in Finance in 1992, then his Ph.D. in Finance at the University of Bourgogne in 1994. He is a member of CREGO-LATEC, a University of Bourgogne research centre associated with CNRS, and CUREGE (University of Besançon). He has been published in congress proceedings and in French academic and professional journals (on topics such as market efficiency, nonlinearities, high frequency data, chaos), including *Finance, Journal de la Société Statistique de Paris, Bulletin de l'Institut des Actuaires Français*.

FELIPE M. APARICIO ACOSTA

In 1987 Felipe M. Aparicio Acosta received the M.Sc. degree in electrical engineering from the Escuela Técnica Superior de Ingenieros de Telecommunicación (ETSIT) at Madrid Polytechnic University (UPM), and the 'Mastère en traitement du signal' at the Ecole Nationale Supérieure des Télécommunications (ENST) in Paris. In May 1995 he obtained a Ph.D. degree from the Signal Processing Laboratory of EPFL (Switzerland). His major interests are in the field of time series analysis and signal modelling.

PETER J. BOLLAND

Peter Bolland is currently a Ph.D. student in the Decision Technology Centre at London Business School. The focus of his thesis is the development of robust non-parametric estimation procedures and their application to financial data.

For the last three years Peter has been an active member of the Computational Finance Programme. He is currently working in collaboration with several financial institutions on the development of a high-speed arbitrage identification system. His research interests include analysis of high frequency financial data, volatility modelling and risk analysis.

JEROME T. CONNOR

For the last two years Jerome has been a research fellow with the Decision Technology Centre at the London Business School modelling financial time series. His research has concentrated on modelling high frequency financial data in the foreign exchange and fixed income markets. Current research interests include modelling risk and factor sensitivity estimation.

Jerome Connor received his Ph.D. from the University of Washington in 1993. His Ph.D. was on the robust nonlinear estimation of noisy time series. Upon completion of the Ph.D., he spent two years as a postdoctorate with Bell Communications Research modelling telecommunications demand and fraud patterns.

ROBERTO DACCO'

Roberto Dacco' holds an M.Sc. in finance and a Ph.D. in economics from Birkbeck College, University of London. He is currently working in the research department of a major investment bank. Previously he was Assistant Professor of Finance at the Graduate Faculty of the New School for Social Research in New York. He has also been research associate in the Department of Applied Economics, University of Cambridge and visiting scholar at the Economic Department of the University of California at San Diego.

MICHEL M. DACOROGNA

Michel M. Dacorogna is one of the founding members of Olsen & Associates (O&A), a research institute in applied economics. He has devoted the past few years to an extensive research and development project involving a real-time, value-added information system in the field of applied economics. His main research interest is the application of computer science and numerical analysis to dynamic systems in various fields in order to gain insight into the behaviour of such systems. In addition to his research duties at O&A, Dr Dacorogna has assumed a leadership role in organizing the first international conference on high frequency data in finance. Dacorogna received his Ph.D. and M.Sc. in physics from the University of Geneva. Prior to joining O&A, he was a postdoctorate in the solid state theory group of the University of California at Berkeley.

JÉRÔME DRUNAT

Jérôme Drunat is a senior researcher with the IREFI Research Group of Paris XII University. He is currently working on the effects of nonlinear dynamics in the

field of finance. Recently published papers discuss applications of ARCH family models to a variety of high frequency data.

GILLES DUFRÉNOT

Gilles Dufrénot is assistant professor at the University of Paris XII, where he received his Ph.D. in economics. His research encompasses nonlinear econometrics and chaotic dynamics applied to macroeconomics and finance. Recently published papers examine the application of bispectral analysis to macroeconomic time series.

CHRISTIAN L. DUNIS

Christian L. Dunis is Executive Vice President, Head of Global Markets Research at Banque Nationale de Paris. BNP's Global Markets Research Group covers foreign exchange and fixed income strategies, quantitative market research and quantitative trading. Its key objective is, on top of the support provided to traders, to be instrumental in the marketing of BNP's trading capabilities. Its 23-strong research staff is spread between London, Paris and Singapore.

Christian L. Dunis was previously Head of Quantitative Research and Trading with Chase Manhattan in London until 1996, having joined Chemical Bank in 1985 and co-headed its Economic and Market Research Group since 1987.

He holds a Diploma in Higher Studies in Economics and International Finance and a Ph.D. in Economics from the University of Paris. He is a member of the Securities and Futures Authority in London, of the French Association of Corporate Treasurers (AFTE) in Paris and of the International Institute of Forecasters (USA).

He is the organiser, with Imperial College, of an Annual International Conference held in London on 'Forecasting Financial Markets: Advances for Exchange Rates, Interest Rates and Asset Management'.

He is a member of the editorial board of *The European Journal of Finance*. He is also the co-author of *Exchange Rate Forecasting* published by Probus Publishing in 1989 and the editor and co-author of *Forecasting Financial Markets* published by John Wiley & Sons in 1996.

MICHAEL GAVRIDIS

Michael Gavridis joined the Global Market Research of the Banque Nationale de Paris from Chase Manhattan Bank in 1996 as a senior quantitative analyst. He is responsible for the evaluation and application of new modelling techniques to the forecasting of financial time series ranging from traditional fundamental economic models to more advanced time series econometric modelling. He is the co-editor of BNP's *Working Papers in Financial Economics*, a quarterly publication in applied quantitative research. He holds a Ph.D. in financial economics from Brunel University and an M.Sc. in project analysis, finance and investment from the University of York.

ERIC GHYSELS

Eric Ghysels is Professor of Economics at the Pennsylvania State University. He was awarded his Ph.D. from Northwestern University in 1984, the thesis was entitled 'Managerial Economics and Decision Science'.

ISABELLE GIRERD-POTIN

Isabelle Girerd-Potin is Associate Professor of Finance, ESA, at the University of Grenoble 2, appointed in 1994. She has a Ph.D. in Finance from the same University, and is a graduate of ENS Cachan. She is a member of CERAG, a University of Grenoble 2 research centre in business administration associated with CNRS. She has been published in congress proceedings and in French academic and professional journals (on topics such as market efficiency, stock market anomalies and chaos) including *Analyse financière, Finance, Journal de la Société Statistique de Paris* and *Revue économique*.

CHRISTIAN GOURIÉROUX

Christian Gouriéroux is Professor of Econometrics and Head of the Finance and Insurance Laboratory at CREST-INSEE. He has published widely in international journals in econometrics, statistics and finance. He has been the winner of the Koopmans prize for the best paper in the *Journal of Econometrics Theory* and has received the gold medal of the Société Statistique de Paris.

DOMINIQUE GUÉGAN

Dominique Guégan obtained his Ph.D. in mathematics in 1977. She is now Professor of Statistics in ENSAE (Ecole Nationale de l'Administration et des Etudes Economiques), Paris, Associate Professor at the University of Paris XIII and a member of CNRS Laboratory UA 742.

ANDREW HARRIS

Andrew Harris, Vice President, is a quantitative analyst in the Quantitative Research and Trading (QRT) Group, Chase Manhattan Bank, London. He holds an MA in operational research from Lancaster and a Ph.D. in pure mathematics from Cambridge. He joined Chemical Bank (now Chase) in 1993 and has been responsible for the software development and implementation of the trading models (on UNIX and PCs) used by QRT. He previously worked for Hill Samuel Investment Management and the London School of Economics.

JOANNA JASIAK

Joanna Jasiak obtained her Ph.D. in Econometrics from the University of Montreal. She is currently affiliated to the University of York, where she is working in the Department of Economics. In 1996 Joanna was awarded the 'Intra-Day Market Activity' award for the best research project on the French stock market, SBF–Bourse de Paris.

SWEE LEONG

Swee Leong, Vice President, is a quantitative analyst in the Quantitative Research and Trading (QRT) Group, Chase Manhattan Bank, London. He holds a B.Sc. in applied mathematics and a Ph.D. in aeronautical engineering, both from the University of London. He is responsible for the detailed specifications of the trading models used by QRT. Dr Leong joined Chemical Bank (now Chase) in 1993. He has extensive experience of quantitative models, having previously worked in similar positions in the City.

LAURENT MATHIEU

Laurent Mathieu is assistant professor at the University of Paris-St Quentin en Yveline. He has written several articles on parametric models for nonlinear times series. His current work centres around the construction of chaotic and nonlinear stochastic models for financial time series.

LUDOVIC MERCIER

Ludovic Mercier is a former student of ENSAE (Ecole Nationale de la Statistique et de l'Administration Economique) and is now Ph.D. student at the CREST statistics laboratory (Malakoff, France) with D. Guégan as adviser. His research focuses on the statistical and algorithmic problems involved in chaotic time series forecasting. He is addressing the problem of choosing a non-parametric method for prediction suited to highly nonlinear time series such as those generated by chaotic dynamical systems. He is working on applications of these methods to simulated as well as real time series, especially in high frequency financial data.

JOHN MOODY

John E. Moody is a Professor of Computer Science and Engineering at the Oregon Graduate Institute of Science and Technology (OGI) and is the Director of OGI's Computational Finance Program. He is also the Founder and President of Nonlinear Prediction Systems located in Beaverton, Oregon.

Dr. Moody's principal areas of research are in computational finance, machine learning, pattern recognition, neural networks, nonparametric statistics, and time series analysis and prediction. He has authored over 50 scientific papers. Dr. Moody has chaired the prestigious Neural Information Processing Systems conference and has served as a member of the organizing committees of the Computational Finance conferences (London Business School and Caltech) and Forecasting Financial Markets (London).

ULRICH A. MÜLLER

Throughout his studies and professional career, Ulrich Müller has worked in Zurich while changing fields several times. He did his undergraduate studies in solid-state physics, became a teaching assistant at the ETH (Swiss Federal Institute of Technology), and wrote his Ph.D. thesis on thermoacoustic oscillations which won the Georg A. Ischer prize. He did quantitative risk analyses at an engineering company and became self-employed.

In 1985, he was a founding member of Olsen & Associates (O&A). Quantitative finance was the new field to which he applied his skills in mathematics and programming. He is (co-)author of most of O&A's scientific publications, among them the recent paper on the HARCH model which describes prices as generated by many market actors with different time horizons. He has given invited talks at conferences and in academic institutions.

POOMJAI NACASKUL

Poomjai Nacaskul took a BA degree with dual majors in Physics and Economics at Western Reserve College, Case Western Reserve University, Cleveland and then an MS in Management Science at the Weatherhead School of Management at the same University. From 1993 he has been a Ph.D. research student at the Imperial College of Science, Technology and Medicine at the University of London, and from 1995 has been a quantitative analyst at the Quantitative Research and Trading Group (QRT), Chase Manhattan Bank, London.

RICHARD B. OLSEN

After completing his studies at the University of Zurich (law) and Oxford (economics), Dr Olsen worked for two years at a private bank in Zurich, initially as legal counsel, then as a financial analyst, and finally as a foreign exchange dealer. During the course of his studies, Dr Olsen had developed a number of theories on financial markets, theories which he then saw supported by the behaviour of foreign exchange practitioners, who seemed to understand certain elements of those theories intuitively. Thus motivated, he founded Olsen & Associates, a private research institute, in August of 1985. There, Dr Olsen and his staff developed a real-time information system providing decision support to foreign exchange dealers.

OLIVIER V. PICTET

After completing his undergraduate studies in architecture and physics, he got his Ph.D. in solid-state physics from the University of Geneva. In addition, he followed a one-year postdoctoral course in artificial intelligence at the Swiss Federal Institute of Technology in Lausanne. His main research interest is the application of numerical analysis and computer science to solve complex problems in various fields.

He joined Olsen & Associates in 1987 to become one of its research group members. Working on large research and development projects, like the O&A's real-time value-added information system, he gained wide experience in applied economics and high quality software development. During recent years, he has played a leadership role in the implementation of a powerful research environment for developing trading models in finance.

APOSTOLOS-PAUL REFENES

Paul Refenes is Associate Professor of Decision Science and Director of the Neurocomputing and Computational Finance Programme at London Business School. He has held previous appointments at University College, London, University of Athens and the DTI. He is a member of the UK's Technology Foresight panel on financial services.

He is the author of over 90 papers and editor of three books on the subjects of neural computing and computational finance. Current research includes neural network design methodologies, model identification, and estimation procedures and application on tactical asset allocation, factor models for equity investment, dynamic risk management, nonlinear co-integration, exchange risk management, etc.

STEPHEN SATCHELL

Stephen Satchell is a fellow of Trinity College and a lecturer in economics at Cambridge University. He holds Ph.D.s from the London School of Economics and Cambridge University. He is interested in finance and econometrics and has written at least 50 papers in this area. He is also an academic adviser to many leading asset management companies and a frequent speaker at City conferences.

OLLIVIER TARAMASCO

Ollivier Taramasco is Professor of Finance, ESA, the University of Martinique. He gained a DEA in Econometrics in 1988 and in Finance in 1993, and his Ph.D. in Statistics at the University of Grenoble 1. He is a member of CERAG, a University of Grenoble 2 research centre in business administration associated with CNRS. He has been published in congress proceedings and in French academic and professional journals (on topics such as market efficiency, stock market anomalies and chaos), including *Analyse financière, Finance, Journal de la Société Statistique de Paris* and *Revue économique*.

LIZHONG WU

Dr. Wu is a Principal Research Scientist in the Department of Computer Science at Oregon Graduate Institute of Science and Technology and a Senior Consulting Scientist at Nonlinear Prediction Systems in Beaverton, Oregon. His research interests include developing forecasting and trading systems based on techniques from neural networks, nonparametric statistics, time series analysis, and adaptive signal processing. He has done extensive work analyzing the foreign exchange, fixed income, and commodities markets.

Dr. Wu holds a Ph.D. in Information Engineering from the University of Cambridge (1992) and M.Sc. and B.Sc. degrees in Electrical Engineering from South China University of Science and Technology (1986 and 1983). From July 1992 to October 1993, he was a Post-Doctoral Research Associate in the Engineering Department of Cambridge University.

BIN ZHOU

Dr Bin Zhou is the founder and the president of BH Technology, Inc. specializing in real-time financial data analysis. Dr Zhou had a Ph.D. in statistics from the University of California, Berkeley. He was an assistant professor at the Sloan School of Management, Massachusetts Institute of Technology, for six years from 1991. He developed a series of methodologies to analyse ultra-high frequency financial data including de-volatilization, normalization and a real-time trading model for currencies. His recent work has been to develop commercial products such as T-vol^{TM} and MSIP^{TM} (most significant intra-day prices) from his de-volatilization theory.

Series Preface

This series aims to publish books which give authoritative accounts of major new topics in financial economics and general quantitative analysis. The coverage of the series includes both macro and micro economics and its aim is to be of interest to practioners and policy-makers as well as the wider academic community.

The development of new techniques and ideas in econometrics has been rapid in recent years and these developments are now being applied to a wide range of areas and markets. Our hope is that this series will provide a rapid and effective means of communicating these ideas to a wide international audience and that in turn this will contribute to the growth of knowledge, the exchange of scientific information and techniques and the development of cooperation in the field of economics.

Stephen Hall
London Business School, UK and
Imperial College, UK

Preface

Nonlinear Modelling of High Frequency Financial Time Series is an edited book written by leading international researchers and market practitioners presenting the latest developments in modelling high frequency data in finance. By 'high frequency', we mean that the financial time series considered are sampled at a granularity of at least *intraday* observations.

Nonlinear modelling is a rather new topic in finance and so is the interest of financial markets for intraday data. Combining the two is an interesting challenge that should attract interest both from academics and market practitioners around the world.

Over the past few years, the use of advanced technologies for trading, risk and asset management has grown exponentially among financial institutions, at a time when the increasing availability of powerful computers has made it ever easier to collect, store and process higher frequency databanks. For a good review on this evolution see Focardi and Jonas (1997).

In the competitive and risky environment of today's financial markets, daily prices and models based upon such low frequency price series do not provide the level of accuracy required by traders and a growing number of risk managers. Even in the field of asset management, recent evidence shows that, with the arrival in Europe of more aggressive management styles, the constant pressure for performance and the increasing attention to risk, some fund managers have already switched to higher frequency data, with some of the more quantitatively oriented firms already using real-time datafeeds (see the recent study commissioned by Barra International on this particular topic, The Intertek Group, 1997).

Still, the analysis of high frequency data remains a real challenge for financial markets analysts and researchers as such data arrive at irregularly spaced time intervals, so that standard econometric and time series techniques relying on fixed time intervals do not apply. In order to deal with this problem, two competing approaches are generally used: either to arbitrarily choose a given fixed time span (i.e. 5-minute, 10-minute, etc. ...), or to devise some time deformation method (every n-ticks for instance) to derive a homogeneous time series based on some tick time or business time scale.

Moreover, in a multivariate context, taking into account the fact that most financial markets do not move independently of each other, the non-synchronicity of such high frequency data arrival clearly poses major practical problems.

Progress in recent years has not been limited to the related fields of computer technology and databanks. Modelling the markets has also experienced significant changes with the implementation of nonlinear analysis in finance.

Indeed, it seems that there is now a growing consensus, not only among market practitioners but also among academics, that most markets are not perfectly efficient in so far as prices of financial assets do not immediately and fully reflect new information.

The higher volatility of interest rates since the early 1980s has spilled over to all other asset classes, because of the links of all interest rate markets via the exchange rate. Clearly, this move has been reinforced by the liberalisation and the globalisation of world asset markets. This greater instability has increased uncertainty, pushing creditors to ask for higher risk premia, a move that has been reinforced by the irresistible rise in indebtedness.

It is this increased uncertainty which has sparked the development of new hedging tools and has been behind the exponential rise of derivative markets since the late 1980s and early 1990s. Whether these new markets have reduced volatility levels by opening new opportunities for risk diversification or whether they have contributed to the rise in global instability in the financial markets remains an open question, but numerous events in the recent past, such as the Procter & Gamble/Bankers Trust case in February 1994, the fall of Barings in February 1995, the demise of the US subsidiary of Daiwa in October 1995, the large loss from interest rate option mispricing incurred by NatWest Markets in March 1997 and UBS's losses in equity derivatives in January 1998 have all demonstrated the necessity for commercial and industrial companies, financial institutions and their regulators to closely monitor their risk positions.

At the same time when uncertainty was increasing, empirical evidence has emerged during the past decade that pockets of predictability do exist in financial markets. Academics have developed new mathematical and statistical tools to help predict future price moves. Combined with extensive databanks (and also higher frequency databanks) and the greater availability of powerful computers, these new techniques which rely heavily on the analysis of nonlinearities now make it possible to devise systems that can help take and manage risk positions in the different asset markets. They are increasingly used by major trading institutions and fund managers and there is also an increasing interest from some large corporates.

Today's financial markets are characterised by a large number of participants, with a different appetite for risk, a different time horizon, different motivations and reactions to unexpected news. In the circumstances, it would come as a surprise if all these complex interactions were to average out in a linear fashion. Furthermore, the introduction of nonlinearities in the modelling approach should allow one to explain some price moves that seemed previously random, without resorting to stochastic mechanisms.

Not so long ago the assumption that price changes in financial markets were unpredictable was still one of the undiscussed pillars of finance. True, the seminal work of Mandelbrot (1963) gave a first blow to the well-established theory of a Gaussian distribution of financial asset returns and underlined the presence of volatility clusters in these time series.

Some 20 years later, Engle (1982) formalised this latter idea with the auto-regressive conditional heteroskedastic or ARCH model: basically, this model states that the variance of asset returns in any given period directly depends on a constant and the previous period's squared random component of the return. This model was later generalised by Bollerslev (1986) and Taylor (1986) to give the generalised autoregressive conditional heteroskedastic or GARCH model: in this case, the variance of asset returns in any given period directly depends on a constant, the previous period's squared random component of the return *and* the previous period's variance. In other words, financial theory had recognised that the variance of asset returns was indeed predictable, if not the returns themselves which remained independently and identically distributed or i.i.d.

This particular area of research has grown exponentially since the early 1990s, giving rise to ever more refined models. These 'refinements' have mostly addressed two different types of issues: on the one hand, the integration of intraday and intraweek seasonality following Baillie and Bollerslev (1991); on the other hand, a finer analysis of persistence properties in order to discriminate between short- and long-term memory with contributions such as Baillie (1996).

One also had to wait until the 1990s, with its easier accessibility to financial databanks and greater computer power, to have a thorough demonstration of the benefits of technical trading rules and, consequently, of the possibility to forecast not only the variance but also the mean of financial asset returns: among others, let us note the contributions of Dunis and Feeny (1989), Neftçi (1991), Brock *et al.* (1992), Taylor and Allen (1992) and Levich and Thomas (1993).

This latter research area paved the way for papers whose aim was precisely to demonstrate that price changes themselves were predictable when models and time frequencies adequate for financial markets were chosen: among the contributions concentrating on frequencies from intraday down to the week, and without being exhaustive, one can note again Taylor (1986), but also LeBaron (1992), Dacorogna *et al.* (1992, 1993, 1996), Pictet *et al.* (1992), Moody and Wu (1995), Dunis (1996a) and Zhou (1996).

Clearly, there has been a growing recognition that the introduction of non-linearities in the modelling approach could allow one to explain certain price moves that seemed previously random. At the same time that it enabled the testing of new categories of models, and particularly nonlinear models, the access to higher frequency databanks has made it possible to explore the microstructure of financial markets.

The Forecasting Financial Markets Conference organised by the Banque Nationale de Paris and Imperial College each year in London has certainly also contributed to this effort, as well as the Conference on Microstructure of Foreign Exchange Markets held in Perugia in July 1994 and the Conference on High Frequency Data in Finance held in Zurich in March 1995 (see also Dunis 1996b).

This book is a further contribution to a better understanding of the dynamics of financial markets. As such, it evolves around four major themes. The first introductory part is descriptive and focuses on the features of high frequency financial data. The second part examines the exact nature of the time series considered: several linearity tests are presented and applied and their modelling implications are assessed. The third and fourth parts are then dedicated to modelling and forecasting these financial time series, discriminating between the use of parametric and non-parametric (nonlinear) models as we deem this categorisation superior to a distinction between stochastic and deterministic models and/or between models integrating nonlinearities in the variance or in the mean.

1 HIGH FREQUENCY MODELS IN FINANCE: MOTIVATIONS AND THEORETICAL ISSUES

This section, as mentioned just above, is an introductory one and contains two chapters, which are respectively:

- 'Modelling with High Frequency Data: A Growing Interest for Financial Economists and Fund Managers' by M. Gavridis: this chapter is a review of the recent literature on high frequency data. The author evaluates the increased insights that the analysis of intraday data allows researchers and market practitioners to obtain. It also addresses the issue of efficiency and predictability of financial time series. The much debated concept of linearity and efficiency of the financial markets, examined by means of low frequency data, tends to give an inaccurate representation of reality. This conclusion results from recent empirical evidence, especially with high frequency financial time series, which points towards nonlinear, if not chaotic, markets where volatility clusters do exist and trading profits can be made. Such evidence has important implications both for the theoretical paradigms that need to be developed to accommodate these empirical findings and for market practitioners who need to allow for these empirical observations in their asset allocation, pricing and trading models.

- 'High Frequency Foreign Exchange Rates: Price Behavior Analysis and "True Price" Models' by J. Moody and L. Wu: this chapter investigates some empirical features of tick-by-tick foreign exchange data and proposes the use of state-space models to study the observed correlation structures. In addition to the usual 'physical' time scale, a 'tick time' business time scale is implemented for analysing short-term price behaviour. An interesting finding is that tick data are slightly trending on short-term time scales of about 15 minutes on average for the USD/DEM exchange rate. State-space models are used to decompose observed prices into unobserved 'true prices' plus observational noise. These models applied to the USD/DEM are able to explain the existence of anticorrelations in successive price changes as well as positive correlation on longer time scales: by so doing, they demonstrate the existence of trends in intraday foreign exchange data.

2 DETECTING NONLINEARITIES IN HIGH FREQUENCY DATA: EMPIRICAL TESTS AND MODELLING IMPLICATIONS

This section presents several linearity tests which are applied to intraday data and it assesses their modelling implications. It also shows how to deal with the presence of noise in high frequency data and the heteroscedasticity of the return distributions. It contains four articles which are respectively:

- 'Testing Linearity with Information-theoretic Statistics and the Bootstrap' by F.M. Aparicio Acosta: this chapter presents a way of testing for linearity which combines frequency-domain bootstrapping with information-theoretic concepts. The methodology consists of bootstrapping the data in the frequency domain and then comparing the values taken by an information-theoretic test statistic evaluated for both the original time series and its bootstrapped linear replica. The linearity test proposed here is not formulated in a regression context and the method chosen therefore avoids the possibility of spectral imbalance which may arise as a consequence of regressing variables with different spectral properties. It is successfully applied to hourly USD/DEM, USD/ESP and DEM/ESP exchange rates where it finds evidence of nonlinearity in the means of the USD/DEM and DEM/ESP series.
- 'Testing for Linearity: A Frequency Domain Approach' by J. Drunat, G. Dufrénot and L. Mathieu: this chapter also presents new developments in linearity testing with high frequency financial data in the frequency domain. The authors propose two statistical tests based on the study of the third-order moments in the frequency domain and using bispectrum analysis. Bispectral F-tests and chi-squared tests are then applied to three high frequency exchange rates: the results clearly indicate that sampling does not modify the usual conclusions about the distribution properties of exchange rates. The Gaussianity assumption is indeed rejected for all three exchange rates as they exhibit a strong departure from Gaussianity. Moreover, it is shown that, in several cases, the use of lower frequency returns instead of the higher intraday returns tends to smooth the nonlinear components of the series considered.
- 'Stochastic or Chaotic Dynamics in High Frequency Financial Data' by D. Guégan and L. Mercier: this chapter is a thorough investigation of the

potential use of both stochastic and deterministic models for modelling high
frequency exchange rates with an empirical application to the DEM/FRF rate
at three different time steps, 10, 20 and 60 minutes respectively, over the
period 01/09/1994 to 31/08/1995. The authors find that, although using a
deterministic approach does not give noise the primordial importance it has
in real data and it is therefore legitimate to consider stochastic models, it
is nevertheless desirable to adopt a modelling approach where the intrinsic
nonlinearities are built into the data-generating process. In order to control
the noise and to discriminate it from the underlying dynamics of the system,
they develop a 'stochastic version' of deterministic chaos. In their simulations,
they also use prediction methods developed for well-known chaotic systems to
yield an optimal forecasting time step, a promising avenue for future research.

- 'F-consistency, De-volatilization and Normalization of High Frequency
  Financial Data' by B. Zhou: this chapter presents a new type of statistical
  consistency, the F-consistency, which takes into account the fact that
  increasing observation frequency while keeping the time span constant does
  not necessarily improve parameter estimation. It also develops a new approach
  to the problem of heteroskedasticity of financial time series by suggesting
  an analysis of a homoskedastic subsequence of the data, i.e. to either 'de-
  volatilize' or 'normalize' the time series. These procedures reduce the noise
  effect as well as the level of heteroscedasticity and both produce a return series
  which is quasi-normally distributed. But they are not equivalent: while 'de-
  volatization' allows for a volatility-varying sampling frequency, with more
  data being collected when the market is more active and less when it shows
  a greater level of inertia, 'normalization' rescales returns from volatile and
  more stable time periods. The use of the distribution characteristics of the 'de-
  volatilized' or 'normalized' returns makes it possible to use many traditional
  financial models which assume homoskedasticity and Gaussian returns, and
  to forecast the markets' evolution accordingly.

3 PARAMETRIC MODELS FOR NONLINEAR FINANCIAL TIME SERIES

This third section is dedicated to the parametric modelling of intraday nonlinear
time series. It contains four chapters which are respectively:

- 'High Frequency Financial Time Series Data: Some Stylized Facts and
  Models of Stochastic Volatility' by E. Ghysels, C. Gouriéroux and J. Jasiak:
  this chapter deals with several specific issues which emerge in the econometric
  modelling of high frequency data via stochastic volatility. After having
  examined three different sets of high frequency data, the authors present
  a detailed example involving the estimation in a business time scale of
  stochastic volatility models for the USD/DEM, USD/JPY and DEM/JPY

intraday exchange rates. Using a formulation whereby volatility is related to both market activity variables and deviations from average market activity, they find that, in the case of the USD/DEM, volatility becomes more persistent and less erratic when market activity is high, and that volatility changes are largely driven by the extent to which actual market activity deviates from its average level. They reach similar conclusions for the USD/JPY. For the DEM/JPY, however, the only variable increasing volatility appears to be the instantaneous excess return, a good enough reason to model DEM/JPY volatility within a different framework.

- 'Modelling Short-term Volatility with GARCH and HARCH Models' by M.M. Dacorogna, U.A. Müller, R.B. Olsen and O.V. Pictet: this chapter presents a new formulation of the HARCH (heterogeneous autoregressive conditional heteroscedasticity) model where market volatility is expressed in terms of partial volatilities representing different market components to global market volatility. These independent volatility components are modelled as exponential moving averages of past squared returns measured at different time frequencies, which brings this new version of the HARCH model closer to the traditional GARCH-type formalism. Using 10 years of 30-minute returns for the USD/DEM, USD/JPY, GBP/USD, USD/CHF and DEM/JPY exchange rates, the new EMA–HARCH model is shown to be more accurate in terms of statistical fit than other competing models including HARCH. Out-of-sample, it is the best predictor of hourly historical (i.e. realised) volatility, outperforming other GARCH-type models and even the earlier version of HARCH and thus giving further empirical evidence of the heterogeneity of financial markets.

- 'High Frequency Switching Regimes: A Continuous-time Threshold Process' by R. Dacco' and S. Satchell: this chapter is concerned with the analysis of high frequency exchange rates using regime-based models. Having stressed the links between the time deformation literature and switching regime models, the authors consider a continuous-time threshold autoregressive (CTAR) process capable of dealing with irregularly spaced observations and accounting for negative autocorrelation, a general empirical feature of foreign exchange tick-by-tick databanks also present in the USD/DEM intraday series which they use for their empirical application. They extend the basic Ornstein–Uhlenbeck continuous time process which is characterised by positive autocorrelation to include more complex autocorrelation patterns and investigate ways of allocating observations between the two regimes considered. They find that short-term returns follow an asymmetric process for positive and negative values and that the model will switch regimes if there is sufficient noise in the data.

- 'Modelling Burst Phenomena: Bilinear and Autoregressive Exponential Models' by J. Drunat, G. Dufrénot and L. Mathieu: this chapter shows how bilinear and exponential autoregressive (EXPAR) models can be used to study the dynamics of intraday exchange rates. As a natural extension of ARMA models in the field of nonlinear analysis, bilinear models are interesting as they constitute a generation of stochastic models that allow for nonlinearities in the mean of the series considered. This is an important point when making investment decisions where assessing risk and the potential evolution of future returns are both necessary steps of the allocation process. EXPAR models are also introduced as a more general formulation for nonlinear stochastic models, making it possible to capture such phenomena as amplitude-dependent frequency, jump behaviours and limit cycles. Using the same databank as in Chapter 4, the authors demonstrate that bilinearity is an empirical feature of the three exchange rates considered. They also show that the bilinear model developed for the USD/FRF exchange rate significantly outperforms some linear benchmark models and the respective EXPAR model not only in-sample, but, more importantly, out-of-sample.

4 NON-PARAMETRIC MODELS FOR NONLINEAR FINANCIAL TIME SERIES

This last section is dedicated to the non-parametric modelling of intraday nonlinear time series. It contains three chapters which are respectively:

- 'Application of Neural Networks to Forecast High Frequency Data: Foreign Exchange' by P.J. Bolland, J.T. Connor and A.-P.N. Refenes: this chapter presents a methodology to model multivariate high frequency financial time series. The model proposed uses a state-space representation of the series considered in real time, as using a time deformation process would prove impractical in the case of multivariate analysis with different time arrivals for the different time series. The state-space framework is refined by allowing the state dynamics to be estimated by a neural network model which does not impose any parametric restriction on the relationships considered, but allows the dynamics to develop in a nonlinear fashion. The authors apply this multivariate framework to model triangular arbitrage between high frequency GBP/USD, USD/DEM and GBP/DEM exchange rates. Their extended Kalman filter procedure makes it possible to track unobserved price moves on less frequently traded exchange rates and to provide reliable estimates of the 'true price' in the presence of data contamination, as well as to successfully identify some market mispricings in the arbitrage relationship.
- 'An Application of Genetic Algorithms to High Frequency Trading Models: A Case Study' by C. Dunis, M. Gavridis, A. Harris, S. Leong and P. Nacaskul: this chapter describes the performance of genetic algorithms applied to high frequency trading models. GA-based systems appear to be particularly suitable for identifying hidden patterns and relationships which can potentially be profitably exploited. The purpose is to develop a trading model such that

profitability and money management criteria are directly measured rather than inferred from forecasting errors. The time series evaluated are intraday observations of the USD/DEM and DEM/JPY exchange rates from January to May 1996. After addressing issues relating to sampling methodology, data filtering, trading hours and optimal population size, the authors examine some in- and out-of-sample performance results of their experiments with GAs, employing this procedure within the context of optimising a given technical trading model: as such, the GA searches over the specified model parameter space in order to optimise a real-time trading performance measure but is not yet entrusted with the task of model building.

- 'High Frequency Exchange Rate Forecasting by the Nearest Neighbour Method' by H. Alexandre, I. Girerd-Potin and O. Taramasco: this chapter examines the forecasting properties of the nearest neighbour methodology. This method is based on the existence of a strange attractor for the series considered and on the fact that, despite the sensitivity to initial conditions characterising chaotic series, very short-term forecasting is nevertheless possible. The authors apply this non-parametric technique to three high frequency exchange rates (USD/DEM, USD/FRF and DEM/FRF) after verifying their chaotic nature by calculating their highest Lyapunov exponent. The USD/DEM is found to be non-chaotic. Yet the quality of the forecasts obtained for the USD/FRF and the DEM/FRF in terms of correlation between forecast and actual values is unfortunately quite weak, even in the case of the DEM/FRF which provides the best results. Consequently, the authors conclude it is impossible to confirm the presence of a chaotic structure in the series considered or at least to make use of such a process to derive high frequency forecasts based on the nearest neighbour methodology.

As mentioned at the beginning of this preface, nonlinear modelling is a rather new topic in finance and so is the interest of financial markets for intraday data. Combining the two is certainly a challenge as many results remain tentative and more research avenues will undoubtedly be opened in the near future.

Having gone through the reasons that have led me to select the four major themes of this book and briefly presented each chapter, I cannot conclude this preface without thanking again all its contributors, and also Richard Baggaley of John Wiley & Sons who asked me to edit it.

I also wish to thank my colleagues of the Global Markets Research group at the Banque Nationale de Paris for their comments and suggestions. They have proved quite helpful. In particular, special thanks go to Michael Gavridis who has helped me to revise several chapters of this book, and to my wife and daughters who have had to put up, yet again, with my usually bad mood which turned for the worse on some occasions while I was preparing and revising the final manuscript.

Christian L. Dunis

REFERENCES

Baillie, R.T. (1996), 'Long Memory Processes and Fractional Integration in Econometrics', *Journal of Econometrics*, **73**, 5-59.

Baillie, R.T. and Bollerslev, T. (1991), 'Intra-day and Inter-market Volatility in Foreign Exchange Rates', *Review of Economic Studies*, **58**, 565-585.

Bollerslev, T. (1986), 'Generalized Autoregressive Conditional Heteroskedasticity', *Journal of Econometrics*, **31**, 307-327.

Brock, W., Lakonishok, J. and LeBaron, B. (1992), 'Simple Technical Trading Rules and the Stochastic Properties of Stock Returns', *The Journal of Finance*, **47**, 1731-1764.

Dacorogna, M.M., Gauvreau, C.L., Müller, U.A., Olsen, R.B. and Pictet, O.V. (1992), *Short Term Forecasting Models of Foreign Exchange Rates*, Technical Report MMD. 1992-05-12, Olsen & Associates, Zurich.

Dacorogna, M.M., Müller, U.A., Nagler, R.J., Olsen, R.B. and Pictet, O.V. (1993), 'A Geographical Model for the Daily and Weekly Seasonal Volatility in the FX Market', *Journal of International Money and Finance*, **12**, 413-438.

Dacorogna, M.M., Müller, U.A., Jost, C., Pictet, O.V., Olsen, R.B. and Ward, J.R. (1996), 'Heterogeneous Real-time Strategies in the Foreign Exchange Market', in Dunis, C. (ed.), *Forecasting Financial Markets — Exchange Rates, Interest Rates and Asset Management*, Wiley, Chichester, pp. 69-92.

Dunis, C. (1996a), 'The Economic Value of Neural Network Systems for Exchange Rate Forecasting', *Neural Network World*, **6**, 43-55.

Dunis, C. (ed.) (1996b), *Forecasting Financial Markets — Exchange Rates, Interest Rates and Asset Management*, Wiley, Chichester.

Dunis, C. and Feeny, M. (1989), *Exchange Rate Forecasting*, Woodhead-Faulkner, Cambridge (particularly Chapter 5, pp. 165-205).

Engle, R.F. (1982), 'Autoregressive Conditional Heteroskedasticity with Estimates of U.K. Inflation', *Econometrica*, **50**, 987-1008.

Focardi, S and Jonas, C. (1997), 'Modeling the Market: New Theories and Techniques', Frank J. Fabozzi Associates, New Hope, Pennsylvania.

LeBaron, B. (1992), 'Forecast Improvements Using a Volatility Index', *Journal of Applied Econometrics*, **7**, 137-149.

Levich, R.M. and Thomas, L.R. (1993), 'The Significance of Technical Trading-Rule Profits in the Foreign Exchange Rate Market: A Bootstrap Approach', *Journal of International Money and Finance*, **12**, 451-474.

Mandelbrot, B.B. (1963), 'The Variation of Certain Speculative Prices', *Journal of Business*, **36**, 394-419.

Moody, J. and Wu, L. (1995), 'Statistical Analysis and Forecasting of High Frequency Exchange Rates', Research Paper, Computer Science Department, Oregon Graduate Institute of Science & Technology.

Neftçi, S.N. (1991), 'Naive Trading Rules in Financial Markets and Wiener-Kolmogorov Prediction Theory: A Study of "Technical Analysis"', *Journal of Business*, **64**, 549-571.

Pictet, O.V., Dacorogna, M.M., Olsen, R.B. and Ward, J.R. (1992), 'Real-Time Trading Models for Foreign Exchange Rates', *Neural Network World*, **2**, 713-744.

Taylor, M.P. and Allen, H. (1992), 'The Use of Technical Analysis in the Foreign Exchange Market', *Journal of International Money and Finance*, **11**, 304-314.

Taylor, S.J. (1986), *Modelling Financial Time Series*, Wiley, Chichester.

The Intertek Group (1997), *Real-Time Data, Analytics and Forecasting Systems*, The Intertek Group, Paris.

Zhou, B. (1996), 'Forecasting Foreign Exchange Rates Subject to De-volatilization', in Dunis, C. (ed.), *Forecasting Financial Markets — Exchange Rates, Interest Rates and Asset Management*, Wiley, Chichester, pp. 51–67.

PART I
High Frequency Models in Finance: Motivations and Theoretical Issues

1

Modelling with High Frequency Data: A Growing Interest for Financial Economists and Fund Managers

MICHAEL GAVRIDIS

1 INTRODUCTION

Even after about four decades of substantial empirical evidence in financial economics,[1] the question of whether financial markets are predictable remains the subject of considerable debate with numerous articles supporting both sides of the issue. Before we proceed with evaluating the insights and new perspectives that high frequency data analysis has provided to the debate, it is worth making the following clarification. There appears to be a considerable degree of misinterpretation with respect to probably the two most talked about concepts in the empirical financial literature: namely, that of *efficiency* and that of *predictability*. Efficiency, after Fama (1970), is generally accepted to refer to the way information is incorporated into asset prices within a competitive market-place comprised of rational participants.[2] Thus, in efficient markets asset prices reflect all the relevant information and there should be no opportunities for abnormal returns. The corollary of this definition is that an investor, either institutional or private, cannot systematically outperform the market over the long run. If all relevant information, current and past, is incorporated into the asset prices then only *new* information should change prices. However, new information, by definition, cannot be deduced from previous information, hence it must be independent over time

Nonlinear Modelling of High Frequency Financial Time Series.
Edited by Christian Dunis and Bin Zhou. © 1998 John Wiley Sons Ltd

and thus unforecastable. Consequently, price changes should be unforecastable. Hence, it is often considered that financial prices follow a random walk which is also interpreted to imply that price changes are unpredictable.

The above generally describes the main financial thinking up until the late 1970s–early 1980s, when evidence started emerging which pointed to the fact that there might be signs of predictability in the financial markets. The evidence grew more and more substantial to the point that nowadays we are talking about the degree of predictability that our tests allow us to unveil. However, despite the varied evidence, we have not yet answered whether identifying predictability implies that the markets are inefficient. If we employ the original definition of efficiency as our benchmark, then we would say that the recent evidence due to its increased sophistication unveils what was always there but we could not depict because of the limits of our then methodologies; however, efficiency does not in itself preclude predictability.

One of the recent explanations of the so-called predictable patterns in financial time series is that they are induced by the structural features of each market. Whether this constitutes inefficiency of the market is a different question altogether which could be argued both ways. The market microstructure research implies that on many instances the results depend rather sensitively on the precise operational technicalities of the market involved: opening and closing arrangements, order- or quote-driven, specialist or competing market makers.

Thus, it would seem a lot more research is required before we can come to any sort of conclusive answers with respect to efficiency and predictability or otherwise of the financial markets and their variables. Recently, important insights into the working of the markets and their series have seemed to emerge by means of analysing frequencies higher than those we have analysed thus far, namely, frequencies higher than daily.

Lately, we have observed a plethora of articles written on the topic of high frequency data. Some may claim that high frequency data and their modelling represent the latest topic of interest for financial economists and fund managers, both eager to find their Holy Grail. The former group believes that high frequency should provide them with the micro perspective that was missing from the analysis so far and enable them to decipher the empirical puzzles of empirical finance. The latter group, equipped with these insights about the movements of speculative prices, could exploit them in their asset allocation or trading models.

A new body of financial literature has started emerging as a result of the availability of financial data at frequencies higher than daily. High frequency data refer to time series sampled at intervals of, say, ever hour, or minute by minute or even *tick by tick*, i.e. as data reach the market. The microstructure literature has unveiled patterns and relationships that, first, would be impossible to uncover at daily or weekly frequencies and, second, this empirical evidence points to the realisation that the prevailing linear paradigm and efficient market hypothesis (EMH) may not only be far from the observed reality, but also adherence to them may severely distort our perspective of how markets effectively operate. Hence, in view of the recent empirical evidence, the popular view at this point in time would appear to be that financial time series are mainly nonlinear, if not chaotic, until proven otherwise. Therefore, since information arrives in the market continuously, a discretely low frequency sampling would involve ignoring a large segment of information. High frequency sampling and its subsequent analysis aim at reducing the discrepancy between actual market information flow and its analysis.

The more the global the markets have become, the finer the frequency at which the analysis is conducted.

In the addition to the above developments in the academic field, growing international trade and the widening search for profit opportunities have driven the integration and globalisation of the markets. Whatever the reasons, globalisation has induced increased uncertainty and therefore volatility. Volatility brings with it risk and risk encourages the use of derivatives which, although designed to manage risk, can hold their own dangers (see, for instance, the recent banking failures — Barings, Daiwa, NatWest, amongst other which in addition indicates lack of thorough management controls.). Bernstein (1996) observes that the boom in derivatives like globalisation, electronic trading and multiplication of markets indicates a transformation not so much in the markets themselves but rather in the way that investors manage funds: 'the way we invest is a function of the theoretical developments and the computer as a vehicle to make the theory into practicality'.

Moreover, recently, performance is linked to and evaluated through the risk perspective.[3] Thus, good performance is rewarded only if it is the result of adhering to given risk limits. Fund managers are required to report their risk levels and incorporate *ex ante* risk considerations in their forecasting and model-building procedures. The aim is to maintain real-time risk control.[4] Market operators, from traders[5] to fund managers, are increasingly paying attention to correlations of the trading risks they undertake.

At the same time, the growing complexity and automation of the markets require greater use of analytic tools (The Intertek Group 1997). In addition, the existence of any pattern in the price or volatility series has profound implications for financial theory and market practitioners because patterns make prediction possible. As Diebold (1996) and others conclude, all of finance deals with risk and risk is just volatility. Asset pricing, options pricing or hedging depend crucially upon the accuracy with which volatility can be modelled.

Furthermore, a greater number of investment managers have started adopting less traditional fundamental asset management methodologies in an attempt to enhance their performance. Modern portfolios are usually comprised of foreign exchange, equity, interest rates and derivatives, and tend to be diversified over many geographical regions and sectors. As portfolios globalise, volatilities tend to grow. At the same time, the frequency over which investments are programmed for, monitored and evaluated over has been substantially reduced over the recent decade. Thus, although long-term performance certainly remains the overriding objective, the yardstick of evaluation has become smaller. There are fully automated funds optimised on the basis of real-time information (The Intertek Group 1997).

This chapter is organised as follows. In the next section, we take a brief account of some of the important underlying issues that the linearity/efficiency paradigm of the financial markets fails to explain in view of the reported empirical regularities (or anomalies). Furthermore, we evaluate the recent evidence of analysing financial data within a nonlinear and chaotic dynamics framework. In section 3, the advent of high frequency data is introduced and its repercussions to empirical finance are evaluated. In section 4, we conclude.

2 FINANCIAL MARKETS AND TIME SERIES ACCORDING TO THE EMH: SOME RECENT EVIDENCE

Let us summarise some of the evidence that the various tests of the EMH have suggested[6] and what the implications of such evidence are for the issue of predictability.

Tests with stock market data over different horizons, including autocorrelation coefficients of price differences, regression tests,[7] variance bounds tests,[8] do not provide us with similar inferences regarding EMH, as they should in principle do. Namely, the first two tests, returns autocorrelations and regression tests, whether univariate or multivariate, examine to what extent past returns (or other variables[9]) can predict current returns. They tend to indicate that *ex post* real returns and excess returns are predictable.[10] Furthermore, regression tests reveal significant predictability in stock returns. Trading strategies based on the forecasts of these tests give rise to profits (transaction costs considered).[11] However, as Cuthbertson (1996) suggests, these profits should be evaluated by means of adequate *ex ante* risk measures.

The variance bounds tests examine whether the variance of stock prices is justified by the variability in fundamental variables. Shiller (1981) strongly rejects the rational valuation formula by means of variance bounds inequalities. However, it should be mentioned that, first, there are certain methodological issues that were raised by the research of Kleidon (1986) with respect to Shiller's variance bounds inequalities. Second, the violations of the rational valuation might be statistically unclear, as Gilles and LeRoy (1991) and Mankiw *et al.* (1991) point out.

In addition, the reason, as suggested in the literature, why the results of the above methodologies cannot be reconciled is that tests with stock data returns are based on different equilibrium models from those based on stock prices. Furthermore, the small sample properties of the statistics differ. However, at this point it would suffice to say that the above evidence, despite some allowances regarding statistical concerns, suggests an ambiguous picture of market efficiency and predictability.

Several studies have uncovered the existence of excess returns in the foreign exchange market by following various technical trading rules, see amongst others Dooley and Shafer (1983), Sweeny (1986), Levich and Thomas (1993) and Osler and Chang (1995). According to these studies, some trading rules give rise to economic and significant excess returns in various currency pairs and over different time intervals.[12] Further evidence of the microstructure of both foreign exchange and equity markets has shown the possibility of certain complicated regularities. Brock *et al.* (1992) provide strong support for technical strategies having predictive power in the stock market, as these rules pick up some of the hidden patterns or unmeasured risk.

2.1 Empirical Puzzles in Financial Time Series

Let us now turn to the often more attention-receiving evidence of inefficiency and patterns in financial time series (early evidence of these patterns, termed anomalies, was provided by Jensen 1978). This evidence refers to empirical puzzles such as the well-documented *weekend* effect and *January* effect,[13] the *small firm* effect,[14] closed-end funds enjoying higher rates of return (Fortune 1991; Malkiel 1977; Lee *et al.* 1990) the strategy of purchasing value-line rank 1 shares giving rise to profits even after accounting for risk and transactions costs (see Holloway 1981), the winner's curse (see de Bondt and Thaler 1985, 1989; Bremer and Sweeney 1988).

Despite the fact that the above evidence of anomalies may be perceived as predominantly present in small-sized stocks, it does, nevertheless, raise some questions about or, according to others, even shake the validity of the EMH.

Additional doubts about the validity of EMH emerged from the evidence on *noise* traders and *herd* behaviour amongst market practitioners (see de Long *et al.* 1990; Shleifer and Summers 1990; Shiller 1989). Summers (1986) documents that a share price series which is artificially generated from a model in which price diverges from fundamentals in a persistent way does give rise to a new series that resembles very closely (random walk-like) the behaviour of an actual share price series. The presence of noise traders also allows share prices to experience persistent swings on the assumption that there is persistence in the agents' perceptions of volatility. Guillaume *et al.* (1994) suggest that the coexistence of different types of traders[15] might explain why price changes are found to contain a unit root, thus becoming globally unforecastable, while forecasts conditional on the volatility are still possible. This latter suggestion seems to explain the observed empirical evidence of persistence in volatility uncovered by the ARCH family of models.[16] This evidence may be consistent with time-varying risk premia and equilibrium returns being influenced by the changing perceptions of risks by the agents.[17]

2.2 Evidence of Nonlinearities and Chaotic Dynamics

In addition, the whole idea of linearity in financial time series has been questioned as evidence that linear structural models do not outperform random walk forecasts (Meese and Rogoff 1983) and as evidence from a new set of methodologies based on chaotic dynamics emerged. A number of empirical articles suggest that nonlinearities might be particularly suited for providing us with information about foreign exchange volatility (see, amongst others, Diebold and Pauly 1988; Hsieh 1988, 1989; LeBaron 1992). Additional empirical evidence suggested that foreign exchange returns may be generated by regime-switching models (Hamilton 1989) and/or bilinear processes (Maravall 1983).[18] Furthermore, Medio (1992) suggested that exchange rates may sometimes be drawn from low dimensional chaotic systems.

Given first the failure of structural, fundamental models to explain the movements in exchange rates,[19] second the limitations of econometric models, the latest chaotic systems provide interesting alternative paradigms of the observed random-like behaviour of the exchange rate series which may be the result of nonlinear deterministic dynamic models.[20] De Grauwe et al. (1993), for instance, report that data from a chaotic system can first be modelled and second provide us with acceptable short horizon forecasts.[21]

Chaos theory examines how nonlinear deterministic systems can generate apparently random and irregular behaviour. Despite their sensitivity to initial conditions and their generation of apparent random patterns in the time domain, chaotic systems have a discernible structure which can be employed to test for the presence of chaos.[22] These nonlinearities cannot easily be detected with the stochastic approach (see Brock et al. 1992). However, stochastic models can formalise nonlinear systems.

Fractal patterns and volatility clustering are compelling evidence that the markets are nonlinear. Within a linear context, effects are proportional to their cause. Whatever the cause of volatility in the markets, the effects are often cumulative and disproportionate. Mandelbrot (1963) and other researchers ever since have uncovered that nonlinearity can cause relatively simple systems to behave in a way that appears highly complex and random. As Weigend (1996) contends, as researchers realised that simple equations can produce complicated behaviours then they started hypothesising that since financial markets exhibit complicated behaviour then the latter could be modelled by means of simple equations.

In the case of exchange rates, the evidence tends to indicate that first, deterministic nonlinear models can give rise to persistent random and irregular time series resembling actual time series. Second, although the reported evidence on deterministic chaos in exchange rates is far from conclusive,[23] it does suggest that nonlinearities are present in the data-generation process.

Although this evidence has pointed to the possibility (or necessity to some) of including nonlinearities in financial equations, an economic theory that is consistent with these nonlinearities remains to be developed (see Pesaran and Potter

1993). What this evidence does point to is alternatives to the rational expectations model.[24] More practically, it is impossible to disregard the implications of the hypothesis that financial markets may exhibit complex, nonlinear dynamics which, amongst other things, also suggest that prior tests, for instance unit roots, may have failed to discover more complicated temporal dependencies caused by differing horizons of differing agents (Goodhart and O'Hara 1995; Hogan and Melvin 1994).

The realisation and acceptance that capital markets and financial/economic time series do not move according to a linear model[25] triggered the investigation of alternative paradigms in the search for explanations of market behaviour. The recent availability of large databanks of financial time series renders this exploration possible. This is the subject of the following section.

3 HIGH FREQUENCY DATA: INSIGHTS AT THE MICRO LEVEL

In view of the issues presented in the preceding section and the evidence of predictability of various empirical studies,[26] then it becomes clear that any analysis at lower frequencies would give rise to at best incomplete (at worst misleading) inferences, given the dynamic and complex character of the current financial market-place.[27] Questions regarding how the market actually evolves in real time, especially the nature of dynamic interaction within the markets, comprising heterogeneous agents, following the arrival of information, could be answered with a greater level of accuracy.[28]

Before we proceed it is worth presenting a characteristic sample of the evidence that empirical research with high frequency data has unveiled regarding, for instance, the distributional properties of returns and volatility, the relationship of news releases and high frequency data, the intraday patterns or seasonalities and the market dynamics.[29]

The obvious advantage of employing high frequency data is that a more detailed examination of both the sources and characteristics of return volatility can be made. A fundamental property of high frequency data is that observations can occur at varying time intervals. Trades are not equally spaced throughout the day, resulting in intraday seasonals in the volume of trade, the volatility of prices and the behaviour of spreads.[30] This characteristic can also be problematic, due to its implications on the security price process, since no uniformly accepted approach is presented in the empirical literature. Namely, how should time (clock vs trade) be treated in high frequency analysis or is the notion of time relevant within this context? In the market microstructure literature, time is treated as irrelevant (as is volume).[31] In other studies, timing of trades is considered as important since it is perceived as a signal in itself, the same way that trade size (volume)[32] is also essential, especially if we also consider their effect on spreads. Dacorogna *et al.* (1992, 1993, 1994) document that the time dimension of global trading is in itself responsible for the trading patterns observed in high frequency foreign exchange data. This element could furthermore be employed in categorising market activity and trades. High frequency data are particularly suited for investigating the extent to which timing is important in financial time series, which at an intuitive level appears evident.

Guillaume *et al.* (1994) provide an excellent account of some stylised facts associated with intraday patterns in foreign exchange markets.[33] Let us present some of these empirical facts regarding autocorrelation, the impact of news releases, spreads and volatility.

3.1 Autocorrelation in High Frequency Data

Goodhart and Figliuoli (1991) examine minute-by-minute foreign exchange rates as they are reported in Reuters' FXFX page and they find clear evidence of *negative* first-order autocorrelation, especially after jumps in the exchange rate level, for up to 4 minutes.[34] This evidence is corroborated by Bollerslev and Domowitz (1993) who also report evidence of negative serial correlation in the returns series calculated from either bid or ask quotes. This negative first-order autocorrelation is also confirmed by Baillie and Bollerslev (1990) using the same data set as Goodhart and Figliuoli (1991) and by Zhou (1992) using a different data set. Low and Muthuswamy (1996) also conclude that 5-minute returns of the USD/JPY, USD/DEM and DEM/JPY exchange rates exhibit significant serial dependencies (i.e. heteroskedastic), possibly nonlinear in nature.

A possible explanation for this observation could be that market participants with diverging opinions revise their views upon the arrival of new information. Other researchers attribute this evidence to the fact that FXFX quote prices are indicative and quotes tend to move depending on the banks' order imbalances, or persistent tendencies of banks to quote high or low, as in Bollerslev and Domowitz (1993), or pure noise, as in Zhou (1992), while Goodhart and Payne (1995) attribute it to the presence of thin markets.

3.2 News Releases in High Frequency Data

Goodhart and Figliuoli (1991) did not identify any relationship between news headlines, as reported on Reuters' AAMM, and the subsequent moves in the relevant foreign exchange rates. Contrarily, when Baestens and van den Bergh (1996) evaluate the impact of news headlines on swap rate returns by means of linear and nonlinear models, they report evidence of some standardised news headlines regularly affecting returns.

Moreover, Ederington and Lee (1993) report that scheduled macroeconomic announcements affect the direction of price adjustment in T-bonds, Eurodollar and DEM foreign exchange futures rates within the first minute, while prices remain volatile for the subsequent 15 minutes.[35] In fact, they conclude that announcements are the most important sources of systematic return volatility.

Eddelbüttel (1997), using a resolution of 1 hour in the operational or θ-time-scale, fits various models to the USD/DEM exchange rate, ranging from a GARCH(1,1) to semi-parametric models using k-nearest neighbours regression and included a news count (relevant to the USD, DEM and global news) and the relevant interest rate differential. He reports that the yield differential does not have a lot of explanatory power at high frequency. However, the frequency of news was important in the conditional variance in the sense that more global news increases the USD/DEM conditional volatility.

3.3 Volatility and Spreads in High Frequency Data

Andersen and Bollerslev (1994) examine the issues of seasonality and volatility persistence in intraday stock market and foreign exchange data. They demonstrate that there is intraday seasonality in high frequency foreign exchange returns that requires to be taken into account so that the relationship between intraday and daily returns can be uncovered. This filtering or deseasonalisation may reconcile the reported persistence in the volatility series of daily data with the rapid decay associated with the news arrival in intraday data (Andersen and Bollerslev 1995). In Andersen and Bollerslev (1996), they extend their analysis of the USD/DEM rate and after accounting for various factors or effects (calendar, holidays, lunch breaks, data gaps), they report that scheduled macroeconomic news releases could in fact explain day-of-the-week seasonalities, concluding that news releases introduce significant but short-lived volatility bursts into the market.

Low and Muthuswamy (1996) document strong evidence of the effects of public information on quote returns volatility and spread changes. In particular, they find that news announcements are a significant explanatory factor influencing volatility. In addition, they present evidence that news releases reduce the spread and increase the volatility of spreads. Their results contradict those of first, Bollerslev and Domowitz (1993), who report no consistent relationship between the arrival of news (or news proxies) and exchange rate spreads,[36] and second those of Goodhart and Figliuoli (1991) who also find no evidence of the spread being related to changes in market conditions. At a theoretical level, we would expect that once information is released, a certain degree of uncertainty resolution would ensue and, consequently, the spread (often regarded as a measure of information asymmetry) should narrow. Thus, the evidence presented would appear to be conflicting. At an intuitive level, this evidence might be indicative of a classification of news releases in the sense that first, not all pieces of information generate a market reaction, and second, the same type of information might be given more or less attention depending on the stage of the economic cycle.[37]

In view of the intraday seasonals observed in high frequency foreign exchange data, several time transformation or deformation procedures have been suggested in the literature. Baillie and Bollerslev (1990) employ one dummy variable for each hour of the day, using a resolution of 60 minutes. Andersen and Bollerslev (1994) suggested a flexible Fourier specification that allows for a relationship between the level of daily volatility and the shape of the intraday seasonal pattern in explaining volatility across different times of the day. Ghysels *et al.* (1995) recommend a stochastic volatility model accounting simultaneously for both average and conditional market activity. Zhou (1996) focuses on the observed heteroscedasticity and proposes a statistical transformation, the so-called devolatilisation procedure which takes a homoscedastic subsequence from high frequency data. However, different time transformation specifications address different intraday structures. Therefore, accounting for intraday volatility seasonals does not eradicate the observed inconsistencies between daily and intra-daily estimates (Drost and Nijman 1993; Andersen and Bollerslev 1994; Guillaume *et al.* 1995; Ghose and Kroner 1996).

Bollerslev (1996) concludes that as with the patterns in volatility, the discovery of this seasonality in the markets has only been possible because of the availability of high frequency data. Scrutiny of tick-by-tick price movements has revealed market dynamics that were simply invisible to previous researchers because they had access to only daily data at best, in a sense 'high-frequency data has determined the direction of today's empirical research'.

4 CONCLUSION

Recently, we have experienced an explosion in the field of financial economics and a keen interest from market practitioners in applying, and ultimately putting to the test, the empirical evidence reported in these articles. In the 1960s and 1970s, financial theory was developed on the basis of traditional, fundamental models and statistical techniques, early computers and low frequency databases. The resulting models, although interesting in that they formed the starting point where later research ensued from, they were at best approximations and simplified perspectives of reality. In the 1980s and 1990s, together with path-breaking technological developments and the availability of extensive databanks, we have reached the point where we can analyse financial time series and markets at almost any speed and frequency, depending upon the desired application.

Real-time trading models epitomise the practical application of this research endeavour. Neural network models and genetic algorithms represent the latest fascinating tools of market practitioners. The development of these methodologies was substantially aided by the availability of large databanks and powerful computers. Perhaps it is too early to examine what the contribution of these methodologies is with respect to financial theory.

At the same time, it would seem that there is an element of scepticism that surrounds their application. This scepticism is healthy as their efficacy remains to be proven. Market practitioners often claim that these technologies failed to deliver. However, with few exceptions, the majority were applied in forecasting, which might not be entirely suitable for these applications. For example, with hindsight high frequency data would appear highly suited for value-at-risk calculations whereby the financial institution knows at any point in time the maximum loss that may potentially be suffered as a result of adverse price movements.[38] It is unlikely that occasional snapshots of a portfolio's composition can serve as a basis for evaluating the riskiness of a dynamic strategy; only a greater understanding of how markets work can improve the models and the management of risk. As Bollerslev (1996) suggests, we need to be able to simulate and replicate events realistically in terms of saying whether a specific observation represents a regular event or is an aberration.

Furthermore, Weigend (1996) suggests that the early success in applying neural networks was short-lived, mainly because the approach that was adopted was too simplistic to deal with such complex problems.[39] Therefore, combinations of mathematical models and tools are recommended, especially if we consider that high frequency data are noisy, which causes problems for machine learning systems, with the possibility of ending up modelling the noise rather than the underlying dynamics. To avoid such pitfalls, a greater comprehension of the financial markets and the underlying structural factors which set prices is required.

According to LeBaron (1996), although the evidence from the latest methodologies might not have resulted in any bold new theoretical insights and, in the case of chaotic systems, it might be too early to conclude that financial time series do exhibit chaotic behaviour, the empirical findings have still shaken the very foundations of established theory. For instance, the discovery of volatility clustering and other forms of statistical predictability when up until recently any deviations from the EMH were considered as statistically irrelevant. This volatility clustering could not be accounted for by most traditional market models. However, it has now become apparent, from evidence with real-time data, that volatility clustering is to be expected in dynamic systems that include learning and evolution.

Given the empirical evidence that has emerged from the analysis of high frequency data, our understanding of how the financial market-place works has substantially been enhanced and serious efforts in bridging the gap between classical theory and market reality are being made. For example, the identification of the various seasonalities in high frequency data has revealed strong biases in the computation of various statistics or estimates of intraday data processes, which, if not controlled for, may generate spurious results (Guillaume et al. 1994). These improved insights are being incorporated into the asset allocation, trading, valuation and risk management decision-making process of market practitioners, traders and fund managers alike, so that, for instance, in the area of forecasting we observe attempts of integrating high frequency forecasting methodologies in near-automatic asset management or trading systems.

Finally, in what precedes, we have not thoroughly examined the role of market participants. However, an understanding of the participants' behaviour is essential to the understanding of the operation of a dynamic system as the financial markets. What is missing at present is a pragmatic model that elucidates first, how the various market operators (informed or noise traders, hedge funds, central banks) respond to various sets of information as they reach the market, and second, how these groups react to each other's response. Such a modelling effort is further complicated by the fact that in some markets, like that for foreign exchange, there is 24-hour trading around the globe. Although we do believe this is not an easy task, we strongly believe that high frequency information will be instrumental.

What is certainly an interesting avenue for future research is to evaluate the relationship between the type of trading rule employed by technical analysts and the nature of fractal, nonlinear features uncovered in the data. Neely *et al.* (1997), by means of a genetic programming methodology, report technical trading rules can result in profitable strategies (see also LeBaron 1992; Goodhart and Curcio 1992; Pictet *et al.* 1992). What remains to be done is to see whether any clear relationship exists between the kind of trading rules actually employed by technical analysts and fund managers and the nature of the fractal, nonlinear characteristics uncovered in the data.

ENDNOTES

1. However, seminal papers were reported much earlier than in the last 40 years, notably, Bachelier (1900) was probably the first who defined security markets as efficient, Cowles (1933) suggested that even professional investors cannot forecast stock price changes, Working (1934), Kendall (1953) and Osborne (1959, 1962) documented random walk-like behaviours in stock and commodity prices, Samuelson (1965) and Mandelbrot (1966) provided the theory behind the efficient market hypothesis (EMH) where unexpected price changes behave as independent random draws in competitive markets and economic profits are zero. In economics, this hypothesis (see rational expectations) was developed independently by Muth (1961).
2. Although beyond the scope of the present chapter, testing the EMH requires an equilibrium pricing model detailing how prices or price changes are set in the market. Acceptance or rejection of the EMH may equally be attributed to the selected equilibrium pricing model.
3. Although the idea of evaluating risk and reward simultaneously is by no means new to the empirical financial literature (see modern portfolio theory by Markowitz 1952, 1959), what is novel is the development of new ways of managing funds.
4. See value-at-risk (VAR) and risk management unit (RMU) methodologies which are often used by practitioners, but neither their use nor their analytical sophistication are uniformly accepted.
5. Although the link between trading and real-time high frequency information would seem obvious, it is only recently that the potential of exploiting this link has emerged as a result of analysing high frequency data and technological advances.
6. The review on the issues of this section is by no means exhaustive of the numerous articles published on the issues.
7. As in Fama and French (1988) and Poterba and Summers (1988) who examine whether there is evidence of mean reversion over long horizons, amongst others.
8. As in Shiller (1979, 1981), LeRoy and Porter (1981), amongst others.

9. Keim and Stambaugh (1986) found, in addition to a January effect, that variables such as the difference in the yield between low-grade corporate paper and the yield on one-month T-bills, the deviation of last period's real S&P Index from its 45-year average, had statistically significant explanatory power.

10. However, this evidence is indicative of market inefficiency only if either equilibrium real or equilibrium excess returns represent the true expected returns model (Cuthbertson 1996).

11. As in Pesaran and Timmermann (1994) who find evidence of profitable switching trading strategies.

12. Nevertheless, since the rules examined in these articles are evaluated *ex post*, there is a risk of bias (Neely *et al.* (1997)). However, Neely *et al.* (1997) present evidence that a sophisticated technical trader can identify *ex ante* trading rules that would generate excess returns in the foreign exchange market during the period 1981–95.

13. Whereby prices on some stocks are systematically found to fall on Fridays (i.e. weekend effect) and similarly, daily returns in January are reported to be higher. Various explanations can be found in Keane (1983) and Reinganum (1983).

14. Reinganum (1983) reports that even after adjusting for risk the rate of return on small firms is higher.

15. Most empirical financial literature distinguishes three types of agents: market traders, informed traders and noise (liquidity) traders. Many researchers believe this classification is inadequate; however, much of the observed activity results from the interplay between and heterogeneity of those groups. It is the latter that could partly explain the fractal patterns and volatility clustering (Goodhart and O'Hara 1995).

16. Evidence of persistence in the conditional volatility is found almost uniformly, see Chou (1988), Sentana and Wadhwani (1992). Nevertheless, ARCH type of models do not provide any theoretical justification for this empirical observation. Hogan and Melvin (1994) link the observed persistence to the heterogeneity and different investment horizons of market participants.

17. Despite the plausibility of such a hypothesis, a capital asset pricing model (CAPM) with time-varying returns does not completely explain equilibrium returns (Attanasio and Wadhwani 1990). As Lamoureux and Lastrapes (1990) found, trading volume might influence expected returns.

18. These approaches are particularly suitable for explaining sudden bursts in exchange rate fluctuations.

19. Mark (1995) demonstrates that monetary fundamental information may provide a useful predictor of the exchange rate behaviour, but this is possible over long rather than short horizons. In addition, Frankel and Froot (1988) and Takagi (1991) provide evidence that expectations are not rational. Furthermore, co-integration tests tend to report that the spot rate of many exchange rates does not have a long run (equilibrium) relationship with economic fundamentals (Baillie and Selover 1987).

20. Within this context shocks or noise are still possible, see de Grauwe *et al.* (1993), as are rational expectations.

21. However, their overall evidence on chaotic behaviour might be weak.

22. See de Grauwe *et al.* (1993) for more on chaotic systems in the foreign exchange market.

23. According to Goodhart (1996), chaos is deterministic and the markets are not!, Guillaume *et al.* (1994), Vassilicos and Demos (1994), amongst others, report no evidence of low-dimensional chaos in the foreign exchange market.

24. Where all agents have homogeneous expectations, know the true model of the economy and use all available information when forecasting (Cuthbertson 1996).

25. Or linear approximations to nonlinear models so that tractability and closed-form solutions are ensured.

26. Where it becomes clear that predictability depends upon the specific models and time frequencies selected, see for example Taylor (1986), LeBaron (1992), Dacorogna *et al.* (1992, 1993), Pictet *et al.* (1992), Moody and Wu (1995) and Dunis (1996).
27. Additionally, the investigation of chaotic dynamics requires the use of a large number of observations.
28. However, with the existing set of data the hypothesis that interactions between agents with differing information sets, investment horizons and objective functions is not likely to be easily tested (Goodhart and O'Hara 1995).
29. For a more detailed account of issues and applications of high frequency data see Goodhart and O'Hara (1995).
30. The sporadic nature of trading makes measuring volatility problematic and this in turn dictates a need to view volatility as a process rather than a number (Goodhart and O'Hara 1995).
31. Kyle (1985), by aggregating the trades, finds that when the order is placed does not affect the resulting equilibrium. Glosten and Milgrom (1985), by not aggregating the trades, contend that as time is not correlated with any variable relevant to the underlying asset's value then trade timing is of no relevance.
32. For the issue of price dependence on time and trade timing see Easley and O'Hara (1992) and Diamond and Verrecchia (1987), for the issue of volatility dependence on volume see Lamoureux and Lastrapes (1990), Campbell *et al.* (1993) and Gallant *et al.* (1992).
33. Müller *et al.* (1990) provided us with evidence on the patterns in intraday foreign exchange data at different geographical regions.
34. If the expected equilibrium asset return is constant through time, statistically small sample autocorrelations may be indicative of market efficiency (Fama 1976). For small intervals, the assumption of approximately constant expected returns might be reasonable (Miller *et al.* 1994).
35. Additional evidence on the impact of macroeconomic news releases for the first hour after opening is reported in Harvey and Huang (1991) and Hakkio and Pearce (1985).
36. Bollerslev and Domowitz (1993) do, however, report that trading activity has a strong influence on the conditional variance of the spread. Both Bollerslev and Domowitz (1993) and Low and Muthuswamy (1996) report that the changes in spreads are highly negatively autocorrelated.
37. On market reaction after major market news see Berry and Howe (1994).
38. Certainly, precise measures of risk will also impact on more efficient asset allocations.
39. Besides treating these approaches as black boxes.

REFERENCES

Andersen, T.G. and Bollerslev, T. (1994), 'Intraday Seasonality and Volatility Persistence in Foreign Exchange and Equity Markets', Working Paper, No. 186, Kellogg Graduate School of Management, Northwestern University.

Andersen, T.G. and Bollerslev, T. (1995), 'Intraday Seasonality and Volatility Persistence in Financial Markets', Presentation Paper, First International Conference on High Frequency Data in Finance, Olsen & Associates, Zurich.

Andersen, T.G. and Bollerslev, T. (1996), 'DM-Dollar Volatility: Intraday Activity Patterns, Macroeconomic Announcements and Longer Run Dependencies', Working Paper, No. 217, Kellogg Graduate School of Management, Northwestern University.

Attanasio, O. and Wadhwani, S. (1992), 'Does the CAPM Explain Why the Dividend Yield Helps Predict Returns?' LSE Financial Markets Group Discussion Paper, No. 4.

Bachelier, L. (1900), *Théorie de la spéculation*, Gauthier-Villars, Paris, reprinted in P. Cootner (ed.) (1964), *The Random Character of Stock Prices*, MIT, Cambridge, Mass.

Baestens, D.E. and van den Bergh, W.M. (1996), 'Money Market Headline News Flashes, Effective News and the DEM/USD Swap Rate: an Intraday Analysis in Operational Time', Presentation Paper, Third Forecasting Financial Markets Conference, London.

Baillie, R. and Bollerslev, T. (1990), 'Intraday and Intermarket Volatility in Foreign Exchange Rates', *Review of Economic Studies*, **58**, 565–585.

Baillie, R. and Selover, D.D. (1987), 'Cointegration and Models of Exchange Rate Determination', *International Journal of Forecasting*, **3**, 43–52.

Bernstein, P. (1996) in *Views from the Frontier: Commentary on the New World of Forecasting and Risk Management*, Olsen & Associates, Zurich.

Berry, T. and Howe, K. (1994), 'Public Information Arrival', *Journal of Finance*, **49**, 1331–1345.

Bollerslev, T. (1996) in *Views From the Frontier: Commentary on the New World of Forecasting and Risk Management*, Olsen & Associates, Zurich.

Bollerslev, T. and Domowitz, I. (1993), 'Trading Patterns and Prices in the Interbank Foreign Exchange Market', *Journal of Finance*, **48**, 1421–1443.

Bremer, M.A. and Sweeney, R.J. (1988), 'The Information Content of Extreme Negative Rates of Return', Working Paper, Claremont McKenna College.

Brock W., Hsieh, D. and LeBaron, B. (1991), *Nonlinear Dynamics, Chaos and Instability*, MIT Press, Cambridge, Mass.

Brock, W., Lakonishok, J. and LeBaron, B. (1992), 'Simple Technical Trading Rules and the Stochastic Properties of Stock Returns', *Journal of Finance*, **47**, 1731–1764.

Campbell, J., Grossman, S. and Wang, J. (1993), 'Trading Volume and Serial Correlation in Stock Returns', *Quarterly Journal of Economics*, **103**, 905–934.

Chou, R.Y. (1988), 'Volatility Persistence and Stock Valuations: Some Empirical Evidence Using GARCH', *Journal of Applied Econometrics*, **3**, 279–294.

Cowles, A. III (1933), 'Can Stock Market Forecasters Forecast?' *Econometrica*, **1**, 309–324.

Cuthbertson, K. (1996), *Quantitative Financial Economics: Stocks Bonds and Foreign Exchange*, Wiley, Chichester.

Dacorogna, M.M., Gauvreau, C.L., Müller, U.A., Olsen, R.B. and Pictet, O.V. (1992), 'Short Term Forecasting Models of Foreign Exchange Rates', *Technical Report MMD.1992-05-12*, Olsen & Associates, Zurich.

Dacorogna, M.M., Müller, U.A., Nagler, R.J., Olsen, R.B. and Pictet, O.V. (1993), 'A Geographical Model for the Daily and Weekly Seasonal Volatility in the Foreign Exchange Market', *Journal of International Money and Finance*, **12**, 413–438.

Dacorogna, M.M., Müller, U.A., Jost, C., Pictet, O.V., Olsen, R.B. and Ward, J.R. (1994), 'Heterogeneous Real-time Trading Strategies in the Foreign Exchange Market', Presentation Paper, Third Forecasting Financial Markets Conference, London.

De Bondt, W.F.M. and Thaler, R.H. (1985), 'Does the Stock Market Overreact?' *Journal of Finance*, **40**(3), 793–805.

De Bondt, W.F.M. and Thaler, R.H. (1989), 'Anomalies: a Mean-Reverting Walk Down Wall Street', *Journal of Economic Perspectives*, **3**(1), 189–202.

De Grauwe, P., Dewachter, H. and Embrechts, M. (1993), *Exchange Rate Theory: Chaotic Models of Foreign Exchange Markets*, Blackwell, Oxford.

De Long, J.B., Shleifer, A., Summers, L.H. and Waldmann, R.J. (1990), 'Noise Trader Risk in Financial Markets', *Journal of Political Economy*, **98**(4), 703–738.

Diamond, D. and Verrecchia, R.E. (1987), 'Constraints on Short Selling and Asset Price Adjustment to Private Information', *Journal of Financial Economics*, **18**, 83–106.

Diebold, F.X. (1996) in *Views from the Frontier: Commentary on the New World of Forecasting and Risk Management*, Olsen & Associates, Zurich.

Diebold, F.X. and Pauly, P. (1988), 'Endogenous Risk in a Rational Expectations Portfolio Balance Model of DEM/USD Rate', *European Economic Review*, No. 32, 27–54.

Dooley, M.P. and Shafer, J.R. (1983), 'Analysis of Short Run Exchange Rate Behaviour: March 1973 to November 1981', in D. Bigman and T. Taya (eds), *Exchange Rate and Trade Instability: Causes, Consequences and Remedies*, Ballinger, Cambridge, Mass, pp. 43–69.

Drost, F.C. and Nijman, T.E. (1993), 'Temporal Aggregation of GARCH Processes', *Econometrica*, **61**(4), 900–927.

Dunis, C. (1996), 'The Economic Value of Neural Network Systems for Exchange Rate Forecasting', *Neural Network World*, **6**, 43–55.

Easley, D. and O'Hara, M. (1992), 'Time and the Process of Security Price Adjustment', *Journal of Finance*, **47**, 577–606.

Eddelbüttel, D. (1997), 'Three Essays in Financial Economics and Econometrics', unpublished PhD thesis, Ecole des Hautes Etudes en Sciences Sociales.

Ederington, L. and Lee, J. (1993), 'How Markets Process Information: News Releases and Volatility', *Journal of Finance*, **48**, 1161–1191.

Fama, E.F. (1970), 'Efficient Capital Markets: a Review of Theory and Empirical Work', *Journal of Finance*, **25**(2), 383–423.

Fama, E.F. (1976), 'Forward Rates as Predictors of Future Spot Rates', *Journal of Economics*, **3**, 361–377.

Fama, E.F. and French, K.R. (1988), 'Permanent and Temporary Components of Stock Prices', *Journal of Political Economy*, **96**, 246–273.

Fortune, P. (1991), 'Stock Market Efficiency: an Autopsy?' *New England Review, Federal Reserve Bank of Boston*, March–April, 17–40.

Frankel, J.A. and Froot, K.A. (1988), 'Chartists, Fundamentalists and the Demand for Dollars', *Greek Economic Review*, **10**, 49–102.

Gallant, R., Rossi, P. and Tauchen, G. (1992), 'Stock Prices and Volume', *Review of Financial Studies*, **5**, 199–242.

Ghose, D. and Kroner, K.F. (1996), 'Components of Volatility in Foreign Exchange Markets: an Empirical Analysis of High-frequency Data', Unpublished manuscript, Department of Economics, University of Arizona.

Ghysels, E., Gourieroux, C. and Jasiak, J. (1995), 'Trading Patterns, Time Deformation and Stochastic Volatility in Foreign Exchange Markets', *Scientific Series 95s-42*, CIRANO, Montreal.

Gilles, C. and LeRoy, S.F. (1991), 'Econometric Aspects of the Variance-bounds Tests: a Survey', *Review of Financial Studies*, **4**(4), 753–791.

Glosten, L. and Milgrom, P. (1985), 'Bid, Ask and Transaction Prices in a Specialist Market with Heterogeneously Informed Traders', *Journal of Financial Economics*, **14**, 71–100.

Goodhart, C.A.E. (1996), in *Views from the Frontier: Commentary on the New World of Forecasting and Risk Management*, Olsen & Associates, Zurich.

Goodhart, C.A.E. and Curcio, R. (1992), 'When Support/Resistance Levels are Broken, Can Profits be Made? Evidence from the Foreign Exchange Market', Discussion Paper, No. 142, LSE Financial Markets Group.

Goodhart, C.A.E. and Figliuoli, L. (1991), 'Every Minute Counts in Financial Markets', *Journal of International Money and Finance*, **10**, 23–52.

Goodhart, C.A.E. and O'Hara, M. (1995), 'High-frequency Data in Financial Markets: Issues and Applications', Introductory Lecture, First International Conference of High-Frequency Data in Finance, Olsen & Associates, Zurich.

Goodhart, C.A.E. and Payne, R. (1995), 'Microstructural Dynamics in a Foreign Exchange Electronic Broking System', Unpublished Paper, No. 142, LSE Financial Markets Group.

Guillaume, D., Dacorogna, M., Dave, R., Müller, U., Olsen, R. and Pictet, O. (1994), 'From the Bird's Eye to the Microscope: a Survey of New Stylised Facts of the Intradaily Foreign Exchange Markets', Discussion Paper, Olsen & Associates, Zurich.

Guillaume, D., Pictet, O. and Dacorogna, M. (1995), 'On the Intraday Performance of GARCH Processes', Presentation Paper, Conference on High Frequency Data organised by Olsen & Associates, Zurich.

Hakkio, G.S. and Pearce, D.K. (1985), 'The Reaction of Exchange Rates to Economic News', *Economic Inquiry*, **23**(4), 621–636.

Hamilton, J.D. (1989), 'A New Approach to the Economic Analysis of Non-stationary Time Series and the Business Cycle', *Econometrica*, **57**, 307–317.

Harvey, C. and Huang, R. (1991), 'Volatility in the Foreign Currency Futures Market,' *Review of Financial Studies*, **4**, 543–569.

Hogan, K. and Melvin, M. (1994), 'Sources of Meteor Showers and Heat Waves in the Foreign Exchange Market', *Journal of International Money and Finance*, **10**, 590–599.

Holloway, C. (1981), 'A Note on Testing an Aggressive Investment Strategy Using Value Line Ranks', *Journal of Finance*, **36**(3), 711–719.

Hsieh, D.A. (1988), 'The Statistical Properties of Daily Exchange Rates: 1974–1983', *Journal of International Economics*, **24**, 129–145.

Hsieh, D.A. (1989), 'Modelling Heteroscedasticity in Daily Foreign Exchange Rates', *Journal of Business and Economic Statistics*, **7**, 307–317.

Jensen, M.C. (1978), 'Some Anomalous Evidence Regarding Market Efficiency', *Journal of Financial Economics*, **6**, 95–101.

Keane, S.M. (1983), *Stock Market Efficiency: Theory, Evidence and Implications*, Philip Allan, Oxford.

Keim, D.B. and Stambaugh, R.F. (1986), 'Predicting Returns in Stock and Bond Markets', *Journal of Financial Economics*, **17**, 357–390.

Kendall, M. (1953), 'The Analysis of Economic Time Series, Part I: Prices', *Journal of the Royal Statistical Society*, **96**, 11–25.

Kleidon, A.W. (1986), 'Variance Bounds Tests and Stock Price Valuation Models', *Journal of Political Economy*, **94**, 953–1001.

Kyle, A. (1985), 'Continuous Auctions and Insider Trading', *Econometrica*, **53**, 1315–1335.

Lamoureux, C.G. and Lastrapes, W.D. (1990), 'Heteroscedasticity in Stock Return Data: Volume vs GARCH Effects', *Journal of Finance*, **45**(1), 221–229.

LeBaron, B. (1992), 'Forecast Improvements Using a Volatility Index', *Journal of Applied Econometrics*, **7**, 137–149.

LeBaron, B. (1996) in *Views From the Frontier: Commentary on the New World of Forecasting and Risk Management*, Olsen & Associates, Zurich.

Lee, C.M.C., Shleifer, A. and Thaler, R.H. (1990), 'Closed-end Mutual Funds', *Journal of Economic Perspectives*, **4**(4), 153–164.

LeRoy, S.F. and Porter, R.D. (1981), 'The Present Value Relation: Tests Based on Implied Variance Bounds', *Econometrica*, **49**, 555–574.

Levich, R. and Thomas, L. (1993), 'The Significance of Technical Trading Rule Profits in the Foreign Exchange Market: a Bootstrap Approach', *Journal of International Money and Finance*, **12**, 452–474.

Low, A. and Muthuswamy, J. (1996), 'Information Flows in High-frequency Exchange Rates', in C. Dunis (ed.), *Forecasting Financial Markets*, Wiley, Chichester, pp. 3–32.

Malkiel, B.G. (1977), 'The Valuation of Closed-end Investment-company Shares', *Journal of Finance*, **32**(3), 357–390.

Mandelbrot, B.B. (1963), 'The Variation of Certain Speculative Prices', *Journal of Business*, **36**, 394–419.

Mandelbrot, B.B. (1966), 'Forecasts of Future Prices, Unbiased Markets and Martingale Models', *Journal of Business*, **39**, 242–255.

Mankiw, N.G., Romer, D. and Shapiro, M.D. (1991), 'Stock Market Forecastability and Volatility: a Statistical Appraisal', *Review of Economic Studies*, **58**, 455–477.

Maravall, A. (1983), 'An Application of Non-linear Time-Series Forecasting', *Journal of Business and Economic Statistics*, **3**, 350–355.

Mark, N.C. (1995), 'Exchange Rates and Fundamentals: Evidence from Long Horizon Predictability', *American Economic Review*, **85**(1), 201–218.

Markowitz, H. (1952), 'Portfolio Selection', *Journal of Finance*, **7**, 77–91.

Markowitz, H. (1959), *Portfolio Selection*, Wiley, New York.

Medio, A. (1992), *Chaotic Dynamics, Theory and Application to Economics*, Cambridge University Press, New York.

Meese, R.A. and Rogoff, K. (1983), 'Empirical Exchange Rate Models of the Seventies: Do They Fit Out-of-sample?' *Journal of International Economics*, **14**, 3–24.

Miller, M., Muthuswamy, J. and Whaley, R. (1994), 'Mean Reversion of S&P's Index Basis Changes: Arbitrage-induced or Statistical Illusion?' *Journal of Finance*, **2**, 479–513.

Moody, J. and Wu, L. (1995), 'Statistical Analysis and Forecasting of High Frequency Exchange Rates', Research Paper, Computer Science Department, Oregon Graduate Institute of Science and Technology.

Müller, U., Dacorogna, M., Olsen, R., Pictet, O., Schwarz, M. and Morgenegg, C. (1990), 'Statistical study of Foreign Exchange Rates, Empirical Evidence of a Price Scaling Law and Intraday Analysis', *Journal of Banking and Finance*, **14**, 1189–1208.

Muth, J. (1961), 'Rational Expectations and the Theory of Price Movements', *Econometrica*, **29**, 315–335.

Neely, C., Weeler, P. and Dittmar, R. (1997), 'Is Technical Analysis in the Foreign Exchange Market Profitable? A Genetic Algorithm Approach', Presentation Paper, Fourth Forecasting Financial Markets Conference, London.

Olsen & Associates (1996), *Views from the Frontier: Commentary on the New World of Forecasting and Risk Management*, Zurich.

Osborne, M.F.M. (1959), 'Brownian Motion in the Stock Market', *Operations Research*, **7**, 145–173.

Osborne, M.F.M. (1962), 'Periodic Structure in the Brownian Motion of Stock Prices', *Operations Research*, **10**, 345–379.

Osler, C.L. and Kevin Chang, P.H. (1995), 'Head and Shoulders: Not Just a Flaky Pattern', Staff Papers, Federal Reserve Bank of New York.

Pesaran, M.H. and Potter, S.M. (1993), *Non-linear Dynamics, Chaos and Econometrics*, Wiley, New York.

Pesaran, M.H. and Timmermann, A. (1994), 'Forecasting Stock Returns: an Examination of Stock Market Trading in the Presence of Transactions Costs', *Journal of Forecasting*, **13**(4), 335–367.

Pictet, O.V., Dacorogna, M.M., Olsen, R.B. and Ward, J.R. (1992), 'Real-time Trading Models for Foreign Exchange Rates', *Neural Network World*, **2**, 713–744.

Poterba, J.M. and Summers, L.H. (1988), 'Mean Reversion in Stock Prices: Evidence and Implications', *Journal of Financial Economics*, **22**, 26–59.

Reinganum, M.R. (1983), 'The Anomalous Stock Market Behaviour of Small Firms in January', *Journal of Financial Economics*, **12**(1), 89–104.

Samuelson, P. (1965), 'Proof that Properly Anticipated Prices Fluctuate Randomly', *Industrial Management Review*, **6**, 41–49.

Sentana, E. and Wadhwani, S. (1992), 'Feedback, Traders and Stock Return Autocorrelations: Evidence from a Century of Daily Data', *Economic Journal*, **102**(411), 415–425.

Shiller, R.J. (1979), 'The Volatility of Long Term Interest Rates and Expectations Models of the Term Structure', *Journal of Political Economy*, **87**(6), 1190–1219.

Shiller, R.J. (1981), 'Do Stock Prices Move Too Much to be Justified by Subsequent Changes in Dividends', *American Economic Review*, **71**, 421–436.

Shiller, R.J. (1989), *Market Volatility*, MIT Press, Cambridge, Mass.

Shleifer, A. and Summers, L.H. (1990), 'The Noise Trader Approach to Finance', *Journal of Economic Perspectives*, **4**(2), 19–33.

Summers, L.H. (1986), 'Does the Stock Market Rationally Reflect Fundamental Values?' *Journal of Finance*, **41**(3), 591–601.

Sweeny, R.J. (1986), 'Beating the Foreign Exchange Market', *Journal of Finance*, **41**, 163–182.

Takagi, S. (1991), 'Exchange Rate Expectations', *IMF Staff Papers*, **8**(1), 156–183.

Taylor, S.J. (1986), *Modelling Financial Time Series*, Wiley, Chichester.

The Intertek Group (1997), *Real-time Data, Analytics and Forecasting Systems*, Summary of results for participants, Study commissioned by BARRA International, The Intertek Group, Paris.

Vassilicos, C. and Demos, A. (1994), 'The Multifractal Structure of High Frequency Foreign Exchange Rate Fluctuations', LSE Financial Markets Group, Discussion Paper, No. 86.

Weigend, A. (1996) in *Views From the Frontier: Commentary on the New World of Forecasting and Risk Management*, Olsen & Associates, Zurich.

Working, H. (1934), 'A Random Difference Series for Use in the Analysis of Time Series', *Journal of American Statistical Association*, **29**, 11–24.

Zhou, B. (1996), 'Forecasting Foreign Exchange Rates Subject to De-volatilisation', in Dunis, C. (ed.), *Forecasting Financial Markets*, Wiley, Chichester, pp. 51–68.

2
High Frequency Foreign Exchange Rates: Price Behavior Analysis and 'True Price' Models

JOHN MOODY and LIZHONG WU

1 INTRODUCTION

The interbank foreign exchange (FX) market is the primary market for foreign exchange transactions, and operates 24 hours per day, 5 days per week. Lacking a centralized exchange, the spot FX market is a distributed, over-the-counter market in which participants trade directly with each other. Tick-by-tick interbank FX data consist of a sequence of bid/ask prices quoted by various firms that function as market makers. While bid/ask price quotes from many market makers are displayed continuously by wire services such as Reuters and Telerate, a single price series can be constructed from the sequence of newly updated quotes. Examples of such *indicative quote* series are the data displayed on the Reuters FXFX and RICS pages. Note that these indicative quotes are nonbinding and do not represent actual transactions. There is no public record of all FX transaction prices and volumes for the interbank market.

Figure 2.1 displays a sequence of bid ask prices during October 1992. Figures 2.2 and 2.3 plot hourly prices and daily tick volumes of the USD/DEM market from October 1992 to September 1993. The data in Figures 2.1–2.3 were collected from the Reuters FXFX page by Olsen & Associates. Business days have about 6000 USD/DEM quotes (ticks) per day on average, or about 250 quotes per hour and about 4 quotes per minute. The weekly cycle of trading activity and the Christmas and New Year holidays are apparent from Figure 2.3.

Nonlinear Modelling of High Frequency Financial Time Series.
Edited by Christian Dunis and Bin Zhou. © 1998 John Wiley Sons Ltd

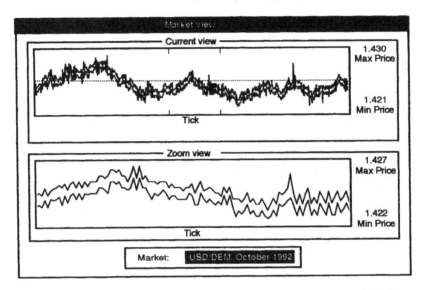

Figure 2.1 Bid and ask USD/DEM prices extracted from 1 October 1992. The upper window displays about 3.5 hours of tick data, while the lower window shows a zoom view of about 25 minutes of data. In both cases the data are plotted in tick time. High frequency oscillations in successive price quotes are clearly apparent in the zoom view. Relative to these oscillations, the local average price levels are slowly varying. These phenomena will be quantified and modeled in later sections of this chapter

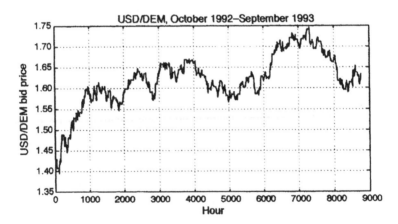

Figure 2.2 Hourly price of the USD/DEM market from October 1992 to September 1993

Figure 2.4 plots the intra-week hourly tick volumes for the USD/DEM and USD/JPY markets from October 1992 to September 1993. As shown in the figure, the three trading peaks correspond to the three major, overlapping, geographical components in the market (Dacorogna *et al.* 1993). The primary market hours in

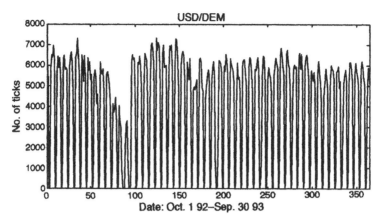

Figure 2.3 Daily quote volume of the USD/DEM market from October 1992 to September 1993

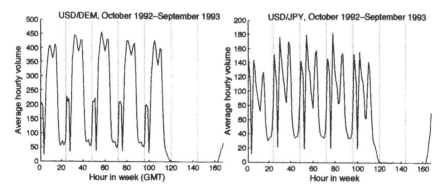

Figure 2.4 Average intra-week hourly quote volumes of the USD/DEM (left) and the USD/JPY (right) markets from October 1992 to September 1993. Weekly seasonality and the overlapping presence of geographical components (East Asia, Europe and America) are apparent. Each small panel separated by the dotted vertical lines corresponds to one day. From left to right, the panels are respectively for Monday to Sunday. As shown, there are very few trades on Saturday. Because early Monday mornings in East Asia correspond to late Sundays in GMT, the weekly trading activity starts late Sunday evening on this plot. The sharp downward spikes in trading volume during East Asian trading hours correspond to the Tokyo lunch break

East Asia and Europe are GMT 23:00–6:00 and GMT 6:00–16:00 respectively, and GMT 12:00–20:00 are the primary market hours in America.

Different from daily or weekly data, tick-by-tick data are randomly spaced in time. One frequently used method to deal with this irregularity is to sample intra-daily data at regular intervals of physical time, often by interpolating the nearest ticks bracketing specified times. Another method is to use business (or intrinsic) time, such as the θ-time discussed by Müller *et al.* (1993) and Dacorogna *et al.* (1993); θ-time dilates physical time according to weekly seasonality patterns in price volatility.

However, in this study, we use 'tick time', a simple and convenient business time scale for analyzing short-term price behaviors. Tick time assigns one time unit per tick. For some purposes, it is useful to first 'reduce' the dual bid and ask series to a single average price series by computing the 'mean price', the average of the bid and ask prices or of the log(bid) and log(ask) prices. The time scales (physical or tick) and data series types we analyze are indicated in the various sections or figure captions that follow.

In this chapter, we present a number of empirical results for the tick-by-tick interbank FX data and present state-space models that describe the observed correlation structures. In section 2, we analyze the short-term behavior of the FX price changes. We examine the probability distributions of bid and ask returns, and the autocorrelation coefficients in short-run windows. In section 3, our study is then extended further by considering up to thousands of ticks. We study the temporal correlation structure of the data via rescaled range analysis and computations of Hurst exponents. To correct for the effects of short-term autocorrelations, we present a new rescaled range statistic R/S^*. In section 4, we explore the relationships between price uncertainty on short time scales, volatility and bid/ask spreads. We find that our proposed measure of uncertainty (tick-by-tick forecast error) is correlated with volatility and bid/ask spreads. In section 5, we present state-space models for FX indicative quotes that are able to explain both the tick-by-tick and longer-term correlation structures described in sections 2 and 3. In these models, the underlying 'true price' is masked by observational noise. True price estimation has a variety of potential applications for dealers, traders and arbitrageurs.

2 SHORT-TERM MEMORY STRUCTURES IN TICK-BY-TICK FX DATA

2.1 Distributions of Bid and Ask Returns

In this section, we present empirical results for the distributions of bid and ask returns and for the autocorrelation structure of USD/DEM indicative quotes on time scales of a few ticks. A typical sample of bid and ask prices is shown in Figure 2.1.

Figure 2.5 shows the temporal evolution of one-dimensional histograms of ask returns for a sequence of frames of length 1024 ticks. Considerable nonstationarity in the one-dimensional histograms is apparent. This corresponds to changes in volatility over time. Two-dimensional histograms of frequencies of bid returns for USD/DEM are shown in Figure 2.6. The histograms also show

USD/DEM Ask_return, first 25 600 ticks in October 1992

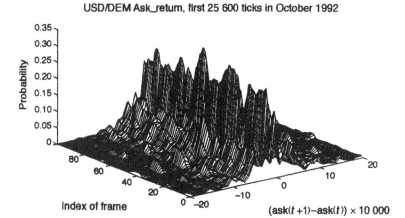

Figure 2.5 Probability distributions for ask returns versus time. Data sample is the first 25 600 ticks of USD/DEM for October 1992. Each time frame is 1024 ticks long and is shifted by 256 ticks from the previous frame. Note the substantial nonstationarity in the distribution, even though the 75% overlap between successive frames smoothes some of the actual nonstationarity. Changes in volatility over time are clearly apparent

the anticorrelation of successive bid returns. Similar results obtain for the ask series. The negative correlations have also been observed on the 1-minute time scale (Goodhart and Figliuoli 1991).

2.2 Autocovariance and Autocorrelation Functions

Figure 2.7 shows the evolution of the autocovariance and autocorrelation coefficients for a sequence of windows of length 1024 ticks successively shifted by 512 ticks. Here, considerable nonstationarity in variance and covariance is apparent. Again, the negative correlation of successive returns is clear. Interestingly, although the correlation coefficients for lags two, three and four appear to be almost statistically insignificant, the data in Table 2.1 suggest that they are on average significant.

Table 2.1 Fractions of frames with autocorrelation coefficients larger in absolute value than the 95% significance levels, based on USD/DEM for October 1992. Note that all numbers are in excess of 0.05, suggesting that, over time, there is significant autocorrelation even at lag nine

Lag	1	2	3	4	5	6	7	8	9
Bid	1.00	0.28	0.18	0.18	0.16	0.15	0.15	0.13	0.11
Ask	1.00	0.29	0.17	0.13	0.14	0.13	0.15	0.14	0.08

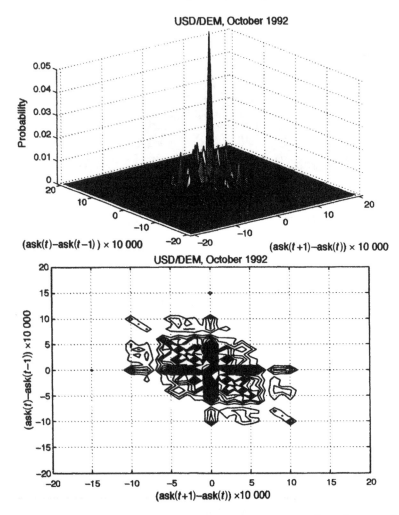

Figure 2.6 Two-dimensional probability distributions for successive ask returns for the USD/DEM exchange rate during October 1992. The lower panel plots the contours of the probability distribution shape in the upper panel

The negative correlation of subsequent returns in bid and ask prices is apparent from the histograms and the first autocorrelation coefficient. Furthermore, the covariance structures of the series are nonstationary, and a daily volatility cycle is apparent. It is interesting to note that the first autocorrelation coefficient fluctuates around a value of approximately -0.43. In the state-space framework developed in section 5, this suggests that one-tick returns are due mostly to observational noise.

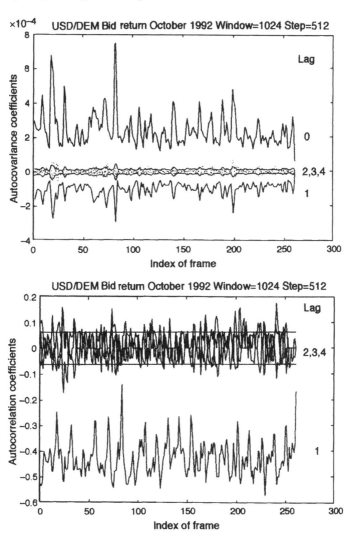

Figure 2.7 Autocovariance and autocorrelation coefficients {0, 1, 2, 3, 4} versus time frame for USD/DEM during October 1992. Each time frame contains 1024 ticks and successive frames overlap by 512 ticks. A typical business day has about 12 overlapping frames. Note the nonstationarities and possible daily variations in the covariance and correlation structures. The 95% significance levels are indicated by solid lines close to zero in the upper figure and the solid horizontal lines in the lower figure. Although the first autocorrelation coefficient is obviously significantly different from zero at all times, the statistical significance for coefficients two, three and four is less obvious. However, the data in Table 2.1 suggest that these higher-order correlations should not be discounted.

3 LONG-TERM PRICE BEHAVIOR

There are three widely used methods for the analysis of long-term dependencies: autocorrelation analysis, fractional difference modeling (Granger and Joyeux 1980; Hosking 1981) and scaling law analysis. The latter includes the rescaled range (R/S) (Hurst 1951), Hurst exponent (Hurst 1951; Mandelbrot and van Ness 1968) and drift exponent (Müller *et al.* 1990) statistics. This section describes R/S analysis and Hurst exponents, which have recently become popular in the finance community largely due to the empirical work of Peters (1989).

Compared to autocorrelation analysis, the advantages of R/S analysis include: (i) detection of long range dependence, (ii) applicability to non-Gaussian time series with large skewness or kurtosis, (iii) almost sure convergence for stochastic processes with infinite variance and (iv) detection of nonperiodic cycles. However, there are also two deficiencies associated with rescaled range analysis and the estimation of Hurst exponents: (i) estimation errors exist when the time scale is very small or very large relative to the number of observations in the time series (Mandelbrot and Wallis 1969; Wallis and Matalas 1970; Feder 1988; Ambrose *et al.* 1993; Moody and Wu 1995; Müller *et al.* 1995), and (ii) the rescaled range is sensitive to short-term dependencies (McLeod and Hipel 1978; Hipel and McLeod 1978; Lo 1991). The second shortcoming will sometimes lead to completely incorrect results.

In this section, we review rescaled range analysis and the Hurst exponent, and present a modified version or rescaled range analysis R/S^* that is insensitive to short-term autocorrelations. We then demonstrate that as indicated by the Hurst exponent, USD/DEM tick data are slightly trending, not mean-reverting, on time scales of 60 ticks (about 15 minutes) or less. This empirical result agrees with that obtained by Müller *et al.* (1990) using the drift exponent for data sampled in θ-time (a deseasonalized physical time scale) on time scales of 10 minutes or more.

3.1 R/S Analysis and Hurst Exponents

The R/S statistic is the range of partial sums of deviations of a time series from its mean rate of change, rescaled by its standard deviation. Denoting a series of returns (one period changes) by r_t, the average m and (biased) standard deviation S of the returns from $t = t_0 + 1$ to $t = t_0 + N$ are[1]

$$m(N, t_0) = \sum_{t=t_0+1}^{t_0+N} r_t/N \qquad (1)$$

$$S(N, t_0) = \left\{ \frac{1}{N} \sum_{t=t_0+1}^{t_0+N} [r_t - m(N, t_0)]^2 \right\}^{1/2} \qquad (2)$$

The partial sum of deviations of r_t from its mean and the range of partial sums are then defined as

$$X(N, t_0, \tau) \equiv \sum_{t=t_0+1}^{t_0+\tau} (r_t - m(N, t_0)) \quad \text{for } 1 \leq \tau \leq N \tag{3}$$

$$R(N, t_0) \equiv \max_\tau X(N, t_0, \tau) - \min_\tau X(N, t_0, \tau) \tag{4}$$

The R/S statistic for time scale N is simply the ratio between the average values of $R(N, t_0)$ and $S(N, t_0)$:

$$[R/S](N) \equiv \frac{\sum_{t_0} R(N, t_0)}{\sum_{t_0} S(N, t_0)} \tag{5}$$

Assuming that a scaling law exists for $[R/S](N)$, we can write

$$[R/S](N) \approx (aN)^H \tag{6}$$

where a is a constant and H is referred to as the Hurst exponent. By estimating H, we can characterize the behavior of time series as follows:

$$\text{if} \quad \begin{array}{ll} H = 0.5 & \text{random walk} \\ H \in (0, 0.5) & \text{mean-reverting} \\ H \in (0.5, 1) & \text{mean-averting (trending)} \end{array}$$

For a more detailed, but readable, discussion of R/S analysis and Hurst exponents, see Feder (1988).

3.2 Rescaled Range Analysis with Unbiased S^*

As mentioned above, the standard rescaled range analysis is sensitive to short-term correlations. Specifically, rejections of the null hypothesis (that the time series is a random walk) on long time scales can be erroneous and can be due instead to bias induced by short-term dependencies. It is possible, in fact, for a trending series to appear mean-reverting if short-term anticorrelations are present.

A widely used alternative approach for avoiding misleading results due to short-term correlations is to filter the data using an autoregressive filter with a short lag structure. This method often works well, but requires an additional processing step.

Another approach was proposed by Lo (1991). Lo's modified R/S analysis rescales the range R using a modified $\tilde{S}$, which is a weighted sum of short-term autocovariances, instead of the standard deviation S. Unfortunately, Lo's rescaling factor $\tilde{S}$ has significant downward bias for small N, and this distorts both $R/\tilde{S}$ and the Hurst exponent H. In fact, Lo's $R/\tilde{S}$ statistics can yield *negative* Hurst exponents, which are not possible theoretically.

To reliably detect the presence of long-term memory structures in financial time series when short-term autocorrelations are present, we proposed a new unbiased rescaled range statistic R/S^* (Moody and Wu 1996) that eliminates the contaminating effects of autocorrelations on time scale q. This addresses the problems with the statistics $[R/S](N)$ and $[R/\tilde{S}](N)$ described above, by using an unbiased rescaling factor S^* that corrects for mean biases in the range R due to short-term dependencies without inducing the distortions on short time scales that S and Lo's $\tilde{S}$ do.

Denoting the standard unbiased estimate of the variance as

$$\hat{\sigma}^2(N, t_0) = \frac{1}{N-1} \sum_{t=t_0+1}^{t_0+N} (r_t - m)^2 \tag{7}$$

our proposed unbiased rescaling factor with weighted covariances up to lag q is

$$S^*(N, t_0, q) = \left\{ \left[1 + 2 \sum_{j=1}^{q} w_j(q) \frac{N-j}{N^2} \right] \hat{\sigma}^2(N, t_0) \right.$$

$$\left. + \frac{2}{N} \sum_{j=1}^{q} w_j(q) \sum_{t=t_0+j}^{t_0+N} (r_t - m)(r_{t-j} - m) \right\}^{1/2} \tag{8}$$

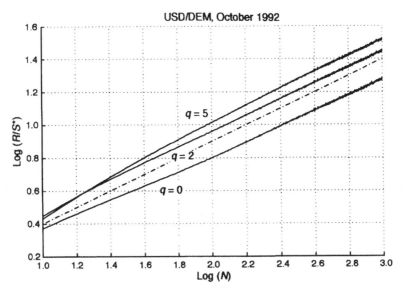

Figure 2.8 $[R/S^*](N)$ for the USD/DEM bid returns for October 1992 using lag parameters $q = \{0, 2, 5\}$. Note that for time scales of less than 60 ticks (about 15 minutes on average during weekdays), the slope H_0 for the $q = 0$ case is less than 0.5, while the slopes H_2 and H_5 for the $q = 2$ and $q = 5$ cases are greater than 0.5. The apparent mean reversion ($q = 0$) on short time scales in the USD/DEM series is actually due to the high frequency oscillations, and that when these are removed on a time scale of five ticks, the series is shown to be slightly trending

where $w_j(q)$ is the weighting function as defined by Lo ($w_j(q) = 1 - j/(q+1)$). This weighting function yields a positive S^*, provided that $q < N$. It is trivial to show that the estimates of the autocovariances in equation (8) have zero mean bias. When $q = 0$, S^* reduces to the unbiased standard deviation $\hat{\sigma}$.

3.3 R/S^* Analysis of USD/DEM Prices

Figure 2.8 shows an R/S^* analysis of USD/DEM indicative prices (Moody and Wu 1996). As explained in the figure caption, the apparent price behavior on time scales up to 60 ticks changes completely as the effects of tick-by-tick negative autocorrelations are removed. The apparent behavior of the tick-by-tick USD/DEM series shifts from mean-reverting to mean-averting (trending). From this experiment, we can see that the spuriously observed mean reversion in the original price series is due to short-term negative autocorrelations, rather than to intrinsic dependencies in the price movements, and that the underlying behavior of the series on longer time scales is actually trending on average. Our empirical result that long-term trends are present in FX data is consistent with results obtained by Müller *et al.* (1990) using the drift exponent on time scales of 10 minutes or more.

4 FORECASTABILITY, VOLATILITY AND BID/ASK SPREADS

There is a well-known relationship between the dealers' bid/ask spreads and price volatility. Dealers widen their spreads when volatility is higher in order to reduce their risk of loss.

We have extended this analysis to compare measures of *price uncertainty* with volatility and bid/ask spreads. One should not confuse short-term price volatility and uncertainty. For example, it is possible to have high short-term volatility and low uncertainty. This can happen if there are large short-term fluctuations in bid and ask prices around a stable underlying value. In the state-space framework of section 5, this situation occurs when the observational noise variance is high relative to the process noise variance.

Our measures of uncertainty are normalized prediction errors of one-tick-ahead univariate autoregressive (AR) predictors of the bid and ask price returns. Although one-tick-ahead AR forecasts are of little interest from the standpoint of most traders, we find that normalized prediction errors are positively correlated with volatilities and bid/ask spreads.

4.1 Tick-by-Tick Univariate AR Prediction and Nonstationarity

To quantify a measure of price uncertainty, we constructed adaptive AR predictors of the bid and ask returns series. The predictors were univariate predictors and were re-estimated for each tick based on a moving window of the 1024

Table 2.2 Summary statistics of USD/DEM AR predictor accuracy. The accuracy measures include normalized MSE, normalized root MSE, normalized mean absolute error (NMAE) and fraction of return directions predicted correctly. The performance measures are computed for frames of 1024 ticks. The summary statistics are for all frames in the year October 1992 to September 1993

	NMSE		NRMSE		NMAE		% Same direction	
	Bid	Ask	Bid	Ask	Bid	Ask	Bid	Ask
Mean	0.7556	0.7507	0.8692	0.8664	0.8976	0.8933	0.5712	0.5781
STD	0.0148	0.0143	0.0085	0.0082	0.0117	0.0121	0.0103	0.0118
Max.	0.7933	0.7892	0.8907	0.8884	0.9294	0.9283	0.5819	0.5882
Min.	0.7417	0.7368	0.8612	0.8584	0.8852	0.8823	0.5439	0.5476
Median	0.7675	0.7630	0.8760	0.8734	0.9073	0.9053	0.5629	0.5679

previous ticks (approximately 4 hours of USD/DEM data). The AR model specifications are summarized as follows: separate models for bid return and ask return; one-tick-ahead forecast horizon; model estimation using the previous 1024 ticks of data; and model order selection via Akaike's information criterion, with the maximum model order being four.

The month-by-month performances for the predictors are summarized in Table 2.2. The '% Same direction' figures are the percentages of cases that the AR models predict {down, no-change, up} directions correctly. The no-change prediction can occur when the previous returns used as input to the AR model are zero. The NMSE is the mean squared error normalized by the variance of observed returns for the training data set, which is the 1024 ticks preceding the current tick. The NRMSE is the normalized root MSE. The NMAE is the mean absolute error (difference of predicted and observed returns) normalized by the mean absolute difference between the observed return and the mean return of the training data set.

Note that all four of the forecasting performance measures are independent of the level of tick-by-tick volatility. NMSE, NRMSE and NMAE are all normalized by appropriate measures of the current volatility and the % same direction statistic is independent of volatility. Hence, *price uncertainty*, as measured by prediction performance, captures properties of the data series not captured by volatility measures.

Figure 2.9 plots the linear regression coefficients of the fourth-order AR predictor for the first 12 000 ticks of the October 1992 USD/DEM bid returns series. Nonstationarity is clearly evident in the four AR model coefficients, suggesting that the short-term price behavior evolves over time.

4.2 Relationship of Bid/Ask Spreads, Volatility and Forecastability

We have found a very high degree of correlation between average bid/ask spreads, volatility and uncertainty (as measured by forecastability). Figure 2.10

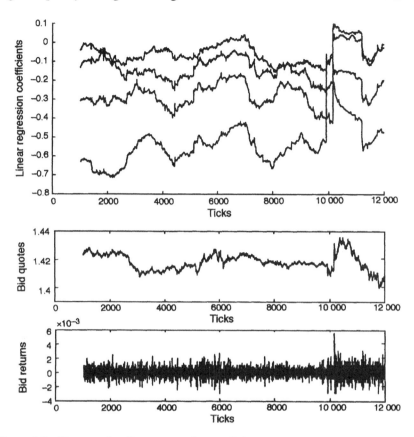

Figure 2.9 Time-varying linear regression coefficients of the fourth-order AR predictor for the first 12 000 ticks in the October 1992 USD/DEM bid returns. The four curves from the bottom to the top correspond to the first, second, third and the fourth regression coefficients, respectively. Note that the shifts in the model shortly before and shortly after the 10 000th tick are due to the price jumps shown in the middle panel. This occurred between 12:30 and 13:30 (GMT) on Friday, 2 October 1992, and were related to the US September employment report. Note also the increase in volatility in the bid returns after these events

shows scatter-plots of our one-tick-ahead prediction accuracy (as measured by the percentage of correctly predicted ups, downs or no-changes), the volatility (defined as the standard deviation of price changes) and the bid/ask spreads. All data were based on daily averages. Table 2.3 gives the correlation coefficients. Note the highly significant correlations for both monthly and daily averages. Spreads are positively correlated with volatility, while forecastability is negatively correlated with both spreads and volatility. In other words, the forecast error is positively correlated with both spreads and volatility.

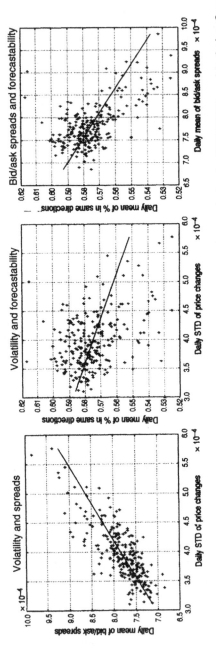

Figure 2.10 Scatter-plots of daily averages of forecastability, volatility and bid/ask spreads for the USD/DEM market during October 1992 to September 1993. Significant correlations between the variables are apparent from the regression lines and from the cross-correlation coefficients (Table 2.3)

Table 2.3 Interactions of monthly and daily average bid/ask spreads, volatility and forecastability. The 95% confidence limits for the cross-correlation coefficients are $\{-0.49, +0.66\}$ for monthly averages and $\{-0.12, +0.13\}$ for daily averages. Thus, all of the cross-correlations are significantly different from zero

Monthly	Forecastability	Volatility	Spreads
Forecastability	1		
Volatility	−0.797	1	
Spreads	−0.912	0.856	1

Daily	Forecastability	Volatility	Spreads
Forecastability	1		
Volatility	−0.402	1	
Spreads	−0.566	0.796	1

These results support the notion that higher volatility is associated with greater uncertainty and increased risk for market makers. To compensate for this increase in risk, market makers increase their bid/ask spreads.

5 STATE-SPACE MODELS OF FX INDICATIVE PRICES

In previous sections, we described statistically significant structures in tick-by-tick interbank foreign exchange (FX) price series on various time scales. These structures include: (i) negative correlations in successive tick-by-tick price changes; see Figures 2.1 and 2.7; (ii) positive autocorrelations on longer time scales of up to 60 ticks (about 15 minutes on average for USD/DEM); see Figure 2.8. This second effect is not necessarily easy to measure, since the strong tick-by-tick anticorrelations can mask it.

The strong anticorrelation at lag 1 in the tick-by-tick returns as shown in Figures 2.1 and 2.7 is believed by financial economists to be caused by market microstructure effects, particularly the inventory effect (Lyons 1993; O'Hara 1995). Regardless of its cause, we will argue that it can be explained empirically as an effect due to additive observational noise in the indicative price quotes.

To account for both the observed short- and longer-term correlation structures, we propose state-space models for financial time series in which the observed price is a noisy version of an unobserved, less noisy 'true price' process. The 'true prices' in our models are stochastic processes with short-term, long-term or multiscale memory structures. The processes we consider include random walks, random or autoregressive trends and fractional Brownian motions. Using the Kalman filter and estimation maximization (EM) algorithms, we can estimate the unobservable underlying true prices (assuming some price process) and remove the observational noise in the indicative quotations.

5.1 State-space Models

State-space or 'true price' models assume that the recorded price quotations can be described by

$$q(t) = p(t) + \varepsilon(t) \tag{9}$$

where $p(t)$ is the underlying 'true price' and $\varepsilon(t)$ is zero mean random noise. Our task is thus to estimate $p(t)$ assuming some model, given the observed series $q(t)$.[2] In this section, we study and compare the following three types of models for the underlying price $p(t)$:

1. *Steady model (random walk+noise).* This model assumes that the underlying prices follow a random walk process, i.e

$$p(t) = p(t-1) + \delta(t) \tag{10}$$

where $\delta(t)$ is a process noise. Assuming that both the observation noise ($\varepsilon(t)$ in equation (9)) and the process noise are white, the autocovariances of the observed returns $r_q(t) = q(t) - q(t-1)$ are

$$E[r_q^2(t)] = 2\sigma_\varepsilon^2 + \sigma_\delta^2 \tag{11}$$

$$E[r_q(t)r_q(t-1)] = -\sigma_\varepsilon^2 \tag{12}$$

$$E[r_q(t)r_q(t-\tau)] = 0 \quad \text{for } \tau \geq 2 \tag{13}$$

It is straightforward to estimate σ_ε^2 and σ_δ^2 from measurements of the auto-covariances. The state $p(t)$ can be estimated via the Kalman filter. The autocorrelation coefficients are $\rho_1 = -\sigma_\varepsilon^2/(2\sigma_\varepsilon^2 + \sigma_\delta^2)$, and $\rho_j = 0$ for $j > 1$. Theoretically, the value of ρ_1 for the steady model can range between -0.5 when $\sigma_\delta^2 = 0$ and 0 when $\sigma_\varepsilon^2 = 0$.

For the USD/DEM returns in Figure 2.7, $\hat{\rho}_1 \approx -0.43$ and $\hat{\rho}_2 \approx \hat{\rho}_3 \approx \hat{\rho}_4 \approx 0$ on average, suggesting that the returns on very short time scales are well described by the steady model, and that the returns are mostly observational noise.

However, the steady model is not completely satisfactory, since: $\hat{\rho}_1 < -0.5$ at some points; $\hat{\rho}_j$ for $j > 1$ are significantly different from 0 too frequently; and weak, positive correlations on longer time scales are not explained.

Figure 2.11 plots the *signal-to-noise ratio* of the model, defined as SNR $= \sigma_\delta^2/\sigma_\varepsilon^2$, for USD/DEM in September 1995. Its nonstationarity requires that our model should be adaptive through time. The observed SNR is remarkable for two reasons: (i) it is usually much less than one and (ii) it varies significantly in magnitude, suggesting that there are periods with significant price movements (high SNR) separated by periods of almost no price movement (low SNR).

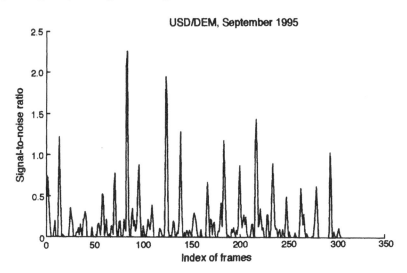

Figure 2.11 SNR in the steady model for USD/DEM in September 1995. Each frame consists of 1024 ticks; the frames overlap by 512 ticks. A daily volatility cycle is apparent

2. *Autoregressive trend model (AR trend + random walk + noise).* This model assumes that the underlying prices follow:

$$p(t) = p(t-1) + \beta(t-1) + \delta_1(t) \tag{14}$$

$$\beta(t) = \alpha\beta(t-1) + \delta_2(t) \tag{15}$$

For the special case $\alpha = 0$, this model is known as the linear growth model. With the assumption that the process and observation noises are white, we can solve this model using the Kalman filter.

3. *Fractional Brownian motion (FBM) model.* Here, the underlying price series is assumed to follow fractional Brownian motion. Fractional Brownian motion is a generalization of the usual Brownian motion or random walk. It was introduced to model processes that have long memory or $1/f$-type spectral behaviors (Beran 1994), and have a statistical self-similarity property (Feder 1988). Since the discovery of the presence of long memory components in asset returns, see for example Mandelbrot and van Ness (1968), there have been many empirical reports to support this finding (Granger 1980; Peters 1989; Diebold and Rudebusch 1989). For FBMs, the dependence between distant observations, though small, is by no means negligible. Compared to short memory series such as autoregressive moving average (ARMA) processes, the dependences of long-term persistent processes decay hyperbolically instead of exponentially. Conventional approaches like ARMA models are therefore inadequate to capture the correlation structures embedded in long memory series.

In the next section, we will study fractional Brownian motion modeling with wavelet representations.

5.2 Estimating FBMs via Wavelet Decomposition and the EM Algorithm

There have been many models developed for FBM processes. Some well-known and recently developed models include: filtered white noise (Mandelbrot and van Ness 1968; Feder 1988), aggregation of short memory models (Granger 1980), fractional difference models (Granger and Joyeux 1980; Hosking 1981), driving white noise through an infinite cascade of pole-zero sections (Keshner 1982) and orthonormal wavelet basis expansions with uncorrelated random coefficients (Mallet 1989; Flandrin 1992; Wornell and Oppenheim 1992). To compare these approaches systematically is another topic of study. However, the latter approach, wavelets, has certain advantages for estimating state-space models. Ramsey and Zhang (1995) and Bjorn (1995) have also used wavelets for financial time series analysis, but not in a state-space context.

The wavelet transform decomposes a signal into self-similar wavelets which are derived from one elementary waveform by means of shifts and dilations. Fractional Brownian motions also exhibit self-similarity, since any portion of a given process can be viewed, in a statistical sense, as a scaled version of a larger or smaller sample of the same process. The above correspondence sets up a bridge between the wavelet transform and FBMs. In fact, the multi-resolution analysis with wavelet decompositions is particularly well suited to analyzing the underlying statistical property of FBMs when observational noise is present.

Taking the wavelet transform of equation (9), see for example Daubechies (1988) and Mallet (1989), we get

$$Q_n^m = P_n^m + \varepsilon_n^m \quad \text{for } m \in \mathcal{M} \text{ and } n \in \mathcal{N}(m) \tag{16}$$

with m representing the scale level and n for the time index of the components. Under the Gaussian assumption, P_n^m can be estimated by Flandrin (1992) and Wornell and Oppenheim (1992):

$$\hat{P}_n^m = \mathbf{E}[P_n^m | Q_n^m] = S(m, \theta) Q_n^m \tag{17}$$

where

$$S(m, \theta) = \frac{\sigma^2 \beta^{-m}}{\sigma^2 \beta^{-m} + \sigma_\varepsilon^2} \tag{18}$$

is a wavelet analog of the Wiener filter that serves as a smoothing function. Denoting the wavelet basis functions as $\psi_n^m(t)$, this yields the following estimate of the 'true price':

$$\hat{p}(t) = \sum_{m,n} \hat{P}_n^m \psi_n^m(t) = \sum_{m,n} S(m, \theta) Q_n^m \psi_n^m(t) \tag{19}$$

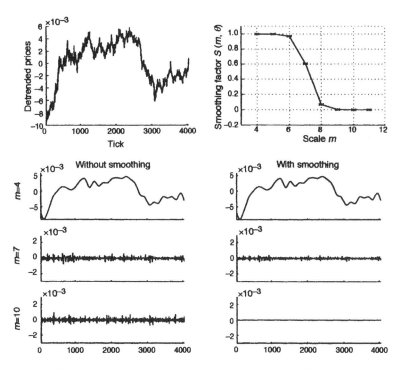

Figure 2.12 Visualizing equation (19) for a set of USD/DEM prices after being detrended as shown in the upper left panel. The smoothing function $S(m, \theta)$ is plotted in the upper right panel. Lower panels compare the original and smoothing reconstructed signals at scales of 4, 7 and 10. The signals are mostly retained at coarser scales (small m), while at finer scales (large m), the signals are mostly removed

The model parameters $\theta = (\beta, \sigma^2, \sigma_\varepsilon^2)$ can be estimated using the EM algorithm. Note that the factor $S(m, \theta)$ has a thresholding or smoothing role: at coarser scales (small m) where the signal predominates, the coefficients Q_n^m are retained, while at finer scales (large m) where noise predominates, the coefficients Q_n^m are attenuated.

In Figure 2.12, we visualize equation (19) for a set of USD/DEM tick-by-tick prices. The smoothing factor $S(m, \theta)$ decays from 1 to 0 as the scale level m goes from coarse to fine. At coarser scales, the signals are mostly retained, while at finer scales, the signals are mostly removed.

5.3 Independent Component Analysis

Since both the observational noise and the changes in the true price series have non-Gaussian distributions, the Kalman filter and EM algorithms are not able to completely separate the observational noise from the true price components. To improve this separation, we perform a neural-network-based independent component analysis (ICA) using algorithms developed for the blind separation of signals (Bell and Sejnowski 1995; Amari, Cichocki and Yang 1996). ICA finds a separation of the signals with reduced statistical dependence at not only second order (cross-correlations), but also at higher orders as well (e.g. fourth-order cross-cumulants). Our ICA is performed by using the true price and observational noise components estimated via the Kalman filter or EM algorithms as reference inputs to the blind separation algorithm. More detailed discussion and empirical results are presented in Moody and Wu (1997) and Wu and Moody (1997).

5.4 Empirical Results and Discussions

Figure 2.13 compares a segment of true prices to the observed prices. We see that the 'true prices' are much smoother and less noisy.

Comparisons between Models

We have estimated three true prices based on different models. The question that arises is: how do these different estimated prices differ and relate to each other? To answer this, we perform pair-by-pair homogeneous χ^2 testings for the distributions of the estimated returns for the different models. As shown in Figure 2.14, our analysis accepts the hypothesis that the returns come from different populations. Thus, all true price return series are significantly different from the observed price return, and the choice of true price model among the three models studied yields significantly different results.

Autocorrelation Analysis

Figure 2.15 shows short-run autocorrelations during September 1995 for the original returns and compares them to autocorrelations for changes in the noise and

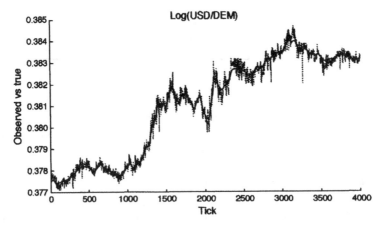

Figure 2.13 Observed USD/DEM (dotted curve) and the true prices estimate under the model of FBM assumption (solid curve)

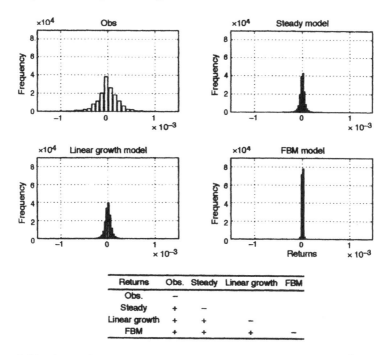

Returns	Obs.	Steady	Linear growth	FBM
Obs.	−			
Steady	+	−		
Linear growth	+	+	−	
FBM	+	+	+	−

Figure 2.14 Comparison of histograms and pair-by-pair homogeneous χ^2 testings for observed returns and denoised and smoothed true price returns for three state-space models. '−' indicates that the hypothesis that the pairs of returns come from different populations is rejected and '+' indicates that the hypothesis is accepted. The significance level is 99%. The data are USD/DEM price quotes for September 1995

true price components. The true price model is estimated under the FBM assumptions, and the autocorrelation analysis is performed after further separating the signals using ICA. Autocorrelations for lags up to 50 ticks (about 8 minutes on average) are computed in windows of length 1024 ticks.

From the figure, we can see that both the noise component returns and the original returns show very similar autocorrelation functions, which are dominated by significantly negative, first-order autocorrelations. The mean values for the other orders are basically equal to zero. The autocorrelations of the true price component show positive correlations except at first order.

The above autocorrelation analysis suggests the following:

1. Changes in the true prices for the FBM model exhibit slight, but significant, trends on tick-by-tick time scales. Whether this is an artifact introduced by the wavelet smoothing must still be determined. However, these results are consistent with those indicated by R/S^* analysis in Figure 2.8.
2. The autocorrelation function of original returns reflects only the anticorrelation of price changes at lag 1 (believed by economists to be due to the

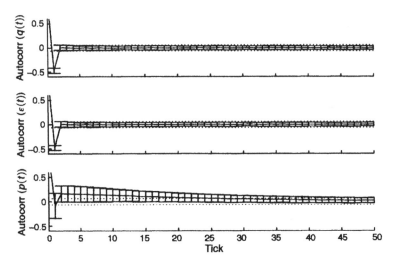

Figure 2.15 Comparison of autocorrelation functions of the returns for the original series (the upper panel), the observational noise component (the middle panel) and the true price component (the lower panel) for the FBM model. USD/DEM data for September 1995 are divided into 293 subsets of 1024 tick windows which overlap by 512 ticks. The autocorrelation results presented here are the means and standard deviations for the 293 windows. The horizontal dotted lines represent the 95% confidence band for a single 1024 tick window

inventory effect). This suggests that the existence of the strong, short-term anticorrelations will foil a standard autocorrelation analysis on longer time scales. These results may be model-dependent and should be considered preliminary. However, they suggest that true price models may be effective in uncovering underlying structure that is obscured by additive noise.

Sonification of True Prices

The statistical differences between the observed price series, estimated true price series and white noise can be easily perceived by playing the price changes through a sound generator. The results are quite striking. In particular, the true prices for the FX markets exhibit periods of relative calm, occasional waves of activity, and intermittent impulse noise (presumably due to news).

6 SUMMARY AND DISCUSSION

In this chapter, we presented a number of empirical results for tick-by-tick interbank FX data and proposed state-space models that describe the observed correlation structures.

In sections 2 and 3, we examined the correlation structures present in high frequency FX data on both very short tick-by-tick and longer time scales. On short time scales, FX indicative price quote returns exhibit significant negative correlation at lag one. On longer time scales (10–1000 ticks), we study the temporal correlation structure of the data via rescaled range analysis and computations of the Hurst exponent. To correct for the effects of short-term autocorrelations, we use a new rescaled range statistic R/S^*. We find that the tick data are slightly trending on time scales of 10–60 ticks (about 15 minutes for USD/DEM on average).

In section 4, we explored the relationships between price uncertainty on short time scales, volatility and bid/ask spreads. We find that our proposed measure of uncertainty (the tick-by-tick forecast error) is correlated with volatility and bid/ask spreads.

In section 5, we proposed using state-space models to analyze high frequency financial data. These models decompose the observed prices into unobserved, underlying true prices plus observational noise. We have presented three such true price models, including random walks, random trends and fractional Brownian motions. The random walk and random trend models are estimated using Kalman filters, while wavelet decompositions and the EM algorithm are used to estimate the FBM models. Since the observational noise and process noise components of the observed prices are non-Gaussian, we use independent component analysis (ICA) to further separate observational noise from the true prices.

These models are able to explain observed correlation structures in the USD/DEM exchange rates. These include anticorrelations in successive price changes and positive correlations (trends) on longer time scales. Our statistical modeling of high frequency intra-day FX price series has demonstrated that trends may in fact exist in noisy FX data and that the conventional random walk models of efficient market theory do not explain the correlation structures that are present in the high frequency data. Further studies are required.

Possible applications of our proposed true price models include discovery of new arbitrage opportunities (Bolland and Connor 1996), obtaining better transaction prices, more competitive FX dealing, and constructing better forecasting and trading models.

ACKNOWLEDGEMENTS

We would like to thank Olsen & Associates, Chemical Bank and Citibank for providing us with the data used in our analysis, and Michel Dacorogna and Yoni Cheifetz for insightful discussions. We gratefully acknowledge support for this work from ARPA and ONR under grant N00014-92-J-4062, NSF under grant CDA-9309728, ARPA under contract DAAH01-96-C-R026, and Nonlinear Prediction Systems.

ENDNOTES

1. The quantity $S(N, t_0)$ conventionally used in R/S analysis is an estimate of the standard deviation that is biased downward by a factor $\sqrt{(N-1)/N}$. The unbiased

estimate of the true standard deviation $\sigma(N, t_0)$ is

$$\hat{\sigma}(N, t_0) = \left\{ \frac{1}{N-1} \sum_{t=t_0+1}^{t_0+N} [r_t - m(N, t_0)]^2 \right\}^{1/2}$$

In section 3.3, we present improved results using the unbiased estimate $\hat{\sigma}(N, t_0)$.
2. Bolland and Connor (1996) have used state-space models to identify triangle arbitrage opportunities in groups of currencies.

REFERENCES

Amari, S., Cichocki, A. and Yang, H. (1996), 'A New Learning Algorithm for Blind Signal Separation', in D. Touretzky, M. Mozer and M. Hasselmo (eds), *Advances in Neural Information Processing Systems 8*, MIT Press, Cambridge, Mass., pp. 757–763.

Ambrose, B., Ancel, E. and Griffiths, M. (1993), 'Fractal Structure in the Capital Markets Revisited', *Financial Economic Review*, 30, 685–704.

Bell, A. and Sejnowski, T. (1995), 'An Information–Maximization Approach to Blind Separation and Blind Deconvolution', *Neural Computation* 7(6), 1129–1159.

Beran, J. (1994), *Statistics for Long-Memory Processes*, Chapman and Hall, New York.

Bjorn, V. (1995), 'Multiresolution Methods for Financial Time Series Prediction', in *Conference on Computational Intelligence for Financial Engineering*, IEEE Press, Piscataway, New Jersey.

Bolland, P. and Connor, J. (1996), 'Identification of fx Arbitrage Opportunities with a Non-linear Multivariate Kalman Filter', in A. Refenes, Y. Abu-Mostafa, J. Moody and A. Weigend (eds), *Neural Networks in the Capital Markets, Proceedings of the Third International Conference* (London, October 1995), World Scientific, London, pp. 122–134.

Dacorogna, M., Müller, U., Nagler, R., Olsen, R. and Pictet, O. (1993), 'A Geographical Model for the Daily and Weekly Seasonal Volatility in the Foreign Exchange Market', *Journal of International Money and Finance*, 12, 413–438.

Daubechies, I. (1988), 'Orthonormal Bases of Compactly Supported Wavelets', *Commun. Pure Appl. Math.*, 41, 909–996.

Diebold, F.X. and Rudebusch, G.D. (1989), 'Long Memory and Persistence in Aggregate Output', *Journal of Monetary Economics*, 24, 189–209.

Feder, J. (1988), *Fractals*, Plenum Press, New York.

Flandrin, P. (1992), 'Wavelet Analysis and Synthesis of Fractional Brownian Motions', *IEEE Transactions on Information Theory*, 38(2), 910–917.

Goodhart, C.A.E. and Figliuoli, L. (1991), 'Every Minute Counts in Financial Markets', *Journal of International Money and Finance*, 10, 23–52.

Granger, C. (1980), 'Long Memory Relationships and the Aggregation of Dynamic Models', *Journal of Econometrics*, 14, 227–238.

Granger, C. and Joyeux, R. (1980), 'An Introduction to Long-memory Time Series Models and Fractional Differencing', *Journal of Time Series Analysis*, 1, 15–29.

Hipel, K. and McLeod, A. (1978), 'Preservation of the Rescaled Adjusted Range. 2. Simulation Studies using Box–Jenkins Models', *Water Resource Research*, 14, 509–516.

Hosking, J. (1981), 'Fractional Differencing', *Biometrika*, 68, 165–176.

Hurst, H. (1951), 'Long-term Storage of Reservoirs', *Transactions of the American Society of Civil Engineers*, 116.

Keshner, M. (1982), '1/f noise', *Proceedings IEEE*, 70, 212–218.

Lo, A.W. (1991), 'Long Term Memory in Stock Market Prices', *Econometrica*, **59**, 1279–1313.

Lyons, R. (1993), 'Tests of Microstructural Hypotheses in the Foreign Exchange Market', Working Paper Series 4471, National Bureau of Economic Research, INC.

McLeod, A. and Hipel, K. (1978), 'Preservation of the Rescaled Adjusted Range. 1. A Reassessment of the Hurst Phenomenon', *Water Resource Research*, **14**, 491–508.

Mallet, S. (1989), 'A Theory for Multiresolution Signal Decomposition: The Wavelet Representation', *IEEE Transactions on Pattern Analysis and Machine Intelligence*, **11**(7), 674–693.

Mandelbrot, B. and van Ness, J. (1968), 'Fractional Brownian Motion, Fractional Noise, and Applications', *SIAM Review*, **10**, 422–437.

Mandelbrot, B. and Wallis, J. (1969), 'Computer Experiments with Fractional Gaussian Noises. Part 3, Mathematical Appendix', *Water Resource Research*, **3**(1), 260–267.

Moody, J. and Wu, L. (1995), 'Price Behavior and Hurst Exponents of Tick-by-tick Interbank Foreign Exchange Rates', in *Conference on Computational Intelligence for Financial Engineering*, IEEE Press, New York.

Moody, J. and Wu, L. (1996), 'Improved Estimates for the Rescaled Range and Hurst Exponents', in A. Refenes, Y. Abu-Mostafa, J. Moody and A. Weigend (eds), *Neural Networks in the Capital Markets, Proceedings of the Third International Conference* (London, October 1995), World Scientific, London, pp. 537–553.

Moody, J. and Wu, L. (1997), 'What is the "True Price"?' in Y. Abu-Mostafa, A. Refenes and A. Weigend (eds), *Neural Networks in the Capital Markets III*, World Scientific, London, pp. 346–358.

Müller, U., Dacorogna, M., Olsen, R., Pictet, O., Schwarz, M. and Morgenegg, C. (1990), 'Statistical Study of Foreign Exchange Rates, Empirical Evidence of a Price Change Scaling Law, and Intraday Analysis', *Journal of Banking and Finance*, **14**, 1189–1208.

Müller, U., Dacorogna, M., Davé, R., Pictet, O., Olsen, R. and Ward, J. (1993), *Fractals and Intrinsic Time — a Challenge to Econometricians*, Technical Report UAM.1993-08-16, Olsen & Associates, Zurich.

Müller, U., Dacorogna, M. and Pictet, O. (1995), *The Error of Statistical Volatility of Intra-daily Quoted Price Changes Observed over a Time Interval*, Technical Report UAM.1995-07-31, Olsen & Associates, Zurich, Switzerland.

O'Hara, M. (1995), *Market Microstructure Theory*, Blackwell Business, Cambridge, Mass.

Peters, E. (1989), 'Fractal Structure in the Capital Markets', *Financial Analysts Journal*, July/August, pp. 32–37.

Ramsey, J. and Zhang, Z. (1995), 'The Analysis of Foreign Exchange Data Using Waveform Dictionaries', in *First International Conference on High Frequency Data in Finance*, Olsen & Associates, Zurich, Switzerland.

Wallis, J. and Matalas, N. (1970), 'Small Sample Properties of H and K, Estimators of the Hurst Coefficient H', *Water Resource Research*, **6**, 1583–1594.

Wornell, G. and Oppenheim, A. (1992), 'Estimation of Fractal Signals from Noisy Measurements Using Wavelets', *IEEE Transactions on Signal Processing*, **40**(3), 611–623.

Wu, L. and Moody, J. (1997), 'Multi-effect Decompositions for High Frequency Financial Data Modeling', in M. Mozer, M. Jordan and T. Petsche (eds), *Advances in Neural Information Processing Systems 9*, MIT Press, Cambridge, Mass., pp. 995–1001.

PART II

Detecting Nonlinearities in High Frequency Data: Empirical Tests and Modelling Implications

3
Testing Linearity with Information-theoretic Statistics and the Bootstrap

F.M. APARICIO ACOSTA

1 INTRODUCTION

An important aspect in the analysis of financial time series is *linearity testing*. On one hand, a test of linearity may point to the existence of higher-order dependencies in the level of the series, and therefore to the possibility of improving standard predictors based on linear autoregressions. This information is particularly appreciated in series with random walk-like behaviour, since the accuracy of forecasts provided by the optimal linear predictor in these cases deteriorates very fast with increasing forecasting horizon. On the other hand, a linearity test can be applied to the residuals from a nonlinear model fitted to the series, in order to check the adequacy of this model.[1] Many tests of linearity could be interpreted as *Lagrange-multiplier tests* against specific nonlinear models (Luukkonen *et al.* 1988; Granger and Terasvirta 1993, p. 62). These tests assess the significance in the regression of the residuals from a linear model fitted to the series, on certain *test* or *moment functions*, $\psi_\mathbf{a}(Y_{t-1})$, generally depending on a parameter vector $\mathbf{a}$, and with $Y_{t-1} = (y_{t-1}, \ldots, y_{t-m})'$ representing a delay or state vector in an appropriate embedding space for y_t. If the moment function happens to represent satisfactorily the true model for a nonlinear series, then the test is *uniformly most powerful* against this alternative. Otherwise, the test may still have power against it. However, this power can be jeopardized if the series has important features that may not be captured very well by the

Nonlinear Modelling of High Frequency Financial Time Series.
Edited by Christian Dunis and Bin Zhou. © 1998 John Wiley Sons Ltd

moment function. The latter situation may lead to an imbalance or mismatch of major properties between both sides of the nonlinear regression equation in the test, which translates into a large probability of type II errors. This problem is called *spectral imbalance*, when the model fitted to a number of variables is unable to describe important spectral features of the latter (Granger 1995).

A commonly used technique to deal with spectral imbalance consists of running the test on the first differences of the series. Unfortunately, this approach may result in the obliteration of relevant information 'living' near the zero frequency (Granger and Joyeux 1980) (see Figure 3.1) unless the true model for the series is $(1 - B)^d y_t = x_t$ with d an integer, and x_t denoting a process with spectral density bounded everywhere. This information could be important in such applications as classification and long-range forecasting, especially if the dynamics are mostly confined to this range of frequencies.

The chapter has a twofold purpose: (i) to introduce a new family of non-parametric linearity tests to economists working in the field of empirical finance; (ii) to apply these techniques to financial time series such as exchange rates, and to see how they perform as compared to standard linearity tests. A key

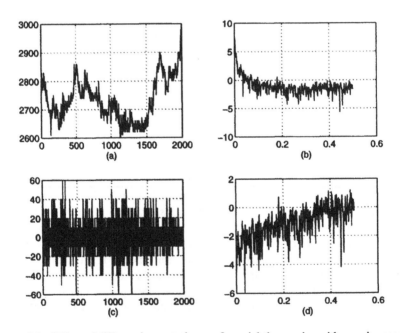

Figure 3.1 Effect of differencing a stationary financial time series with a major spectral feature at the origin: (a) hourly series from USD/CAD exchange rate; (b) log-periodogram of (a); (c) series of first differences from (a); (d) log-periodogram of (c). The plot in (d) shows how the low frequency information in the series is severely damped by differencing

idea underlying these new testing schemes is that of *bootstrapping* the data in the frequency domain and comparing the values of an *auxiliary test statistic*, evaluated for the original series and for the bootstrapped linear replica. The other important idea is the application of information-theoretic concepts such as the *entropy* and the *transinformation* or *mutual information* in forming one such test statistic. We will show that entropy-based measures are very sensitive to linear departures from the Gaussianity assumption. As a consequence, they are not suitable for linearity testing. On the contrary, the mutual information in pairs of random variables (r.v.'s) from the same process, which is a general measure of serial dependence, does not appear to be handicapped by these ambiguities. Based on this fact, we propose a linearity test which, by design, is not being formulated in a regression context, and thus it is free of spectral imbalance problems.

The rest of the chapter is organized as follows. Section 2 explains the methodology of linearity testing using the bootstrap method, and section 3 introduces an information-theoretic framework for testing linearity. The implementation of the major blocks in the latter is considered in section 4. Section 5 shows the performance of our test on both simulated series and real data of foreign exchange rates, respectively. Finally, section 6 concludes.

2 LINEARITY TESTING USING THE BOOTSTRAP

In this section, we present a family of non-parametric tests where the main idea consists of comparing the values taken by a test statistic when evaluated on the original time series y_t, and on a *linear surrogate replica*, x_t, of y_t. The surrogate replica has the same linear correlation structure as y_t and can be obtained by randomizing the phase spectrum (the Fourier phases) of y_t while preserving its power spectrum. Of course, when using this technique, we are implicitly assuming that part of the nonlinearity (if any) lives in the phase spectrum (i.e. higher-order statistical information) of the series.

The previous method for generating surrogate data is somehow equivalent to parametric bootstrapping in the temporal domain, whereby the residuals from an estimated parametric linear model fitted to the series, are randomized and later filtered by this model. However, there is an advantage in randomizing the phase spectrum over (parametric) temporal bootstrapping of the series. Indeed, since it postulates no model at all, the former avoids the problems of an eventual misspecification of the linear model adjusted to the series.

Let
$$X = (x_1, x_2, \ldots, x_N)' \quad \text{and} \quad Y = (y_1, y_2, \ldots, y_N)'$$

with X denoting a linear surrogate replica of Y and N the sample size. Also let $t_N(Y)$ denote the value taken at Y by an auxiliary test statistic, and consider the stochastic difference $\eta_N(Y, X) = t_N(Y) - t_N(X)$. A linearity test can be constructed by requiring $\eta_N(Y, X)$ to approach zero when y_t is linear, and to be comparatively large in magnitude otherwise.

In order to reduce the sampling variability of $\eta_N(Y, X)$, we may consider some sort of ensemble averaging by generating a number, say P, of linear surrogate replicas of y_t, say $x_t^{(i)}$, for $i = 1, \ldots, P$, and forming the new test statistic:

$$\eta_{N,P}(Y) = P^{-1} \sum_{p=1}^{P} \eta_N(Y, X^{(p)}) \tag{1}$$

To obtain a consistent test, we may try scaling our test statistic as $P^{1/2}\eta_{N,P}(Y)$. Assuming that a central limit theorem (CLT) holds, this statistic will converge to a normal random variable with zero mean, under H_0, and diverge with probability one under H_1. In the rest of the chapter we assume this limit behaviour for our test statistic, since our concern is merely exploratory.

3 LINEARITY TESTING WITH INFORMATION-THEORETIC STATISTICS

The family of tests that will be described in this section follow the previous strategy of constructing a test statistic involving linear surrogate replicas of the original time series Y. Here, we consider for the auxiliary test statistic, some non-parametric measures of variability and dependence, such as the entropy and the mutual information. As these quantities can be estimated non-parametrically, the resulting testing device is purely non-parametric, and might be preferred to a parametric linearity test, whose power depends on the relevance of the test function as a model for the series on which the test is applied.

Henceforth we will adopt the following point of view. Let us suppose a time series given in vector form, Y, which has been obtained by sampling the output of a nonlinear system acting on a linear input, X. We are now interested in 'measuring' the amount of information (which we will allow to be either positive, negative or zero) contributed by the system. We can define this information as the difference between the *uncertainty* in X and that in Y. In fact, we are viewing the union of the input and the system as an *information source*, and we want to estimate that part of the information contributed only by the system. Alternatively, we may view X as the source, the system as a *distorting channel*, and our problem as that of estimating the amount of distortion introduced by the channel.

Shannon (1948) stated the concept of uncertainty, and thereby that of information, by applying ideas from probability theory. He defined the entropy of a discrete r.v. or source x as

$$H(x) = H(p_1^{(x)}, \ldots, p_N^{(x)}) = -\sum_{i=1}^{N} p_i^{(x)} \log p_i^{(x)} \tag{2}$$

for a source alphabet of symbols $\{x_1, \ldots, x_N\}$ having probabilities $\{p_1^{(x)}, \ldots, p_N^{(x)}\}$, respectively. For a continuous r.v. x, having a marginal probability density function (p.d.f.) $f_x(\cdot)$, it is possible to define a *differential* entropy (e.g. Cover and Thomas 1991, p. 224) as

$$H(x) = H(f_x) = - \int_{-\infty}^{\infty} f_x(x) \log f_x(x) \, dx \qquad (3)$$

When we deal with sequences of r.v.'s or with stochastic processes, the entropy of the sequence grows indefinitely with the number of r.v.'s in it. Thus a more operative concept is that of *entropy rate* (e.g. Gray 1990, p. 37), which measures how this entropy grows with increasing size of the sequence. For example, for a sequence $X = (x_1, \ldots, x_N)'$, the entropy rate would be defined as

$$H(x) = N^{-1} H(x_1, \ldots, x_N) \qquad (4)$$

where $H(x_1, \ldots, x_N) = H(X)$ is the joint entropy of the r.v.'s in X, which must be expressed in terms of the joint p.d.f. of this variate, $f_x(X)$, that is

$$H(X) = -N^{-1} \int f_x(X) \log f_x(X) \, dX \qquad (5)$$

It is clear that when the r.v.'s are independent and identically distributed (i.i.d.) then the entropy rate identifies with the entropy of a single variable. But in general, this is not the case, since there is usually a certain amount of serial dependence among the variables in the sequence.

The entropy function could be interpreted as a measure of *general variability* or *disorder* in the data, in contrast to the variance, which could be regarded as a measure of 'linear variability'. It can be shown (e.g. Morgera 1985), that in the i.i.d. Gaussian case these two measures are related by

$$H(X) \propto \log \sigma_x \qquad (6)$$

where σ_x denotes the standard deviation for the sequence x_t, and '$\propto$' means 'equal to up to a scaling constant'.

However, in contrast to the variance, the entropy can reflect both the serial dependence and the higher-order moment information in the series. In particular, when there is only linear serial dependence, the entropy function has the form (Morgera 1985)

$$H(X) = 0.5N + 0.5N \log(2\pi) + 0.5 \log |\mathbf{C}_{x,x}| \qquad (7)$$

where $\mathbf{C}_{x,x}$ denotes the $N \times N$ covariance matrix of the vector X, and $|\cdot|$ stands for the determinant of the argument matrix.

An interesting property of the entropy function, $H(f_x)$, relates to how it behaves under transformations of the variate X. To explain, let the action of the system be represented by a (deterministic) mapping $g(\cdot)$, so that $Y = g(X)$. In this case, the entropy $H(Y)$ of Y can be easily shown to be

$$H(Y) = H(X) + \int f_x(X) \log \left(\left| \frac{\partial g}{\partial X} \right| \right) \, dX \qquad (8)$$

where $|\partial g / \partial X|$ represents the Jacobian of the transformation $g(\cdot)$.

Equation (8) suggests that it may be possible to detect the presence of nonlinearity in Y if one has access to the input X. This is because the effect of a nonlinear transformation, $g(\cdot)$, applied to X is, in general, that of subtracting a certain amount of information from X. This follows from a result of information theory known as the *data processing inequality* (e.g. Gray 1990, p. 44), which states that $H(X) \geq H(g(X))$ for any transformation g. In this case, the system may be called *passive* or *resistive*, in the sense that no information is created through its action. If $H(Y) \approx H(X)$ the system could be declared *linear* in an information-theoretic sense, since its output preserves the amount of information carried by the input.

Notice from equation (8) that the entropy is not generically invariant to linear transformations. Therefore, the previous definition of linearity is not adequate unless we constrain the form of the relationship between the variates X and Y. We will see later that this sort of constraint is not needed if X is a linear bootstrapped replica of Y.

A model such as $Y = g(X)$ may seem too restrictive, but could be generalized to $Y = g(X, \aleph)$, where the parameter vector $\aleph$ may evolve stochastically and independently of X. An example of a time series model reflecting this sort of data-generating mechanism is the *stochastic unit-root model* (Granger and Swanson 1994). In this case, the system can contribute information to the input (*active system*), and thus lead to $H(Y) > H(X)$.

An alternative method for quantifying the amount of information contributed by our imaginary dynamical system consists of measuring how the action of such a system affects the serial dependence structure in the data. For this, we will use a most general measure of dependence known as the *mutual information or transinformation* statistic. Given two variates Y and X, the mutual information $I(X, Y)$ measures the amount of information that one of the variates conveys on the other, or in other words, the decrease in the uncertainty about X implied by the observation of Y (e.g. Cover and Thomas 1991, p. 231; Kullback 1968, p. 6).

The mutual information is defined in terms of the marginal and joint p.d.f.'s of the variables as follows:

$$I(X, Y) = \int f_{x,y}(X, Y) \log \left(\frac{f_{x,y}(X, Y)}{f_x(X) f_y(Y)} \right) \, dX \, dY \tag{9}$$

Using this information-theoretic statistic, a possible way of assessing the nonlinearity in the series is by comparing the quantities $I(Y_t, Y_{t-k})$ and $I(X_t, X_{t-k})$, where k is a non-zero integer.

3.1 Linearity Test Based on the Entropy

In order to estimate the contribution of the system alone to the entropy in the output of the previous model, we must somehow reconstruct the input. Although in reality this is not possible, since we ignore the system characteristic response (in fact, this is the problem to be solved), for our purposes we just need to construct a sequence X having the same properties as the real input, as regards the entropy. One may suggest that X be a linear surrogate replica of Y, as defined in section 2.

A heuristically appealing test statistic could be derived from $\eta_N(X, Y) = H(X) - H(Y)$, which measures the amount of *compression* of the information in X performed by the system which has Y as output and X as input. If $\eta_N(X, Y) > 0$ the system acts as an *encoder* (i.e. it reduces the variability in the source, or equivalently, creates dependencies among the input variables). If $\eta_N(X, Y) = 0$ then the system leaves the entropy of its input unchanged. Finally, if $\eta_N(X, Y) < 0$ the system acts as a *corrupting channel* (i.e. it expands the variability in the input, or equivalently, introduces additional randomness).

In summary, we may think of linearity as the case where the system does not leave its imprint on the input's entropy, that is, when $\eta_N(X, Y) = 0$, whereas nonlinearity corresponds to the encoder and corrupting channel cases, that is, when either $\eta_N(X, Y) > 0$ or $\eta_N(X, Y) < 0$. This is the basis for the construction of a linearity test.

Remarks
1. Notice that, by considering the linear surrogate series X as the input to the system, we are implicitly assuming that the latter leaves the (linear) correlation structure of this input unchanged, and just alters its higher-order features. We are therefore attempting to construct a *linearity index* based on the information contained in higher-order moments of the series. Thus the idea is the same that has fostered so much interest over the years in higher-order spectra. That is, since linear dependencies cannot 'live' beyond second-order statistics, nonlinearity could be resolved by 'looking' at the higher-order statistical information in the series.
2. Since x_t is constructed in such a way that the corresponding spectral densities verify $S_x(\lambda) = S_y(\lambda) \; \forall \; \lambda$, then $\sigma_x^2 = \sigma_y^2$, thereby excluding the possibility that $Y = aX$ with $|a| \neq 1$. As a consequence, the sensitivity of the entropy functional to scaling is not an issue here.

One problem with the previous test statistic is that the entropy is a highly distribution-dependent measure. For example, it is known (e.g. Lasota and Mackey 1994) that among those sequences x_t of i.i.d. r.v.'s, for which $E(|x_t|) < \infty$ the maximum entropy is achieved for the uniform p.d.f., that is, when $f_x(x) = c$, with c being a constant over some interval. But it reaches a maximum for the Gaussian p.d.f., if these processes verify $E(x_t^2) < \infty$. Therefore, even though under the hypothesis $H_{0,1}$ of Gaussianity in the output Y, $\eta_N(X, Y)$ will be close to zero, this will not generally be the case under $H_{0,2}$ of linearity and non-Gaussianity, since the linear surrogate sequence x_t will tend to be a Gaussian replica of y_t, thus yielding $\eta_N(X, Y) \neq 0$. If, in addition, y_t has a finite second-order moment then $\eta_N(X, Y) > 0$. As a consequence, the previous test statistic will be unable to discriminate between cases of $H_{0,2}$ and cases of nonlinearity (H_1). The following proposition summarizes these properties of the entropy as regards linearity testing.

Assumption AS1:

Let x_t, y_t be wide sense stationary time series such that $S_y(\lambda) = S_x(\lambda)$, where $S_z(\lambda)$, $z = x$, y denotes the spectral density of the sequence z_t.

Proposition 1

$H(Y) \leq H(X)$ under linearity, with equality in the Gaussian case under AS1.

Proof:

That $H(Y) = H(X)$ in the Gaussian case is trivial, since the entropy depends, on the one hand, on the shape of the distribution (which in this case is the same for Y and X), and on the other on the serial dependence structure in the data (in the Gaussian case, this is fully encoded in the covariances, which are the same for X and Y under assumption AS1).

That $H(Y) < H(X)$ in the linear non-Gaussian case follows by noting that x_t is 'Gaussianized' by the bootstrapping. To see this, let the spectral representation of y_t be $y_t = \int \exp(j\omega t)\, dZ_y(\omega)$, where $Z_y(\omega)$ denotes the *spectral distribution function* of y_t (e.g. Rosenblatt 1974, p. 163). Writing $dZ_y(\omega) = |dZ_y(\omega)| \exp(j\phi_y(\omega))$, we have for x_t, $dZ_x(\omega) = |dZ_y(\omega)|v(\omega)$, where $v(\omega)$ represents a complex random process (indexed by ω) independent of Y. Discretization of the spectral representation for x_t leads to

$$x_t \approx \sum_{i=0}^{N} \exp(j\omega_i t)|\Delta Z_y(\omega_i)|v(\omega_i) \qquad (10)$$

where $v(\omega_i)$ is an i.i.d. sequence. By applying a classical CLT result for sequences of partial sums of complex r.v.'s, we may conclude on the asymptotic (as $N \to \infty$) normality of x_t.

3.2 Linearity Test Based on the Transinformation

The entropy test has the drawback of being very sensitive to the shape of the variate's p.d.f. An attempt to cope with this problem consists of using a general measure of serial dependence such as the mutual information in pairs of variates, instead of a measure of general variability such as the entropy.

A measure of 'default' or 'excess' dependencies in Y with respect to X could be embodied in a test statistic having the form

$$\eta_n^{(n)}(Y, X) = I(Y^n, Y_{(-1)}^n) - I(X^n, X_{(-1)}^n) \qquad (11)$$

where $Z^n (Z = Y, X)$ denotes a generic n-dimensional delay vector or variate extracted from the sample of data, so that if $Z^n = (z_{t+1}, \ldots, z_{t+n})'$, then $Z_{(-1)}^n =$

$(z_t, \cdots, z_{t+n-1})'$. In particular, X^n represents a generic n-dimensional delay vector of r.v.'s formed from a linear surrogate replica x_t of y_t. Henceforth we will deliberately omit the superscript n, thereby assuming that the number of components in the variates X and Y was fixed in advance.

The statistic in equation (11), which yields a measure of the effect of nonlinearity on the serial dependence structure in y_t, could be generalized to higher lags:

$$\eta_n^{(m)}(Y, X) = I(Y^n, Y_{(-m)}^n) - I(X^n, X_{(-m)}^n) \tag{12}$$

Accordingly, a more general test statistic could be

$$\eta_n(Y, X) = \sum_{m=1}^{M} a_m \eta_n^{(m)}(Y^n, X^n) \tag{13}$$

where a_m could be an appropriate weighting sequence, chosen so as to maximize the magnitude of $\eta_n(Y, X)$.

A consistent estimator of the mutual information $I(Z^n, Z_{(-m)}^n)$ for a stationary sequence, z_t, of size N, is (Robinson 1991)

$$\hat{I}(Z^n, Z_{(-m)}^n) = N_\gamma^{-1} \sum_{i \in S} c_i(\gamma) \log \left(\frac{\hat{f}_{z,z}(Z_i^n, Z_{i-m}^n)}{\hat{f}_z^2(Z_i^n)} \right) \tag{14}$$

where $Z_i^n = (z_{i+1}, \ldots, z_{i+n})'$, $\hat{f}_{z,z}(\cdot, \cdot)$ and $\hat{f}_z(\cdot)$ denote estimates of the bivariate and the univariate joint densities, respectively, and the set S is introduced to make explicit the exclusion of certain innocuous summands, which may occur, for example, when $\hat{f}_{z,z}(., .) \leq 0$ or $\hat{f}_z(\cdot) \leq 0$, that is, when logarithms cannot be taken. Finally, the coefficients c_i are given by

$$c_i(\gamma) = \begin{cases} 1 + \gamma & \text{for } i \text{ odd} \\ 1 - \gamma & \text{for } i \text{ even} \end{cases}$$

with $\gamma \geq 0, N_\gamma = N$ for N even, and $N_\gamma = N + \gamma$, for N odd.

Now, we may synthesize a number, P, of linear surrogate replicas $x_{i,t}$, $(i = 1, \ldots, P)$, of y_t, from which P n-dimensional delay vectors ($n \ll N$), $\{X_1, X_2, \ldots, X_P\}$, can be obtained and used in forming the statistic

$$\eta_{n,P}^{(m)}(Y) = I(Y^n, Y_{(-m)}^n) - P^{-1} \sum_{p=1}^{P} I(X_p^n, X_{P_1(-m)}^n) \tag{15}$$

Assuming a standard CLT applies, it may be possible to conclude on the convergence of $P^{1/2} \eta_{n,P}^{(m)}(Y)$ towards a normally distributed zero-mean r.v., whereas it will diverge with probability one under nonlinearity, as $P \to \infty$.

4 SOME IMPLEMENTATION ISSUES

In the exploratory analysis that follows with the transinformation linearity test, the mutual information in pairs of variates was estimated using formula (14), with the p.d.f.'s approximated using *kernel smoothers* (e.g. Breiman *et al.* 1977).

Given a set of $N-n$ n-dimensional vectors Y_i, $i = 1, N-n$, a kernel density estimator with kernel K and bandwidth α, has the form

$$\hat{f}(Y) = (N-n)^{-1}\alpha^{-1}\sum_{i=1}^{N-n} K[\alpha^{-1}(Y-Y_i)] \tag{16}$$

where the kernel K is a function verifying $\int_{\Re^n} K(Y)\,dY = 1$.

In our experiments we used Gaussian kernels:

$$K(Y) = (2\pi)^{-n/2}\exp(-Y'Y/2) \tag{17}$$

Even though the form of the kernel is not critical to the results, the bandwidth is. To deal with this drawback, we use adaptive bandwidths (that is, $\alpha_i = \alpha(Y_i)$). This means that the kernels are allowed to shrink in rather densely populated regions of the embedding space, and to widen in regions with few data points. In this way, the smoothing is applied where needed, and never in excess, so that important biases are not introduced into the estimates. Specifically, we proceed by first obtaining an initial estimate of the densities, using a fixed bandwidth, α_0, for the kernels, and then adapting this parameter to the structure at different regions of the embedding space. For example, we may take for the local bandwidth parameters

$$\alpha(y) \propto 1/\hat{f}_{\alpha_0}(y) \tag{18}$$

where $\hat{f}_{\alpha_0}(y)$ denotes a rough estimate of the p.d.f. at y using a kernel smoother with fixed bandwidth, α_0.

The linear surrogate replicas y_t' of y_t were constructed in the following way:

1. Take the Fourier transform of the series, $s_j = \text{DFT}(y_k)$, with DFT standing for 'discrete Fourier transform'.
2. Randomize the Fourier phases in s_j. For example, take for the new Fourier estimates $s_j' = |s_j|\exp(i\phi_j)$, with ϕ_j representing a sequence of i.i.d. r.v.'s, uniformly distributed on the interval $(0, 2\pi)$.
3. Symmetrize the phase so as to obtain the Fourier estimates of a real r.v. For this, we define s_j'' such that $\mathcal{R}(s_j'') = 0.5\,\mathcal{R}(s_j' + s_{n+1-j}')$, and $\mathcal{I}(s_j'') = 0.5\,\mathcal{I}(s_j' - s_{n+1-j}')$, where $\mathcal{R}, \mathcal{I}$ stand for real and imaginary parts, respectively.
4. Finally, define $x_k = \text{DFT}^{-1}(s_j'')$, as the inverse Fourier transform of the previous sequence.

5 EXPERIMENTS ON SIMULATED AND FINANCIAL DATA

To assess the robustness of the transinformation test (T_0) to spectral imbalance, we run the test, on series, from a battery of near-unit root models. These models were the following:

- *Model 1:* $y_t = ay_{t-1} + x_t$, with $x_t \sim$ i.i.d. $\mathcal{N}(0, 1)$ and $a \in (0.9, 1.0)$
- *Model 2:* $y_t = (0.9 + 0.1 \exp[-d_0 y_{t-1}^2])y_{t-1} + x_t$, with x_t as in Model 1
- *Model 3:* $y_t = (0.9 + 0.1 d^2/y_{t-1}^2)y_{t-1} + x_t$, where $d = d(y_{t-1})$ and x_t is as in Model 1. Here $d = d_0 = cte > 0$ if $|y_{t-1}| > d_0$, and $d = 0$ otherwise
- *Model 4:* $y_t = (0.9 + 0.1\xi_t)y_{t-1} + x_t$, with x_t as in Model 1, and ξ_t is chosen at random between 0 and 1

Model 1 is linear and its spectral density has a major feature at the zero frequency when $a \approx 1$. We used this model to check the stability in the size of the test near the non-stationary border. We deliberately avoided non-stationarity in all models by forcing the autoregressive root to be strictly smaller than 1, but close to 1 so as to preserve the major spectral features that cause imbalance. Models 2 and 3 have nonlinearities, and model 4 has a stochastic near-unit root.

For the purposes of comparison with our testing device, we again used Keenan's (T_1) and Tsay's (T_2) tests. These tests are sensitive to spectral imbalance, since they both proceed by projecting the residuals from a linear AR model fitted to the series on a nonlinear function of the original series. This nonlinear function generally preserves the low-frequency energy contents in the transformed series, whereas the residuals do not.

The outcomes of both Keenan's and Tsay's tests depend on the significance of the interaction terms in a second-order Volterra expansion of y_t,

$$y_t \approx \mu + \sum_{i=1}^{\infty} b_i \varepsilon_{t-i} + \sum_{i=0}^{\infty} \sum_{j=0}^{\infty} b_{i,j} \varepsilon_{t-i} \varepsilon_{t-j} \qquad (19)$$

However, their approaches differ in the way they assess this significance. While in Keenan's test the residuals from a linear model fitted to the series are regressed on $\hat{y}_t^2$ (the square of the fitted value of y_t based on the entertained linear model), in Tsay's these residuals are projected on the individual cross-terms.

The linear predictor order in these tests was fixed to 2, and we took $P = 10$. The sample size was $N = 1024$, and the power was estimated from 500 replications of each model. Using the critical values of the standard normal for the standardized transinformation test statistic, the power of our test against the linear near-unit root time series model 1 was 0.06. On the other hand, the nonlinearity in models 2, 3 and 4 was detected at the 5% level in 65, 87 and 90% of the replications, respectively. Table 3.1 summarizes our results on the power of these tests against models 1–4, at the 5% significance level.

Table 3.1 Power comparisons for Keenan's (T_1), Tsay's (T_2) and the transinformation test (T_0) on some near-unit root time series

Linearity tests	(T_1)	(T_2)	(T_0)
Model 5	0.04	0.0	0.06
Model 6 $(d_0 = 100)$	0.04	0.02	0.65
Model 7 $(d_0 = 10)$	0.15	0.06	0.87
Model 8	0.01	0.02	0.9

In the following, we discuss the results obtained with the transinformation linearity test when applied to hourly financial time series, and compare these results to those obtained with some standard linearity tests. These series, shown in Figure 3.2, were the hourly rates of exchange of the US dollar (USD/ESP), and the Deutschmark (DEM/ESP) against the Spanish peseta, and of the US dollar against the Deutschmark (USD/DEM) starting from 1 November 1994. They were obtained by taking the hourly averages from data recorded at higher frequency.

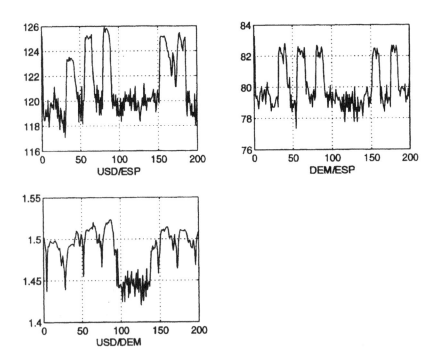

Figure 3.2 Hourly exchange rate data from 1 November 1994: USD/ESP (US dollar/Spanish peseta), DEM/ESP (Deutschmark/Spanish peseta) and USD/DEM (US dollar/Deutschmark)

The two apparently different regimes of stationary mean behaviour suggest the possibility of nonlinearity in these series. On the contrary, their linear surrogate replicas, obtained through randomization of their spectral phases, and shown in Figure 3.3, exhibit stationary near-unit root AR(1)-type behaviour. To justify the assumption of stationarity, it may be enough to notice that the first differences of the series in 2 have spectral densities that exhibit a null close to the origin (Figure 3.4 shows the log-periodograms of these series), that is, the hallmark of overdifferencing. By construction, the first differences of the linear surrogates in Figure 3.3 have the same spectral behaviour.

Moreover, as the residuals of a stationary linear model fitted to the series will tend to have a flat spectrum, we may expect that the power of regression-based linearity tests be affected by spectral imbalance.

To test for linearity, we first run two standard parametric linearity tests on the original series. These were Keenan's (T_1) and Tsay's (T_2) tests, with a predictor order of $p = 10$. With a sample size of 1024, we found that T_1 rejected the null of linearity only on DEM/ESP at the 1% level. However, it was unable to reject it on USD/DEM and USD/ESP. On the other hand, T_2 rejected linearity on both USD/DEM and DEM/ESP, but failed to do so on USD/ESP, also at the

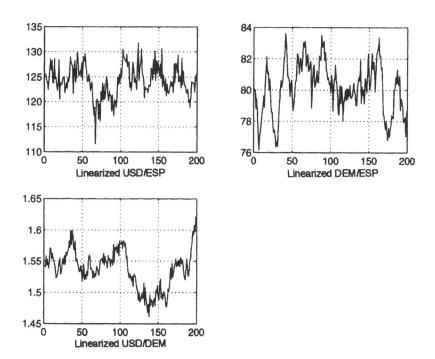

Figure 3.3 Linear surrogate replicas of series in Figure 3.2, obtained by randomization of their Fourier phases

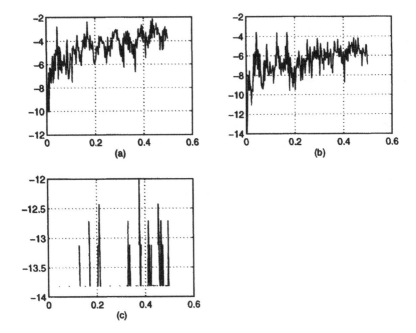

Figure 3.4 Log-periodograms of the first differences of the series in Figure 3.2, showing a null near the zero frequency

1% significance level. To check that the linear surrogate replicas of these series were truly linear, we also ran the tests on the series in Figure 3.3. Tables 3.2 and 3.3 show the significance levels of the tests, obtained for each set of series, and for a sample size of $N = 1024$. In Table 3.3, the significance levels are large for both tests, thus we cannot confidently reject the linearity hypothesis for the series in Figure 3.3.

Table 3.4 shows the mean and standard deviation (between brackets) of the transinformation statistic

$$\eta_{n,P}^{(1)}(Y) = I(Y^n, Y_{(-1)}^n) - P^{-1} \sum_{i=1}^{P} I(X_i^n, X_{i(-1)}^n)$$

Table 3.2 Significance probability of H_0 of linearity obtained with Keenan's (T_1) and Tsay's (T_2) tests applied to the three exchange rate series in Figure 3.2

Series	USD/ESP	DEM/ESP	USD/DEM
T_1 significance	0.0462	0.0	0.3147
T_2 significance	0.3797	0.0	0.0010

Table 3.3 Significance probability of H_0 of linearity obtained with Keenan's (T_1) and Tsay's (T_2) tests applied to the linear surrogate replicas of the three exchange rate series in Figure 3.2

Series	USD/ESP	DEM/ESP	USD/DEM
T_1 significance	0.2192	0.2864	0.6204
T_2 significance	0.9986	0.9996	0.9990

Table 3.4 Mean and standard deviation of $\eta_{1,10}^{(1)}(Y)$ on simulated AR(1) time series with i.i.d. and conditionally heteroscedastic errors

Series	AR(1) with i.i.d. errors	AR(1) with ARCH errors
$\eta_{1,10}^{(1)}(Y)$	0.019 (0.021)	−0.00089 (0.022)

where X_i represents the ith linear surrogate replica of Y. These quantities were estimated from 100 simulated linear AR(1) time series, with both i.i.d. innovations and heteroscedastic errors, and with $P = 10$, $N = 1024$, $\gamma = 1$, $n = 1$. The i.i.d. innovations were generated as for model 1 in Table 3.1, while for the ARCH errors we used the model $x_t = \varepsilon_t b_t$, with $\varepsilon_t \sim$ i.i.d. $\mathcal{N}(0, 1)$, $\sigma_t^2 = 1 + c y_{t-1}^2$, with c chosen at random in the interval $(0.01, 0.1)$. Finally, in Tables 3.5 and 3.6, we give the values of $\eta_{1,10}^{(1)}(Y)$ for the three exchange rate series and their linear surrogate replicas, respectively. We remark that except for USD/ESP, the values in Table 3.5 are large compared to those obtained for the simulated linear AR(1) series, given in Table 3.4. In fact, they fall outside three standard deviations from the reference mean in Table 3.4, thereby supporting the evidence of nonlinearity. In contrast, the values in Table 3.6 are small and lie within a three standard deviation confidence interval for the reference mean. Accordingly, the hypothesis of linearity cannot be rejected for the surrogate data, as expected.

Table 3.5 Values taken by $\eta_{1,10}^{(1)}(Y)$ on the three exchange rate series of Figure 3.2

Series	USD/ESP	DEM/ESP	USD/DEM
$\eta_{1,10}^{(1)}(Y)$	0.0260	−0.4426	0.2415

Table 3.6 Values taken by $\eta_{1,10}^{(1)}(Y)$ on the linear surrogate replicas of the three exchange rate series in Figure 3.2

Series	USD/ESP	DEM/ESP	USD/DEM
$\eta_{1,10}^{(1)}(Y)$	−0.0166	0.0042	0.0287

6 CONCLUSION

In this chapter, we proposed a new methodology for testing linearity in time series. This methodology is rooted in the bootstrap and in information-theoretic concepts. It consists of bootstrapping the data in the frequency domain and later comparing the values of an information-theoretic test statistic, evaluated for both the original series and the bootstrapped linear replica. By virtue of adopting a non-regression formulation, our method avoids the possibility of spectral imbalance, which may arise as a consequence of regressing variables with very different spectral features. On simulated stationary near-unit root time series, our test compares favourably with some standard linearity tests, such as Keenan's and Tsay's. Finally, in our experiment with hourly financial data, it points to the same conclusion as Tsay's test, namely that the change between the two apparent regimes in series USD/DEM and DEM/ESP is caused by nonlinearity in the mean behaviour.

ACKNOWLEDGEMENTS

This research was initiated in collaboration with Prof. C.W.J. Granger (Aparicio and Granger 1995) at the Department of Economics and the Institute for Nonlinear Science of the University of California at San Diego. We are grateful to the Chemical Bank in London for providing the high frequency exchange rate series for our experiments.

ENDNOTES

1. If linearity is rejected then a linear model must be discarded.

REFERENCES

Aparicio Acosta, F.M. and Granger, C.W.J. (1995), 'Information-theoretic Schemes for Linearity Testing under Long-range Dependence and Under Cointegration', Working Paper (Dept. of Economics of the University of California at San Diego), March.

Breiman, L., Meisel, W.S. and Purcell, E. (1977), 'Variable Kernel Estimates of Multivariate Densities and their Calibration', *Technometrics*, **19**, 135–144.

Cover, T.M. and Thomas, J.A. (1991), *Elements of Information Theory*, Wiley, New York.

Granger, C.W.J. (1995), 'Modelling Nonlinear Relationships between Extended-memory Variables', *Econometrica*, **63**(2), 265–279.

Granger, C.W.J. and Joyeux, R. (1980), 'An Introduction to Long Memory Time Series Models and Fractional Differencing', *Journal of Time Series Analysis*, **1**(1), 15–29.

Granger, C.W.J. and Swanson, N.R. (1994), 'An Introduction to Stochastic Unit Root Processes', Discussion Paper 92-53R (Dept. of Economics of the University of California at San Diego), May.

Granger, C.W.J. and Terasvirta, T. (1993), *Modeling Nonlinear Economic Relationships*, Oxford University Press, Oxford.

Gray, R.M. (1990), *Entropy and Information Theory*, Springer-Verlag, New York.

Kullback, S. (1968), *Information Theory and Statistics*, Dover, New York.

Lasota, A. and Mackey, M.C. (1994), *Chaos, Fractals and Noise*, vol. 97 of Applied Mathematical Sciences, Springer-Verlag, New York.

Luukkonen, R., Saikkonen, P. and Terasvirta, T. (1988), 'Testing Linearity in Univariate Time Series Models', *Scandinavian Journal of Statistics*, **15**, 161–175.

Morgera, S.D. (1985), 'Information Theoretic Complexity and its Relation to Pattern Recognition', *IEEE Trans. on Systems, Man and Cybernetics*, **15**(5), 608–619.

Robinson, P.M. (1991), 'Consistent Nonparametric Entropy-based Testing', *Review of Economic Studies*, **58**, 437–453.

Rosenblatt, M. (1974), *Random Processes*, Springer-Verlag, New York.

Shannon, C.E. (1948), 'A Mathematical Theory of Communication', *Bell Systems Technical Journal*, **27**, 379–423, 623–656.

4

Testing for Linearity: A Frequency Domain Approach

JÉRÔME DRUNAT, GILLES DUFRENOT and LAURENT MATHIEU

1 INTRODUCTION

Over the last 20 years, linear models have appeared to be privileged in economic applications of time series analysis. Not only have they become more than a benchmark, but their popularity also comes from their practical application on software.

In the classical statistical methodology, testing for autocorrelation usually requires the estimation of a model from which the residuals are fitted. Several procedures have been suggested in this area by Box and Jenkins who developed linear time series algorithms. Their methodology implies checking whether the fitted residuals of a linear model are generated by a white noise process, by studying the statistical properties of the second-order moments.

Even though linear models have been a major issue in time series analysis, there is no reason why the use of nonlinear models should not be questioned (see Brockett, Hinich and Patterson 1988). Indeed, in some cases white noise tests do not help much to discriminate between linear and nonlinear processes. This can be illustrated by the following example, suggested by Priestley (1981, p. 868).

Suppose, for instance, that $\{\varepsilon_t\}_1^T$ is a time series with a stationary mean and assume further that the data are generated by a white noise process:

$$\varepsilon_t = \alpha u_{t-1} u_{t-2} + u_t \quad \text{where } u_t \approx \text{i.i.d.}(0, \sigma_u^2) \tag{1}$$

Nonlinear Modelling of High Frequency Financial Time Series.
Edited by Christian Dunis and Bin Zhou. © 1998 John Wiley Sons Ltd

It is equivalent to show that $\{\varepsilon_t\}$ is a white noise process, or to check that the random variables ε_t and ε_s are not correlated for all $t \neq s$. This can be seen in the calculation of the covariance, because the components of u_t are random:

$$E[\varepsilon_t] = 0 \quad \text{and} \quad \text{cov}[\varepsilon_t, \varepsilon_s] = E[\varepsilon_t, \varepsilon_s] = 0 \quad \text{for all } t \neq s \qquad (2)$$

However, this conclusion no longer holds when we look at the third-order moment:

$$E[\varepsilon_t \varepsilon_{t-1} \varepsilon_{t-2}] = \alpha E[u_{t-1}^2 u_{t-2}^2] = \alpha \sigma_u^2 \qquad (3)$$

Assume now that ε_t is the residual of a linear model. Then, the standard tests based on the study of the autocovariance function would lead us to conclude that the fitted model is adequate. One thus sees that a nonlinear process may be wrongly confounded with a process whose observations are temporally independent.

In fact, as noticed by Ashley and Patterson (1985), both definitions of whiteness and independence are not usually distinguished when they are used to characterise economic time series. The assumption of independence implies that $X_t, X_{t-1}, \ldots, X_{t-T}$ are independent random variables for all $t, t-1, \ldots, t-T$, while the assumption of whiteness only requires that X_t and X_s be uncorrelated for all $t \neq s$. A white noise process should not therefore be assimilated to a pure white noise process (see Grenander and Rosenblatt 1957, p. 42). Both concepts are similar solely when the time series is Gaussian.

These introductory remarks highlight the need for a test which helps to distinguish linear from nonlinear processes. In this chapter, we present two tests based on the study of the third-order moments in the frequency domain. Both use bispectrum analysis but are based on different methodologies. To facilitate discussion of the tests, we begin with a brief presentation of the basic definitions relating to bispectral analysis. We examine further Subba Rao and Gabr's (1980) approach (SG henceforth) and present Hinich's (1982) test which improved the computation and the power of the SG test. Several applications are provided for high frequency exchange rates.

2 DEFINITIONS AND BASIC CONCEPTS

Let $\{X_t\}$ be a discrete-time random process, that is a process whose observations are equally spaced in time. Suppose further that $\{X_t\}$ is a zero-mean third-order stationary process, that is the statistical properties of the first three moments are assumed not to change with time t. The power spectral density function can be written as the discrete Fourier transform of the autocovariance function:

$$f(\omega) = \sum_{s=-\infty}^{\infty} \gamma(s) \exp(-i 2\pi s \omega) \quad -\pi \leq \omega \leq \pi \qquad (4)$$

where the autocovariance function $\gamma(s)$ is given by the expression

$$\gamma(s) = E[X_t.X_{t+s}] = \text{cov}(X_t, X_{t+s}) \quad s = 0, \pm 1, \pm 2, \ldots \quad (5)$$

The spectral density function exists if $\gamma(s)$ is absolutely summable for all ω, that is $\Sigma_{s=-\infty}^{+\infty}|\gamma(s)| < +\infty$. In other words, one assumes an exponential decrease of $\gamma(s)$.

If $\{X_t\}$ is linear and Gaussian, then the spectral density function (whose determination is based on the first two moments of the series) will contain the overall information concerning the dynamics $\{X_t\}$. Conversely, for a nonlinear and/or non-Gaussian process the second-order spectrum will not characterise the series, thereby suggesting the use of higher-order spectra.

Similarly to the definition of the spectral density function, the bispectral density function, noted $f(\omega_1, \omega_2)$, is defined as the Fourier transform of the third-order cumulant $C(\tau, s)$ which is a function of two lags τ and s. Assuming that

$$\sum_{\tau=-\infty}^{\infty} \sum_{s=-\infty}^{\infty} C(\tau, s) \exp(-i2\pi(\tau\omega_1 + s\omega_2)) < +\infty,$$

the bispectrum exists and one has the following expressions:

$$f(\omega_1, \omega_2) = \sum_{\tau=-\infty}^{\infty} \sum_{s=-\infty}^{\infty} C(\tau, s)e^{(-i2\pi(\tau\omega_1 + s\omega_2))} \quad -\pi \leq \omega_1, \omega_2 \leq \pi \quad (6)$$

$C(\tau, s)$, the bi-covariance function, can be written as

$$C(\tau, s) = E[X_t.X_{t+\tau}.X_{t+s}] \quad (7)$$

To test for linearity and Gaussianity in the frequency domain, one needs the description of the bispectral representation of linear processes. This requires first, an estimation of the third-order cumulant of a time series and second, examination of the contribution of the different pairs of frequencies. In what follows, the linear process $\{X_t\}$ is written, according to Wold's theorem, as an infinite moving average process:

$$x_t = \sum_{j=0}^{+\infty} \alpha_j u_{t-j} \quad \text{with } u_t \approx \text{i.i.d.}(0, \sigma_u^2) \quad \text{and} \quad \sum_{j=0}^{+\infty}(\alpha_j)^2 < \infty \quad (8)$$

If we now define the transfer function as

$$H(\omega) = \sum_{j=0}^{+\infty} \alpha_j \exp(-i2\pi\omega j) \quad (9)$$

then the bispectrum is rewritten as follows:

$$f(\omega_1, \omega_2) = \mu_3 H(\omega_1)H(\omega_2)H^*(\omega_1 + \omega_2) \quad (10)$$

where $\mu_3 = E[u_t^3]$ and $H^*(\cdot)$ is the complex conjugate function of $H(\cdot)$.

Under the assumption of stationarity, it is easily shown that the following symmetry relations hold for both the third-order cumulant and the bispectrum (see Brillinger and Rosenblatt 1967):

$$C(\tau, s) = C(s, \tau) = C(-\tau, s - \tau) = C(\tau, -s, -s) \tag{11}$$

$$f(\omega_1, \omega_2) = f(\omega_2, \omega_1) = f(\omega_1, \omega_1 - \omega_2) = f(-\omega_1 - \omega_2, -\omega_2) \tag{12}$$

This last expression is now written

$$f(\omega_1, \omega_2, \omega_3) = \mu_3 H(\omega_1) H(\omega_2) H^*(\omega_3) \tag{13}$$

with $\omega_3 = \omega_1 + \omega_2$.

This expression is invariant to permutations of ω_1, ω_2 and ω_3 and leads to the three symmetry lines: $\omega_1 - \omega_2 = 0$, $2\omega_1 + \omega_2 = 0$ and $\omega_1 + 2\omega_2 = 0$. Furthermore, one has

$$\begin{aligned}
f(\omega_1, \omega_2, \omega_3) &= \mu_3 H(-\omega_1) H(-\omega_2) H^*(-\omega_3) \\
&= \mu_3 H^*(\omega_1) H^*(\omega_2) H(\omega_3) \\
&= f^*(\omega_1, \omega_2, \omega_3) \tag{14}
\end{aligned}$$

where $f^*(\cdot)$ is the complex conjugate function of $f(\cdot)$. Since $f^*(\cdot)$ is invariant to permutations of its arguments, we have

$$f^*(\omega_1, \omega_2, \omega_3) = f^*(\omega_2, \omega_3, \omega_1) \tag{15}$$

and so

$$f(-\omega_1, -\omega_2, -\omega_3) = f^*(\omega_2, \omega_3, \omega_1) \tag{16}$$

Indeed, assuming that $\omega_1 = -\omega_2$, $\omega_3 = -\omega_1$ and $\omega_2 = -\omega_3$, one has

$$\begin{aligned}
f^*(-\omega_2, -\omega_3, -\omega_1) &= \mu_3 H(\omega_2) H^*(\omega_3) H(\omega_1) \\
&= \mu_3 H^*(-\omega_2) H(-\omega_3) H^*(-\omega_1) \tag{17}
\end{aligned}$$

These equalities allow us to define three other symmetry lines: $\omega_1 + \omega_2 = 0$, $\omega_1 = 0$ and $\omega_2 = 0$. All six symmetry lines can be drawn in the complex plane (see Figure 4.1).

The bispectrum is therefore evaluated in one of the 12 regions and the principal domain is represented by the shaded area. We thus write:

$$0 < \omega_2 < 2/3 \quad \text{and} \quad \omega_2 < \omega_1 < -\tfrac{1}{2}\omega_2 + \pi \tag{18}$$

The strict inequalities mean that the frequencies which are located on the borderlines of the shaded area are not considered. However, it would be possible to define the principal domain within the regions I, II or III. These are not used

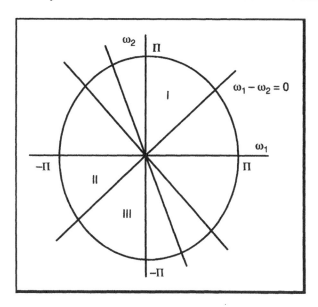

Figure 4.1 Symmetry lines and definition of the principal domain

in practice because they are too small to allow the construction of a sufficient number of uncorrelated variables.

Once the properties of the bispectrum have been specified, one has to construct the test statistic. We first remark that the spectrum of the linear process $\{X_t\}$ can be written as a function of the transfer function $H(\cdot)$:

$$f(\omega) = \sigma_u^2 |H(\omega)|^2 \tag{19}$$

Then, from expression (10) we have, for all the frequencies in the principal domain:

$$R^2(\omega_1, \omega_2) = \frac{|f(\omega_1, \omega_2)|^2}{f(\omega_1) \cdot f(\omega_2) \cdot f(\omega_1 + \omega_2)} = \frac{(\mu_3)^2}{(\sigma_u^2)^3} \tag{20}$$

This expression, which is the square of the skewness function of $\{X_t\}$, helps in understanding the basic intuition of the tests. According to the remarks made in the introduction, a series which conforms to a Gaussian process (in which case it must necessarily conform to a linear model) has its higher than second-order moments equal to zero (see Brillinger 1965). So the bispectrum of a Gaussian process is null at all frequencies and this conclusion also holds for the skewness function. For a linear time series $\{X_t\}$ the value of the skewness function does not vary with the frequencies (ω_1, ω_2) and hence is constant in the whole principal domain. These observations are the basis of both the Gaussianity and linearity tests used by SG and Hinich.

3 SUBBA RAO AND GABR'S APPROACH

In most circumstances, Subba Rao and Gabr's (1980, 1984) approach can be used to test for both the hypotheses of Gaussianity and linearity. Their methodology relies on some results of complex analogues of T^2 and R^2 tests which were developed by Giri (1965) and Khatri (1965). The reader is referred to these papers for a detailed discussion. Our presentation is, by necessity, rather brief and gives an overview which enables understanding of the key points of their methodology. Applications to exchange rates are considered as illustrations.

3.1 Gaussianity Test

Theoretical Considerations

To begin with, it seems natural to inquire as to the number of frequencies in the principal domain that are needed to construct the test. This raises the following question: how can we define a sufficient number of frequencies, while avoiding at the same time an overabundance that would cause an overlapping of bispectral estimates? SG have suggested a procedure which consists of two stages.

In the first stage, the interval $[0, \pi]$ is divided into K sub-intervals and a first set of frequencies is selected:

$$\omega_1^i = \frac{\pi i}{K} \qquad \omega_2^j = \frac{\pi j}{K} \quad i = 1, \ldots, X; \; j = i+1, \ldots, Y$$

$$\text{with } X = \frac{2K}{3} \quad \text{and} \quad Y = K - (i/2) - 1 \tag{21}$$

The second stage is carried out by forming a set of frequencies which are defined around the pairs (ω_1^i, ω_2^j). One needs a distance parameter d and a parameter which defines the number of frequencies to be constructed around (ω_1^i, ω_2^j). SG found that it was convenient to proceed as follows:

$$\omega_{1p}^i = \omega_1^i + pd\pi/T \qquad \omega_{2q}^j = \omega_2^j + qd\pi/T \tag{22}$$

where $p, q = -r, -r-1, \ldots, 0, 1, \ldots, r$. T is the number of observations of the original time series. d must be chosen so that $\pi d/T$ is greater than the bandwidth of the spectral window used. To ensure that the different pairs of frequencies do not overlap, one further requires $d \leq T/K(2r+1)$. Also the quantity $(4r+1)K^2/3$ must be less than T. This is due to the fact that there are $(4r+1)$ points and that the number of 'grids' defined at the first stage is equal to $K^2/3$.

Following this procedure, one forms a set of bispectral estimates:

$$\hat{f}\left(\omega_1^i - \frac{rd\pi}{T}, \omega_2^j\right), \hat{f}\left(\omega_1^i - \frac{(r-1)d\pi}{T}, \omega_2^j\right), \ldots,$$

$$\ldots \hat{f}(\omega_1^i, \omega_2^j), \ldots, \hat{f}\left(\omega_1^i, \omega_2^j - \frac{rd\pi}{T}\right), \ldots, \hat{f}\left(\omega_1^i, \omega_2^j + \frac{rd\pi}{T}\right) \tag{23}$$

These estimates are combined into a data matrix G which can be viewed as a set of S vectors $\hat{f}_k, k = 1, \ldots, S$, each including P elements. Testing for Gaussianity requires the introduction of an S-variate random variable, denoted ϕ_s, which for large S has a complex Gaussian distribution with mean and covariance matrix, respectively, defined by

$$E(\phi_s) = \overline{f} = \frac{1}{S} \sum_{k=1}^{S} \hat{f}_k \quad \text{and} \quad \Sigma_{\phi_s} = E[(\phi_s - \overline{f})(\phi_s - \overline{f})^*] \tag{24}$$

$(\phi_s - \overline{f})^*$, the adjoint of $(\phi_s - \overline{f})$, is obtained by transposing the matrix of co-factors of $(\phi_s - \overline{f})$. The probability density function of ϕ_s is given by

$$p(\phi_s) = \frac{1}{\pi^S (\det \Sigma_{\phi_s})} \exp[-(\phi_s - \overline{f})^* \Sigma_{\phi_s}^{-1} (\phi_s - \overline{f})] \tag{25}$$

Under the null hypothesis that the original series is Gaussian, the mean vector has all its components equal to zero. Thus, we define the null hypothesis as $H_0 : \overline{f} = 0$ and the alternative as $H_1 : \overline{f}^* \Sigma_{\phi_s}^{-1} \overline{f} > 0$ (which means that the elements of $\overline{f}$ are significantly different from zero and strictly positive). Any sample $\phi_{S1}, \phi_{S2}, \ldots, \phi_{SP}$, yields a likelihood function of the form

$$L(\phi_{S1}, \phi_{S2}, \ldots, \phi_{SP}) = \frac{P}{(\pi^S (\det \Sigma_{\phi_s}))^P}$$

$$\exp[- \operatorname{tr}[\Sigma_{\phi_s}^{-1}(A + P(\overline{\phi}_S - \overline{f})(\overline{\phi}_S - \overline{f})^*)]] \tag{26}$$

The derivation of this expression is based on the following assumptions:

1. $\overline{\phi}_S$ is the maximum likelihood estimate of $\overline{f}$:

$$\overline{\phi}_S = \frac{1}{P} \sum_{j=1}^{P} \phi_{Sj} \tag{27}$$

2. $P^{-1}A$ is the maximum likelihood estimate of Σ_{ϕ_s}:

$$P^{-1}A = \sum_{j=1}^{P} (\phi_{Sj} - \overline{\phi}_S)(\phi_{Sj} - \overline{\phi}_S)^* \tag{28}$$

The reader is referred to Goodman (1963) for a proof of these conditions. Two essential motivations lead us to consider equation (27) instead of (24). First, one can use Neyman's criterion according to which $(\overline{\phi}_S, A)$ is a sufficient statistic for $(\overline{f}, \Sigma_{\phi_s})$. In this case, the summations in the expressions of the mean and the covariance are taken over the P observations and not over the S vectors (see Halmos and Savage 1949 for a detailed discussion). Second, this formulation allows us to use the known result that any function Γ of the form defined below is maximum at $B = nI$, where I is the identity matrix, α is a constant and B is a positive definite Hermitian matrix.

$$\Gamma(B) = \alpha(\det B)^n \exp(-\text{tr } B) \tag{29}$$

Therefore, if we suppose that there exists a square complex matrix M, such that $M^*\Sigma_{\phi_S}M$ is diagonal with the characteristic roots of Σ_{ϕ_S} as diagonal elements, then it is seen that equation (27) can be rewritten as follows:

$$\Gamma(\Sigma_{\phi_S}^{-1}) = \alpha_1[\alpha_2 \det \Sigma_{\phi_S}^{-1}]^P \exp[-\text{tr}(\alpha_2\Sigma_{\phi_S}^{-1})] \tag{30}$$

where

$$\begin{cases} \alpha_1 = [\pi^S[A + P(\overline{\phi}_S - \overline{f})(\overline{\phi}_S - \overline{f})^*]]^{-P} \\ \text{and} \\ \alpha_2 = A + P(\overline{\phi}_S - \overline{f})(\overline{\phi}_S - \overline{f})^* \end{cases} \tag{31}$$

If $\Sigma_{\phi_S}^{-1}$ is a Hermitian matrix, then $M^*\Sigma_{\phi_S}M$ is diagonal with the elements of α_2 as diagonal elements. Further, for every definite positive Hermitian matrix B there exists a non-singular matrix N, such that $NBN^* = I$. This suggests that under the null hypothesis, $\Gamma(\Sigma_{\phi_S}^{-1})$ is maximum at

$$\hat{\Sigma}_{\phi_S}^{-1} = I + P\overline{\phi}_S^*A^{-1}\overline{\phi}_S \tag{32}$$

Under the alternative, we have

$$\hat{\Sigma}_{\phi_S}^{-1} = I + P(\overline{\phi}_S - \overline{f})^*A^{-1}(\overline{\phi}_S - \overline{f}) \tag{33}$$

and since $\overline{\phi}_S$ is the maximum likelihood estimate of $\overline{f}$, this equality is reduced to $\Sigma_{\phi_S}^{-1} = I$. It can be shown that the difference between the maximum value of the likelihood function under H_0 and the maximum under H_1 (that is $T_c^2 = P\overline{\phi}_S^*A^{-1}\overline{\phi}_S$), multiplied by a factor $2(S-P)/2P$ is distributed as $F(2P, (S-P))$. The null hypothesis of Gaussianity is thereby rejected at a $\beta\%$ level if the value of the statistic $Z1 = T_c^2 \times [2(S-P)/2P]$ is higher than the theoretical value of the distribution $F(2P, 2(S-P))$.

An Application to High Frequency Exchange Rates

We illustrate the use of the procedure with data on three exchange rates, sampled at 30- and 60-minute frequencies (all series come from the Chemical Bank Database). The exchange rates are the US dollar/Deutschmark, the US dollar/French franc and the Deutschmark/French franc. The sample period begins in January and ends in September of 1996. The exchange rates are transformed in logarithmic returns, in order to ensure stationarity both in the mean and variance.

Before applying the procedure described above, one needs to calculate the sample estimate of the bispectrum. But similar to the estimation of the spectral density function, this estimate, although asymptotically unbiased, is not consistent (see Brillinger and Rosenblatt 1967). Thus, we need to smooth the estimate by using a bispectral window:

$$\lambda(\tau, s) = \lambda(\tau)\lambda(s)\lambda(\tau - s) \tag{34}$$

Now we can write the estimate of the bispectrum, which is biased but consistent:

$$\hat{f}(\omega_1, \omega_2) = \sum_{\tau=-(T-1)}^{T-1} \sum_{s=-(T-1)}^{T-1} \lambda\left(\frac{\tau}{M}, \frac{s}{M}\right) \hat{C}(\tau, s) \exp(-i2\pi(\tau\omega_1 + s\omega_2))$$

$$\text{and} \quad -\pi \leq \omega_1, \omega_2 \leq \pi \tag{35}$$

where M is the truncation point and the expression of the estimate of the third-order cumulant $\hat{C}(\tau, s)$ is given by

$$\hat{C}(\tau, s) = \frac{1}{T} \sum_{t=1}^{T-\theta} (x_t - \overline{\mu})(X_{t+\tau} - \overline{\mu})(X_{t+s} - \overline{\mu}) \tag{36}$$

where $\theta = \max(\tau, s)$ and $\overline{\mu}$ is the sample mean of the series.

In practice, one needs to choose a value of M which allows us to minimise both the variance and the bias of the bispectrum. SG have shown that these two expressions can be written as functions of M:

$$\text{Var}[\hat{f}(\omega_1, \omega_2)] = \varphi\left(\frac{M^2}{T}\right) \quad \text{and} \quad \text{bias}[\hat{f}(\omega_1, \omega_2)] = \varphi\left(\frac{1}{M^2}\right) \tag{37}$$

Various lag windows have been proposed in the literature (Parzen 1957; Tukey 1959) but an optimal two-dimensional lag-window is the one defined by SG:

$$\lambda(\tau, s) = \frac{8}{7\pi^3}[h(\tau, s) + h(-\tau, s - \tau) + h(\tau - s, -s)] \tag{38}$$

where the function h is defined by

$$h(\tau, s) = \left(\frac{2\tau^2 + 2s^2 + \tau s}{\pi\tau^3 s^3}\right)\cos(\tau - s)\pi - \left(\frac{\tau - s}{\tau^2 s^2}\right)\sin(\tau - s) \tag{39}$$

We next examine how the bispectrum estimates can be used to apply the test of Gaussianity to high frequency exchange rates. The results for the statistic $Z1$ are shown in Table 4.1.

The bispectral estimates were computed using $r = 1$ and $S = 5$. We have further fixed the value of K to 4, and so $P = 2$. Following SG, we have chosen a value of M equal to the square root of the number of observations

Table 4.1 Subba Rao and Gabr Gaussianity test (Z1 statistic)

	30-Minute			60-Minute		
	USD/FRF	USD/DEM	DEM/FRF	USD/FRF	USD/DEM	DEM/FRF
January	$0.14E+04$	$0.73E+03$	$0.30E+02$	$0.16E+04$	$0.11E+05$	$0.32E+02$
February	$0.20E+03$	$0.60E+02$	$0.52E+03$	$0.22E+04$	$0.68E+03$	$0.91E+03$
March	$0.34E+03$	$0.89E+03$	$0.11E+04$	$0.59E+04$	$0.35E+04$	$0.24E+04$
April	$0.89E+03$	$0.64E+03$	$0.48E+03$	$0.47E+02$	$0.51E+04$	$0.30E+04$
May	$0.11E+04$	$0.42E+04$	$0.29E+03$	$0.68E+03$	$0.20E+04$	$0.84E+03$
June	$0.80E+04$	$0.24E+04$	$0.88E+02$	$0.68E+03$	$0.55E+03$	$0.68E+03$
July	$0.17E+03$	$0.22E+03$	$0.30E+04$	$0.36E+04$	$0.27E+04$	$0.90E+03$
August	$0.20E+03$	$0.14E+04$	$0.56E+02$	$0.12E+04$	$0.29E+04$	$0.90E+03$
September	$0.82E+02$	$0.65E+03$	$0.36E+03$	$0.16E+03$	$0.91E+03$	$0.16E+03$

Note: The critical value of $F(6, 4)$ at the 5% level is equal to 4.53.

T, that is $M = 33$ at the 30-minute frequency and $M = 23$ at the 60-minute frequency. Under the null hypothesis of Gaussianity the statistic $Z1$ is therefore distributed as $F(4, 6)$. The upper 5% of this F-distribution is 4.53. The results in Table 4.1 lead to overwhelming evidence of a strong rejection of the Gaussianity hypothesis. This reflects, of course, the fact that many exchange rate series are usually seen to have skewed and fat-tailed distributions (see Bollerslev, Chou and Kroner 1992; Diebold and Lopez 1995). The rejection of Gaussianity which is a stylised fact of monthly, weekly and daily exchange rates, also applies to high frequency data. Clearly, high periodicity sampling does not affect the asymmetry of the distribution of foreign exchange rates. So, at the very least, one should expect short-term returns to be volatile and thus difficult to forecast. That finding is usually confirmed for daily returns when their evolution is studied using (G)ARCH type of models. Those models include nonlinearities in the conditional variance of the series. However, the rejection of the null hypothesis of Gaussianity may also indicate the presence of nonlinear components in the mean of the series.

3.2 Linearity Test

Theoretical Considerations

In the previous paragraph, the test of Gaussianity required the construction of a fine grid of frequencies. These were used to generate a set of uncorrelated bispectral estimates. The approach for linearity testing is similar, but the data-generating process applies to the asymmetry function. The normalised bispectrum estimates $R(\omega_{1p}^i, \omega_{2q}^j)$ are used to form S vectors $R_k = (R_{1k}, R_{2k}, \ldots, R_{pk})'$, $k = 1, \ldots, S$ and are combined into a data matrix. With S sufficiently large, the random variables R_k have a joint distribution which is normal with mean vector and covariance matrix respectively given by

$$\bar{R} = \frac{1}{S}\sum_{k=1}^{S} R_k \quad \text{and} \quad \Sigma_R = \frac{1}{S}\sum_{k=1}^{S}(R_k - \bar{R})(R_k - \bar{R})' \qquad (40)$$

Let us partition R_k into two subsets R_k^1 and R_k^2, which include respectively Q and $(S - Q)$ uncorrelated variables. The covariance matrix can thus be partitioned into four sub-matrices:

$$\Sigma_R = \begin{pmatrix} \Sigma_{QQ} & \Sigma_{QV} \\ \Sigma_{VQ} & \Sigma_{VV} \end{pmatrix} \qquad (41)$$

where $V = S - Q$. Testing for linearity is equivalent to see whether there exists any dependence between the variables contained in the vector R_k^1 and those of the vector R_k^2. Considering the fact that the square correlation coefficient can be written as

$$\rho^2 = \frac{\Sigma_{QV} \Sigma_{VV}^{-1} \Sigma_{QV}'}{\Sigma_{QQ}} \qquad (42)$$

the null hypothesis of linearity H_0 is $\Sigma_{QV} = 0$ (or $\rho^2 = 0$) and the alternative H_1 is $\rho > 0$.

It must be pointed out that the rejection of H_0 is an indication of nonlinearity. Indeed, the bispectrum estimates at certain frequencies have an influence on the estimations at other frequencies. This can be interpreted as frequency multiplication or intermodulation distortion, which typically characterises nonlinear systems (see Priestley 1988 for a detailed discussion). Testing procedures of H_0 have already been proposed by Giri (1965) and Khatri (1965) in the case of multivariate complex variables. Their argument can be applied to real processes since a real variable is a complex variable with no imaginary part.

The test is carried out in two stages. First, we assume that the mean vector $\bar{R}$ is known and has all its components equal to a constant α. This constant is 0 if we define the following transformation: $z = MR_k$ where the matrix M has the following structure:

$$M = \begin{pmatrix} 1 & 1 & 0 & \dots & 0 & 0 \\ 0 & 1 & -1 & \dots & 0 & 0 \\ \vdots & \vdots & \vdots & \vdots & \vdots & \vdots \\ 0 & 0 & 0 & \dots & 1 & -1 \end{pmatrix} \qquad (43)$$

Under this transformation, one can define an S-variate random variable θ_s which has a normal distribution with a mean vector whose components are 0 and a covariance matrix $\Sigma_{\theta_s} = M\Sigma_s M'$. Then the test construction requires the expression of a statistic that leads us to accept or reject the null hypothesis. As the formulation is along the line of the arguments given above for the Gaussianity test, we only report here the critical region (the reader is referred to Giri 1965 for a detailed discussion). Assuming that $\bar{\theta}_s$ and PC^{-1} are the maximum likelihood estimates of $\bar{R}$ and Σ_{θ_s}, the null hypothesis of linearity is rejected if

$$R^2 = P\bar{\theta}_s' C^{-1}\bar{\theta}_s > \alpha_2 \qquad (44)$$

where α_2 is a constant whose determination depends on the significance level of the test. Under the null hypothesis of linearity, it can be shown that the statistic $Z2 = R^2[(S - (P - 1))/(P - 1)]$ has a Fisher distribution $F(P - 1, S - (P - 1))$.

An Application to High Frequency Exchange Rates

The test of linearity raises the problem of an appropriate choice of the parameter K, that is the number of equidistant points in the interval $[0, \pi]$. Following SG's suggestion, we may retain a small value for K when the normalised bispectrum is almost constant at all frequencies. But this rule does not always lead to a clear acceptance of the hypothesis of linearity. What is more, the values of $Z2$ are not stable under the alternative hypothesis. The higher the value of K chosen, the stronger the likelihood of the null hypothesis being rejected. Indeed, $Z2$ becomes very large when the values of K are increased. One is therefore confronted with fast changes in the bispectrum estimates. The values of the distance parameter d were computed as $d = P/((2r + 1)K)$. Table 4.2 shows the values of the statistic $Z2$ for exchange rates examined here.

The values for K and r are the same as in section 3.1. The upper 5% of the $F(1, 4)$ distribution is 7.71. As can be seen, the null hypothesis of linearity is rejected in most of the cases for the 30-minute series, less often for the 60-minute series. This makes a great difference with low frequency data (daily, monthly) which are often shown to follow a random walk. It is therefore important to distinguish low and high frequency data when the problem of linear and nonlinear modelling is under examination. Here, we can refer to the fact that the linearity hypothesis is accepted for nearly 30% of the 60-minute frequency data, while this proportion decreases to 10% when the 30-minute frequency series are considered. These results suggest a possible smoothing effect inherent to the nonlinear components in exchange rates. It would be interesting to provide a relevant nonlinear aggregation theory. However, this is an ambitious objective since there does not seem to exist a

Table 4.2 Subba Rao and Gabr linearity tests ($Z2$ statistic)

	30-Minute			60-Minute		
	USD/FRF	USD/DEM	DEM/FRF	USD/FRF	USD/DEM	DEM/FRF
January	$0.28E + 04$	$0.34E + 02$	$0.32E + 02$	$0.99E - 01$	$0.15E + 02$	$0.91E + 01$
February	$0.47E + 02$	$0.29E + 02$	$0.28E + 03$	$0.41E + 01$	$0.35E + 03$	$0.88E - 01$
March	$0.28E + 04$	$0.78E + 03$	$0.27E + 04$	$0.51E + 03$	$0.85E + 03$	$0.43E + 03$
April	$0.32E + 03$	$0.99E + 02$	$0.84E + 04$	$0.53E + 02$	$0.77E + 02$	$0.17E + 03$
May	$0.14E + 04$	$0.94E + 00$	$0.12E + 02$	$0.15E + 03$	$0.11E + 04$	$0.69E + 03$
June	$0.31E + 02$	$0.94E + 00$	$0.94E + 00$	$0.73E + 02$	$0.23E + 04$	$0.14E + 03$
July	$0.60E + 02$	$0.82E + 01$	$0.19E + 04$	$0.50E + 01$	$0.50E - 01$	$0.59E + 01$
August	$0.37E + 04$	$0.49E + 03$	$0.19E + 04$	$0.54E + 01$	$0.23E + 01$	$0.89E + 02$
September	$0.39E + 04$	$0.13E + 02$	$0.13E + 02$	$0.12E + 00$	$0.72E + 01$	$0.68E + 00$

Note: The critical value of $F(1, 4)$ at the 5% level is equal to 7.71. The shaded cells indicate that the null hypothesis of linearity is accepted at the 5% significance level.

logical approach of estimating the degree of nonlinearity in the data. Furthermore, it is usually argued that the time series approach is less promising than the structural nonlinearity hypothesis-testing approach in providing inference results about the properties of the data. In this case, if we seek to study the implications of the smoothing effect, there is a fundamental necessity for the construction of nonlinear models that reproduce the evolution of the exchange rates studied here (for some examples, see Chapter 10).

4 HINICH'S APPROACH

As remarked by Hinich (1982), SG's test statistic is quite sensitive to outliers when the values of the spectrum are too small. Further, the conclusions depend heavily on both the choice of the bispectral window and the construction of the frequency grid. To overcome these problems, Hinich recommends the use of the asymptotic covariance matrix of the bispectrum instead of the second sample moment matrix as in SG's approach.

Assume that $\{x_t\}_1^T$ is a sample of T observations that has been generated from the stationary process $\{X_t\}$. One defines for each pair of integers (j, k) the following estimate of the bispectrum:

$$F(j, k) = \frac{1}{T}\Lambda(\omega_j)\Lambda(\omega_k)\Lambda^*(\omega_{j+k}) \tag{45}$$

where $\Lambda(\omega_j)$ is the Fourier transform of the sample and $\Lambda^*(\omega_j)$ is its complex conjugate. A consistent estimate of the bispectral density is obtained by averaging the different estimates for all pairs of frequencies over a domain of M^2 points:

$$L = \left\{ (2m-1)M/2, (2n-1)M/2 : \text{ for} \right.$$
$$\left. m = 1, \ldots, n \quad \text{and} \quad m \leq \frac{T}{2M} - \frac{T}{2} + \frac{3}{4} \right\}$$

This procedure is similar to the approach usually adopted for obtaining a consistent estimate of the spectrum (see Priestley 1988). We therefore have

$$\hat{f}(m, n) = \left(\frac{1}{M}\right)^2 \sum_{j=(M-1)}^{mM-1} \sum_{s=(n-1)M}^{nM-1} F(j, k) \tag{46}$$

Define now an estimate of the ratio $R(\omega_1, \omega_2)$:

$$\hat{R}(m, n) = \frac{M}{T^{0.5}} \frac{\hat{f}(m, n)}{[\hat{f}(g_m) \cdot \hat{f}(g_m) \cdot \hat{f}(g_{m+n})]^{0.5}} \tag{47}$$

where we note $g_i = (2i-1)M/2T$.

From this expression, Hinich suggested testing both the hypotheses of Gaussianity and linearity:

- *Gaussianity.* First, Hinich showed that $\hat{R}(\omega_1, \omega_2)$ has a complex normal distribution with unit variance. Therefore, the statistic $2|\hat{R}(m, n)|^2$ is asymptotically distributed as a $\chi^2(2)$. This statistic allows the testing of the significance of each peak in the bispectral density. Furthermore, under the null hypothesis of Gaussianity the bispectrum is equal to zero for each pair of frequencies, which implies that the test statistic H

$$H = 2\sum_m \sum_n |\hat{R}(m, n)|^2 \tag{48}$$

is asymptotically distributed as a $\chi^2(2P)$, where P is the number of squares in the principal domain. H can be approximated by a normal law with zero mean and unit variance when $P > 15$.

The rejection of the null hypothesis implies that H is greater than the theoretical χ^2. However, further investigations are necessary before assessing the hypothesis of nonlinearity. Indeed, $\{X_t\}$ may be linear but non-Gaussian. In this case, the statistic $2|\hat{R}(m, n)|^2$ is asymptotically distributed as a $\chi^2(2, \lambda)$ where λ is a non-centrality parameter. An estimate of λ is given by the expression

$$\hat{\lambda} = \frac{H}{P} - 2 \tag{49}$$

- *Linearity.* Under the null hypothesis of linearity, the statistic $2|\hat{R}(m, n)|^2$ can be used to construct P independent peaks, each of which is distributed as a $\chi^2(2, \hat{\lambda})$ with the same non-centrality parameter. However, the non-centrality parameters differ for each pair of frequencies, if the null hypothesis of linearity is rejected. In this case, the sample distribution exceeds the distribution under H_0. Ashley, Hinich and Patterson (1986) used time series generated by processes that were either deterministic or stochastic and showed, using Monte Carlo simulations, that the best dispersion measure was the one given by the 80th quantiles. More specifically, David (1970) demonstrated that the 80th quantile, denoted $\hat{\varepsilon}_{0.8}$, is asymptotically distributed as a normal law $N(\xi, \sigma_\xi^2)$, where an estimate of σ_ξ^2 is given by

$$\hat{\sigma}_\xi^2 = \frac{1}{P}0.8(1 - 0.8)f^{-1}\hat{\xi}_{0.8} \tag{50}$$

where f is the $\chi^2(2, \hat{\lambda})$ density function. Therefore, to test for linearity one needs to compute the statistic

$$Z = \frac{\hat{\xi}_{0.8}}{\hat{\sigma}_\xi^2} \tag{51}$$

Under the null hypothesis of linearity, this statistic is distributed as an $N(0, 1)$.

Ashley, Patterson and Hinich (1986) and Chan and Tong (1986) investigated different simulations to determine the size and the power of both tests of Gaussianity and linearity, leading to the following conclusions:

- For samples of less than 256 observations, the tests are not consistent.
- The power of the test increases with the size of the sample.
- The optimal value for the truncation point M is approximately equal to $0.7\sqrt{T}$ where T is the number of observations.
- The linearity test should be applied as a test of adequacy of a linear model for an empirical series.
- For a non-stationary process, the null hypothesis of linearity may not be rejected wrongly (the opposite argument is not true). However, this nonstationarity does not allow the detection of low frequency cycles from a graphical study.
- Ashley, Patterson and Hinich (1986) have proposed the following theorem:

Equivalence Theorem: Let $\{X(t)\}$ be a zero-mean, discrete-time stochastic process which is third-order stationary and whose third-order cumulant function is absolutely summable. If $\{Y(t)\}$ is generated by passing $\{X(t)\}$ through a fixed, causal, linear filter with absolutely summable impulse response weights, then $\{X(t)\}$ and $\{Y(t)\}$ have identical squared skewness functions.

This theorem means that the bispectrum test can be applied either to the raw series or to the fitted residual of a model. Furthermore, the conclusions are true for all linear filters that can be applied to the raw series.

Before discussing the application of the tests to the exchange rates of this study, it is desirable to point out the practical significance of linearity from

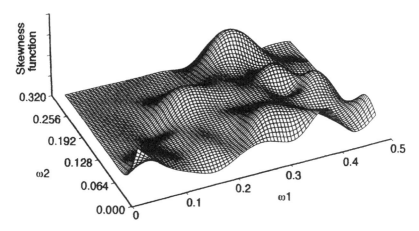

Figure 4.2 Asymmetry function (DEM/FRF September, frequency 60 min)

Table 4.3 Hinich Gaussianity tests (H statistic)

	30-Minute			60-Minute		
	USD/FRF	USD/DEM	DEM/FRF	USD/FRF	USD/DEM	DEM/FRF
January	11.98	6.93	8.15	5.37	4.33	7.34
February	12.74	8.56	12.79	10.06	6.60	8.84
March	15.42	11.33	14.88	9.05	15.57	8.20
April	10.45	10.89	17.03	3.91	5.21	9.11
May	14.62	11.68	11.68	7.19	7.32	5.91
June	9.91	7.68	8.07	5.30	5.84	5.50
July	8.54	8.37	17.65	6.87	6.40	10.62
August	11.02	9.17	14.43	4.84	5.78	8.48
September	18.74	18.34	18.34	10.87	10.01	7.79

Note: The critical value of $N(0, 1)$ at the 5% level is equal to 1.96.

a graphical interpretation. Figure 4.2 describes the asymmetry function corresponding to a linear and non-Gaussian process regarding the H and Z test statistics (Tables 4.3 and 4.4). As can be seen, one frequency dominates the others and most bispectral estimates are defined around $\omega_1 \approx \omega_2 \approx 0.35$, which corresponds approximately to 3 days. As has previously been noted, the symmetry properties of the bispectrum imply that the frequencies are chosen in the triangular principal domain. The asymmetry function is therefore not defined outside this domain.

Figure 4.3 shows the example of a nonlinear and non-Gaussian process. The estimated asymmetry function appears to be very irregular, not flat at all as it should be if the process was linear.

Tables 4.3 and 4.4 show the results for the Gaussianity and the linearity tests. The values of the test statistics have to be compared with standard normal

Table 4.4 Hinich linearity tests (Z statistic)

	30-Minute			60-Minute		
	USD/FRF	USD/DEM	DEM/FRF	USD/FRF	USD/DEM	DEM/FRF
January	4.15	3.51	2.91	4.07	2.09	4.68
February	4.36	3.95	4.07	4.76	2.97	1.67
March	6.83	3.30	3.81	2.41	1.94	4.11
April	1.37	3.18	5.60	2.57	2.51	3.50
May	5.92	3.28	3.28	0.58	3.43	1.80
June	0.36	3.24	7.40	6.38	3.57	4.05
July	4.25	4.54	1.97	6.47	0.47	1.81
August	1.47	2.95	6.64	0.99	2.34	6.16
September	5.89	4.31	4.31	3.22	2.95	0.99

Note: The critical value of $N(0, 1)$ at the 5% level is equal to 1.96. The shaded cells indicate that the null hypothesis of linearity is accepted at the 5% significance level.

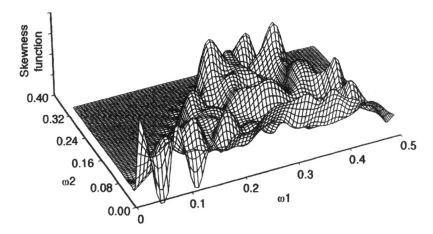

Figure 4.3 Asymmetry function (DEM/FRF September, frequency 30 min)

variables, that is 1.96 at the 5% level. As can be seen immediately, the hypothesis of Gaussianity for all the series is rejected since the test statistic is higher than 1.96. This result, as noted in the previous paragraph, is not surprising since the data have higher peaks and fatter tails than the normal distribution.

The general conclusions in terms of nonlinearity are about the same as for SG's test: the higher the frequency, the more often the hypothesis of linearity is rejected (except for USD/FRF). However, the two approaches sometimes differ in the result for a particular series.

5 CONCLUDING REMARKS

It is often concluded that many financial time series are non-Gaussian and nonlinear. This chapter presents new developments in linearity testing with high frequency financial data. Tests of Gaussianity and linearity must be considered before starting modelling. There exists an abundance of procedures developed to test for linearity in the time domain. Meanwhile, frequency domain analysis is also necessary for investigating the link between the nonlinear components and the moments of orders higher than two in a time series. As argued by Granger and Terasvirta (1993), bispectral analysis is a recommended technique whenever one has plenty of data, which is typically the case for high frequency financial data. Applications of bispectral F-tests and chi-squared tests to three exchange rates has been considered here for illustration. The results seem to indicate that there may be a strong reason for believing that sampling does not affect the usual conclusions about the distributions of exchange rates. Moreover, for those series, the hypothesis of Gaussianity is indeed always rejected. The evidence exhibits a strong departure from Gaussianity. Moreover, for many series the use of low frequency returns instead of high frequency series smooths the nonlinear components.

REFERENCES

Ashley, R. and Patterson, D. (1985) 'Linear versus Nonlinear Macroeconomics: A Statistical Test', *International Economic Review*, 3, 685–704.

Ashley, R., Patterson, D. and Hinich, M. (1986), 'A Diagnostic Test for Nonlinearity and Serial Dependence in Time Series Fitting Errors', *Journal of Time Series Analysis*, 7(3), 165–178.

Bollerslev, T., Chou, R.Y. and Kroner, K.F. (1992), 'ARCH Modelling in Finance: a Review of the Theory and Empirical Evidence', *Journal of Econometrics*, 52, 5–50.

Brillinger, D.R. (1965), 'An Introduction to Polyspectra', *Annals of Mathematics and Statistics*, 36, 1351–1374.

Brillinger, D.R. and Rosenblatt, J. (1967), 'Asymptotic Theory of Kth Order Spectra', in B. Harris (ed.), *Spectral Analysis of Time Series*, Wiley, New York, p. 153–188.

Brockett, R.W., Hinich, M.J. and Patterson, D. (1988), 'Bispectral-based Tests for the Detection of Gaussianity and Linearity in Time Series', *Journal of the American Statistical Association*, 83(403), 657–684.

Chan, W.S. and Tong, H. (1986), 'On Tests for Nonlinearity in Time Series Analysis', *Journal of Forecasting*, 5, 217–228.

David, H.A. (1970) *Order Statistics*, Wiley, New York.

Diebold, F. and Lopez, J.A. (1995), 'Modelling Volatility Dynamics', NBER Technical Working Paper, 173.

Giri, N. (1965), 'On the Complex Analogues of T^2- and R^2-Tests', *Annals of Mathematical Statistics*, 36, 664–670.

Goodman, N.R. (1963), 'Statistical Analysis Based on a Certain Multivariate Complex Gaussian Distribution', *Annals of Mathematical Statistics*, 34, 152–177.

Granger, C.W.J. and Terasvirta, T. (1993), *Modelling Non-linear Economic Relationships*, Oxford University Press, Oxford.

Grenander, U. and Rosenblatt, J. (1957), *Statistical Analysis of Stationary Time Series*, Wiley, New York.

Halmos, P.R. and Savage, L.J. (1949), 'Application of the Radon–Nikodyn Theorem to the Theory of Sufficient Statistic', *Annals of Mathematical Statistics*, 34, 152–177.

Hinich, M.J. (1982), 'Testing for Gaussianity and Linearity of a Stationary Time Series', *Journal of Time Series Analysis*, 3, 169–176.

Hinich, M.J. and Patterson, D. (1985), 'Evidence of Nonlinearity in Stock Returns', *Journal of Business and Economic Statistics*, 3, 69–77.

Khatri, C.G. (1965), 'Classical Statistical Analysis Based on a Certain Multivariate Complex Gaussian Distribution', *Annals of Mathematical Statistics*, 36, 98–107.

Parzen, E. (1957), 'On Choosing an Estimate of the Spectral Density Function', *Annals of Mathematical Statistics*, 28, 921–932.

Priestley, M.B. (1981) *Spectral Analysis and Time Series*, 2 vols, Academic Press, London.

Priestley, M.B. (1988) *Nonlinear and Nonstationary Time Series Analysis*, Academic Press, London.

Subba Rao, T. and Gabr, M.M. (1980), 'A Test for Linearity of Stationary Time Series', *Journal of Time Series Analysis*, 1, 145–158.

Subba Rao, T. and Gabr, M.M. (1984), *An Introduction to Bispectral Analysis and Bilinear Time Series Models*, Springer Lecture Notes in Statistics, 24, Berlin.

Tukey, J.W. (1959), 'An Introduction to the Measurement of Spectra', in U. Grenanger (ed.), *Probability and Statistics*, Wiley, New York, pp. 300–330.

5

Stochastic or Chaotic Dynamics in High Frequency Financial Data

DOMINIQUE GUÉGAN and LUDOVIC MERCIER

1 INTRODUCTION

In recent years, there has been a growing interest in the search for models of nonlinear behaviour in financial markets. These nonlinear models tend to display very complex patterns. Indeed, it is now widely accepted that the linear approach does not allow us to take into account the particularly irregular behaviour that can be observed on numerous financial assets. Both in finance and economics, many types of nonlinearities can be observed. Let us mention, among others, the intrinsic nonlinearities to be seen in those credit offers that are sensitive to the effects of asymmetric information, the nonlinearities due to edge effects and natural nonlinearities occurring in profit rates or in shocks. These nonlinearities stem from some stylised facts like leptokurtocity, aggregate phenomena, persistence, level effects, information arrival or volatility co-movements (see Ghysels *et al.* 1996).

One of the main interests of financial data modelling lies in the opportunity to make predictions. Several approaches can be concurrently considered to tackle the complexity of financial data. Traditional models are stochastic and have generated nonlinearities that have become increasingly complex. Moreover, they do not always make sense from the viewpoint of economic theory; notably, bilinear models, threshold models, EXPAR models, fractional models or ARCH models. A presentation and an interesting bibliography on the latter can be found in Tong (1990) and Guégan (1994a).

More recently, various stochastic volatility models have appeared, including the EGARCH, SARV and FIGARCH models. They are interesting mainly

Nonlinear Modelling of High Frequency Financial Time Series.
Edited by Christian Dunis and Bin Zhou. © 1998 John Wiley Sons Ltd

because they force the noise to act directly on the volatility. This, in turn, allows more flexibility in the modelling of data and in separating the different sources of noise. See Chapter 7 for more details on the subject. Stochastic volatility models, however, present a major problem because of the overabundance of parameters present in the model. Those parameters are necessary in order to model the nonlinearity observed, but they are also difficult to use in a theory of identification. To get around this problem, constraints are often added to the models that are being built, which results in relatively simple but identifiable models, and the original complexity is reduced.

These models are relevant not only because they provide a better understanding of the nature of the series studied but also because predictions can be made. Indeed, when these models are thoroughly investigated, the confidence intervals that are obtained yield more precise predictions. So far, however, these models have not been adequately developed and the best results serve only as approximations (see Ghysels *et al.* 1996).

In this context, another approach can be contemplated so as to understand and predict the dynamics of highly nonlinear data: that of deterministic nonlinear dynamics. An essential aspect of this theory concerns the study of the dynamic instability of stationary states. With this approach, seemingly periodic fluctuations that are linked with the notion of attractor as defined by Poincaré (1908) can be considered. It also allows the study of the random fluctuations that, in turn, bring in the notion of chaos. At this point, we are talking of structural instability. The latter point of view can be very useful in the study of financial data.

The modelling of financial data on a deterministic basis amounts to giving more importance to the estimation of the hidden dynamic structure of the series than to the estimation of its stochastic components. Hopefully, in this context, a deterministic model of some fluctuations that would have otherwise been classed as a noise can be obtained.

Whatever method is used, the modelling of nonlinearities on data requires a great number of points for the underlying theoretical results to fall within asymptotic theory. That is why the two aforementioned theories (stochastic or deterministic) can be used with high frequency data series.

In the present chapter, the tick-by-tick data come from the interbank FX market. The interbank FX market is the spot market for foreign exchange transactions and operates 24 hours a day. Tick-by-tick interbank FX data consist of a sequence of bid/ask prices quoted by various firms that function as market makers. While bid/ask price quotes from many market makers are displayed simultaneously by wire services such as Reuters and Telerate, a single price series can be constructed from the sequence of newly updated quotes.

Due to the overlapping periods of activity of market makers located over the three continents — America, Europe and Asia — a sequential pattern of intraday trading is observed. A simple inspection of the series indicates that the time scales observed vary from one or two ticks to thousands of ticks per minute.

Thus, the choice of time scale is very important and the results can accordingly be very different.

We analyse a full year of such tick-by-tick interbank FX prices quotes for one series: the Deutschmark/French franc exchange rate. The data were provided by the Chemical Bank of London and its sample includes every tick from September 1994 to August 1995, that is to say 420 134 ticks. Here, we have chosen to work with regularly spaced data and we use a physical scale; a discussion on the choice of the scale for this kind of data can be found in Chapter 8.

Given the choice of time scale, we can now consider the problems of prediction and knowledge of the underlying model for the given data. In the first part, we present the data, the sampling method, how slack periods are taken into account and the main statistical characteristics of the data. The latter point is explained below in section 2. We then proceed to analyse the data using the two points of view that were developed earlier.

We begin from a deterministic viewpoint. From this approach we adopt an original procedure: we use prediction methods that yield an optimal prediction time step according to a certain number of parameters and we specify the prediction criterion. This result is obtained in the case of deterministic — and therefore highly nonlinear — chaotic systems. The idea behind this is not to detect a chaotic behaviour in intra-day financial data but to use prediction methods that have been developed for known chaotic systems in order to predict data series whose behaviour is rather complex.

In section 3, we define the notion of a chaotic system and the characteristics of such systems that we use in this chapter. We give some examples of well-known chaos.

In section 4, we briefly present the non-parametric prediction methods that we bring into play, as well as the prediction criterion considered. Some of these methods are explained in more detail in Chapters 11 and 13. We illustrate these methods with simulations carried out on well-known chaotic systems. We also provide a definition of the notion of optimal sampling time step with a view to obtaining an optimal prediction horizon. We illustrate this method with simulations carried out on the Lorenz attractor.

Section 5 is devoted to the applications of these different methods to the real data.

In section 6 we make predictions using a parametric nonlinear model: the fractional autoregressive model. We consider the classical criterion of mean square error of prediction. We compare the results with those obtained with the deterministic approach.

At this point it would indeed be interesting to be at last in a position to say whether the series are chaotic or not. The question then is linked to the fundamental problem of the existence of noise in real data. Indeed, noise does perturb all experimental data — that is why it is legitimate to consider the stochastic kind of approaches. Using a deterministic approach does not give noise the primordial importance it has in the stochastic approach. Rather, we tend to favour the intrinsic nonlinearity there is in the mechanism that generates the data.

Thus, the aim of the approach we consider here is also to obtain an explanation for the nonlinear behaviour of the data that is different from a stochastic model.

In the last part we develop a stochastic version of deterministic chaos by attempting to show why it is necessary to control the noise and to separate it from the dynamics of the system. We suggest various ways of trying to identify it.

2 PRESENTATION OF THE DATA

In this chapter we investigate tick-by-tick interbank foreign exchange rates. We have selected the Deutschmark/French franc exchange rates. Our empirical investigation covers the period 1 September 1994 to 31 August 1995 and we use Chemical Bank's database (Figure 5.1). The total of the datapoints is 420 134. On this amount of data we have suppressed 1443 outliers which correspond to a difference between the high and the low values greater than 0.01, knowing that the mean value of this difference corresponds to 0.00051.

The importance of intra-day prices lies in the large number of independent observations which enhances the significance of a statistical study. It is also important because it increases the ability to analyse finer details of the behaviour of the data we consider.

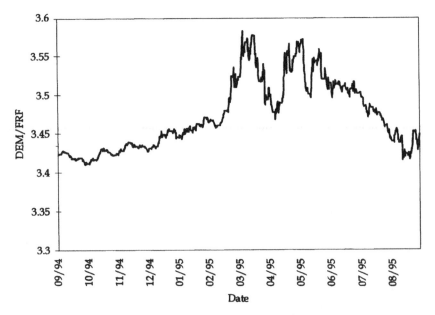

Figure 5.1   DEM/FRF exchange rate between Sept. 1994 and Aug. 1995

One of the most important problems in the use of tick data is that they are not regularly spaced in time. Still, we need regularly spaced data for the methods we use. Various possibilities have been studied for building a regularly spaced time series from tick-by-tick data. The choice is limited here since we have to work in calendar time in order to make predictions that can be compared later. This means that a sampling time step h has to be chosen. Here we took three different values for h: 600 s, 1200 s and 3600 s. This divides the year into 52 560, 26 280 and 13 140 intervals, respectively.

We suppose that in continuous time, the exchange rate is equal to the latest available quote. So, in each interval, the series can take several values as there can be none to a hundred of quotes between two time steps. This continuous time series is then sampled at the rate h in order to build the regularly spaced series.

If t denotes the date in seconds and $x(t)$ the continuous time series, then $x(t)$ is equal to the latest available quote before t. The discrete time series x_i is equal to $x(i.h)$.

Presently, we use the average of the bid and ask quotes to build x_i. We study x_i and the first differences of the logarithm of the series $\log(x_i) - \log(x_{i-1})$.

Some simple statistics on the data $x(t)$: min. = 3.410, first quarter = 3.434, median = 3.462, mean = 3.473, third quarter = 3.509, max. = 3.588, standard deviation = 0.0448.

3 CHAOTIC TIME SERIES

In this section, we present briefly the notion of chaos and the characteristics of the chaos that we use in this chapter. Then we give examples of chaotic systems that we use to generate chaotic time series.

3.1 Definitions and Notations

The study of dynamic systems has undergone a lot of development during the last 10 years. Here, we use this approach with a view to optimising the optimal horizon of prediction for financial data.

By dynamic system we denote a series of observations X_i in $\Re^m$ starting from some initial condition X_0 such that

$$X_i = \varphi(X_{i-1})$$

Here φ is some nonlinear map from D to D, where D is a compact subset of $\Re^m$ and φ is measurable with respect to the Borel field $B(D)$.

In fact, when we observe data sets, we have a univariate data set. For the dynamic approach, this information is not enough. We need to know how many components can characterise the data. We need to know the number of degrees of freedom of the data set that we have to investigate. Thus we must embed the data in the state-space whose dimension corresponds to this number of degrees of freedom. This dimension is called the embedding dimension. The theoretical properties of this state-space have been studied by Takens (1981). Generally the embedding dimension is not known. We can use different methods to estimate it, see for instance Grassberger and Procaccia (1983), Bosq and Guégan (1994) and Guégan and Léorat (1996).

We are going to assume here that the function φ is chaotic. Following Eckmann and Ruelle (1985), we call chaos a dynamic system which is sensitive to initial conditions and ergodic. Sensitivity means that if two identical systems are started at initial conditions X and $X + \varepsilon$, respectively, where ε is a very small quantity, their dynamic states will diverge from each other very quickly in state-space. Their separation increases exponentially on average. We say that a dynamic system is ergodic if there exists an invariant and unique measure for it. For more details on these notions the reader can consult the work of Lasota and MacKey (1987).

Our work concerns essentially short-term predictions. If we know $X_1 \ldots X_N$, we can expect to forecast $X_{N+1} \ldots X_{N+p}$, with small values of p. Actually, even for a chaotic system, we can compute a short-term prediction if the function φ which generates the system has been well reconstructed. However, the future of a nonlinear system in the chaotic phase is not predictable for a mean term time interval because forecasting errors grow exponentially fast. We can say that we make a long-term prediction when the prediction horizon is longer than several pseudo-periods (when pseudo-periods can be defined). In that case, provided the historical data are long enough, we can compute the density of the prediction if we know the invariant measure.

The time series to which we apply the different methods are generated by the following chaotic systems: the Lorenz attractor and the Rössler chaos. Various representations of these systems exist. The parameters chosen are the 'historical' ones. These systems are continuous time processes. We consider here a sampled version of these systems.

3.2 The Lorenz Attractor

The differential equation we chose for the Lorenz attractor (Figure 5.2) is the following in $\mathfrak{R}^3$:

$$
\begin{cases}
\dfrac{dx}{dt} = 16(y(t) - x(t)) \\[2mm]
\dfrac{dy}{dt} = x(t)(45.92 - z(t)) - y(t) \\[2mm]
\dfrac{dz}{dt} = x(t)y(t) - 4z(t)
\end{cases}
$$

We produce the data by integrating this system numerically, starting from initial conditions close to the attractor. Once the transients are eliminated, the data are sampled with a constant time step h.

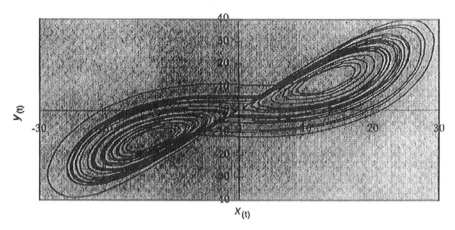

Figure 5.2 A trajectory of the Lorenz system projected on the plane $z = 0$. Successive points are linked with a continuous line

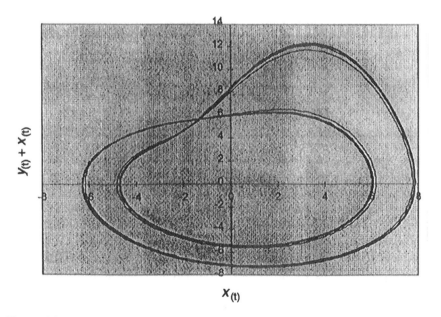

Figure 5.3 A trajectory of the Rössler system projected on the plane $y - z = 0$. Successive points are linked with a continuous line

3.3 The Rössler Chaos

The continuous time representation we chose for the Rössler chaos (Figure 5.3) is the following in $\mathfrak{R}^3$:

$$\begin{cases} \dfrac{\mathrm{d}x}{\mathrm{d}t} = -y(t) - z(t) \\[2mm] \dfrac{\mathrm{d}y}{\mathrm{d}t} = x(t) + 0.15\,y(t) \\[2mm] \dfrac{\mathrm{d}z}{\mathrm{d}t} = 0.2 + z(t)(x(t) - 4) \end{cases}$$

4 NON-PARAMETRIC METHODS OF PREDICTIONS

In this section, we present briefly the different prediction methods we consider. Suppose that the time series under study is a scalar $x(t)$ sampled at rate h. We then have N points $x_1 \ldots x_N$ coming from a dynamic process giving rise to a strange attractor lying on an invariant manifold of the dynamic system. To reconstruct this state-space, we use the standard technique of delay coordinates. The delay state vector is defined as

$$X_i = (x_i, x_{i-\tau}, x_{i-2.\tau}, \ldots, x_{i-(m-1).\tau})'$$

where m is the embedding dimension, τ a time lag and we use the notation V' to represent the transpose of vector V. Note that for the simulated systems, no embedding is needed since we can take the dimension in which the system is defined, that is dimension 3.

Thus, forecasting amounts to solving an interpolation or approximation problem in the state-space. From the system $X_i = \varphi_h(X_{i-1})$, we observe the data set $X_1 \ldots X_N$, and we need to construct an estimate of φ_h denoted $\hat{\varphi}_h$. We are going to use the prediction approach to construct such an estimate.

Classically, the prediction approaches to estimate φ can be classified in three groups. These have been reviewed in the article of Lillekjendlie, Kugiumtzis and Christophersen (1994). We can distinguish the local, the semi-local and the global methods. The local approach has been developed and discussed in the papers of Farmer and Sidorowich (1987), Jimenez, Moreno and Ruggieri (1992), Murray (1994), Doerner, Hübinger and Martiensen (1994) and Finkenstädt and Kuhbier (1995), among others. A review of the semi-local approach can be found in the papers of Smith (1992) and Stockbro and Umberger (1992) and the global approach, for instance by Casdagli (1989), LeBaron and Weigend (1995) and Fang and Cao (1995). Other methods have also been developed using marginal densities; see for example El Gamal (1987) and Geweke (1988). Experimental algorithms have been proposed in the works of Sugihara and May (1990) and Meyer and Packard (1991).

Here, we choose a local and a semi-local method because the global approach is too time consuming. We assume that the data set $X_1 \ldots X_N$ is one realisation of the system $X_i = \varphi_h(X_{i-1})$ starting from an initial condition X_0.

On the basis of the data set, we examine the hypothesis that the target function $\hat{\varphi}$ is chosen among two different classes of functions: the first class is the nearest neighbours, the second is the radial basis functions. We also tried a certain type of feedforward neural network but we do not develop it here; for more comments see section 4.4. We present the details of the methods used in this chapter to make predictions. In the following section we apply these methods on the simulated systems to understand how they perform. Finally, we are going to use these results to try to make predictions on real data.

4.1 The Nearest Neighbours

This method is a local one. It is relatively easy to implement. If we want to use only one neighbour, we search among the set $X_1 \ldots X_{N-1}$ for the point $X_{(1)}$ which is the closest to X_N in the sense of a certain norm (for example, the Euclidean norm) then we define: $\hat{X}_{N+1} = X_{(1)+1}$.

It is possible to use more than one neighbour, to take more than one past value for each one or to consider various weights. Since the dynamics are assumed to be continuous in the state-space, we use K neighbours, a weighting function w and the Euclidean norm in $\mathfrak{R}^m$. Then we get

$$\hat{X}_{N+1} = \sum_{i=1}^{K} w(||X_N - X_{(i)}||) X_{(i)+1}$$

Here, when more than one neighbour is implied, we use the method chosen by Finkenstädt and Kuhbier (1995). That is, we assume that the importance of each neighbour is proportional to the exponential of its distance to X_N. The weighting function w is then

$$w(||X_N - X_{(i)}||) = \frac{\exp(-||X_N - X_{(i)}||)}{\sum_{k=1}^{K} \exp(-||X_N - X_{(k)}||)}$$

4.2 Radial Basis Functions

With this semi-local method, we approach φ with a set of radial basis functions (see Casdagli 1989 for more details). This method is often related to neural networks but its expression is a lot simpler. We construct $\hat{\varphi}$ in the following way:

$$\hat{\varphi}(X_N) = \sum_{c=1}^{C} \lambda_c w_c(||X_N - Y_c||)$$

where the C points are chosen in the state-space via a clustering method (mobile centres) on $X_1 \ldots X_N$; these points are the centres of the radial basis functions. The functions w_c are radial functions like a Gaussian or a multiquadric function. The choice of the function is arbitrary as with the nearest neighbours weights before. Here, we chose multiquadric functions for computational efficiency like $w_c(r) = 1/\sqrt{r^2 + r_c^2}$ where r_c is the radius of the centre Y_c. Here we use the estimated standard deviation of its class, which is defined as the set of points closer to Y_c than to any other centre. The parameters l_c are estimated using a simple regression on the past values.

4.3 Criteria for Comparison

There exist several ways of comparing the efficiency of the predictors. The classical one is the mean square error of the prediction for a given prediction time. We can also compare the coefficients of correlation between the real values and the predictors, see e.g. Sugihara and May (1990). In Diebold and Mariano (1995), we can find other comparisons.

In effect, for chaotic systems, it seems reasonable to consider different criteria with respect to the prediction barrier that we specify below. We can consider the previous methods but it also seems interesting to find out what is the limit of the term *small* for chaotic systems. For the systems we are studying, we can conjecture that the prediction will become exponentially worse as the horizon increases. For each system, we first calculate its diameter, that is the largest distance between two points on the attractor. We then define the 1% horizon (respectively 5%) as the date when the prediction differs by more than 1% of the diameter (or 5%) from the true value. We use these last criteria here. It is also more relevant than the mean square error because we have to compare predictions made with different time steps. Note that this prediction horizon can also be called predictability time.

4.4 Simulations

In this subsection, we present the main results of interest concerning the simulations we performed with the two chaotic systems using the previous forecasting methods. Details about these and other simulations can be found in Guégan and Mercier (1996a).

We generate series taken from the chaotic systems described above with various length, starting points and time steps. Iterative predictions are made from various initial conditions close to the attractor. The 1% and 5% horizons are then computed.

We employed 1, 3 and 10 neighbours for the local method and 50, 100 and 150 centres for the radial basis functions. We also tried various neural networks ranging from 2 layers of 9 neurons to 3 layers of 20 neurons. The results concerning neural networks were not satisfactory because they were about a thousand times slower than the radial basis functions method. This did not allow us to make enough simulations to compare neural networks to other methods with statistically significant results, thus we do not give results with this method here.

The relative quality (Figure 5.4) of nearest neighbours and radial basis functions methods depends on the chosen system but also on the chosen parameters. The use of one neighbour is on average better than many but this may well change in the presence of noise. The quality of radial basis functions increases as the

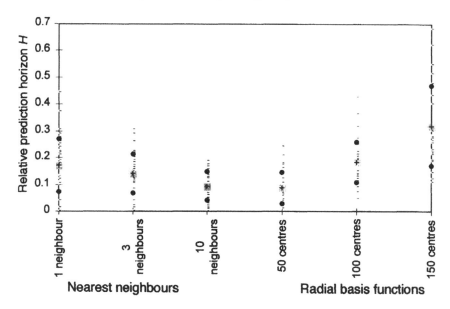

Figure 5.4 The relative prediction horizon is drawn by calculating for each set of parameters and each system the six predictability times $H_1, H_2, \ldots, H_6$ for 1, 3 and 10 neighbours, 50, 100 and 150 radial basis functions centres. For each prediction method p, a dot represents $H_p/(H_1 + \ldots + H_6)$. A cross is the mean, a circle represents the standard error

number of centres increases but so does the computational load. The barrier of 1 or 5% yields globally the same results. Of course, the 1% horizon is always smaller than the 5% one.

The role of the sampling time step appears to be very important and deserves more investigation. If we denote Hh as the prediction horizon for continuous time, N the size of the series and h the time step chosen for sampling, we observed the following (Figure 5.5):

- For a fixed h, the prediction horizon Hh increases with the sample size N but it seems to reach a maximum value.
- For a fixed N, the prediction horizon Hh increases as the sampling time step h increases (more orbits are built), but after a threshold the prediction horizon Hh diminishes (the points are more and more random on the attractor). The existence of a unique optimal time step h is not proven. First investigations show $h^* \propto N^{-1/d}$ where d is the 'local' embedding dimension (thus $d \leq m$) but this result is established only in a very restrictive case (for one nearest neighbour; the proof for a more general context is in progress).

The same phenomenon is observed in the case of the Rössler system with both prediction methods. We can see that the prediction horizon depends strongly on

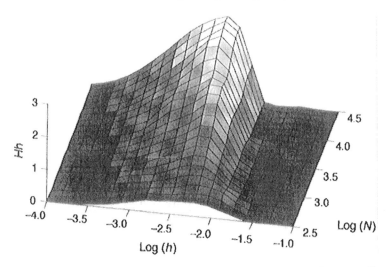

Figure 5.5 Prediction horizon for the Lorenz system as a function of the sampling time step h and the number of points N. Each point is the mean horizon of 100 predictions. To obtain this figure 12 100 predictions are necessary. We used the nearest neighbours method for this figure

the sampling time step h. Choosing the right sampling is more important than increasing the amount of data studied, increasing the amount of parameters in $\hat{\varphi}$ or tuning the estimation method. We can expect to have the same kind of phenomenon in other highly nonlinear real data. We obtained the same map using the radial basis functions method.

5 PREDICTIONS USING A NON-PARAMETRIC APPROACH

In this section, we apply the methods developed previously for chaotic systems and we use the results obtained concerning the optimal sampling time step h. But there is still no way to estimate this optimal time step directly from the database, and there is no evidence that the data under study represent a chaotic system. By conventional statistical standards, there presently exists no econometric test for chaos neither as a type I nor type II error.

We use the data described in section 2. We construct two time series: $x_i = x(ih)$ and $\log(x_i) - \log(x_{i-1})$. These series are sampled at rates $h = 600$ s, $h = 1200$ s and $h = 3600$ s. This divides one year's observations into 52 560, 26 280 and 13 140 intervals, respectively. We used three time lags t for the embedding: $t = 600$ s, $t = 1200$ s and $t = 3600$ s. We used only two embedding dimensions $m = 3$ and $m = 6$. Looking at the series in dimension 1 or 2 shows that it is certainly too small, embedding the series in a dimension greater than 7 would need more than one million points, even dimension 6 is quite high. Dimensions 4 and 5 were not used because of the computational load involved. According to the simulation results, we used 3 nearest neighbours and 100 centres radial basis functions for predictions.

This set of various parameters involves $2 \times 3 \times 3 \times 2 \times 2 = 72$ different cases. For each case, we made 100 out-of-sample predictions at various locations between July 1995 and September 1995. This gave 100 prediction horizons. We took out the predictions that took place when the market is idle, and it yielded 6110 valid predictions. Table 5.1 summarises these results: it gives for each case the average prediction horizon and its standard error. The horizon here is at the 1% level: in this case, it means that the predicted values differ by less than 0.0005 from the real value.

The best mean predictability time is 3140 s which is obtained with a 100 centres radial basis functions predictor for a sampling time step $h = 1200$ s, a time lag $t = 1200$ s and an embedding dimension $m = 3$. In this case the series studied was $\log(x_i) - \log(x_{i-1})$ but the predictability time is calculated once the series and the predicted values are taken back to the real scale x_i. This means that between two and three predictions 20-minute steps ahead are feasible with an absolute error below 0.0005. However, the standard error on the predictability time is quite large (4102 s).

The effects of h and t are different: a change in h can drastically affect the quality of predictions but the choice of t does not seem to be as important. Improving the predictions implies optimising both in h and t but according to this table, the constraint $h = t$ seems irrelevant, which goes against the usual practice that takes $h = t$.

The results for the 1 hour sampling time step are always below 1 hour predictability time on average, which means good predictions less than one step ahead on average. This is a fair indication that 1 hour predictions may be better in the MSE sense using a shorter time scale and generating predictions two or three steps ahead instead of deriving directly 1 hour predictions.

Another way to improve the predictions, besides optimising in h and t, would be to study what happens with embedding dimensions 4 and 5.

These results emphasise the role of the sampling time step in terms of prediction quality but require more testing in order to yield significant results for the other parameters. This can be done only with other time series or a much longer series in order to avoid the lack of testing intervals for out-of-sample prediction tests.

In the case of the intra-day series studied here it seems that the noise is too great to reconstruct the underlying dynamic system properly (if it exists). Methods that proved successful for pure chaotic time series have to be adapted for real data. Still, the DEM/FRF is not the only series that could exhibit chaos. By its structure (it is a cross rate), it is likely to include more noise than other series like the DEM/USD or SP500 and the consequences of the Single European Market on the model are not clear.

Table 5.1 Mean predictability time in seconds for the 1% level

Hh		Series:	$\log(x_i)-\log(x_{i-1})$				x_i			
		m	3		6		3		6	
h	τ	Method:	NN	RBF	NN	RBF	NN	RBF	NN	RBF
600	600	Mean	1731^{1}	1749^{1}	1333^{1}	2225^{2}	1620^{1}	722^{7}	1952^{1}	439^{4}
		Std. Error	2097^{2}	2080^{2}	1979^{1}	3652^{3}	2789^{2}	2007^{2}	3265^{3}	935^{9}
	1200	Mean	1251^{1}	2297^{2}	2186^{2}	2958^{2}	1722^{1}	704^{7}	1592^{1}	617^{6}
		Std. Error	1833^{1}	3662^{3}	2930^{2}	3530^{3}	2382^{2}	2200^{2}	2624^{2}	1435^{1}
	3600	Mean	1911^{1}	2479^{2}	1542^{1}	2256^{2}	1440^{1}	908^{9}	1586^{1}	321^{3}
		Std. Error	2374^{2}	2956^{2}	1923^{1}	2624^{2}	1987^{1}	2450^{2}	2402^{2}	784^{7}
1200	600	Mean	2335^{2}	2700^{2}	1768^{1}	2319^{2}	1907^{1}	1233^{1}	1946^{1}	1378^{1}
		Std. Error	3710^{3}	4037^{4}	2845^{2}	3538^{3}	2645^{2}	3105^{3}	3195^{3}	2655^{2}
	1200	Mean	1600^{1}	$\mathbf{3140}^{3}$	2059^{2}	2844^{2}	1841^{1}	1216^{1}	2011^{2}	810^{8}
		Std. Error	2482^{2}	4102^{4}	2929^{2}	3153^{3}	2940^{2}	2836^{2}	2858^{2}	1634^{1}
	3600	Mean	2032^{2}	2729^{2}	2064^{2}	2400^{2}	1816^{1}	1137^{1}	1476^{1}	379^{3}
		Std. Error	2712^{2}	3494^{3}	2883^{2}	2835^{2}	2530^{2}	2614^{2}	2532^{2}	924^{9}
3600	600	Mean	2141^{2}	2663^{2}	2332^{2}	2870^{2}	1775^{1}	1846^{1}	2452^{2}	1824^{1}
		Std. Error	3470^{3}	3500^{3}	3995^{3}	4084^{4}	3067^{3}	3658^{3}	3830^{3}	3761^{3}
	1200	Mean	2256^{2}	2832^{2}	2132^{2}	2481^{2}	2022^{2}	1959^{1}	1942^{1}	2000^{2}
		Std. Error	3916^{3}	4239^{4}	3175^{3}	3572^{3}	3174^{3}	3637^{3}	3549^{3}	3270^{3}
	3600	Mean	2255^{2}	3000^{3}	2466^{2}	2928^{2}	2000^{2}	1935^{1}	1995^{1}	866^{8}
		Std. Error	3779^{3}	4440^{4}	3693^{3}	4130^{4}	3517^{3}	3528^{3}	3582^{3}	2173^{2}

6 PREDICTIONS USING FRACTIONAL MODELS

In this section, we investigate a stochastic model for the data we have considered to examine whether predictions can be generated. We use the same data set as in the previous section sampled at rate $h = 1200$ s. In fact, we try to see if there exists some evidence of a long memory process for these data so that we can compare the predictions obtained with this approach with those obtained using chaotic systems. To identify a long memory behaviour, we fit a FARIMA process as defined in Granger and Joyeux (1980) or Hosking (1981). This model is as follows:

$$(1 - B)^d x_t = \varepsilon_t$$

where B is the backward operator B $x_t = x_{t-1}$ and ε_t some centred white noise. We want to estimate the parameter d or $H = d + \frac{1}{2}$. We have a long memory process if $d \neq 0$ or $H \neq \frac{1}{2}$. To estimate d we use different methods in order to be sure that our results are meaningful. The methods used are the R/S method introduced by Hurst (1951), the periodogram method presented by Geweke and Porter-Hudack (1983), the aggregated variance described in Taqqu, Teverodovsky and Willinger (1994) and the Higuchi method presented by Higuchi (1988). In a recent paper, Bisaglia and Guégan (1996), we have applied these methods to simulated data to provide a comparison basis for the estimated values of d that we obtain. It is very difficult indeed to assess the true value of d since there exists no confidence interval for its estimated value with the previous methods. Using the benchmark obtained in this paper, we can give some results concerning our real data. In Table 5.2, we can observe that for the real data x_t, all the heuristic estimation methods give an H value close to 0.5. This is in agreement with the fact that this series does not show evidence of long-range dependence. This result also agrees with the efficient market hypothesis that stock market returns contain little serial correlation (Fama 1970; Taylor 1986).

Nevertheless, this does not mean that the series is not i.i.d. but it does not present any evidence of long memory behaviour. The above results show that we cannot propose predictions for x_t with this approach. Accordingly, the method

Table 5.2 Estimation results for H, for the series of simple returns of DEM/FRF

Method	H for x_t
R/S method	0.468
R/S method + scrambling	0.507
Periodogram method	0.500
Periodogram method + scrambling	0.497
Aggregated variance	0.463
Aggregated variance + scrambling	0.477
Higuchi method	0.467

Table 5.3 Estimation results for H, for the series of absolute and squared returns of DEM/FRF

Method	H for $|x_t|$	H for $|x_t|^2$
Periodogram method	0.788	0.713
Periodogram method + scrambling	0.497	0.418
Aggregated variance	0.968	0.883
Aggregated variance + scrambling	0.526	0.471

developed in the previous section seems more suitable. But in order to give more information concerning the long memory behaviour of this data set, we have also considered transformations of x_t, that is its absolute value $|x_t|$ and its squared absolute value $|x_t|^2$. Actually, if x_t is i.i.d., then its transformations should also be i.i.d. We applied the same methods as before and obtained in that case a value for H that is greater than 0.5.

Table 5.3 shows that each method gives a value of H greater than 0.5. Although we obtain estimates of H which are different from each other, the fact that these values are very far above 0.5 is an indication of long memory.

These results allow us to confirm that the behaviour of the mechanism which generates the original data is certainly complex. We can see that trying to adapt a nonlinear fractional model to these data does not allow any predictions for x_t. We can only have predictions for the transformed series $|x_t|$ and $|x_t|^2$. Thus, from a forecasting point of view, the chaotic approach seems more relevant than the stochastic approach (in the case of fractional models).

Note that if the series is a long memory process, the order of the data is very important. By randomly scrambling the data, we should *destroy* the correlation structure and consequently, the H estimated should be closer to 0.5. We can observe in Tables 5.2 and 5.3 that, for the series of simple returns, all the H estimates remain around 0.5, confirming that there is no long memory in this series. For the transformations of the returns, scrambling the data *destroys* the long memory structure and leads to independent series.

7 NOISE IN CHAOS

In this section, we focus upon the prediction approach in an ergodic dynamic system of the type studied above. The natural approach is to consider the observation data set $Y_1 \ldots Y_N$ to consider that it is generated by the following system:

$$Y_i = X_i + \varepsilon_i$$

where

$$X_i = \varphi(X_{i-1})$$

with Y_i and ε_i random variables and X_i deterministic. Here, we have focused upon the prediction of the data X_i in section 5.

Another approach would be to consider that the data $Y_1 \ldots Y_N$ is generated by

$$Y_i = \varphi(Y_{i-1}) + \varepsilon_i$$

where Y_i and ε_i are random variables. We have considered this approach in section 6. This study is not concerned with a 'noisy' chaotic approach because we do not know if the function j is chaotic. Other discussions can be found in Guégan (1994b), Yao and Tong (1994) and Guégan and Léorat (1995).

If we look at the different methods presented in this chapter, we can distinguish different kinds of noise that we are going to specify now.

Some noise is inherent to this approach, as far as simulations are concerned. With respect to the real data, the difficulty is to be able to separate the noise from the dynamics when we consider the chaotic approach. Let us evaluate these different points in more detail.

7.1 Comments on Chaotic Time Series Simulation

In this section, we discuss the different types of errors introduced when chaotic systems are simulated. We discuss the type of errors and the theoretical problems that appear in the context of simulations.

The problems encountered within that context are fundamental when we want to compare the predictions obtained by different methods between them and also with the real data. Most of the problems of errors that we discuss here lose their interest when we work with real data, because the errors introduced in the context of simulations do not appear in real data.

Nevertheless, we often use results obtained from simulations to interpret results obtained with real data, thus it is necessary to know exactly what happens in the former context.

Here, we rely on numerical results to provide information about the asymptotic behaviour of real systems. The problem is that numerical results for chaotic systems can be misleading. The sensitivity to initial conditions results in the repeated enlargement of small rounding errors which cannot be avoided in a numerical setting. Eventually, the computed orbit diverges from the desired true orbit. However, the numerical orbit often exhibits the same general behaviour as the true orbit.

7.1.1 Discretisation Error

The first error encountered when simulating a continuous time process is the discretisation error. Here, we employ the usual forward-Euler algorithm which discretises the following differential equation system $\dot{X}(t) = \Phi(X(t))$ with

$$X(t + \theta) = X(t) + \theta\Phi(X(t))$$

for small values of θ.

Thus, when we discretise, we introduce an error due to the approximation of the discretisation. It is an error on the function Φ. Then, we investigate an approximation of Φ. This discretisation time step is different from the sampling time step, here we take it 1000 times smaller to diminish the approximation error.

7.1.2 Truncation Error

This type of error is due to the limited precision of computers. This limited precision introduces systematic rounding errors during calculations. We do not calculate $X(t)$ but $X(t) + \eta_t$ where η_t is a small noise. We have to assume that this systematic truncation error does not affect the global properties of the chaotic series under study. Here we used 64 bits as a compromise between truncation error and data storage.

These two structural errors do not appear in the real case. The only kind of error when real chaotic data are observed is a measurement error, we observe $\tilde{X}_{i+1} = X_i + v_i$. When a continuous time series is observed, this measurement error also appears on the time index. At the instant t we do not observe $X(t)$ but $X(t + dt)$ where dt is a time error. We can formulate these ideas in the following way for discrete time systems:

- In the case of a simulated system: if the starting value is X_0, $X_1 = \tilde{\varphi}(X_0) + \eta_1$ and more generally: $X_t = \tilde{\varphi}(X_{t-1}) + \eta_t$.
- In the case of a real system: if the starting value is X_0, $X_1 = \varphi(X_0)$, we observe $\tilde{X}_1 = X_0 + v_0$ and more generally: $X_t = \varphi(X_{t-1})$ and $\tilde{X}_{t+1} = X_t + v_t$ is observed.

7.2 Noise in Real Data

In the previous section, we have shown that the amplitude of the structural error can be magnified by the system, which is an important transformation of the system that we want to reproduce. This is important to know when simulating chaotic systems. How should we take into account this kind of error? Nevertheless, this kind of error does not appear with real data.

With respect to real data, another problem is important. It concerns the difference between a chaotic deterministic system and a dynamic system with noise, which is a stochastic model. The prediction approach depends on the type of system at hand.

In the deterministic case the data X_t that we observe corresponds to a chaotic deterministic system with a measurement error that we can describe in the following way:

$$\tilde{X}_{t+1} = \phi(X_t, \varepsilon_t)$$

the possible representation of which is the following: $\tilde{X}_t = X_t + \varepsilon_t$ and the underlying process is given by $X_t = \phi(X_{t+1})$. Here, we predict X_{t+H}.

In the stochastic case, it is the data that we observe that are generated by

$$X_{t+1} = \phi(X_t, \varepsilon_t)$$

and the noise directly affects the underlying dynamics. In this last case, we are close to the so-called 'noisy chaos', which is in fact a stochastic system. The prediction concerns X_{t+H} which is completely different from the previous one. The latter can be computed in terms of conditional expectation, which is not the case for the former.

More complete comments can be found in Tong's discussion paper by Guégan (1994a, 1995a, c), examples are given in Guégan (1995b) and Guégan and Léorat (1995).

With respect to the simulations, the likely existence of an optimal sampling time step for a fixed amount of data is promising. The existence of this optimum in the presence of noise remains to be proven.

In this empirical approach we show that we can use different algorithms for simulated data but we now need to explain the results in terms of the presence of noise so that we can use the results in a real context.

In the case of intra-day data studied here, it seems that noise is too great to reconstruct the underlying dynamic system. The nearest neighbours and the radial basis functions methods that are successful in the case of chaotic systems do not provide as reliable predictions here, essentially for the long term. A small change in the parameters yields globally the same results: we tried periods from 10 to 60 minutes, embedding dimensions 3 and 6 and various numbers of neighbours or centres. None of them gave good results in the mean and long-term predictions.

Our results are globally good for short-term predictions. Two ways are currently being studied to improve the predictions: the first is to find an equivalent of the optimal time step that we have in the chaotic systems that should be around 1200 s, the second is to choose better variables to build the state-space. It is in that sense that we are going to work now.

ACKNOWLEDGEMENT

We are grateful to C. Dunis for giving us the data of the exchange rates that we use in this study and Luisa Bisaglia for her support in conducting the long memory estimations.

REFERENCES

Bisaglia, L. and Guégan, D. (1996), 'A Review on Techniques of Estimation in Long Memory Processes: Application to Intra-day Data', Preprint University of Padua, Italy.
Bosq, D. and Guégan, D. (1994), 'Estimation of the Embedding Dimension of a Dynamic System', Working Paper INSEE 9451, Paris.
Casdagli, M. (1989), 'Non-linear Prediction in Chaotic Time Series', *Physica D*, **35**, 335–359.

Diebold, F.X. and Mariano, R.S. (1995), 'Comparing Predictive Accuracy', *Journal of Business & Economic Statistics*, **13**, 253-263.

Doerner, R., Hübinger, B. and Martiensen, W. (1994), 'Advanced Chaos Forecasting', *Physical Review E*, **50**, R12-R15.

El Gamal, M.A. (1987), 'Simple Estimation and Forecasting Methods in Systems Characterised by Deterministic Chaos: the Univariate Case', Preprint, Univ. of Wisconsin.

Eckmann, J.P. and Ruelle, D. (1985), 'Ergodic Theory of Chaos and Strange Attractors', *Reviews of Modern Physics*, **57**, 617.

Fama, E.F. (1970), 'Efficient Capital Markets: A Review of Theory and Empirical Work', *Journal of Finance*, **25**, 383-417.

Fang, H.P. and Cao, L.Y. (1995), 'Predicting and Characterising Data Sequences from Structure-variable Systems', Preprint, CCAST, Beijing.

Farmer, J.D. and Sidorowich, J.J. (1987), 'Predicting Chaotic Time Series', *Physical Review Letters*, **59**, 845-848.

Finkenstädt, B. and Kuhbier, P. (1995), 'Forecasting Non-linear Economic Time Series: A Simple Test to Accompany the Nearest Neighbour Approach', *Empirical Economics*, **20**, 243-263.

Geweke, J. (1988), 'Inference and Forecasting for Deterministic Non-linear Time Series Observed with Measurement Error', Preprint, Duke University, Durham, NC.

Geweke, J. and Porter-Hudack, S. (1983), 'The Estimation and Application of Long-Memory Time Series Models', *JTSA*, **4**, 221-237.

Ghysels, E., Harvey, A. and Renault, E. (1996), 'Stochastic Volatility', to appear in *Handbook of Statistics*, Vol. **14**, Wiley.

Granger, C.W.J. and Joyeux, R. (1980), 'An Introduction to Long-range Time Series Models and Fractional Differencing', *JTSA*, **1**, 15-30.

Grassberger, P. and Proccacia, I. (1983), 'Measuring the Strangeness of Strange Attractor', *Physica D*, **9**, 189-208.

Guégan, D. (1994a), 'Modèles de séries chronologiques non linéaires à temps discret', *Economica*, Paris.

Guégan, D. (1994b), 'Stochastic Versus Deterministic Systems', Working Paper INSEE 9438, Paris.

Guégan, D. (1995a), 'Discussion on Tong's Paper', *Scandinavian Journal of Statistics*, **22**, 25-27.

Guégan, D. (1995b), 'Robust Estimation in Discrete Time Chaotic Systems', *Proceedings of the IEEE Signal Processing ATHOS Workshop on Higher Order Statistics*, Begur, June 1995, pp. 376-380.

Guégan, D. (1995c), 'How Can Noise be Brought out in Dynamic Chaos?' To appear in the *Proceedings of the Workshop: Methods of Non Equilibrium Processes in Economics and Environment Sciences*, Matrafured, Hungary.

Guégan, D. and Léorat, G. (1995), 'Consistent Estimation to Determine the Embedding Dimension in Financial Data', Preprint, Paris XIII, 95-07.

Guégan, D. and Léorat, G. (1996), 'What is the Good Way to Identify Noisy Chaos? An Empirical Approach', Working Paper INSEE 9619, Paris.

Guégan, D. and Mercier, L. (1996a), 'Rising and Falling Prediction in Financial Intra-day Data', *Proceedings of the Third International Conference Sponsored by Chemical Bank and Imperial College: Forecasting Financial Markets*, London, Ch. 2, 1-24.

Guégan, D. and Mercier, L. (1996b), 'Prediction in Chaotic Time Series: Methods and Comparisons Using Simulations', Working Paper INSEE 9616, Paris.

Higuchi, T. (1988), 'Approach to an Irregular Time Series on the Basis of the Fractal Theory', *Physica D*, **31**, 277-283.

Hosking, J.R.M. (1981), 'Fractional Differencing', *Biometrika*, **68**, 165-176.

Hurst, H.E. (1951), 'Long-term Storage Capacity of Reservoirs', *Trans. Am. Soc. Civil Engineers*, **116**, 770–799.

Jimenez, J., Moreno, J.A. and Ruggieri, G.J. (1992), 'Forecasting in Chaotic Time Series: A Local Optimal Linear-reconstruction Method', *Physical Review A*, **45**, 3553–3558.

Lasota, J. and MacKey, O. (1987), 'Probabilistic Properties of Deterministic Systems', *Cambridge Ltd.*, J. Wiley.

LeBaron, B. and Weigend, A.S. (1995), 'Evaluating Neural Network Predictors by Bootstrapping', Preprint, Univ. of Madison.

Lillekjendlie, B., Kugiumtzis, D. and Christophersen, N. (1994), 'Chaotic Time Series: System Identification and Prediction', Preprint, Oslo.

Meyer, T.P. and Packard, N.H. (1991), 'Local Forecasting of High Dimensional Chaotic Dynamics', Preprint, Los Alamos Inst.

Murray, D.B. (1994), 'Forecasting a Chaotic Time Series Using an Improved Metric for Embedding Dimension', *Physica D*, **68**, 318–325.

Poincaré, H. (1908), *Science et méthode*, Ernest Flammarion, Paris.

Smith, L.A. (1992), 'Identification and Prediction of Low Dimensional Dynamics', *Physica D*, **58**, 50–76.

Stokbro, K. and Umberger, D.K. (1992), 'Forecasting with Weighed Maps', in M. Casdagli and S. Eubank (eds) *Non-linear Modelling and Forecasting*, Addison-Wesley, New York.

Sugihara, G. and May, R.M. (1990), 'Non-linear Forecasting as a Way of Distinguishing Chaos from Measurement Error in Time Series', *Nature*, **344**, 734–741.

Takens, F. (1981), 'Detecting Strange Attractors in Turbulence', *Lecture Notes in Mathematics*, **898**, 366–381.

Taqqu, M., Teverodosky, V. and Willinger, W. (1994), 'Estimators for Long-range Dependence: An Empirical Study', Preprint, Boston University (USA).

Taylor, S. (1986), *Modelling Financial Time Series*, Wiley, New York.

Tong, H. (1990), *Non-linear Time Series: A Dynamic System Approach*, Oxford Statistical Science Series.

Yao, Q. and Tong, H. (1994), 'Quantifying the Influence of Initial Values on Non-linear Predictions', *J. R. Statist. Soc. B*, **56**, 701–725.

6
F-consistency, De-volatilization and Normalization of High Frequency Financial Data
BIN ZHOU

1 INTRODUCTION

As computers have become increasingly powerful and storage media increasingly affordable, financial data have become available at higher and higher frequencies. Foreign exchange rates, for example, are quoted every few seconds (Goodhart and Figliuoli 1991). However, increasing observation frequency does not make the task of modeling and forecasting financial markets any easier. Increasing noise level and heteroscedasticity remain obstacles in modeling financial time series. In this chapter, we discuss two approaches to reduce heteroscedasticity in using high frequency data, de-volatilization and normalization. A related topic regarding using high frequency data is *f-consistency*, which is the consistency of an estimation as the observation frequency increases to infinity without increasing the length of the observation timespan.

In this chapter, I assume that the high frequency data are the observations of a continuous process with micro-level deviations. That is

$$S(t) = P(t) + \varepsilon_t \quad t \in [a, b] \tag{1}$$

where $S(t)$ is the logarithm transformation of the price process and $P(t)$ is a diffusion process

$$dP(t) = \mu(t) + \sigma(t) \, dW_t \tag{2}$$

and ε_t is a stochastic process independent of the price process $P(t)$. When the observation frequency increases, a financial price process increasingly

---

Nonlinear Modelling of High Frequency Financial Time Series.
Edited by Christian Dunis and Bin Zhou. © 1998 John Wiley Sons Ltd

deviates from a continuous process. For example, as the observation frequency increases, the variance of price change does not approach zero and the first-order autocorrelation of price change becomes strongly negative. When using low frequency data such as daily or monthly prices, the deviation is relatively small and negligible. However, it becomes increasingly significant when examining high frequency data. We call the diffusion process in equation (1) a signal process and ε_t the observation noise. Many factors contribute to the observation noise. In the currency market, for example, nonbinding quoting errors are part of the noise. In other markets, bid and offer differences contribute to the observation noise. Other micro-structural behaviors are also included in this observation noise. For low frequency observations, the observation noise is overwhelmed by the signal change. For high frequency observations, the signal change becomes smaller and smaller while the size of the noise remains the same. Therefore the noise eventually dominates the price change in ultra-high frequency data. Viewing high frequency data as observations with noise can capture the various basic characteristics of high frequency financial time series as mentioned above.

This chapter is organized as follows. In section 2, we present the concept of f-consistency and construct an f-consistent estimator of volatility. In section 3, we present the de-volatilization and the normalization procedures. In section 4, we discuss applications of these two procedures in the foreign exchange market. Section 5 includes a discussion and conclusion.

2 VOLATILITY ESTIMATION AND F-CONSISTENCY

Empirical financial analysis has gone through stages of analyzing decades of quarterly data, and years of daily data to today, where we use days of tick-by-tick data to explore market inefficiency. As the observation frequency increases while the observation timespan remains constant or even decreases, we face a new statistical challenge, the consistency of parameter estimation. To illustrate the problem, let us take a simple example. Suppose we need to estimate the diffusion parameters of a simple diffusion process $dB(t) = \mu\,dt + \sigma\,dW(t)$, where $W(t)$ is a standard Wiener process. If the timespan is constant, does high frequency observation improve the estimation of the diffusion parameters? It may surprise some people that increasing observation frequency with a fixed length observation interval does not always improve parameter estimation. In the case of estimating the mean parameter when the variance parameter σ is given, increasing observation frequency does not reduce the mean square error of the estimator. The minimum sufficient statistic for the mean parameter is the increment of the process over the observation interval. This change remains constant as observation frequency increases. Therefore increasing observation frequency does not provide any extra information for estimating the mean parameter. However, when we estimate the variance parameter σ^2, increasing observation frequency does improve the estimation. The quadratic variation estimator is a consistent estimator in this case. This example presents a new type of statistical consistency, the f-consistency, which is defined as the consistency of an estimation as the observation frequency increases to infinity while the observation timespan is held constant.

In this section, we concentrate only on the issue of f-consistency of the volatility estimation. Without losing generality, we assume that the timespan considered here is [0, 1], which can be one hour, one day or one month. The volatility is defined by the variance of the price change

$$\sigma^2 = \int_0^1 \sigma^2(t)\,dt = \text{Var}(P(1) - P(0)) \tag{3}$$

To simplify the discussion, we also assume that

$$S(t) = \mu(t) + W(\tau(t)) + \varepsilon_t \quad t \in [0, 1] \tag{4}$$

where $W(\tau)$ is a standard Wiener process and ε_t are independent Gaussian random variables with mean zero and variance η_t^2. Taking $n + 1$ observations within a time interval [0, 1] and denoting their logarithm transformations as $\{S_{0,n}, S_{1,n}, \ldots, S_{n,n}\}$ and returns as $\{X_{1,n}, X_{2,n}, \ldots, X_{n,n}\}$, we have

$$X_{i,n} = S_{i,n} - S_{i-1,n} = \mu_i + \sigma_i Z_i + \varepsilon_i - \varepsilon_{i-1} \tag{5}$$

where Z_i are standard Gaussian random variables. The joint distribution of $\{X_{1,n}, \ldots, X_{n,n}\}$ is a multivariate normal distribution with mean $\mu_1, \ldots, \mu_n$ and

$$\Sigma_n = \text{diag}(\sigma_1^2, \ldots, \sigma_n^2) + E_n \tag{6}$$

where

$$E_n = \begin{pmatrix} \eta_1^2 + \eta_0^2 & -\eta_1^2 & 0 & \cdots & 0 \\ -\eta_1^2 & \eta_2^2 + \eta_1^2 & -\eta_1^2 & \cdots & 0 \\ \vdots & \vdots & \vdots & \vdots & \vdots \\ 0 & 0 & 0 & \cdots & \eta_n^2 + \eta_{n-1}^2 \end{pmatrix} \tag{7}$$

Define a quadratic estimator of equation (3) as an estimator that has the form of

$$\hat{\sigma}_Q^2 = X^T Q X \tag{8}$$

where $X = (X_{1,n}, \ldots, X_{n,n})^T$ and Q is any $n \times n$ matrix. If $\mu_t = 0$, $\hat{\sigma}_Q^2$ has mean and variance:

$$E\hat{\sigma}_Q^2 = \text{tr}(Q\Sigma_n) \tag{9}$$

$$\text{Var}(\hat{\sigma}_Q^2) = 2\,\text{tr}(Q\Sigma_n Q\Sigma_n) \tag{10}$$

To obtain an f-consistent estimator, we further assume that $\sigma_i^2 = \sigma^2/n$ and $\eta_i^2 = \eta^2$. Under these assumptions, we can construct an f-consistent estimator as follows. Let

$$Q = V_n \, \text{diag}(\tilde{q}_{ii}) V_n \qquad (11)$$

where V_n is an $n \times n$ matrix with its (i, j)-element defined as

$$V_{ij} = \sqrt{\frac{2}{n+1}} \sin\left(\frac{ij\pi}{n+1}\right)$$

and the element of diagonal matrix

$$\tilde{q}_{ii} = \frac{\alpha + \beta \lambda_i}{2(1/n + \lambda_i r)^2} \qquad (12)$$

where

$$\lambda_i = 4 \sin^2\left(\frac{i}{2(n+1)}\right)$$

and α and β satisfy

$$2n = \alpha \sum \frac{1}{(1/n + \lambda_i r)^2} + \beta \sum \frac{\lambda_i}{(1/n + \lambda_i r)^2} \qquad (13)$$

$$0 = \alpha \sum \frac{\lambda_i}{(1/n + \lambda_i r)^2} + \beta \sum \frac{\lambda_i^2}{(1/n + \lambda_i r)^2} \qquad (14)$$

Theorem 1 *For a given parameter* r, *the quadratic estimator defined in equations (11)–(14) is an unbiased of equation (3) with the asymptotic convergence rate*

$$\text{Var}(\hat{\sigma}_Q^2) = \left(8\sqrt{r} + 4\frac{\gamma - r}{\sqrt{r}} + \frac{(\gamma - r)^2}{\sqrt{r^3}}\right) \frac{\sigma^4}{\sqrt{n}} + o\left(\frac{1}{\sqrt{n}}\right) \qquad (15)$$

where $\gamma = \eta^2/\sigma^2$, *the reciprocal of the signal-to-noise ratio and* $o(\cdot)$ *is a higher-order term as* n *goes to infinity.*

The proof is given in the Appendix.

Let $Y = V_n X$, the above quadratic estimator can be written as

$$\hat{\sigma}_Q^2 = \sum_i \tilde{q}_{ii} Y_i^2 \qquad (16)$$

where $\tilde{q}_{ii}$ is defined in equation (12).

From Theorem 1, for any given r, the quadratic estimator $\hat{\sigma}_Q^2$, with Q defined in equations (11)–(14) is f-consistent. The preferred value of r is γ, although it is unknown. r should be close to γ, but not too small.

In applications to financial markets, both assumptions of constant variance and Gaussian noise are not valid. The variance of the price changes over time, especially among high frequency observations. The noise is rarely Gaussian.

However, it is very difficult to find a closed form f-consistent estimator without the assumption of constant variances. In the remaining section, we empirically examine the sensitivity of the quadratic estimator to the assumptions of constant variance and Gaussian noise. We simulated six different types of time series and estimated the variance parameter using the quadratic estimator:

- Series I: $\sigma_{i,n}^2 = \sigma^2/n$ and the noises ε_i are i.i.d. $\eta t(5)$, a t random variable with a scale factor.
- Series II: $\sigma_{i,n}^2 = \sigma^2/n$ and the noises ε_i are i.i.d. ηBernoulli(p) with $p = 0.5$.
- Series III: $\sigma_{i,n}^2$ is sampled from a uniform distribution $U(0, 1)$ and then is rescaled to $\Sigma\sigma_{i,n}^2 = \sigma^2$, the noises ε_i are i.i.d. $\eta t(5)$.
- Series IV: $\sigma_{i,n}^2$ is sampled from lognormal distribution $LN(0, 1)$ and then rescaled to $\Sigma\sigma_{i,n}^2 = \sigma^2$, the noises ε_i are i.i.d. $\eta t(5)$.
- Series V: $\sigma_{i,n}^2$ is sampled from Bernoulli(p) with $p = 0, 1$ and then rescaled to $\Sigma\sigma_{i,n}^2 = \sigma^2$ and the noises ε_i are i.i.d. ηBernoulli(p) with $p = 0.5$.
- Series VI: $\sigma_{i,n}^2 = \sigma^2/n$ and the noises ε_i are MA(1) with moving average (MA) coefficient 0.5 and noises $\eta t(5)$.

In the simulation, the following values are used for various parameters: $\sigma^2 = 1$, $\eta^2 = 0.01$ and $n = 100, 500$ and 1000. The empirical results are listed in Table 6.1.

The first two series have non-Gaussian noise. The noise has a t and a Bernoulli distribution. The following three series have unequal variances over time. When n is small, the estimator slightly underestimates the variance. The bias disappears as the observation frequency increases. More variation in $\sigma_{i,n}^2$ causes more bias in the estimator. Series VI has correlated observation noise. The quadratic estimator again provides a close estimate of the parameter. There

Table 6.1 Sensitivity of σ_Q^2 to various assumptions

	n	100		500		1000	
	$\hat{\theta}$	$E\hat{\theta}$	var($\hat{\theta}$)	$E\hat{\theta}$	var($\hat{\theta}$)	$E\hat{\theta}$	var($\hat{\theta}$)
Series I	$\hat{\sigma}_Q^2$	0.985	0.1862	0.987	0.0797	1.003	0.0573
Series II	$\hat{\sigma}_Q^2$	0.961	0.2528	0.997	0.0938	1.047	0.0519
Series III	$\hat{\sigma}_Q^2$	0.944	0.1288	1.0239	0.104	0.976	0.0535
Series IV	$\hat{\sigma}_Q^2$	0.939	0.1621	0.981	0.0820	0.993	0.061
Series V	$\hat{\sigma}_Q^2$	0.892	0.2614	0.969	0.0757	0.991	0.0692
Series VI	$\hat{\sigma}_Q^2$	1.052	0.2176	1.105	0.0911	1.157	0.0591

Note: This table lists empirical means and variances of the quadratic estimator for six different types of time series. All series use $\sigma^2 = 1$, $\eta^2 = 0.01$. $r = 0.1$ is used in equations (12)–(14) for σ_Q^2. The variance of the estimator has the convergence rate $1/\sqrt{n}$.

is a possible bias. However, the bias seems not significant. The variance of $\hat{\sigma}_Q^2$ for all examples converges at the rate of $1/\sqrt{n}$. Therefore, the quadratic estimator is not sensitive to weak serial correlation among noises. The simulation indicates that the above quadratic estimator can retain the asymptotic convergence rate even if the assumptions used to construct the estimator are slightly violated. Some empirical findings here have been proved theoretically (Zhou 1995).

3 DE-VOLATILIZATION AND NORMALIZATION

One of the most significant characteristics of a financial time series is heteroscedasticity, which tends to become more severe as sampling frequency increases. Some nonlinear structures of financial time series, such as ARCH structures, are entirely due to heteroscedasticity, which poses a great difficulty in modeling financial markets. The availability of high frequency data gives us new tools to deal with the problem. One way to minimize the heteroscedasticity is to analyze observation at unequally spaced time periods. By taking more observations in a volatile market and less observations in a steady market, we can reduce or eliminate heteroscedasticity. This procedure of obtaining time series with constant volatility apart is called *de-volatilization*. The time series obtained by the procedure is called *dv-series* and the return of a dv-series is called *dv-returns*.

To carry out a de-volatilization procedure, we need to estimate the volatility process to determine when data should be taken. When computation time is not a concern, the f-consistent estimator presented in the last section can be used to estimate incremental volatility. However, when a de-volatilization procedure is implemented in real time, we need a volatility estimator that can be calculated recursively when new data arrive. Zhou (1996b) has proposed another volatility estimator for this purpose:

$$\text{Var}(P(b) - P(a)) = \frac{1}{k} \sum_{t_i \in [a,b]} [X^2(t_{i-k}, t_i) + 2X(t_{i-k}, t_i)X(t_{i-2k}, t_{i-k})] \qquad (17)$$

where $X(s, t) = S(t) - S(s)$, and k is a constant. This is also a quadratic estimator. However, it is not f-consistent. The mean square error of the estimator diverges as the observation increases to infinity. We may produce an opposite effect when tick-by-tick price is used in the volatility estimation. The parameter k in equation (17) can be adjusted for the optimal standard error.

Given a volatility estimator, the de-volatilization procedure can be carried out in the following steps:

Algorithm 1 (De-volatilization)

Suppose that $\{S(t_i)\}$ is a series of observations from process (1). This algorithm takes a subsequence from the series $\{S(t_i)\}$ and forms a dv-series, denoted as

r_τ. The return of the dv-series has near constant volatility and dv-returns have a Gaussian distribution.

1. Let the initial value $r_0 = S(t_0)$;
2. Assume that the most recent element of the dv-series is obtained at time t_m, i.e. $r_\tau = S(t_m)$;
3. Estimate the volatility increment $\mathrm{Var}(P(t_{m+i}) - P(t_m))$ by $S(t_m), \ldots, S(t_{m+i})$ for $i = 1, \ldots$, until the increment $\mathrm{Var}(P(t_{m+i}) - P(t_m))$ exceeds the threshold v, a predetermined constant. Let

$$k = \min\{i; \mathrm{Var}(P(t_{m+i}) - P(t_m)) \geq v \quad \text{and} \quad |S(t_{m+i}) - S(t_{m+i-1})| < \sqrt{v}\} \tag{18}$$

   $r_{r+1} = S(t_{m+k})$ is taken as the next element of the dv-series.
4. Repeat step 3 until the end of series $\{S(t_i)\}$.

Since high frequency financial data are characterized by excessive noise, the condition (18) is necessary to reduce the sensitivity of the procedure to noise. Instead of picking data whenever the price jumps, waiting for one or two ticks to get prices confirmed can avoid taking noise into the dv-series. Other steps can also be adopted to reduce the sensitivity to noise. After selecting a volatility estimator, one can easily implement the de-volatilization. The de-volatilization threshold v can be arbitrarily chosen to meet the different needs of a variety of analyses. However, it should be large enough so that there is a reasonable amount of data for each volatility estimation. The signal-to-noise ratio $v/\mathrm{Var}(\varepsilon_{t_i})$ should also be large enough so that the noise ε_t in the dv-series is no longer significant. We discuss an example of de-volatilizing exchange rates in the next section.

The de-volatilization procedure can reduce or eliminate the heteroscedasticity of a financial time series. Under the specification of (1) and (2), the dv-series also has Gaussian returns. Some nonlinear price structure due to the heteroscedasticity can now be analyzed using a linear model. However, some situations require equally spaced observations. In these cases, an alternative to de-volatilization is normalization. To normalize an equally spaced time series, we need to estimate the volatility of any two consecutive prices and then rescale the return by its standard deviation. For example, when daily prices are required in an empirical analysis, we can use high frequency data in every 24-hour period to estimate daily volatility. We then normalize daily returns by the square root of the estimated volatility. Since normalization does not require to estimate volatility every tick, computational time is less a concern. We can use the f-consistent quadratic estimator presented in the previous section. The estimator is not only f-consistent, but also less sensitive to various assumptions used in constructing the estimator. The parameter r can be estimated in various ways and is not essential as long as it is not too small. The normalization procedure can also eliminate the heteroscedasticity and can simplify the empirical analysis. However, there is an essential difference between de-volatilization and normalization, which we will discuss later.

4 APPLICATIONS IN THE FOREIGN EXCHANGE MARKET

In this section, we discuss applications of de-volatilization and normalization. We first apply de-volatilization and then normalization to foreign exchange rate. The data set used in this section are the tick-by-tick exchange rate of the Deutschmark versus the US dollar (DEM/USD) of 1995 provided by Chemical Bank. The data set has more than 2.1 million observations. The variance of the year is estimated at 0.015 using daily sample variance, and the average noise level $\mathrm{Var}(\varepsilon) \approx 2.7e-8$.

To implement the de-volatilization procedure, we choose $v = 3e-6$ as the de-volatilization threshold. This gives an average of 500 observations to estimate the volatility between two dv-series data points. The volatility estimator used in the de-volatilization is given by formula (17) with $k = 7$. The basic statistics of the returns of the dv-series are listed in Table 6.2. The statistics of the equally spaced time series for every 90 minutes are also listed in the same table for comparison. The 90-minute time series has approximately the same number of data points as

Table 6.2 Descriptive statistics of dv-returns and 90-minute returns

	N	Mean	Median	Variance	Skewness	Kurtosis
dv-series	4320	$-1.3e-5$	0.0	$3.84e-6$	0.01	0.15
90-minute	4157	$-1.8e-5$	0.0	$4.11e-6$	0.53	20.41

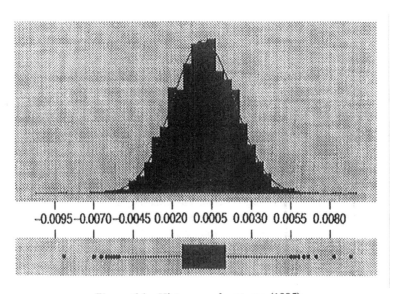

Figure 6.1 Histogram: dv-returns (1995)

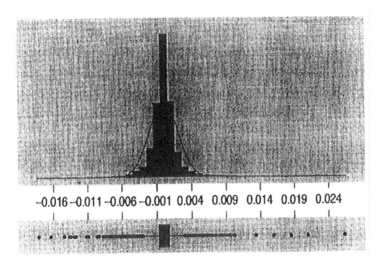

Figure 6.2 Histogram: 90-minute returns (1995)

the dv-series. The variance of dv-return is always above the threshold v because we wait until the increment of the volatility crosses above the threshold before incorporating a price into the dv-series. The histograms of both dv-series and 90-minute time series are plotted in Figures 6.1 and 6.2.

In the above example, de-volatilization achieved both homoscedasticity and Gaussian returns. The Anderson–Darling normality test yields $p = 0.057$ for the dv-returns. De-volatilization also reduced the ARCH effect. There is only a little autocorrelation in squared dv-returns or absolute dv-returns. The Box–Pierce Q statistic of both dv-returns and 90-minute returns is listed in Table 6.3. The de-volatilization also helps to detect nonrandom walk periods in foreign exchange market (Zhou 1996a).

To eliminate heteroscedasticity in equally spaced time series, we can normalize the returns by their volatility. Suppose we need to analyze daily prices. To carry out the normalization, we first estimate daily volatility from tick-by-tick data. Each daily volatility is estimated from data within a 24-hour period. The volatility estimator used here is the f-consistent quadratic estimator defined in equations (11)–(14). With annual volatility estimated at 0.015 and noise level $\text{Var}(\varepsilon) \approx 2.7e - 8$, the daily signal-to-noise ratio is about $2.1e + 4$ or $\gamma = 5e - 5$.

Table 6.3 The Box–Pierce Q statistics of dv-returns and 90-minute returns

Q_{10}	X_i	(p)	X_i^2	(p)	$|X_i|$	(p)
dv-series	14.31	(0.16)	21.95	(0.02)	20.32	(0.03)
90-minute	29.30	(0.00)	66.04	(0.00)	377.22	(0.00)

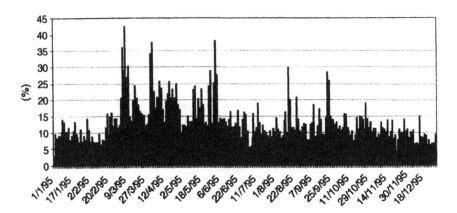

Figure 6.3 Daily volatility estimates of USD/DEM (1995)

Table 6.4 Descriptive statistics of daily and normalized daily returns

	N	Mean	Median	Variance	Skewness	Kurtosis
Daily prices	248	$-3.0e - 4$	0.0	$6.7e - 5$	0.03	2.39
Normalized	248	$-3.8e - 2$	0.0	0.99	0.10	-0.54

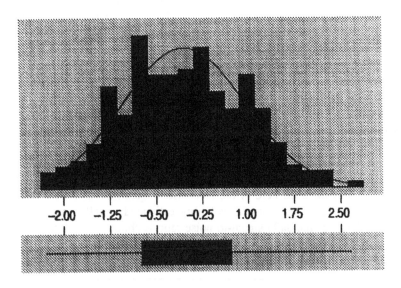

Figure 6.4 Histogram: normalized daily returns (1995)

Since daily volatility has large fluctuations, we choose $r \approx 0.0005$ to ensure r will not be too small. The annualized daily volatility is plotted in Figure 6.3. The descriptive statistics of normalized returns and daily returns are listed in Table 6.4. The histograms of normalized return and daily return are plotted in Figures 6.4 and 6.5. The p-value of the Anderson–Darling normality test is 0.21. We cannot reject the hypothesis that normalized returns follow a normal distribution.

The normalization also reduces the complexity of the time series structure and increases the chance of detecting linear patterns. In the above example, normalized returns show a marginal significant autocorrelation in the first lag. The first lag autocorrelation is -0.16 with a t-ratio of 2.47. The autocorrelation functions for both daily returns and normalized returns are plotted in Figures 6.6 and 6.7.

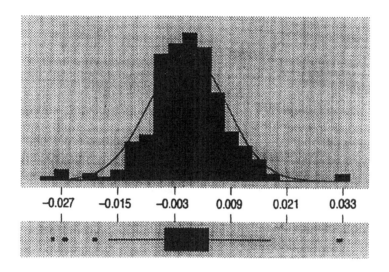

Figure 6.5 Histogram: daily returns (1995)

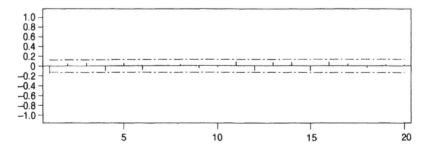

Figure 6.6 Autocorrelation function of normalized daily returns

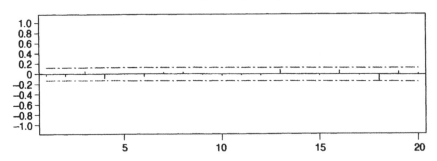

Figure 6.7 Autocorrelation function of daily returns

5 DISCUSSION AND CONCLUSION

One misperception about using high frequency data is that the more data there are, the better. Increasing observation frequency while keeping the timespan constant does not always help parameter estimation. An estimator developed for low frequency data is often not usable for high frequency data. The observation noise, which does not decrease as the observation frequency increases, is the key obstacle. The term 'observation noise' used here is different from its normal use in the financial literature. It is widely recognized that currency spot quotes have noise. However, a stock transaction price recorded precisely can also contain a noise component as defined in this article. The noise is simply the deviation of the price from an assumed underlying continuous process. This observation noise can include micro-activities of the market that do not interest us in a given application.

The de-volatilization and normalization procedures utilize high frequency data and reduce the heteroscedasticity. They also transform returns to Gaussian random variables. Since many financial models assume homoscedasticity and Gaussian returns, de-volatilization and normalization increase the power of many existing models. However, there is a major difference between the two procedures. On one hand, de-volatilization lengthens volatile periods and analyzes more data in those periods. Equivalently, analyzing de-volatilized time series places more weight on data during volatile periods. On the other hand, the normalization procedure 'equalizes' returns from volatile time periods with returns from more stable time periods. The procedure does not reflect the particular importance of data from different market conditions. Therefore de-volatilization and normalization are not equivalent and should be chosen accordingly.

As we have seen in this chapter, both de-volatilization and normalization help in reducing the impact of noise in high frequency data analysis. They also go a long way towards reducing heteroscedasticity.

APPENDIX

Proof of Theorem 1: Under the assumptions of equal volatility $\sigma_i^2 = \sigma^2/n$ and Gaussian noise with variance $\eta_i^2 = \eta^2$, the variance matrix of X is

$$\Sigma_n = \frac{\sigma^2}{n}I_n + \eta^2 A_n \tag{19}$$

where I_n is an identity matrix and

$$A_n = \begin{pmatrix} 2 & -1 & 0 & \cdots & 0 & 0 \\ -1 & 2 & -1 & \cdots & 0 & 0 \\ 0 & -1 & 2 & \cdots & 0 & 0 \\ \vdots & \vdots & \vdots & \vdots & \vdots & \vdots \\ 0 & 0 & 0 & \cdots & 2 & -1 \\ 0 & 0 & 0 & \cdots & -1 & 2 \end{pmatrix} \tag{20}$$

The eigenvalues and eigenvectors of this matrix are known (Gregory and Karney 1969)

$$\lambda_i = 4\sin^2\left(\frac{i}{2(n+1)}\right) \tag{21}$$

and

$$v_i = (2/(n+1))^{1/2}\begin{pmatrix} \sin(i\pi/(n+1)) \\ \sin(2i\pi/(n+1)) \\ \vdots \\ \sin(ni\pi/(n+1)) \end{pmatrix} \tag{22}$$

Let $V_n = (V_i \ldots V_n)$

$$\Sigma_n = \frac{\sigma^2}{n}I_n + \eta^2 A_n = V_n \operatorname{diag}\left(\frac{\sigma^2}{n} + \lambda_i\eta^2\right)V_n$$

where V_n and λ_i are defined in equations (21) and (22). V_n is symmetric, therefore $V_n^T = V_n$. Let

$$\tilde{Q}_n = V_n Q_n V_n \tag{23}$$

then

$$E\hat{\sigma}_Q^2 = \sum_i \tilde{q}_{ii}\left(\frac{\sigma^2}{n} + \lambda_i\eta^2\right) \tag{24}$$

$$\operatorname{Var}(\hat{\sigma}_Q^2) = 2\sum_{ij} \tilde{q}_{ij}^2\left(\frac{\sigma^2}{n} + \lambda_i\eta^2\right)^2 = 2\sigma^4\sum_{ij} \tilde{q}_{ij}^2\left(\frac{1}{n} + \lambda_i\gamma\right)^2 \tag{25}$$

where $\gamma = \eta^2/\sigma^2$, the signal-to-noise ratio. Obviously, $\hat{\sigma}_Q^2$ is unbiased if and only if

$$\sum_i \tilde{q}_{ii} = n \quad \text{and} \quad \sum_i \tilde{q}_{ii}\lambda_i = 0 \tag{26}$$

It can be proved that

$$\sum \frac{1}{(1/n + \lambda_i r)^2} = \frac{n^{5/2}}{4\sqrt{r}} + o(n^{5/2})$$

$$\sum \frac{\lambda_i}{(1/n + \lambda_i r)^2} = \frac{n^{3/2}}{4r^{3/2}} + o(n^{3/2})$$

$$\sum \frac{\lambda_i^2}{(1/n + \lambda_i r)^2} = \frac{n}{r^2} + o(n)$$

where little $o(n^\gamma)$ is defined as $o(n^\gamma)/n^\gamma \to 0$ as $n \to \infty$. Therefore

$$\alpha = (2n)\left(\frac{n}{r^2} + o(n)\right) \Big/ \left(\frac{n^{5/2}}{4\sqrt{r}}\frac{n}{r^2} + o(n^{7/2})\right) = \frac{8\sqrt{r}}{n^{3/2}} + o(n^{-3/2})$$

$$\beta = (2n)\left(-\frac{n^{3/2}}{4r^{3/2}} + o(n^{3/2})\right) \Big/ \left(\frac{n^{5/2}}{4\sqrt{r}}\frac{n}{r^2} + o(n^{7/2})\right) = -\frac{2r}{n} + o\left(\frac{1}{n}\right)$$

Rewrite the variance

$$\mathrm{Var}(\hat{\sigma}_Q^2) = \sigma^4 \sum_i \tilde{q}_{ii}^2 \left(\frac{1}{n} + \lambda_i \gamma\right)^2 = \sigma^4 \sum_i \tilde{q}_{ii}^2$$

$$\times \left[\left(\frac{1}{n} + \lambda_i r\right)^2 + 2(\gamma - r)\left(\frac{1}{n} + \lambda_i r\right) + (\gamma - r)^2 \left(\frac{1}{n} + \lambda_i r\right)^2\right]$$

It is easy to check that the first term

$$\sum_i \tilde{q}_{ii}^2 \left(\frac{1}{n} + \lambda_i r\right)^2 = \frac{\alpha^2}{4} \sum_i \left(\frac{1}{n} + \lambda_i r\right)^{-2} + o\left(\frac{1}{n}\right)$$

$$= \frac{1}{4}\left(\frac{8\sqrt{r}}{n^{3/2}}\right)^2 \frac{n^{5/2}}{4\sqrt{r}} + o\left(\frac{1}{\sqrt{n}}\right)$$

$$= \frac{4\sqrt{r}}{\sqrt{n}} + o\left(\frac{1}{\sqrt{n}}\right).$$

The other two terms can be argued similarly. It is a long and tedious calculus manipulation. Numerically, one can easily verify the following equations:

$$\sum_i \tilde{q}_{ii}^2 \left(\frac{1}{n} + \lambda_i r\right)\lambda_i = \frac{1}{\sqrt{rn}} + o\left(\frac{1}{\sqrt{n}}\right)$$

$$\sum_i \tilde{q}_{ii}^2 \lambda_i^2 = \frac{1}{2\sqrt{r^3}\sqrt{n}} + o\left(\frac{1}{\sqrt{n}}\right)$$

Therefore

$$\text{Var}(\hat{\sigma}_Q^2) = 2\sigma^4 \sum_{ij} \tilde{q}_{ij}^2 \left(\frac{1}{n} + \lambda_i \gamma \right)^2$$

$$= \left(8\sqrt{r} + 4\frac{\gamma - r}{\sqrt{r}} + \frac{(\gamma - r)^2}{\sqrt{r^3}} \right) \frac{\sigma^4}{\sqrt{n}} + o\left(\frac{1}{\sqrt{n}} \right)$$

A more detailed proof can be found in Zhou (1995).

REFERENCES

Goodhart, C.A.E. and Figliuoli, L. (1991), 'Every Minute Counts in Financial Markets', *Journal of International Money and Finance*, **10**, 23–52; *Econometrica*, **46**, 1293–1302.

Gregory, R.T. and Karney, D.L. (1969), *A Collection of Matrices for Testing Computational Algorithms*, Wiley, New York.

Zhou, Bin (1995), 'Estimating the Variance Parameter from Noisy High Frequency Financial Data', MIT Sloan School Working Paper 3739.

Zhou, Bin (1996a), 'Forecasting Foreign Exchange Rates Subject to De-volatilization', in C. Dunis (ed.) *Forecasting Financial Markets*, Wiley, Chichester, pp. 51–68.

Zhou, Bin (1996b), 'High Frequency Data and Volatility in Foreign Exchange Rates', *Journal of Business and Economics Statistics*, **14**, 45–52.

PART III
Parametric Models for Nonlinear Financial Time Series

———— 7 ————

High Frequency Financial Time Series Data: Some Stylized Facts and Models of Stochastic Volatility

ERIC GHYSELS, CHRISTIAN GOURIÉROUX
and JOANNA JASIAK

1 INTRODUCTION

Computer technology has not only changed the structure of trading, it has also made the collection, storage and retrieval of financial market data more widespread at levels of detail never seen before. Until only a few years ago most empirical studies involved daily, weekly or monthly time series. As high frequency data, henceforth denoted HF data, become more easily available it is now possible to study how financial markets evolve in real time. While data sets a researcher in microstructures would dream of involving identity, motives and portfolio positions of those transacting, are not available yet, it is clear that continuous record observations which are now easy to obtain already contain a vast amount of information. There are at least two key challenges one faces in modelling these newly available data sets. First, unlike daily, weekly or monthly series, quote or tick-based data are by their very nature irregularly spaced. The great majority of empirical asset pricing models or models of market volatility such as ARCH-type models are constructed on the basis of equally spaced data points such as daily observations. This simplification no longer suits HF data and therefore needs to be modified. It is particularly important to note that the spacing

Nonlinear Modelling of High Frequency Financial Time Series.
Edited by Christian Dunis and Bin Zhou. © 1998 John Wiley Sons Ltd

of time between quotes is not a purely technical issue. Indeed, the recent vintage of microstructure models use the length of time elapsed between consecutive transactions as a signal revealing information known to market participants (see Easly and O'Hara 1992). A second challenge one faces with the analysis of markets in real time is the sheer number of data points. A typical data set of daily observations spanning a number of years contains a couple of thousand observations. In contrast, there are an average of roughly between four to five thousand new quotes on a single market like the USD/DEM spot exchange recorded by the Reuters FXFX screen page every working day. Hence, data sets run into millions of records and are easier to measure in terms of the disc space they occupy rather than the number of observations. With such large data sets there is obviously also a great need to identify and summarize empirical regularities in trading patterns and returns.

This chapter deals with HF data and stochastic volatility, henceforth denoted SV. We do not try to be exhaustive, either on the subject of HF data or on that of SV models. Two recent surveys, one on HF data and models by Goodhart and O'Hara (1995) and the other dealing with SV by Ghysels, Harvey and Renault (1996), provide a detailed coverage of the literature. The purpose of this chapter is to be complementary to those surveys as it tries to isolate several specific issues which emerge in the econometric modelling of HF data via SV.

In section 2 we examine three different examples of HF data sets. These examples serve two purposes: (i) uncovering some stylized facts and (ii) illustrating the modelling issues one faces with HF data. The second point is also the subject of section 3 which provides a brief review of some models. Section 4 provides the details of a specific example worked out in detail involving the estimation of SV models for HF data. Section 5 reports empirical results.

2 HIGH FREQUENCY DATA: SOME EXAMPLES AND THEIR EMPIRICAL PROPERTIES

In this section we discuss three specific examples which are used for illustrative purposes. The first example is taken from the interbank FX market, the second involves trades from the Bourse de Paris of Alcatel shares, a French telecommunications company which figures among the most actively traded stocks on the exchange, and last but not least tick-by-tick data for shares in IBM recorded on the NYSE and options on IBM's stocks traded on the Philadelphia Stock Exchange.[1] The three columns of Table 7.1 provide a snapshot of each of the three data sets. The first column covers data of the interbank FX market for foreign exchange bid/ask price quotes from various firms and banks which are recorded 24 hours a day and displayed worldwide. These data have a GMT time stamp, a bid and ask price and an identity of the quoting source. The next column shows similar features for Alcatel except that we now have trade data instead of quotations giving a price and the volume of transactions. Another difference is the fact that the Paris Bourse is not a 24-hour market, hence some of the data displayed in the column have a 10 a.m. time stamp corresponding to the opening price, which reflect overnight orders, while the data after 10 a.m. represent regular trading hour transactions. We do notice that several orders can arrive simultaneously with the same time identification (for a more detailed analysis of the Alcatel stock and the Paris market structure, see Gouriéroux, Jasiak and Le Fol 1996). The third and final data set with IBM displays properties similar to Alcatel. It has the additional feature that it not only shows trades in the primitive asset but also trades in the derivative securities written on the stock. These reflect information regarding the stock which do not appear as trades in IBM but option contracts written on IBM stocks.

The snapshots of data appearing in Table 7.1 provide an illustration of several issues encountered in HF data; they are:

Table 7.1 Snapshots of three HF data sets: (1) FX interbank quotations, (2) trades in Alcatel and (3) trades in IBM and its stock options

Time (GMT)	(1) The FX interbank quotations		Country	City	Bank	(2)Alcatel			(3)IBM		
	Bid	Ask				Time	Price	Quantity	Code	Price	Time
00:00:14	1.4116	1.4121	392	01	0058	10:00:00	458.1	500	IBM	54.875	9:36:30
00:00:54	1.4108	1.4118	036	02	0130	10:00:00	458.1	2000	IBM	54.875	9:36:30
00:01:00	1.4110	1.4120	392	01	0452	10:00:00	458.1	1000	IBM	54.875	9:36:30
00:01:18	1.4115	1.4120	392	01	0041	10:00:00	458.1	30	IBMGJ	7.000	9:36:30
00:01:24	1.4107	1.4117	036	02	0130	10:01:37	458.1	440	IBM	54.875	9:36:30
00:01:30	1.4115	1.4125	036	02	0089	10:01:37	458.1	440	IBM	54.750	9:36:30
00:01:36	1.4113	1.4123	392	01	0041	10:03:11	458	10	IBM	54.875	9:36:30
00:01:42	1.4110	1.4120	392	01	0053	10:03:11	458	20	IBM	54.875	9:37:02
00:01:54	1.4118	1.4128	344	01	0041	10:03:11	458	10	IBMSJ	2.063	9:37:02
00:02:06	1.4113	1.4123	702	01	0055	10:05:16	457.1	150	IBM	54.750	9:37:02
00:02:18	1.4115	1.4130	036	01	0126	10:05:23	457.1	10	IBM	54.875	9:37:02
00:02:24	1.4105	1.4115	344	02	0130	10:05:48	458	2000	IBM	54.875	9:37:02
00:02:30	1.4115	1.4125	392	01	0089	10:08:02	457.1	50	IBM	54.875	9:37:02
00:02:48	1.4115	1.4125	036	01	0041	10:09:29	457.8	40	IBM	54.875	9:37:02
00:02:54	1.4116	1.4121	702	03	0070	10:09:35	457.8	360	IBM	54.875	9:37:02
00:03:06	1.4110	1.4120	036	01	0119	10:10:45	457.8	400	IBM	54.750	9:37:02
00:03:20	1.4105	1.4115	392	02	0130	10:11:45	458	260	IBM	54.875	9:37:02
00:03:26	1.4115	1.4125	036	01	0041	10:11:59	457.8	240	IBM	54.750	9:37:02
00:03:52	1.4108	1.4118	036	02	0130	10:12:17	457.5	3000	IBMGL	2.313	9:37:02
00:03:58	1.4114	1.4121	344	02	0032	10:12:51	458	40	IBMGL	2.313	9:37:02
00:04:04	1.4113	1.4118	392	01	0003	10:12:51	458	10	IBM	54.875	9:37:30
00:04:10	1.4114	1.4121	036	01	0041	10:12:58	458	960	IBM	54.875	9:37:30
00:04:28	1.4102	1.4112	391	02	0130	10:12:58	458	1040	IBM	54.875	9:37:30
00:04:34	1.4112	1.4117	344	01	0058	10:14:18	458	950	IBM	54.875	9:37:30
00:04:46	1.4105	1.4115	344	01	0089	10:14:18	458	1050	IBM	54.875	9:37:30
00:05:00	1.4113	1.4123	036	01	0000	10:14:34	457.1	90	IBM	54.875	9:37:30
00:05:14	1.4103	1.4113	344	02	0130	10:15:06	458	10	IBM	54.875	9:37:30
00:05:26	1.4110	1.4120	702	01	0089	10:15:30	458	10	IBMJK	54.875	9:37:30
00:05:40	1.4110	1.4125	036	01	0126	10:15:44	457.1	20	IBMJJ	5.625	9:37:30
00:05:48	1.4105	1.4115	392	02	0130	10:16:05	458	10	IBM	8.375	9:37:30

1. Unequal time spacing of data.
2. Multiple simultaneous prices such as bids and asks.
3. Multiple simultaneous trades or quotes.
4. Multiple assets, primitive and derivative, traded simultaneously.
5. Overnight market closures.

It is coping with each of these issues which makes modelling of HF data challenging. Let us start with points (1) and (2), for instance, using the data displayed in the first column. For the purpose of calculations we consider the entire data set which covers price quotes from 1 October 1992 until 30 September 1993 for three exchange rates: the US dollar/Deutschmark (USD/DEM), the Japanese yen/US dollar (USD/JPY) and the Deutschmark/yen (DEM/JPY) rate. The number of observations in the three samples are, respectively, 1 472 266, 570 839 and 159 004. Although the ask and bid sequences are reported simultaneously, a vast majority of researchers study a single price series constructed as a geometric average of asks and bids. Following the notation adopted by Dacorogna *et al.* (1993), the returns on the foreign exchange market are thus defined as

$$\Delta x(t) = x(t) - x(t-1)$$
$$= \tfrac{1}{2}[(\log \text{ask}(t) + \log \text{bid}(t)) - (\log \text{ask}(t-1)$$
$$+ \log \text{bid}(t-1))]$$

or

$$\Delta x(t) = \tfrac{1}{2}[(\log \text{ask}(t) - \log \text{ask}(t-1)) + (\log \text{bid}(t)$$
$$- \log \text{bid}(t-1))]$$
$$\Delta x(t) = \tfrac{1}{2}[\Delta \log \text{ask}(t) + \Delta \log \text{bid}(t)]$$

Usually, it is assumed that the dynamics of the $x(t)$ series reflect the general pattern of market activity. One could argue, however, that the logarithmic middle price averages outcomes of distinct trading strategies of buyers and sellers. Indeed, the real time data reveal several differences between asks and bids. Table 7.2 presents the summary statistics of $\Delta \log \text{ask}(t)$ and $\Delta \log \text{bid}(t)$, the two components of $\Delta x(t)$ compared across markets in real time. Table 7.3 contains the same statistical summary over a fixed 20-minute interval of time scale. We report the mean, variance, standard deviation, skewness coefficient, excess kurtosis (i.e. the empirical kurtosis -3), the minimum and maximum values as well as the range. A 95% confidence interval of the mean and variance estimators is also provided.

In real time, we find in general that $\Delta \log \text{ask}(t)$ has a higher mean and a larger variance than $\Delta \log \text{bid}(t)$. However, the first two moments of ask and bid differ only marginally as compared to the discrepancies reported in moments of order 3 or 4. In fact, the most relevant differences arise in terms of asymmetry and tail properties. On the USD/JPY and DEM/JPY markets, the ask series is skewed to the right, while the bids are skewed to the left. The quotes on the USD/DEM

Table 7.2 Summary statistics (real time (tick-by-tick) data)

	Mean	Variation	Std. dev.	Skewness	Excess kurtosis	Min.	Max.	Range
USD/DEM								
Δ log ask(t)	0.992E-07 (−0.345E-06, 0.543E-06)	0.754E-07 (0.752E-07, 0.755E-07)	0.00027	0.04352	5.4334	−0.00603	0.00972	0.01576
Δ log bid(t)	0.900E-07 (−0.337E-06, 0.517E-06)	0.697E-07 (0.696E-07, 0.699E-07)	0.00026	0.05181	4.5265	−0.00660	0.00923	0.01584
Δx(t)	0.992E-07 (−0.302E-06, 0.501E-06)	0.617E-07 (0.615E-07, 0.618E-07)	0.00024	0.05438	6.0310	−0.00616	0.00947	0.01565
USD/JPY								
Δ log ask(t)	−0.218E-06 (−0.119E-05, 0.760E-06)	0.141E-06 (0.140E-06, 0.141E-06)	0.00037	0.02470	21.9921	−0.00944	0.00939	0.01885
Δ log bid(t)	−0.233E-06 (−0.117E-05, 0.705E-06)	0.130E-06 (0.129E-06, 0.130E-06)	0.00036	−0.00158	6.5750	−0.00907	0.00916	0.01824
Δx(t)	−0.217E-06 (−0.109E-05, 0.655E-06)	0.112E-06 (0.112E-06, 0.113E-06)	0.00033	−0.00174	10.7756	−0.00921	0.00925	0.01847
DEM/JPY								
Δ log ask(t)	−0.260E-03 (−0.344E-03, −0.175E-03)	0.293E-03 (0.291E-03, 0.296E-03)	0.01714	167.02110	31359.7910	−0.03059	3.21939	3.24999
Δ log bid(t)	−0.166E-05 (−0.338E-05, 0.481E-07)	0.121E-06 (0.120E-06, 0.122E-06)	0.00034	−0.38500	20.5896	−0.00975	0.00995	0.01971
Δx(t)	−0.169E-05 (−0.337E-05, −0.236E-07)	0.115E-06 (0.114E-06, 0.116E-06)	0.00033	−0.39260	18.8470	−0.00968	0.00662	0.01631

Notes: The data cover one year of exchange rate quotes assembled by Olsen and Associates. The figures between parentheses are 95% confidence interests.

Table 7.3 Summary statistics (20-minute sampling interval)

	Mean	Variation	Std. dev.	Skewness	Excess kurtosis	Min.	Max.	Range
USD/DEM								
Δ log ask(t)	0.769E-05 (−0.547E-05, 0.208E-04)	0.846E-06 (0.829E-06, 0.864E-06)	0.00092	0.2974	9.0182	−0.00841	0.01344	0.02186
Δ log bid(t)	0.757E-05 (−0.554E-05, 0.207E-04)	0.840E-06 (0.824E-06, 0.858E-06)	0.00091	0.2048	9.1872	−0.00842	0.01345	0.02187
Δx(t)	0.770E-05 (−0.533E-05, 0.207E-04)	0.830E-06 (0.813E-06, 0.847E-06)	0.00091	0.2496	9.3027	−0.00842	0.01344	0.02186
USD/JPY								
Δ log ask(t)	−0.663E-05 (−0.200E-04, 0.681E-05)	0.873E-06 (0.856E-06, 0.891E-06)	0.00093	0.17402	12.6636	−0.00923	0.01097	0.02021
Δ log bid(t)	−0.663E-05 (−0.198E-04, 0.655E-05)	0.841E-06 (0.824E-06, 0.858E-06)	0.00091	0.01485	10.2305	−0.00924	0.01000	0.01925
Δx(t)	−0.664E-05 (−0.197E-04, 0.641E-05)	0.824E-06 (0.807E-06, 0.841E-06)	0.00090	0.09053	10.9400	−0.00924	0.01049	0.01973
DEM/JPY								
Δ log ask(t)	−0.161E-04 (−0.313E-04, −0.100E-05)	0.100E-05 (0.979E-06, 0.102E-05)	0.00100	−0.06358	7.3136	−0.00988	0.01143	0.02132
Δ log bid(t)	−0.162E-04 (−0.311E-04, −0.126E-05)	0.972E-06 (0.951E-06, 0.993E-06)	0.00098	−0.22131	7.1505	−0.01003	0.01028	0.02032
Δx(t)	−0.161E-04 (−0.311E-04, −0.123E-05)	0.963E-06 (0.949E-06, 0.990E-06)	0.00098	−0.13480	7.1586	−0.00996	0.01086	0.02082

Notes: The data cover one year of exchange rate quotes assembled by Olsen and Associates. The figures between parentheses are 95% confidence interests.

exchange rates are both skewed to the right and show little differences in absolute values of the skewness coefficients. In contrast, on the DEM/JPY market, we report a 434 times higher absolute value of the skewness coefficient of asks compared to bids. More excess kurtosis is found in the ask series as well. The difference is either slight, as is the case of the most active USD/DEM market, moderate in the USD/JPY quotes, where the excess kurtosis in asks is almost 3.5 times higher than in bids, or extreme on the DEM/JPY market where the ask coefficient is almost 1523 times larger than the excess kurtosis of the bid series.

Two observations can be made regarding the third and fourth moment statistics reported in Tables 7.2 and 7.3. First, the differences in skewness and kurtosis for bid and ask in the tick-by-tick data indicate that there are far more extreme changes in the ask quotations than there are in the bid. As noted before, these differences are particularly important for the DEM/JPY and USD/JPY markets. A second observation is with respect to the comparison of the kurtosis statistics obtained from real time and 20-minute sampling.[2] The results in Tables 7.2 and 7.3 show that this is the case for the USD/DEM series and for the bid series of the USD/JPY market. All other series do not have this feature.

The geometric average price seems to follow the asymmetric pattern of the bid quotes, both in terms of the sign and the magnitude of skewness coefficients. The thickness of tails in the $\Delta x(t)$ series also appears to be determined by bids rather than asks at least on those markets where the largest bid–ask discrepancies in terms of excess kurtosis were reported, i.e. USD/JPY and DEM/JPY.

The descriptive statistics resulting from the data sampled over 20-minute intervals, presented in Table 7.3, provide us some insights on the time scale adjustment effects. The results in Tables 7.2 and 7.3 indicate that the sampling scheme has an immediate and very strong impact on the distributional properties of the data. We report largely different values of the first four moments of quotes on the same exchange rates sampled on the adjusted time scale.[3] Besides, data show much less variety across the markets in a sense that the basic statistics defining the distinct character of the three data sets become much less dissimilar. It seems that on the aggregated time scale, some of the properties identifying the individual series are becoming attenuated. Accordingly, we do not observe either the bid–ask discrepancies, at least to the extent reported in real time. For this reason, statistics on both quote sequences and their geometric average appear more coherent as well.

To visualize the differences between the $\Delta \log \text{ask}(t)$, $\Delta \log \text{bid}(t)$ and $\Delta x(t)$ series in terms of their distributional properties, we present plots of the corresponding empirical univariate densities (see Figure 7.1). For clarity of exposition, we cover only one market, namely DEM/JPY featuring extreme bid–ask discrepancies in real time.

The three graphs on the left in Figure 7.1 show a much larger pile-up of zeros in comparison to the 20-minute observations, indicating the fact that tick-by-tick series have a considerable fraction of the no-change quote arrivals. Obviously,

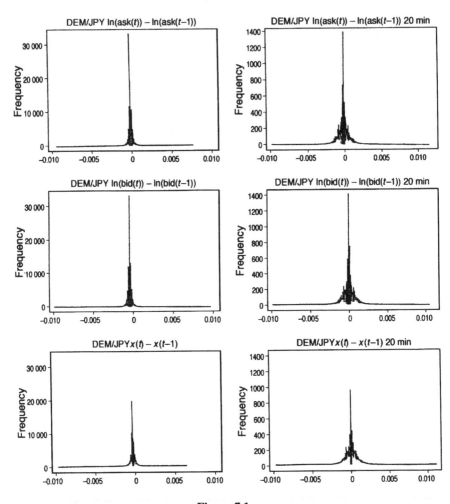

Figure 7.1

part of this is due to point (3), the fact that trades and quotes are recorded simultaneously involving the same price. How much these repeated observations bias and/or affect measures of persistence and other statistical inferences is unclear.

Figures 7.2 and 7.3 display the bivariate distributions of $[\Delta \log \text{ask}(t), \Delta \log \text{bid}(t)]$, the univariate distributions of the two series, as well as the contour plots of quotes recorded both in real time and on the adjusted time scale. A typical shape of the bivariate density can be described as a sudden, very pronounced peak surrounded by some smaller ones within a large domain of infrequently quoted values. In all data sets, the empirical densities are stretched out along one axis of the ellipse, indicating a strong positive correlation between $\Delta \log \text{ask}(t)$ and

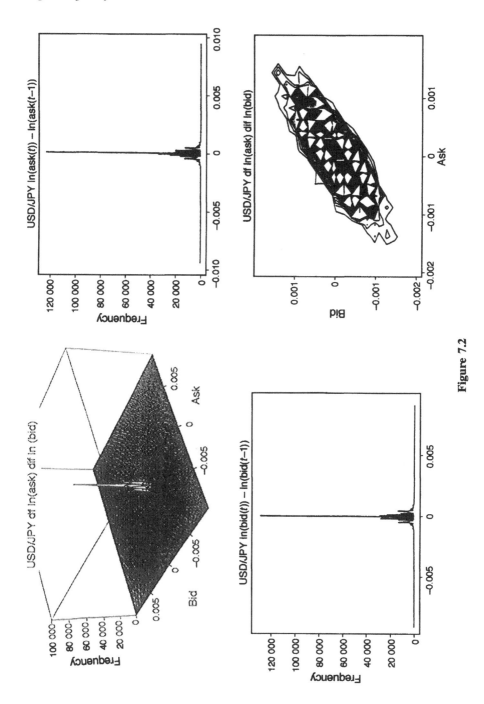

Figure 7.2

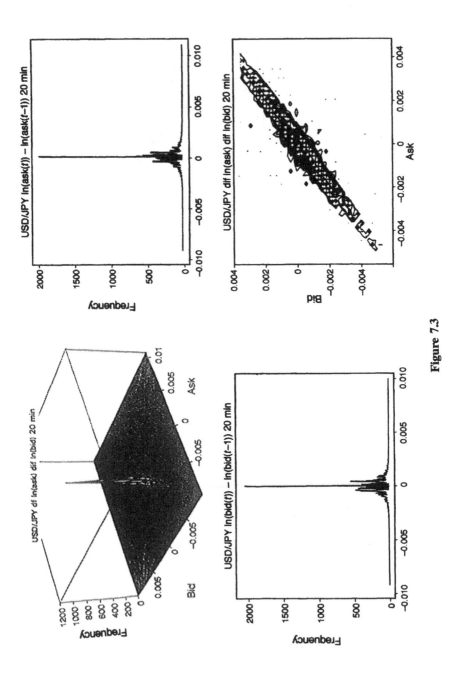

Figure 7.3

$\Delta \log \text{bid}(t)$. The shapes shown on the contour plots confirm a higher variance of data sampled at 20-minute intervals and suggest more correlation between both quote sequences on the 20-minute grid.

So far we have analyzed data sampled over an entire year to examine the behavior of bid and ask price quotes. Any analysis of HF data has to cope with another problem, namely the strong seasonal patterns, particularly intradaily patterns. There is an extensive literature on the stylized facts of intradaily patterns in financial time series. Wood, McInish and Ord (1985) and Harris (1987) documented the existence of a distinct U-shaped pattern in return volatility over the trading day for financial markets operating on a daily business hour schedule such as stock markets. The case of FX markets is more complicated due to the 24-hour trading cycle.

3 MODELLING ISSUES

The purpose of this section is to discuss modelling issues without going into the details of actual model specifications. The previous section highlighted data features and the challenges one faces. The nature of the data and the purpose of modelling greatly affect the type of model being developed. Indeed, some HF data models only serve the purpose of predicting the timing of market transactions while others predict volatility for hedging and so on. While both the nature of the data and the purpose of the model used determine the type of model, we will focus primarily on the former of the two. To facilitate the presentation and provide a guidance to the discussion, we produce a summary table, namely Table 7.4, with data- and model-type entries.

For the data one finds several entries beginning with tick-by-tick data as the first entry in Table 7.4 followed by equally spaced calendar time data where transaction intensities such as quote arrivals or trading volume over fixed time intervals are recorded. The analysis of the FX data at 20-minute time intervals with quote arrivals combined with changes in ask, bid or any combination of it as discussed in section 2 would be a specific example. Next, we list the types of data most often encountered in HF intradaily data studies involving univariate series of bid, ask or returns. Finally, at the more aggregate level one also finds daily, weekly and monthly data. While we do not distinguish models according to their final use, we defined two broad categories in Table 7.4. These are: (i) market transactions models and (ii) financial time series models. The second category is probably the best known and researched as it includes the large class of standard ARCH and SV models listed in the second column bottom entry of Table 7.4. There are several surveys which cover this extensive literature: for ARCH models, see Bera and Higgins (1995), Bollerslev, Chou and Kroner (1992), Bollerslev, Engle and Nelson (1994) and Diebold and Lopez (1995), while Ghysels, Harvey and Renault (1996) cover SV models. All other entries in Table 7.4 are less densely populated with examples and will be studied case by case.

Table 7.4 Data features and modelling issues

Data	Models	
	Market transactions models	Financial time series models
Tick-by-tick data	Point processes, durations and hazard models	
Intradaily equally spaced data prices (volume) and number of transactions	Subordinated processes with transaction-based time deformation	Unequally spaced ARCH and time deformed SV models
Intradaily equally spaced data prices (volume) but no transactions information	Latent variable subordinated processes	Standard ARCH and SV models
Daily, weekly and monthly series	Volume-return models	Standard ARCH and SV models (temporal aggregation)

Before turning our attention to the specific models, it is important to note there is at the outset an important difference between market transactions models and the broad class of volatility models such as ARCH and SV. Indeed, the latter are a relatively uniform class involving the same fundamental structure, like ARCH, which may not necessarily lend itself easily to temporal aggregation. The situation is quite different for market transactions models where depending on the specific context and purpose one encounters point processes counting transaction events, data, duration and hazard models, continuous time jump processes, among many others. Such models clearly do not share the same parametric structure and typically little is known about their temporal aggregation features (see Gouriéroux, Jasiak and Le Fol 1996 for more details).

The models for tick-by-tick data focus on a sequence of times $\{t_1, t_2, \ldots, t_n\}$ at which quotes arrive or transactions occur. Such arrival times are called point processes. There is an extensive statistics literature on such processes, see e.g. Cox and Miller (1965). Moreover, microeconometric models of labor markets are based on many related models, see e.g. Lancaster (1990). These models are not directly suitable for modelling arrivals of quotes or the occurrence of transactions in financial markets as the arrival event is assumed to be independently distributed, an assumption which does not apply here. Recently, Engle and Russell (1995) suggested autoregressive conditional duration models where conditional durations $t_i - t_{i-1}$ depend on past lagged durations $(t_j - t_{j-1})_{j<i}$ in an autoregressive way.

Market transactions models based on equally spaced sampling of returns or bid/ask movements which involve quote arrival data are indirectly related to the previous class of models as both rely on some notion of time deformation distinguishing so-called market time from calendar time. The concept of time deformation or subordinated processes is particularly apt to address some of the challenges posed by HF data. The idea originated in the work by Mandelbrot and Taylor (1967) and Clark (1973), among others, who argued that since the number of transactions in any time period is random, one may think of asset price movements as the realization of a process $Y_t = Y_{z_t}^*$ where z_t is a directing process. This positive non-decreasing stochastic process z_t can, for instance, be thought of as related to the number of transactions or more fundamentally, the cumulated volume of trades, the cumulated volatility or to the arrival of information. This by now familiar concept of subordinated stochastic processes, originated by Bochner (1960), was used by Mandelbrot and Taylor (1967) and later refined by Clark (1973) to explain the behavior of speculative prices. Originally, it was mostly applied to daily observations since HF data were not available. A well-known example in finance is the considerable amount of empirical evidence documenting nontrading day effects. Such phenomena can be viewed as time deformation due to market closure.[4] Obviously, as pointed out by Mandelbrot and Taylor (1967), time deformation is also directly related to the mixture of distributions model of Tauchen and Pitts (1983), Harris (1987), Foster and Viswanathan (1993) among others. More to the point regarding HF data, one should mention that in foreign exchange markets, there is also a tendency to rely on activity sales determined by the number of active markets around the world at any particular moment. Dacorogna *et al.* (1993a) explicitly describe a model of time deformation for intraday movements of foreign exchange rates. Besides these relatively simple examples, there are a number of more complex ones. Ghysels and Jasiak (1994) proposed a stochastic volatility model with the volatility equation evolving in an operational time scale. They use trading volume and leverage effects to specify the mapping between calendar and operational time. In Ghysels, Gouriéroux and Jasiak (1998) this framework is extended and applied to intraday foreign exchange data, providing an alternative to the Dacorogna *et al.* time scale transformation. Madan and Seneta (1990) and Madan and Milne (1991) introduced a Brownian motion evaluated at random (exogenous) time changes governed by independent gamma increments as an alternative martingale process for the uncertainty driving stock market returns. Geman and Yor (1993) and Leblanc (1994) also used time-changed Bessel processes to compute path-dependent option prices such as is the case with Asian options. It is also worth nothing that there is some research specifically examining the time between trades; see Hausman and Lo (1990), Han, Kalay and Rosenfeld (1994), Engle and Russell (1995) for instance.

Another class of models also involves equally spaced returns modelled as subordinated processes but with latent Z_t. Such models can essentially be viewed as latent factor models. As X_T is no longer tied to observable processes it is clear that more stringent identification assumptions must be imposed to estimate subordinated processes as latent factor models. Clark (1973) originally assumed that Z_t was an i.i.d. process. In the most recent work, see for instance Conley et al. (1997) and Ghysels, Gouriéroux and Jasiak (1995), it is assumed that Z_t is independent of the Y^* process. The assumption and its implications are discussed in more detail in Ghysels, Gouriéroux and Jasiak (1998).

The last category in the first column of Table 7.4 corresponds to models of asset returns and trading volume, typically estimated with daily data; see for instance Karpoff (1987), Gallant, Rossi and Tauchen (1992), Lamoureux and Lastrapes (1993), among others.

4 TRADING PATTERNS, TIME DEFORMATION AND STOCHASTIC VOLATILITY IN FOREIGN EXCHANGE MARKETS

Different types of HF data suggest specific modelling strategies. In this section we provide a detailed example, using one of the HF data sets presented in section 2. The example we develop involves data on equally spaced time sampling supplemented with market activity data such as average quote arrivals. Hence it is a market transactions model, as discussed in section 3, involving transaction-based series. In the first subsection we describe the models, and then in section 4.2 we discuss several possible directing processes for market activity.

4.1 Stochastic Volatility and Time Deformation

In this section we provide a brief summary of the stochastic volatility model with time deformation presented in Ghysels and Jasiak (1994) and Ghysels, Gouriéroux and Jasiak (1998). Following the work by Hull and White (1987), Johnson and Shanno (1987), Scott (1987), Chesney and Scott (1989), Stein and Stein (1991), we call a stochastic volatility model the following set of equations:

$$dy(t) = \mu y(t)\, dt + \sigma(t)y(t)\, dW_1(t) \tag{1a}$$

$$d \log \sigma(t) = a(b - \log \sigma(t))\, dt + c\, dW_2(t) \tag{1b}$$

where $W_1(t)$ and $W_2(t)$ are two independent, standard Wiener processes. Ghysels and Jasiak (1994) suggested adopting the framework of equations (1a) and (1b) and define the volatility process as a subordinated stochastic process evolving in a time dimension driven market activity. This approach has been motivated by the works of Mandelbrot and Taylor (1967), as well as Clark (1973). The complex and quite frequently irregular behavior of asset prices becomes simpler and hence easier to model once we assume that the volatility is tied to some observed or unobserved variables, like the information arrival, which determines the dynamics of tradings.[5] Hence, we assume that there exists an operational time scale of the volatility process, with $s = g(t)$, a mapping between operational and calendar time t, such that[6]

$$dy(t) = \mu y(t) \, dt + \sigma(g(t)) y(t) \, dw_1(t) \tag{2a}$$

$$d \log \sigma(s) = a(b - \log \sigma(s)) \, ds + c \, dw_2(s) \tag{2b}$$

Following Stock (1988), we use the notation $g(t)$ for the directing process to indicate some *generic* time deformation, which may include trading volume besides other series that help to determine the pace of the market. Before discussing what might determine $g(t)$, we would like to make some observations regarding equations (1a) and (1b). Indeed, it should first be noted that the equations collapse to the usual stochastic volatility model if $g(t) = t$. Obviously, there are several possible specifications of $\sigma(g(t))$. Moreover, one could correctly argue that defining volatility as a subordinated process amounts to suggesting a more complex law of motion in comparison to the Ornstein–Uhlenbeck (henceforth O–U) specification appearing in (2b). This interpretation is valid, yet it should be noted that, through $g(t)$, one can associate many series other than the security price $y(t)$ to explain volatility; hence, one implicitly deals with a multivariate framework. Moreover, as we have pointed out, the time deformation setup enables us to handle rather complex structures through the subordinated representation.

To enhance our understanding of the mechanism of the process, we first consider the system (2) in its continuous and discrete time versions. To simplify the presentation, let us set $b = 0$ and discuss a continuous time AR(1). An investor's information can be described by considering the probability space $(\Omega, \mathcal{F}, \mathcal{P})$ and the nondecreasing family $F = \{\mathcal{F}\}_{t=0}^{+\infty}$ of sub-σ-algebras in calendar time. Furthermore, we let Z_t be an m-dimensional vector process adapted to the filtration F, i.e. Z_t is F_{t-1} — measurable via the logistic transformation:[7]

$$\Delta g(t) \equiv g(t) - g(t-1) \equiv \exp(c' Z_{t-1}) \Big/ \left\{ \frac{1}{T} \sum_{t=1}^{T} \exp(c' Z_{t-1}) \right\} \tag{3}$$

Equation (3), setting the speed of changes in operational time as a measurable function of calendar time process Z_{t-1}, is completed by the additional identification assumptions:

$$0 < g(\tau; Z_{t-1}) < \infty \quad \forall \tau \tag{4}$$

$$g(0) = 0 \tag{5}$$

$$\frac{1}{T} \sum_{t=1}^{T} \Delta g(t) = 1 \tag{6}$$

These three conditions guarantee that the operational time clock progresses in the same direction as calendar time without stops or jumps.[8] Given that g is constant between consecutive calendar time observations via equation (3), its discrete time analog: $\Delta g(t) \equiv g(t) - g(t-1)$ takes the same logistic form appearing in equation (3). At this point, we will not present the components of the Z_{t-1} vector. As we will discuss this issue in the next section, let us just indicate that, in principle, Z_{t-1} consists of any processes related to the information arrival. Ghysels and Jasiak (1994) show that the solution in calendar time can be expressed as

$$\Delta \log y_t - a_1 \Delta \log y_{t-1} - \lambda = e^{ht} \varepsilon_t \tag{7}$$

$$h_t = [(1 - \exp(a\Delta g(t)))]^b + \exp(a\Delta g(t)) h_{t-1} + v_t \tag{8}$$

$$v_t \sim N(0, -\Sigma(1 - \exp(2a\Delta g(t))/2a) \tag{9}$$

Equations (7) and (8) constitute the basic set of equations for the discrete time representation of the SV model with subordinated volatility process which evolves at a pace set by $\Delta g(t)$. A linear state-space representation of the system (7)–(8) can be estimated by maximizing the conditional maximum likelihood function within the Kalman filter framework. Following Harvey, Ruiz and Shephard (1994), we rewrite equation (9) as:

$$\log[\Delta \log y_t - a^1 \Delta \log y_{t-1} - \lambda]^2 = h_t + \log \varepsilon_t^2 \tag{10}$$

where $E \log \varepsilon_t^2 = -1.27$ and $\mathrm{Var} \log \varepsilon_t^2 = \pi^2/2$. Defining $\varsigma_t = \log \varepsilon_t^2$, we obtain

$$\log[\Delta \log y_t - a_1 \Delta \log y_{t-1} - \lambda]^2 = -1.27 + h_t + \varsigma_t \tag{11}$$

Apart from the parameter λ, treatment of which is discussed for instance by Gouriéroux, Monfort and Renault (1993), the coefficients of this state-space model are time-varying and hence, similar to the specification proposed by Stock (1988), except for the properties of the ς_t process which is no longer Gaussian. Consequently, the estimation procedure based on the Kalman filter will result here in a quasi-maximum likelihood estimate (QMLE), as pointed out by Harvey, Ruiz and Shephard (1994). The details of the QMLE algorithm for the time-deformed SV models are discussed in Ghysels and Jasiak (1994), while Ghysels, Gouriéroux and Jasiak (1995a) present a detailed account of subordinated process theory and their estimation.

4.2 Directing Processes for Market Activity

The model structure described in the previous section is a generic one where, apart from some regularity conditions and the logistic form, the specification of $\Delta g(t)$ was left open. Clark (1973), Tauchen and Pitts (1983) and Ghysels and Jasiak (1994) studied stock returns and used a time deformation model with trading volume as a proxy for market activity. It is well known that for foreign exchange markets trading volume is difficult to obtain. Hence, we need to consider other series. The *Olsen and Associates* database provides several possibilities of modelling market activity. The purpose of this section is to discuss the different approaches one could consider.

Our strategy will consist of distinguishing 'regular' or average market activity, and deviations from the expected level of activity. For example, when European financial markets open and start active trading in say the USD/DEM, each market participant has a certain expectation of the number of quotes arriving during the first 5 minutes, the next 5 minutes, and so on.[9] Some mornings, the market activity is more brisk or even frenzy-like. On other mornings, the market activity is down relative to its usual rhythm. Every part of the trading day has a certain reference norm of activity against which one portrays the latest quote arrivals. What is true for quote arrivals also holds for other market indicators like bid–ask spreads, returns, absolute value of returns, etc. The model specification strategy which we will adopt is to incorporate into $\Delta g(t)$ measures of 'regular' or average market activity and series representing deviations from average trading patterns. To continue with the quote arrival example, we can formulate $\Delta g(t)$ as

$$\Delta g(t) = \exp(c'Z_{t-1}) \equiv \exp(\Theta_{qa} nqa_{t-1} + \Theta_{qd}(nqa_{t-1} - nq_{t-1})) \tag{12}$$

where the scaling constant appearing in equation (5) has been omitted from (12). Hence from equation (12) we have that $Z_{t-1} = (nqa_{t-1}, (nqa_{t-1} - nq_{t-1}))$ where nqa_{t-1} is the mean number of quotes arriving over the interval $t-1$, while nq_{t-1} is the actual number of quotes which arrived in $t-1$.

To clarify this, let us consider the plots appearing in Figure 7.4. The figure consists of six plots; the left-hand side displays graphs with results from data sampled at 5-minute intervals and the right panel contains the equivalent 20-minute sampling frequency. We study the three markets of the Olsen data set, namely USD/DEM, DEM/JPY and USD/JPY. Each plot covers a span of a week, omitting the weekends, and displays the average number of quotes, computed over the entire sample, for each 5 (left) or 20 (right) minute time intervals of the week. The plots display the repetitive intraday cycle which is so typical for HF exchange rate data. The 5-minute plots are, of course, more jagged than the 20-minute ones, but each clearly shows the patterns of quote arrivals repeated over a 24-hour cycle. The graphs displayed in Figure 7.4 represent the nqa_{t-1} series used to model $\Delta g(t)$. The number of quote arrivals is one candidate series to measure market activity, besides other series which we shall discuss shortly.

Before turning to these other series, it is worth drawing attention to a special case of time deformation. Suppose for the moment that $\Theta_{qd} = 0$ in equation (12). Then, $\Delta g(t)$ is purely a function of the repetitive daily pattern of $\{nqa_t\}$ which amounts to volatility being a periodic autoregressive process:

$$h_t = \gamma_t + \alpha_t h_t + W_t \tag{13}$$

where γ_t and α_t are changing every 5 or 20 minutes, depending on the sampling frequency, with a 24-hour repetitive cycle, i.e. $\gamma_t = \gamma_s$, $\alpha_t = \alpha_s$, with $s = t + 24$ hours.[10] A periodic model like (13) resembles the class of periodic ARCH

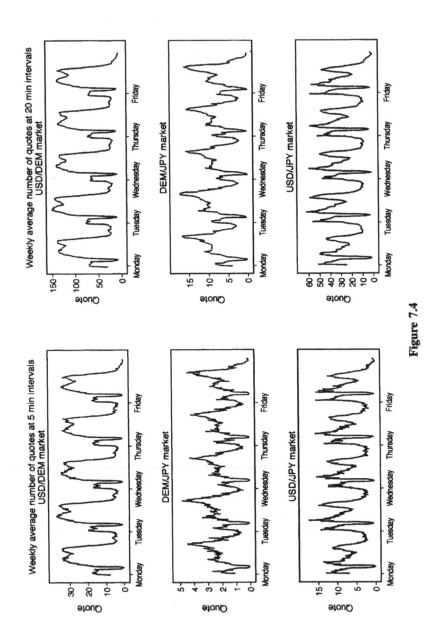

Figure 7.4

processes proposed by Bollerslev and Ghysels (1996) by analogy with periodic ARMA models for the mean which have been extensively studied. Of course, the parameter variation in (13) is determined by $\gamma_t = (1 - \exp(a\Delta g(t)))$ and $\alpha_t = (a\Delta g(t))$.

We noted that quote arrivals are not the only measure of market activity, and indeed several other series in the Olsen data file could be considered. Figure 7.5 displays the intradaily pattern of bid–ask spreads. The figure has the averages computed on a weekly basis of the average bid–ask spreads during 5- or 20-minute intervals. We notice in Figure 7.5(a) a reasonably regular 24-hour pattern for bid–ask spreads but by far not as pronounced and regular as the quote arrivals displayed in Figure 7.4. Following the example in equation (12), we can formulate a directing process as follows, using the same principle:

$$\Delta g(t) \equiv \exp(\Theta_{sa} spa_{t-1} + \Theta_{sd}(spa_{t-1} - sp_{t-1})) \tag{14}$$

where spa_{t-1} is the sample average computed on weekly basis of the mean spread over the interval $t - 1$, while sp_{t-1} is the mean spread actually realized.

Last, but certainly not least, we can use absolute return. The weekly averages are displayed in Figure 7.6. The absolute return series has been used by Müller *et al.* (1990) to model an activity scale. These authors have observed that absolute returns exhibited clear structures reflecting market activity through the repetitive cycles of business hours. Indeed, we recover such a pattern in absolute returns, although it again appears not to be as regular as in the case of quote arrivals. If we were to use only absolute returns, we could construct a directing process:

$$\Delta g(t) \equiv \exp(\Theta_{ra} ara_{t-1} + \Theta_{rd}(ara_{t-1} - ar_{t-1})) \tag{15}$$

where ara_{t-1} is the sample average of absolute returns while ar_{t-1} is the actual realization for time interval $t - 1$.

Whatever measure is best suited to formulate the directing process is ultimately an empirical question of model specification and diagnostics. In equation (12)–(15) we considered each of the series separately in their expected value format and deviations from the mean. However, one could easily combine the series and create a generic directing process:

$$\Delta g(t) \equiv \exp(c'Z_{t-1}) \equiv \exp[(\Theta_{qa} nqa_{t-1} + \Theta_{sa} spa_{t-1} + \Theta_{ra} ara_{t-1}$$
$$+ \Theta_{qd}(nqa_{t-1} - nq_{t-1}) + \Theta_{sd}(spa_{t-1} - sp_{t-1})$$
$$+ \Theta_{rd}(ara_{t-1} - ar_{t-1})] \tag{16}$$

A priori one should expect that the formulation (16) has a lot of redundancy, particularly with respect to the *nqa* and *ara* time series. Presumably, the best representation is to pick one of the averages as representative to measure market activity as a combination of the selected average processes and add the series measuring deviations from the regular market activity. The latter could be represented either by one, two or all three surprise variables in equation (16). This is precisely the modelling strategy which we will adopt in the next section.

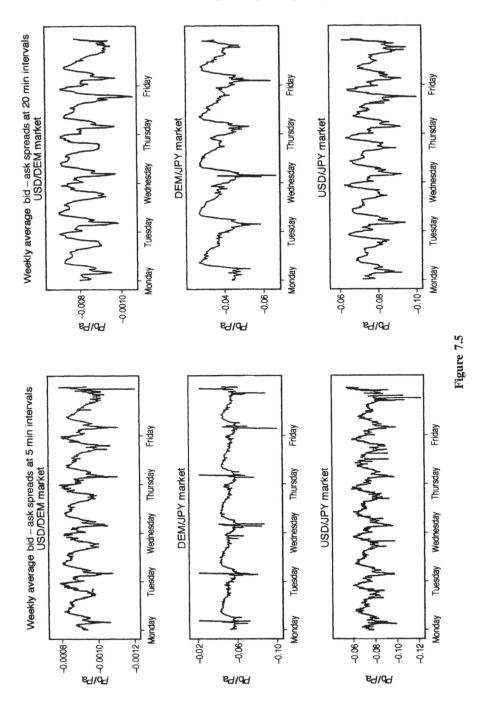

Figure 7.5

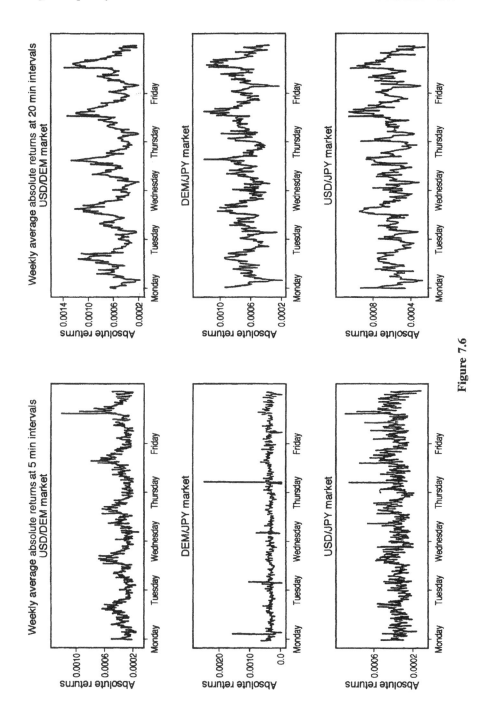

Figure 7.6

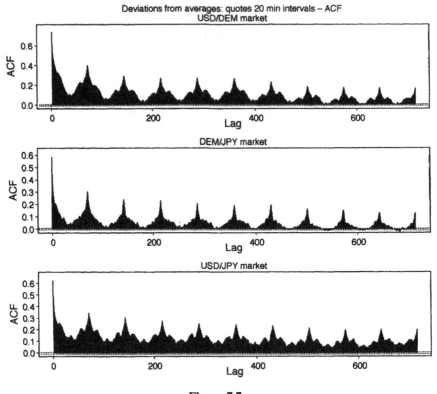

Figure 7.7

Before presenting the estimation results, we need to discuss the time series properties of the $(nqa_t - nq_t)$, $(spa_t - sp_t)$ and $(ara_t - ar_t)$ series, i.e. the series measuring deviations from regular market activity. To do this, we examine the autocorrelation function (ACF) of each series. These are plotted in Figures 7.7–7.9, and are complementary to the plots of the weekly averages. The first of the three figures covers the ACF of the $\{nqa_t - nq_t\}$ series. We notice a very strong and repetitive pattern in all three markets. This means that average quote arrivals, as displayed in Figure 7.4, are not the only source of periodic patterns appearing in equation (14), since the deviations from market average are also strongly autocorrelated with seasonal patterns. When we turn our attention to Figure 7.8, which covers the bid–ask spread series $\{spa_t - sp_t\}$, we observe less seasonal autocorrelations, at least on a daily basis, but still within a weekly lag. Since weekends were deleted prior to computing the autocorrelation functions, one recovers a positive autocorrelation at around 360 lags. This weekly pattern is present on both the USD/DEM and USD/JPY markets. On the DEM/JPY market, we find a daily seasonal pattern, however, quite similar to that in

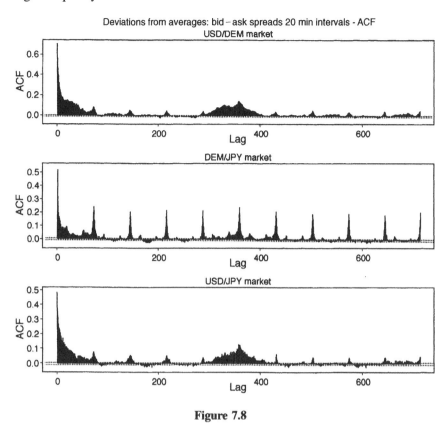

Figure 7.8

Figure 7.7. Finally, we turn our attention to the absolute return market deviation series $\{ara_t - ar_t\}$ in Figure 7.9. Unlike the two previous series, it exhibits no particular regular patterns in the corresponding ACF. Instead, we find a slowly decaying pattern starting from a first-order autocorrelation which is much higher than the previous ones, namely 0.25 instead of around 0.05 as those appearing in Figures 7.7 and 7.8. Even after 800 lags, we still have an autocorrelation above 0.05.

5 EMPIRICAL RESULTS

There are three currency exchange markets available in the Olsen and Associates data set, and hence we will devote a subsection to each market. We begin with the most active USD/DEM market which is covered in section 5.1 followed by DEM/JPY and finally, USD/JPY markets which are covered in section 5.2. Before discussing the actual results, a few observations are in order regarding estimation. It was noted in the previous section that the details of the QMLE

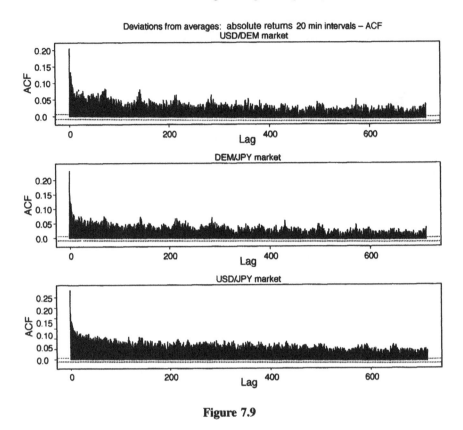

Figure 7.9

algorithm are omitted here as they appear in Ghysels and Jasiak (1994). The numerical optimization of the quasi-likelihood function was accomplished via simulated annealing. The algorithm, which is described in Goffe *et al.* (1994), appeared to be the best equipped to deal with the multiplicity of local maxima which tricked most other conventional algorithms we tried. Also, for reasons of numerical stability, we rescaled the quote and spread series by $1.e-03$ while the absolute return series was rescaled by $1.e-01$.

5.1 The USD/DEM Foreign Exchange Market

In section 4 we noted that our modelling strategy of the mapping between calendar time and operational time would consist of picking one of the three series measuring anticipated market activity and combine it with the set of series reflecting deviations from averages. Table 7.5 reports the estimation results obtained from the 20-minute sampling interval for three model specifications, each involving different measures of market activity, as appearing in equations (3)–(7), completed with several combinations of the deviations from

Table 7.5 QML estimates of stochastic volatility models with time deformation 20-minute sampling intervals — USD/DEM market

Model: $\log[\Delta \log y_t - a_1 \Delta \log y_{t-1} - \lambda]^2 = -1.27 + h_t + \varsigma_t; h_t$
$$= [(1 - \exp(a\Delta g(t)))]b + \exp(a\Delta g(t))h_{t-1} + v_t$$
$$\Delta g(t) \approx \exp[\Theta_{qa} nqa_{t-1} + \Theta_{qd}(nqa_{t-1} - nq_{t-1}) + \Theta_{sd}(spa_{t-1} - sp_{t-1}) + \Theta_{rd}(ara_{t-1} - ar_{t-1})]$$
$$v_t \sim N(0, -\Sigma(1 - \exp(2a\Delta g(t)))/2a)$$

	(1) Est.	(1) St. Er.	(2) Est.	(2) St. Er.	(3) Est.	(3) St. Er.	(4) Est.	(4) St. Er.
Θ_{qa}	−0.0106	0.0011	−0.0107	0.0011	−0.0114	0.0032	−0.0148	0.0016
Θ_{qd}	−0.0197	0.0029	−0.0196	0.0029	0.0320	0.0057	—	—
Θ_{sd}	−1.5040	0.0054	−1.4805	0.0053	—	—	−1.6044	0.0262
Θ_{rd}	−4.5236	0.0049	—	—	—	—	−4.7899	0.0050
a	−0.4206	0.0050	−0.3800	0.0053	−0.1357	0.0305	−0.6455	0.0226
Σ	1.1714	0.0049	1.0581	0.0049	0.3758	0.1050	1.7842	0.0114
b	−14.9361	0.0050	−14.9369	0.0050	−14.9702	0.0773	−14.8807	0.0375

$$\Delta g(t) \approx \exp[\Theta_{ra} ara_{t-1} + \Theta_{qd}(nqa_{t-1} - nq_{t-1}) + \Theta_{sd}(spa_{t-1} - sp_{t-1}) + \Theta_{rd}(ara_{t-1} - ar_{t-1})]$$

	(1) Est.	(1) St. Er.	(2) Est.	(2) St. Er.	(3) Est.	(3) St. Er.	(4) Est.	(4) St. Er.
Θ_{ra}	2.2965	0.0050	−2.3450	0.0050	−2.2099	0.6004	−1.8602	0.0049
Θ_{qd}	−0.0270	0.0028	−0.0270	0.0028	−0.0268	0.0047	—	—
Θ_{sd}	−1.7471	0.0161	−1.7464	0.0157	—	—	−1.8360	0.0142
Θ_{rd}	−3.0309	0.0049	—	—	—	—	−2.6463	0.0049
a	−0.7601	0.0269	−0.7418	0.0245	−0.1257	0.0189	−0.8759	0.0276
Σ	2.0766	0.0115	2.0260	0.0106	0.3382	0.0629	2.2712	0.0120
b	−14.8290	0.0060	−14.8193	0.0119	−14.8360	0.0614	−14.6385	0.0106

the average market activity. To avoid reporting too many empirical results, we present models with nqa and ara variables of average market activity and omit those with spa which yield quite similar results. The three surprise terms appear either simultaneously or separately in models summarized in Table 7.5. Besides the point estimates, we also report standard errors which were computed using a heteroscedasticity consistent QMLE covariance matrix estimator. One should recall that the QMLE procedure is asymptotically inefficient, yet the standard errors in Table 7.5 reveal that all series entering $\Delta g(t)$, no matter what specification is used, appear significant. Hence, the standard errors do not give us much guidance on what model specification to chose. Before elaborating further on model choice, let us first discuss the interpretation of the estimates. One can note immediately that all the coefficients Θ_{ij} have negative signs. Obviously, each coefficient measures a partial effect. However, from microstructure models we know, for instance, that as the time interval between quotes decreases, one expects spreads to increase (see, for instance, Easly and O'Hara 1992 for further discussion). Hence, each of the series reflects movements that are obviously not related. The mapping between calendar time and operational time we investigate is, of course, one based on statistical fit. Let us distinguish first the coefficients related to average market activity from those related to deviations from the normal pace. The first example covers average quotes. Negative coefficients Θ_{qa} and a

imply that when the average number of quotes is high, market volatility becomes more persistent and less erratic. Obviously, high quote arrivals do not necessarily reflect a high information content, but it often means that many markets are active simultaneously. Comparing Figures 7.4 and 7.5, we note that high average quote arrivals appear to be associated with the higher bid–ask spreads, at least for the USD/DEM market discussed here. Likewise, comparing Figures 7.4 and 7.5, we make the same observation for absolute returns, at least again on the USD/DEM market.

The coefficients related to the deviations from normal market activity are also negative. Since deviations are measured as average minus actual realizations, it is clear that, with negative a coefficient, above-normal market activity increases volatility and vice versa. Also, operational time increases (decreases) when market activity is above (below) average. It must also be noted that each specification of $\Delta g(t)$ involves lagged values of the deviations from market activity. This is, of course, done in order to guarantee that $\Delta g(t)$ is based on variables that are measurable with regard to $t-1$ information. From the autocorrelation functions in Figures 7.7–7.9, we also know, however, that the first-order autocorrelations for each of the market activity deviation processes are positive.

With all entries being significant for the 20-minute USD/DEM specifications, we must rely on other criteria to discriminate among models. In the remainder

Table 7.6 QML estimates of stochastic volatility models with time deformation 20-minute sampling intervals — USD/JPY market

Model:
$$\log[\Delta \log y_t - a_1 \Delta \log y_{t-1} - \lambda]^2 = -1.27 + h_t + \varsigma_t; h_t$$
$$= [(1 - \exp(a\Delta g(t)))]b + \exp(a\Delta g(t))h_{t-1} + v_t$$
$$\Delta g(t) \approx \exp[\Theta_{qa} nqa_{t-1} + \Theta_{qd}(nqa_{t-1} - nq_{t-1}) + \Theta_{sd}(spa_{t-1} - sp_{t-1}) + \Theta_{rd}(ara_{t-1} - ar_{t-1})]$$
$$v_t \sim N(0, -\Sigma(1 - \exp(2a\Delta g(t)))/2a)$$

	(1) Est.	St. Er.	(2) Est.	St. Er.	(3) Est.	St. Er.	(4) Est.	St. Er.
Θ_{qa}	−0.0153	0.0043	−0.0167	0.0066	−0.0070	0.0024	−0.0070	0.0042
Θ_{qd}	−0.0239	0.0036	−0.0243	0.0083	—	—	—	—
Θ_{sd}	−0.2002	0.0049	—	—	0.2970	0.1401	—	—
Θ_{rd}	−0.8204	0.0049	—	—	—	—	−0.5879	0.0049
a	−0.2189	0.0053	−0.2152	0.0411	−0.1943	0.0069	−0.1983	0.0399
Σ	0.6899	0.0111	0.6777	0.1756	0.5801	0.0239	0.5951	0.0079
b	−14.9240	0.0050	−14.9306	0.0596	−14.7899	0.0212	−14.7950	0.0050

$$\Delta g(t) \approx \exp[\Theta_{ra} ara_{t-1} + \Theta_{qd}(nqa_{t-1} - nq_{t-1}) + \Theta_{sd}(spa_{t-1} - sp_{t-1}) + \Theta_{rd}(ara_{t-1} - ar_{t-1})]$$

	(1) Est.	St. Er.	(2) Est.	St. Er.	(3) Est.	St. Er.	(4) Est.	St. Er.
Θ_{ra}	6.2526	0.0049	6.2884	2.6309	6.0877	3.8865	5.2324	0.0049
Θ_{qd}	−0.0178	0.0041	−0.0181	0.0054	—	—	—	—
Θ_{sd}	−0.2864	0.0050	—	—	−0.3251	0.1398	—	—
Θ_{rd}	−0.7404	0.0049	—	—	—	—	−0.5565	0.0049
a	−0.2063	0.0161	−0.2063	0.0202	−0.1921	0.0068	−0.1943	0.0154
Σ	0.6357	0.0643	0.6354	0.0804	0.5702	0.0234	0.5777	0.0596
b	−14.8784	0.0339	−14.8860	0.0388	−14.7786	0.0213	−14.7838	0.0024

Table 7.7 QML estimates of stochastic volatility models with Time Deformation 20-minute sampling intervals — DEM/JPY market

Model: $\log[\Delta \log y_t - a_1 \Delta \log y_{t-1} - \lambda]^2 = -1.27 + h_t + \varsigma_t; h_t$
$$= [(1 - \exp(a\Delta g(t)))]b + \exp(a\Delta g(t))h_{t-1} + v_t$$
$$\Delta g(t) \approx \exp[\Theta_{qa} nqa_{t-1} + \Theta_{qd}(nqa_{t-1} - nq_{t-1}) + \Theta_{sd}(spa_{t-1} - sp_{t-1}) + \Theta_{rd}(ara_{t-1} - ar_{t-1})]$$
$$v_t \sim N(0, -\Sigma(1 - \exp(2a\Delta g(t)))/2a)$$

	(1) Est.	(1) St. Er.	(2) Est.	(2) St. Er.	(3) Est.	(3) St. Er.	(4) Est.	(4) St. Er.
Θ_{qa}	0.0273	0.0074	0.0022	0.0132	0.0186	0.0134	−0.0050	0.0131
Θ_{qd}	−0.0204	0.0097	0.0201	0.0111	—	—	—	—
Θ_{sd}	0.4924	0.0054	—	—	0.4822	0.0800	—	—
Θ_{rd}	−0.2240	0.0052	—	—	—	—	0.1387	0.5881
a	−0.1773	0.0098	−0.1743	0.0088	−0.1781	0.0091	−0.1767	0.0089
Σ	0.3195	0.0272	0.3163	0.0212	0.3232	0.0215	0.3241	0.0216
b	−14.3923	0.0022	−14.3674	0.0202	−14.4061	0.0199	−14.3817	0.0196

$$\Delta g(t) \approx \exp[\Theta_{ra} ara_{t-1} + \Theta_{qd}(nqa_{t-1} - nq_{t-1}) + \Theta_{sd}(spa_{t-1} - sp_{t-1}) + \Theta_{rd}(ara_{t-1} - ar_{t-1})]$$

	(1) Est.	(1) St. Er.	(2) Est.	(2) St. Er.	(3) Est.	(3) St. Er.	(4) Est.	(4) St. Er.
Θ_{ra}	6.6248	5.4780	7.7326	5.6690	6.4390	3.0797	7.6165	0.0052
Θ_{qd}	−0.0214	0.0116	0.0195	0.0111	—	—	—	—
Θ_{sd}	−0.4577	0.0787	—	—	−0.4573	0.0978	—	—
Θ_{rd}	−0.2292	0.6664	—	—	—	—	−0.1189	0.0054
a	−0.1805	0.0093	−0.1748	0.0088	−0.1812	0.0171	−0.1750	0.0147
Σ	0.3276	0.0220	0.3178	0.0212	0.3309	0.0417	0.3199	0.0356
b	−14.4100	0.0198	−14.3696	0.0196	−14.4160	0.0252	−14.3790	0.0133

of this section, we will focus on the models appearing in the first column of Tables 7.5–7.7. These models contain all three measures of deviations from average market activity combined with each of the three measures of average market activity. We first turn our attention to the plots of squared returns paired with the sample paths of market time as obtained from the estimated $\Delta g(t)$ processes. These appear in Figure 7.10. The three $\Delta g(t)$ processes appear quite similar, although upon closer examination, it is clear that the time deformation involving average quotes looks quite distinct from the other two specifications.

Since we have computed the $\Delta g(t)$ process, we may also proceed as in Müller *et al.* (1993) and analyze returns not in calendar time, but rather in operational time. It is a useful tool, as Müller *et al.* (1993) suggest, to study 'deseasonalized' returns. It should be noted though that while the Olsen and Associates activity scale is based purely on average (repetitive) patterns, our approach uses direct dynamic effects. We compute the ACF in operational time estimated from our models, by using an approximation, namely, by defining the $[\Delta \log y_t - a_1 \Delta \log y_{t-1} - \lambda]^2/\Delta g(t)$ process as being the normalized returns, relative to market time. Obviously, when $\Delta g(t) \equiv 1$, we recover the calendar time process. Otherwise, we recover a squared return process adjusted for serial dependence and drift which is normalized by operational time changes. This normalized process is used to compute an ACF. For comparison, we plot first the

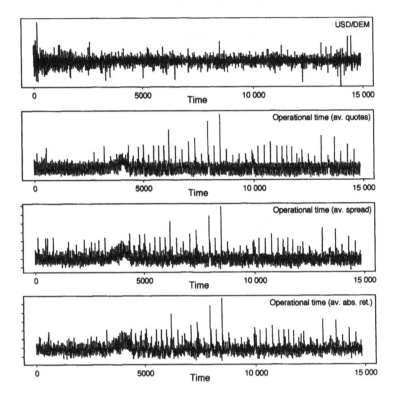

Figure 7.10

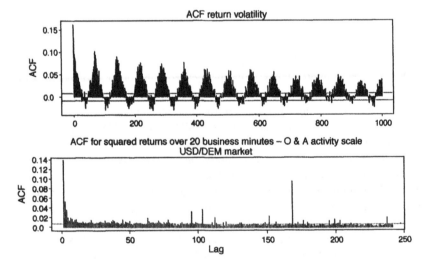

Figure 7.11

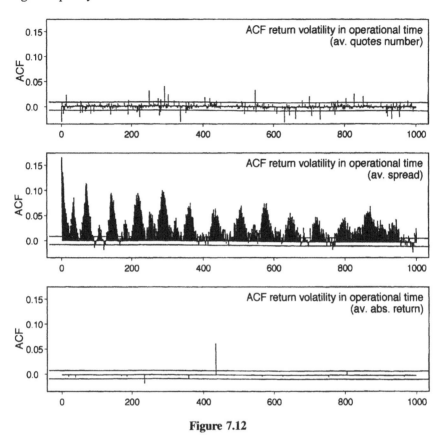

Figure 7.12

squared returns ACF in calendar time followed by the ACF computed from the Olsen and Associates time scale[11] (see Figures 7.11 and 7.12). We observe that all operational time ACFs corresponding to the Olsen and Associates and our specifications look very different. Those involving average spreads which were not reported in Table 7.5 show significant autocorrelations at weekly, biweekly, lags. In sharp contrast, the ACFs involving operational time scales with average quotes and particularly with absolute returns, indicate that the normalized squared returns are almost white noise series which do not show any long memory properties. Judging on the basis of these ACFs, it appears that the model involving absolute returns is probably the most appealing to estimate from the USD/DEM data.

5.2 The USD/JPY and DEM/JPY Foreign Exchange Markets
We now turn our attention to Tables 7.6 and 7.7, each covering empirical results from our market. Again, we present model specifications involving two different measures of average market activity, *nqa* and *ara*, combined with three measures of deviations introduced in the previous section.

There are several differences between the parameter estimates based on the USD/DEM sample and those reported on the USD/JPY and DEM/JPY markets. In Tables 7.6 and 7.7 we immediately notice positive as well as negative signs of Θ_{ij} and we also see that some coefficients became insignificant. Exceptionally, the parameter estimates of the USD/JPY model involving the nqa variable (Table 7.6 top panel) have similar signs as the coefficients of the analog specification estimated from the USD/DEM data. Consequently, both models yield a similar interpretation of the volatility behavior. The operational time slows down when the number of expected quotes increases and it accelerates while the current number of quotes, the current level of spread or returns exceeds the expected values. Thus, changes in the volatility appear to be driven by the extent to which the actual market activity deviates from the average level. The results presented in the bottom panel of Table 7.6 indicate that the surprise terms have the same effect in the specification involving the ara variable. A high level of expected returns, contrary to the average quote arrival, speeds up the operational time and the volatility adjustments.

The results based on the DEM/JPY sample are difficult to interpret. In section 2 we pointed out several distinct distributional properties of DEM/JPY quotes. Some particular seasonal patterns of the series have also been discussed in section 4. It appears that the only variable accelerating the operational time and, hence, changes in the volatility process, is the instantaneous excess return. The coefficients on the remaining variables are positive throughout both specifications, indicating an opposite effect. It may also be worth recalling from section 2 that the excess kurtosis statistics for the tick-by-tick data in comparison to the equally sampled data do not conform with a time deformation framework $X(\Delta g(t))$ where $\Delta g(t)$ is independent of X, on the DEM/JPY market. This fact may also help to explain the poor performance. In conclusion, the DEM/JPY market. This fact may also help to explain the poor performance. In conclusion, the DEM/JPY model yields results which are not plausible, and it seems appropriate to estimate volatility on this particular market within a different framework.

ACKNOWLEDGEMENT

The first author would like to acknowledge the financial support of CREST as well as the SSHRC of Canada and the Fonds FCAR of Québec.

ENDNOTES

1. The first data set distributed by Olsen and Associates, Zurich, and is described in detail by Dacorogna *et al.* (1993). The second is extracted from the CD-ROM data made public by the Paris Bourse while the third is distributed by ISSM (Institute for the Study of Security Markets, Memphis, Tenn.).

2. In Ghysels, Gouriéroux and Jasiak (1998) it is shown that for a time-deformed process $X(\Delta g(t))$ there is an increase in kurtosis due to time deformation when the mechanism $\Delta g(t)$ is independent of X. This would yield larger excess kurtosis for the 20-minute sampled series in comparison with the tick-by-tick series.

3. This phenomenon has been documented for series aggregated from daily to weekly or to monthly sampling frequencies (see Drost and Nijman 1993).

4. Examples of such evidence include Schwert (1990) who argues that returns on Monday are systematically lower than on any other day of the week, while French and Roll (1986), French, Schwert and Stambaugh (1987) and Nelson (1991) demonstrate that daily return volatility on the NYSE is higher following nontrading days.

5. Microfoundations for the time deformation and the process of price adjustments can be found most explicitly in Easly and O'Hara (1992).

6. The mapping $s = g(t)$ must satisfy certain regularity conditions which will be discussed later.

7. The fact that the denominator in equation (3) contains a sample average may suggest that $\sigma(g(t))$ is not measurable with respect to the filtration $\mathcal{F}_t$ in calendar time. However, the denominator in equation (3) is there for reasons of numerical stability of the algorithms. Since it is only a scaling factor, its presence is of no conceptual importance.

8. See Stock (1988) for a detailed discussion of the identification assumptions.

9. Strictly speaking, market participants, depending on their expectations, have an idea about the level of activity not the number of quotes per 5-minute intervals.

10. Since the averages nqa_t were computed on a weekly basis, there might be some slight differences from one day to the next over an entire week. Yet, judging on the basis of Figure 7.4, those differences appear minor.

11. We are grateful to Michel Dacorogna for providing us with the ACF. It should be noted that the sample used in Müller *et al.* (1993) and the one used here are not exactly the same. We ignore this aspect here.

REFERENCES

Bera, A.K. and Higgins, M.L. (1995), 'On ARCH Models: Properties, Estimation and Testing', in L. Exley, D.A.R. George, C.J. Roberts and S. Sawyer (eds), *Surveys in Econometrics*, Basil Blackwell, Oxford.

Bollerslev, T., Chou, Y.C. and Kroner, K. (1992), 'ARCH Modelling in Finance: A Selective Review of the Theory and Empirical Evidence', *Journal of Econometrics*, **52**, 201–224.

Bollerslev, T., Engle, R. and Nelson, D. (1994), 'ARCH Models', in R.F. Engle and D. McFadden (eds), *Handbook of Econometrics*, Vol. IV, North-Holland, Amsterdam.

Bollerslev, T. and Ghysels, E. (1996), 'On Periodic Autoregressive Conditional Heteroskedasticity', *Journal of Business and Economic Statistics* **14**, 139–152.

Bochner, S. (1960), *Harmonic Analysis and the Theory of Probability*, University of California Press, Berkeley.

Chesney, M. and Scott, L. (1989), 'Pricing European Currency Options: A Comparison of the Modified Black-Scholes Model and a Random Variance Model', *Journal of Financial Quantitative Analysis*, **24**, 267–284.

Clark, P.K. (1973), 'A Subordinated Stochastic Process Model with Finite Variance for Speculative Prices', *Econometrica*, **41**(1), 135–156.

Conley, T., Hansen, E., Luttmer, E. and Scheinkman, J. (1997), 'Estimating Subordinated Diffusions from Discrete Time Data', *Review of Financial Studies*, **10**, 525–577.

Cox, D.R. and Miller, H.D. (1965), *The Theory of Stochastic Processes*, Chapman and Hall, London.

Dacorogna, M.M., Müller, U.A., Nagler, R.J., Olsen, R.B. and Pictet, O.V. (1993), 'A Geographical Model for the Daily and Weekly Seasonal Volatility in the Foreign Exchange Market', *Journal of International Money and Finance*, **12**, 413–438.

Diebold, F.X. and Lopez, J.A. (1995), 'Modelling Volatility Dynamics', in K. Hoover (ed.), *Macroeconomics: Developments, Tensions and Prospects*, Kluwer, Boston, pp. 427–472.

Drost, F.C. and Nijman, T.E. (1993) 'Temporal Aggregation of GARCH Processes', *Econometrica*, **61**, 909–998.

Easley, D. and O'Hara, M. (1992), 'Time and the Process of Security Price Adjustment', *Journal of Finance*, **XLVII**(2), 577–605.

Engle, R.F. and Russell, J.R. (1995), 'Autoregressive Conditional Durations: A New Model for Irregularly Spaced Time Series Data', *Econometrica* (forthcoming).

Foster, D. and Viswanathan, S. (1993), 'The Effect of Public Information and Competition on Trading Volume and Price Volatility', *Review of Financial Studies*, **6**, 23–56.

French, K. and Roll, R. (1986), 'Stock Return Variances: The Arrival of Information and the Reaction of Traders', *Journal of Financial Economics*, **17**, 5–26.

French, K.R., Schwert, G.W. and Stambaugh, R.F. (1987), 'Expected Stock Returns and Volatility', *Journal of Financial Economics*, **19**, 3–29.

Gallant, A.R., Rossi, P.E. and Tauchen, G. (1992), 'Stock Prices and Volume', *Review of Financial Studies*, **5**, 199–242.

Geman, H. and Yor, M. (1993), 'Bessel Processes, Asian Options and Perpetuities', *Mathematical Finance*, **3**, 349–375.

Ghysels E., Gouriéroux, C. and Jasiak, J. (1995), 'Trading Patterns, Time Deformation and Stochastic Volatility in Foreign Exchange Markets', Discussion Paper, CIRANO, 95s–42. Montreal, Canada.

Ghysels, E., Gouriéroux, C. and Jasiak, J. (1998), 'Market Time and Asset Price Movements: Theory and Estimation', in D. Hand and S. Jacka (eds), *Statistics in Finance*, Edward Arnold, London.

Ghysels, E., Harvey, A. and Renault, E. (1996), 'Stochastic Volatility', in G.S. Maddala (ed.), *Handbook of Statistics*, Vol. 14 — *Statistical Methods in Finance*, North-Holland, Amsterdam, Ch. 5, pp. 119–191.

Ghysels, E. and Jasiak, J. (1994), 'Stochastic Volatility and Time Deformation: An application to Trading Volume and Leverage Effects', Working Paper, CRDE.

Goffe, W.L., Ferrier, G.D. and Rogers, J. (1994), 'Global Optimization of Statistical Functions with Simulated Annealing', *Journal of Econometrics*, **60**, 65–100.

Goodhart, C.A.E. and O'Hara, M. (1995), 'High Frequency Data in Financial Markets: Issues and Applications', *Journal of Empirical Finance* (forthcoming).

Gouriéroux, C., Jasiak, J. and Le Fol, G. (1996), 'Intra-Day Market Activity', Discussion Paper, CREST Paris, France.

Gouriéroux, C., Monfort, A. and Renault, E. (1993), 'Indirect Inference', *Journal of Applied Econometrics*, **8**, S85–S118.

Han, S., Kalay, A. and Rosenfeld, A. (1994), 'The Information Content of Non Trading', Discussion Paper, University of Utah.

Harris, L. (1987), 'Transaction Data Tests of the Mixture of Distributions Hypothesis', *Journal of Financial and Quantitative Analysis*, **88**, 127–141.

Harvey, C.R., Ruiz, E. and Shephard, N. (1994), 'Multivariate Stochastic Variance Models', *Review of Economic Studies*, **61**, 247–264.

Hausman, J. and Lo, A. (1990), 'A Continuous Time Discrete State Stochastic Process for Transactions Stock Prices: Theory and Empirical Evidence', Discussion Paper, MIT.

Hull, J. and White, A. (1987), 'The Pricing of Options on Assets with Stochastic Volatilities', *Journal of Finance*, **42**, 281–300.

Johnson, H. and Shanno, D. (1987), 'Option Pricing When the Variance is Changing', *Journal of Financial Quantitative Analysis*, **22**, 143–152.

Karpoff, J. (1987), 'The Relation between Price Changes and Trading Volume: A Survey', *Journal of Financial and Quantitative Analysis*, **22**, 109–126.

Lamoureux, C. and Lastrapes, W. (1993), 'Endogenous Trading Volume and Momentum in Stock Return Volatility', Working Paper, J.M. Ohlin School of Business, Washington University.

Lancaster, T. (1990), *The Econometric Analysis of Transaction Data*, Cambridge University Press.

Leblanc, B. (1994), 'Une Approche Unifiée pour une Forme Exacte du Prix d'une Option dans les Différents Modèles à Volatilité Stochastique', Discussion Paper, CREST Paris, France.

Madan, D.B. and Milne, F. (1991), 'Option Pricing with V.G. Martingale Components', *Mathematical Finance*, **1**, 39–55.

Madan, D.B. and Seneta, E. (1990), 'The V.G. Model for Share Market Returns', *Journal of Business*, **63**, 511–524.

Mandelbrot, B. and Taylor, H. (1967), 'On the Distribution of Stock Prices Differences', *Operations Research*, **15**, 1057–1062.

Müller, U.A., Dacorogna, M.M., Olsen, R.B., Pictet, O.V., Schwarz, M. and Morgenegg, C. (1990), 'Statistical Study of Foreign Exchange Rates. Empirical Evidence of a Price Change Scaling Law and Intraday Analysis', *Journal of Banking and Finance*, **14**, 1189–1208.

Müller, U.A., Dacorogna, M.M., Davé, R.D., Pictet, O.V., Olsen, R.B. and Ward, J.R. (1993), 'Fractals and Intrinsic Time — A Challenge to Econometricians', Discussion Paper, O & A, Zurich.

Nelson, D.B. (1991), 'Conditional Heteroscedasticity in Asset Returns: A New Approach', *Econometrica*, **59**, 347–370.

Scott, L.O. (1987), 'Option Pricing When the Variance Changes Randomly: Theory, Estimation and an Application', *Journal of Financial Quantitative Analysis*, **22**, 419–438.

Schwert, G.W. (1990), 'Indexes of U.S. Stock Prices from 1802 to 1987', *Journal of Business*, **63**, 399–426.

Stein, E.M. and Stein, J. (1991), 'Stock Price Distributions with Stochastic Volatility: An Analytic Approach', *Review of Financial Studies*, **4**, 727–752.

Stock, J.H. (1988), 'Estimating Continuous Time Processes Subject to Time Deformation', *Journal of the American Statistical Association*, **83**, 77–84.

Tauchen, G.E. and Pitts, M. (1983), 'The Price Variability Volume Relationship on Speculative Markets', *Econometrica*, **51**(2), 485–505.

Wood, R., McInish, T. and Ord, J.K. (1985), 'An Investigation of Transaction Data for NYSE Stocks', *Journal of Finance*, **40**, 723–739.

—————— 8 ——————

Modelling Short-term Volatility with GARCH and HARCH Models

MICHEL M. DACOROGNA, ULRICH A. MÜLLER, RICHARD B. OLSEN and OLIVIER V. PICTET

1 INTRODUCTION

One of the many challenges posed by the study of high frequency data in finance is to build models that can explain the empirical behavior of the data at any frequency from minutes to months at which they are measured. For instance, the well-documented clustering of volatility of financial assets. The most popular model among researchers in the field for this behavior is undoubtedly the GARCH (generalized autoregressive conditional heteroscedasticity) model (Bollerslev et al. 1992). This model was originally developed to study data measured at daily or lower frequencies (Engle 1982; Bollerslev 1986). The persistence of volatility has, on the one hand, also been seen with high frequency data, and, on the other, the aggregation properties of GARCH models have been theoretically derived by two groups (Nelson 1990; Drost and Nijman 1993). Yet the question remains whether the GARCH models are able to reproduce the heteroscedastic behavior under aggregation. Recent studies of this problem show the failure of simple GARCH models in this respect (Andersen and Bollerslev 1994; Guillaume et al. 1994; Ghose and Kroner 1995) even after a correct treatment of the intra-day seasonality of the volatility. The level of volatility clustering is relatively constant under aggregation. In other words, the volatility memory seems quite short-lived when measured with high frequency data while it seems

Nonlinear Modelling of High Frequency Financial Time Series.
Edited by Christian Dunis and Bin Zhou. © 1998 John Wiley Sons Ltd

long-lived when measured with daily or lower frequency data. We attribute this, along with other authors (Andersen and Bollerslev 1996), to the presence of many independent volatility components in the data. We identify these components as heterogeneous market agents following various investment strategies depending on their institutional constraints, geographical location and risk profile (Müller et al. 1993).

Moreover, in a recent paper (Müller et al. 1997), we have shown that there is asymmetry in the interaction between volatilities measured at different frequencies. A coarsely defined volatility predicts a fine volatility better than the other way around. This effect is not present in a simple GARCH model. All these reasons speak for the development of a new and more complex type of ARCH model that would be able to account for the heterogeneity found in high frequency data. We propose to use for this the HARCH (heterogeneous autoregression conditional heteroscedasticity) model. We presented a first formulation of this model together with its stationarity properties in two papers (Müller et al. 1997; Dacorogna et al. 1996a). Because of the long memory detected in high frequency data (Dacorogna et al. 1993), this initial formulation of HARCH requires numerous sums of returns measured at different frequencies going from 30 minutes to a few weeks. This makes the model optimization heavy and requires a lot of computational power when the model is evaluated on high frequency data. To overcome this dilemma, we propose here a reformulation of the model in terms of exponential moving averages, which both simplifies the numerical estimation of the model and preserves the stationarity condition derived for the original form of the process equation. This new formulation also preserves the idea of modelling the impacts of market components by defining 'partial' volatilities originating from each component. We compare the new and the old formulation of the process in terms of their optimization results (impacts and likelihoods) and show that they give rise to similar impacts for the same market component.

The real challenge for a model is its ability to forecast the future behavior of the modelled quantity. The difficulty in volatility models is a good definition of the quantity to which the forecast should be compared. We develop in this chapter a framework to test the forecasting accuracy of various models. This framework is used to analyze the performance of GARCH and HARCH models in predicting the hourly realized volatility out-of-sample.

In section 2, the new formulation of the HARCH process is presented and discussed. The estimation of the model parameters is explained in section 3, together with the results obtained for both formulations, over a sample of 10 years of 30-minute returns. Section 4 deals with the forecasting performance of volatility models both in establishing the framework and presenting the results for various models. The conclusions are drawn in section 5. In a technical appendix, we give some additional results for the estimation of HARCH models on four different foreign-exchange (FX) rates and the respective forecasting performance.

2 A NEW FORMULATION OF THE HARCH PROCESS EQUATION

The original formulation of the HARCH process has a variance equation based on price changes over intervals of *different sizes*. The returns $r(t)$ of a HARCH(n) process are defined with the help of the random variable $\varepsilon(t)$ which is i.i.d. and follows a distribution function with zero expectation and unit variance (in this chapter, we take a normal distribution).

$$r(t) = \sigma(t)\varepsilon(t)$$

$$\sigma^2(t) = c_0 + \sum_{j=1}^{n} c_j \left(\sum_{i=1}^{j} r(t - i\Delta t) \right)^2 \tag{1}$$

where

$$c_0 > 0, c_n > 0, c_j \geq 0 \quad \text{for} \quad j = 1 \ldots n - 1 \tag{2}$$

and Δt is the grid interval of the original time series. The returns are computed from the logarithmic price x as follows: $r(t) = x(t) - x(t - \Delta t)$ (Guillaume *et al.* 1997). The equation for the variance $\sigma^2(t)$ is a linear combination of the squares of *aggregated* returns. Aggregated price changes may extend over some long intervals from a time point in the distant past up to time $t - \Delta t$. The heterogeneous set of relevant interval sizes leads to the process name HARCH for 'heterogeneous interval, autoregressive, conditional heteroscedasticity'. The first 'H' may also stand for the heterogeneous market if we follow that hypothesis as proposed in Müller *et al.* (1993). The HARCH process belongs to the wider ARCH family, but differs from all other ARCH-type processes in the unique property of considering the volatilities of price changes measured over different interval sizes. The quadratic ARCH process (Sentana 1991) is an exception; although it was not developed for treating different interval sizes, it can be regarded as a generalized form of HARCH.

In Müller *et al.* (1997), the coefficients $c_1 \ldots c_n$ are not regarded as free parameters of the model. The heterogeneous market approach leads to a low number of free model parameters which determine a much higher number n of dependent coefficients modelling the long memory of volatility.

The new idea is to keep in the equation only a handful of representative interval sizes instead of keeping all of them, and replace the influence of the neighboring interval sizes by an exponential moving average (EMA) of the returns measured on each interval. This also has the advantage of including a memory of the past intervals. Let us now introduce the concept of *partial* volatility σ_j^2, which can be regarded as the contribution of the jth component to the total market volatility σ^2. Here the volatility σ_j^2 is defined as the volatility observed over an interval of size $k_j\Delta t$. We can reformulate the HARCH equation in terms of σ_j

as follows:

$$r(t) = \sigma(t)\varepsilon(t)$$

$$\sigma^2(t) = c_0 + \sum_{j=1}^{n} C_j \sigma_j^2(t) \tag{3}$$

where n is now the number of time components in the model. We choose here seven as in Müller *et al.* (1997). In the latter, we reported that adding an eighth component did not improve the likelihood and the coefficient for this component was not significant. Similar results were obtained with the new formulation. The notation is slightly changed to C_j instead of c_j in the old formulation to reflect the different meaning of the coefficients. Unlike the standard HARCH, but similar to the generalized HARCH introduced in Müller *et al.* (1997), the partial volatility σ_j^2 has a memory of the volatility of *past* intervals of size $k_j \Delta t$. The formal definition of σ_j^2 is

$$\sigma_j^2(t) = \mu_j \sigma_j^2(t - \Delta t) + (1 - \mu_j) \left(\sum_{i=1}^{k_j} r(t - i\Delta t) \right)^2 \tag{4}$$

where k_j is the aggregation factor of the returns and takes n possible values following the relation

$$k_j = p^{j-2} + 1 \quad \text{for} \quad j > 1 \quad \text{with} \quad k_1 \equiv 1 \tag{5}$$

The same value $p = 4$ as in Müller *et al.* (1997) is chosen here. Thus, k_j can only take the values 1, 2, 5, 17, 65, 257, 1025, ..., $4^{n-2} + 1$. Equation (4) is the iterative formula for an exponentially weighted moving average. The volatility memory is defined as a moving average of recent volatility. The depth of the volatility memory is determined by the constant μ_j:

$$\mu_j = \exp[-(\Delta t / M(k_j \Delta t))] \tag{6}$$

where the memory decay time constant of the component is given as the function M of the component's volatility interval $k_j \Delta t$. Instead of introducing new parameters for the characterization of $M(k_j \Delta t)$, it is simply chosen as

$$M(k_j \Delta j) = \frac{(k_{j+1} - k_j)\Delta t}{2} \tag{7}$$

The memory is defined by the start and the end point of the component interval k_j. In principle, a more complicated function M can be chosen with independent parameters.

It is easy to prove that a necessary stationarity condition for the new formulation is

$$\sum_{j=1}^{n} k_j C_j < 1 \qquad (8)$$

The proof relies on the fact that the expectation of the EMA is the same as the expectation of the underlying time series and that the expectation of cross terms is zero. A similar proof as in Dacorogna *et al.* (1996a) can be given for the sufficiency of this condition.

We can now define the impact I_j of each component:

$$I_j = k_j C_j \qquad (9)$$

There is no need for a summation here since each time component is represented by only one coefficient.

An iterative formula needs an initial value for σ_j^2 at the very beginning of the time series. A reasonable assumption of that initial value is the unconditional expectation of $\sigma_j^2(t)$, but the first value is computed here from a data sample prior to the first optimization point. We term this sample the 'buildup' sample.

3 OPTIMIZATION OF HARCH — DETERMINING MARKET COMPONENTS

We use time series homogeneous in ϑ-time (Dacorogna *et al.* 1993) to remove the seasonal pattern of intra-day volatility. In this section, the basic time interval is 30 minutes which means only some 7 minutes during the daily volatility peaks around 14:00 GMT, some 80 minutes during the Far Eastern lunch break, and even more during weekends and holidays with their very low volatility. Our optimization sample includes 10 years of data from 1 January 1987 to 31 December 1996. To obtain a reasonable starting value for the iterations of equation (4), some data before the first point in the optimization sample are used.

To achieve parsimony in the old HARCH formulation, we chose only seven market components. The choice was guided by the typical horizons of traders present in the market from intra-day market makers to long-term investors and central banks. We settled on seven components because the optimization did not show any significant improvement of the likelihood when adding an eighth. For the computation of the new HARCH, we optimize the model with seven components. This time, the component is built from only one time interval but includes, according to equation (4), a moving average that extends over a certain range which should account for the neighboring time intervals. In fact, we now have two parameters controlling the component definition: the time interval size over which price changes are computed, $k_j \Delta t$, and the range of the moving average, $M(k_j \Delta t)$. We fix both of them and let the optimization find the C_j parameters.

The optimization is done by searching for the maximum of the log-likelihood function. The method we follow to find this maximum is a two-step method — first a genetic algorithm (GA) search (Pictet *et al.* 1995) and then the use of the Berndt, Hall, Hall and Hausman (BHHH) algorithm (Berndt *et al.* 1974).

We initialize a first generation of potential solutions for the parameters and store them in 'genes' which will form an initial population. The log-likelihood of these solutions are evaluated and constitutes the 'fitness' of the genes. Starting from this population, the GA constructs a new population using its selection and reproduction method (Pictet *et al.* 1995). The best solutions found by the GA are then used as initial solutions for the BHHH algorithm. The BHHH algorithm is a variant of gradient descent which helps the convergence to the local maximum. Once convergence of the BHHH is achieved, the next generation of the GA is computed on the basis of the previous solutions obtained with the BHHH algorithm and the set of solutions of the previous generation. This iterative procedure continues until no improvement of the solution is found. The two-step procedure ensures that the optimization algorithm is not trapped in a local minimum.

The result of the optimization procedure is a set of C_j coefficients from which we can compute the component impact using equation (9). The sum of impacts I_j must be below 1 for stationarity of the process (equation (8)). In Table 8.1, the coefficients for both the HARCH and EMA–HARCH are shown with their t-statistics for USD-DEM. They are obtained on the exact same data set. The likelihoods (here log-likelihoods) can be compared since both models have the same number of independent coefficients (the values displayed in Table 8.1 are per observation). Clearly, the log-likelihood is improved by going to EMA–HARCH. In both cases, all coefficients are highly significant according to the t-statistics and contribute to the variance equation. The stationarity property is fulfilled in both cases. The HARCH has a sum of impacts of 0.8567 and the EMA–HARCH 0.9386. The impacts of the different components are remarkably similar. Two small differences are worth noticing: the relative importance of the long-term components is slightly higher for EMA–HARCH (37% instead of 35%) and the minimum for the fourth component is more pronounced in EMA–HARCH. The t-statistics are also consistently smaller for EMA–HARCH than for HARCH, but still highly significant in all cases. In the Appendix, we present similar tables for four other FX rates which show the same behavior: improved log-likelihood, slightly stronger long-term components, more pronounced minimum for the fourth component, stationarity condition fulfilled in all cases. The residuals in both formulations still present an excess kurtosis as was noticed in Müller *et al.* (1997) for HARCH.

These results show that we have achieved the goal of redesigning the HARCH process in terms of moving averages. We are able to keep and even improve on the properties of the original HARCH and to considerably reduce the computational time to optimize the model. The new formulation of the process equation reduces

Table 8.1 Comparison between the coefficients and impacts of the two HARCH processes, fitting a half-hourly USD–DEM series which is equally spaced in ϑ-time over 10 years. Instead of the coefficients C_i, the impacts I_i are given. These provide a direct measure of the impacts of the market components on the HARCH variance. The market components are those defined in Müller *et al.* (1997) for HARCH and as in equations (4) and (6) for EMA–HARCH. The distribution of the random variable $\varepsilon(t)$ is normal with zero mean and unit variance

USD–DEM	HARCH			EMA–HARCH		
coefficient	Estimate	Standard error	t-statistics	Estimate	Standard error	t-statistics
c_0	1.276×10^{-7}	0.03994×10^{-7}	31.94	0.529×10^{-7}	0.04399×10^{-7}	21.01
I_1	0.1309	0.007151	18.30	0.1476	0.008295	17.80
I_2	0.1930	0.010010	19.28	0.1875	0.012297	15.25
I_3	0.1618	0.009179	17.62	0.1829	0.012545	14.58
I_4	0.0703	0.007363	9.55	0.0507	0.010324	4.91
I_5	0.1003	0.006774	14.81	0.1434	0.010952	13.10
I_6	0.1014	0.006892	14.71	0.1120	0.011835	9.47
I_7	0.0990	0.006118	16.18	0.1145	0.010540	10.86
Log-likelihood	5.794741			5.801367		

this time by a factor of 1000, making the problem of computation of HARCH volatility much more tractable even with limited CPU power. In the next section, we will explore the forecasting ability of these models and compare it to a more traditional approach to volatility.

4 FORECASTING PERFORMANCE OF ARCH-TYPE MODELS

The true test of the veracity of a volatility model is its ability to forecast future movements. Since the seminal work of Meese and Rogoff in 1983, the forecasting quality of a model of financial data is known to be best measured out-of-sample. This means that the data used to test the model are distinct from the data used to find the model parameters. All the analyses described in this section are performed out-of-sample.

There is some added complexity in the case of volatility models: the definition of the quantity against which the model should be tested. There is no unique definition of volatility. We choose here a path similar to that proposed in Taylor and Xu (1997). We construct a time series of realized hourly $v_h(t)$ from our time series of returns as follows:

$$v_h(t) = \sum_{i=1}^{a_h} r^2(t - i\delta t) \tag{10}$$

where a_h is the aggregation factor and δt the time interval size. In this case, we use data every $\delta t = 10$ minutes in ϑ-time so the aggregation factor is $a_h = 6$. We do not need any factor in front of the summation if we assume Gaussian random walk aggregation properties for the variance.

We produce a forecast using different models that are compared to the realized volatility of equation (10). In order to simply test the one-step ahead forecast, we consider models based on *hourly returns*, $\Delta t = 1$ h in ϑ-time to treat the seasonality. The advantage of using hourly returns instead of 30-minute returns as in the previous section is that hourly forecasts are compatible with the historical hourly volatility defined in equation (10). Four models are studied here.

1. The first model, which is also used as a benchmark, is a naive historical model inspired by the effect described in Müller *et al.* (1997): low frequency volatility predicts high frequency volatility. We compute the historical volatility over 1 day measured from returns computed over 1 hour (lower frequency than the volatility we want to predict). This quantity, properly normalized, is used as a predictor for the next hour volatility, $v(t + \Delta t)$, as defined in equation (10). Formally the forecasting model v_b is

$$v_b(t) = \frac{1}{24} \sum_{j=1}^{24} \left(\sum_{i=6(j-1)+1}^{6j} r(t - i\delta t) \right)^2 \qquad (11)$$

where the factor in front of the summation here is to normalize v_b to hourly volatility.

2. GARCH(1,1):

$$v_{\text{GARCH}}(t) = h(t) = \alpha_0 + \alpha_1 \varepsilon^2(t - \Delta t) + \beta_1 h(t - \Delta t) \qquad (12)$$

where $\varepsilon(t)$ is i.i.d. and follows a normal distribution function with zero expectation and unit variance.

3. The old HARCH model following equation (1) and the seven components proposed in Müller *et al.* (1997).

4. The new EMA–HARCH model following equations (3) and (4) with seven components.

The three parameter-dependent models are optimized over a sample of 5 years of hourly data using the fitting procedure described in section 3. The forecast is then analyzed over the 5 remaining years. We term this procedure the static optimization. To account for possible changes in the model parameters, we also recompute them every year using a moving sample of 5 years. We term this procedure dynamic optimization. In this case, the performance is always tested outside of the gliding sample to ensure that the test is fully out-of-sample. In both studies, we use an out-of-sample period of 5 years of hourly data which represents more than 43 000 independent observations.

We compare the accuracy of the four forecasting models to the realized hourly volatility of equation (10). The quantities of interest are the forecasting signal

$$s_f = \tilde{v}_f(t) - v_h(t) \qquad (13)$$

where $\tilde{v}_f$ is any of the forecasting models, and the real signal

$$s_r = v_h(t + \Delta t) - v_h(t) \qquad (14)$$

The quantity $\tilde{v}_f(t)$ can be used as is or could be rescaled by the ratio of the averages $\langle v_h \rangle$ and $\langle \tilde{v}_f \rangle$ taken in the optimization sample. This makes the forecast values on average closer to the historical volatility and does not imply using any future information. In the rest of the chapter we call the quantity $\bar{v}_f(t).\langle v_h \rangle / \langle \bar{v}_f \rangle$ the rescaled forecast.

Formulated like this, performance measures proposed in Dacorogna *et al.* (1996b) can be applied because the quantities defined in equations (13) and (14) can take positive and negative values contrary to the volatilities which are positive definite quantities. One of these measures is the direction quality:

$$Q_d = \frac{\mathcal{N}(\{\tilde{v}_f | s_f \cdot s_r > 0\})}{\mathcal{N}(\{\tilde{v}_f | s_f \cdot s_r \neq 0\})} \qquad (15)$$

where $\mathcal{N}$ is a function that gives the number of elements of a particular set of variables. It should be noted that this definition does not test the cases where either the forecast is the same as the current volatility or when the volatility at time $t + \Delta t$ is the same as the current one. This occurrence is, of course, unlikely to occur in our particular case. A detailed statistical discussion of this measure can be found in Pesaran and Timmerman (1992).

In addition to this measure, we use a measure that combines the size of the movements and the direction quality. It is often called the *realized potential*:

$$Q_r = \frac{\sum \text{sign}(s_f \cdot s_r)|s_r|}{\sum |s_r|} \qquad (16)$$

In fact, the measures Q_r and Q_d are not independent and Q_r is a weighted average of sign $(s_f \cdot s_r)$ whereas $2Q_d - 1$ is the corresponding unweighted average. It is easy to show that if

$$Q_r > 2Q_d - 1 \qquad (17)$$

the forecast of the sign of s_r for large $|s_r|$ values is better than average.

A more traditional measure is also used: the comparison of the absolute error of a model to a benchmark model. This benchmark model is chosen to be the historical volatility as defined in equation (11), v_b. We compute the following quantity:

$$Q_f = 1 - \frac{\sum |s_r - s_f^{\text{ARCH}}|}{\sum |s_r - s_f^{\text{benchmark}}|} \qquad (18)$$

This particular form is chosen to have a quality measure that increases with increasing performance of the model. If $Q_f > 0$, the model outperforms the benchmark. If $Q_f < 0$, the benchmark outperforms the model. The subtracted part of equation (18) is similar to the known Theil's U-statistic (Makridakis *et al.* 1983) except that we use the absolute value instead of the squared errors.

The summations (including $\mathcal{N}$) in equations (15), (16) and (18) are over all hours in the out-of-sample period. The number of independent observations is so large that all the statistical results presented in this study are highly significant. We did not use performance measures based on squares such as the signal correlation or squared errors since we are testing a forecast for essentially squared returns and the fourth moment of the distribution of returns does not converge (Dacorogna *et al.* 1994).

In Table 8.2, the results for the different performance measures are presented for the most traded FX rate, USD–DEM, in the case of static and dynamic optimization. In parentheses, we also give the results for the scaled forecasts. For all measures, the three parameter-dependent models perform better than the benchmark and the new model, EMA–HARCH, performs best. The forecast accuracy is remarkable for all ARCH-type models. The significance of the values shown on Table 8.2 is very high since the number of independent observations is 43 230 which means that the 95% significance level for a Gaussian random walk for Q_d is less than 0.5%. The significance levels for the two other measures (Q_r and Q_f) are more difficult to compute, but the relative error, in Gaussian approximation, is $1/\sqrt{n}$ which, in our case, is about 5×10^{-3}. One of the advantages of working with high frequency data is to be able to achieve very high statistical significance.

In more than two-thirds of the cases, the forecast direction is correctly predicted and the mean absolute errors are smaller than the benchmark errors for all models. The realized potential measure shows that the forecast of volatility change is good not only for small $|s_r|$ but also for large ones. The condition expressed in equation (17) is always satisfied for all models. Neither the scaled forecast nor the dynamic optimization seem to significantly improve the

Table 8.2 Forecasting accuracy of various models in predicting short-term market volatility. The performance is measured every hour over 5 years which means 43 230 independent observations. In parentheses, the accuracy of rescaled forecasts is shown

USD–DEM	Q_d	Q_r	Q_f
Static optimization			
Benchmark	67.7% (67.6%)	54.2% (54.3%)	0.000
GARCH(1,1)	67.8% (67.3%)	58.5% (59.7%)	0.085 (0.072)
HARCH(7c)	69.2% (68.7%)	58.3% (59.2%)	0.134 (0.129)
EMA–HARCH(7c)	69.4% (68.8%)	60.7% (62.5%)	0.140 (0.128)
Dynamic optimization			
Benchmark	67.7% (67.4%)	54.2% (54.6%)	0.000
GARCH(1,1)	67.0% (66.0%)	59.5% (59.8%)	0.074 (0.057)
HARCH(7c)	67.7% (66.8%)	60.1% (60.8%)	0.113 (0.102)
EMA–HARCH(7c)	68.8% (67.7%)	62.4% (62.9%)	0.133 (0.117)

forecasting accuracy; the best results achieved so far are with the plain models. The realized potential Q_r is the only measure that consistently improves with dynamic optimization. Examining the model coefficients computed in moving samples shows that they oscillate around mean values. No structural changes in the coefficients were detected. The accuracy improvement in Q_r, together with the loss in Q_f in the case of dynamic optimization, shows that the prediction of large movements is improved at the cost of the prediction of direction of small real movements. From the point of view of forecasting short-term volatility, the EMA–HARCH is the best of the models considered in this study and compares favorably to HARCH. Similar conclusions can be drawn from the results shown in the table of Appendix B for four other FX rates. The cross rate JPY–DEM presents results slightly less good than the other currencies, but it should be noted that the early half of the sample has been synthetically computed from USD–DEM and USD–JPY. This may lead to noise in the computation of hourly volatility and affect the forecast quality.

5 CONCLUSION

By introducing partial volatilities, the HARCH formalism can be significantly improved both from the computational point of view and its ability to describe the real market volatility both in-sample (higher maximum likelihood) and out-of-sample (more accurate forecasts). The partial volatility can be interpreted straightforwardly as the contribution of one market component to the market volatility. The optimization results allow us to assess the relative impacts of all components which are very close to those published in Müller *et al.* (1997). Formulating σ_j^2 as a function of its past values introduces an element that was missing in the early formulation of HARCH and brings it slightly closer to a GARCH-type of model.

In general ARCH-type models are able to significantly predict the realized hourly short-term volatility out-of-sample with a limited optimization effort. Models including volatility measured at different temporal resolutions (as in HARCH and EMA–HARCH) outperform those that do not consider this effect. This is further evidence of market heterogeneity. It also emphasizes the need for high frequency data to properly analyze financial markets. The next research step will be to study how from the EMA–HARCH one can model volatilities measured at low temporal resolution such as daily or even monthly.

With EMA–HARCH, the use of volatility measured at different temporal resolutions becomes relatively cheap to implement as far as computational time is concerned. It can be a good starting point to extend the formalism for predicting daily or even longer-term volatilities which are needed for option-pricing, risk management and other portfolio management purposes. Another important use of HARCH models can be the study of market structures and possible changes in the influence of various market components over time.

ACKNOWLEDGEMENT

The authors would like to thank Paul Breslaw for a careful reading of the manuscript.

REFERENCES

Andersen, T.G. and Bollerslev, T. (1994), '*Intraday Seasonality and Volatility Persistence in Foreign Exchange and Equity Markets*', Kellogg Graduate School of Management, Northwestern University, Working Paper 186, 1–30.

Andersen, T.G. and Bollerslev, T. (1996), '*Heterogeneous Information Arrivals and Return Volatility Dynamics: Uncovering the Long-run in High Frequency Returns*', Kellogg Graduate School of Management, Northwestern University, Working Paper 216, 1–42.

Berndt, E., Hall, B., Hall, R. and Hausman, J. (1974), 'Estimation and Inference in Nonlinear Structural Models', *Annals of Economic and Social Measurement*, **3**, 653–665.

Bollerslev, T. (1986), 'Generalized Autoregressive Conditional Heteroskedasticity', *Journal of Econometrics*, **31**, 307–327.

Bollerslev, T., Chou, R.Y. and Kroner, K.F. (1992), 'ARCH Modeling in Finance', *Journal of Econometrics*, **52**, 5–59.

Dacorogna, M.M., Embrechts, P., Müller, U.A. and Samorodnitsky, G. (1996a), '*How Heavy are the Tails of a Stationary HARCH(k) Process?*', to be published in a book in memory of Stamatis Cambanis, edited by Yannis Karatzas, 1–31.

Dacorogna, M.M., Gauvreau, C.L., Müller, U.A., Olsen, R.B. and Pictet, O.V. (1996b), 'Changing Time Scale for Short-term Forecasting in Financial Markets', *Journal of Forecasting*, **15**(3), 203–227.

Dacorogna, M.M., Müller, U.A., Nagler, R.J., Olsen, R.B. and Pictet, O.V. (1993), 'A Geographical Model for the Daily and Weekly Seasonal Volatility in the FX Market', *Journal of International Money and Finance*, **12**(4), 413–438.

Dacorogna, M.M., Pictet, O.V., Müller, U.A. and de Vries, C.G. (1994), 'The Distribution of Extremal Foreign Exchange Rate Returns in Extremely Large Data Sets', Internal document UAM.1992-10-22, Olsen & Associates, Seefeldstrasse 233, 8008 Zurich, Switzerland.

Drost, F. and Nijman, T. (1993), 'Temporal Aggregation of GARCH Processes', *Econometrica*, **61**, 909–927.

Engle, R.F. (1982), 'Autoregressive Conditional Heteroskedasticity with Estimates of the Variance of U.K. Inflation', *Econometrica*, **50**, 987–1008.

Ghose, D. and Kroner, K.F. (1995), 'Temporal Aggregation of High Frequency Financial Data', *Proceedings of the HFDF-I Conference*, Zurich, Switzerland, 29–31 March 1995, **2**, 1–31.

Guillaume, D.M., Dacorogna, M.M., Davé, R.D., Müller, U.A., Olsen, R.B. and Pictet, O.V. (1997), 'From the Bird's Eye to the Microscope: A Survey of New Stylized Facts of the Intra-daily Foreign Exchange Markets', *Finance and Stochastics*, **1**, 95–129.

Guillaume, D.M., Pictet, O.V. and Dacorogna, M.M. (1994), 'On the Intra-day Performance of GARCH Processes', Internal document DMG.1994-07-30, Olsen & Associates, Seefeldstrasse 233, 8008 Zurich, Switzerland.

Makridakis, S., Wheelwright, S.C. and McGee, V.E. (1983), *Forecasting Methods and Applications*, 2nd edn, Wiley, New York.

Meese, R.A. and Rogoff, J. (1983), 'Empirical Exchange Rate Models of the Seventies, Do They Fit out of Sample?' *Journal of International Economics*, **14**, 3–24.

Müller, U.A., Dacorogna, M.M., Davé, R.D., Olsen, R.B., Pictet, O.V. and von Weizsäcker, J.E. (1997), 'Volatilities of Different Time Resolutions — Analyzing the Dynamics of Market Components', forthcoming in the *Journal of Empirical Finance*.

Müller, U.A., Dacorogna, M.M., Davé, R.D., Pictet, O.V., Olsen, R.B. and Ward, J.R. (1993), 'Fractals and Intrinsic Time — A Challenge to Econometricians', invited presentation at the XXXIXth International AEA Conference on Real Time Econometrics, 14–15 Oct. 1993 in Luxembourg, and the 4th International PASE Workshop, 22–26 Nov. 1993 in Ascona (Switzerland); also in B. Lüthje (ed.), *Erfolgreiche Zinsprognose*, Verband öffentlicher Banken, Bonn 1994, UAM.1993-08-16, Olsen & Associates, Seefeldstrasse 233, 8008 Zurich, Switzerland.

Nelson, D. (1990), 'Arch Models as Diffusion Approximations', *Journal of Econometrics*, **45**, 7–39.

Pesaran, M.H. and Timmerman, A. (1992), 'A Simple Nonparametric Test of Predictive Performance', *Journal of Business and Economic Statistics*, **10**(4), 461–465.

Pictet, O.V., Dacorogna, M.M., Chopard, B., Oussaidène, M., Schirru, R. and Tomassini, M. (1995), 'Using Genetic Algorithms for Robust Optimization in Financial Applications', *Neural Network World*, **5**(4), 573–587.

Sentana, E. (1991), 'Quadratic ARCH Models: A Potential Re-interpretation of ARCH Models', LSE Financial Markets Group Discussion Paper, **122**, 1–45.

Taylor, S.J. and Xu, X. (1997), 'The Incremental Volatility Information in One Million Foreign Exchange Quotations', forthcoming in the *Journal of Empirical Finance*.

APPENDIX A   TABLES OF COMPARATIVE OPTIMIZATION RESULTS

Table 8.3   Comparison between the coefficients and impacts of the two HARCH processes, fitting a half-hourly USD–JPY series which is equally spaced in ϑ-time over 10 years. Instead of the coefficients C_i, the impacts I_i are given. These provide a direct measure of the impacts of the market components on the HARCH variance. The market components are those defined in Müller *et al.* (1997) for HARCH and as in equations (4) and (6) for EMA–HARCH. The distribution of the random variable $\varepsilon(t)$ is normal with zero mean and unit variance

USD–JPY	HARCH			EMA–HARCH		
coefficient	Estimate	Standard error	t-statistics	Estimate	Standard error	t-statistics
c_0	1.291×10^{-7}	0.03706×10^{-7}	34.83	0.640×10^{-7}	0.3962×10^{-7}	16.17
I_1	0.1342	0.006346	21.14	0.1520	0.007589	20.03
I_2	0.1979	0.009112	21.72	0.1829	0.011498	15.90
I_3	0.1815	0.009688	18.73	0.2292	0.013041	17.57
I_4	0.0942	0.008671	10.86	0.0868	0.011622	7.47
I_5	0.1360	0.007412	18.35	0.1642	0.011366	14.45
I_6	0.0932	0.006845	13.62	0.1063	0.011687	9.10
I_7	0.0486	0.004448	10.93	0.0376	0.008709	4.31
Log-likelihood		5.824818			5.833673	

Table 8.4 Comparison between the coefficients and impacts of the two HARCH processes, fitting a half-hourly GBP–USD series which is equally spaced in ϑ-time over 10 years. Instead of the coefficients C_i, the impacts I_i are given. These provide a direct measure of the impacts of the market components on the HARCH variance. The market components are those defined in Müller et al. (1997) for HARCH and as in equations (4) and (6) for EMA–HARCH. The distribution of the random variable $\varepsilon(t)$ is normal with zero mean and unit variance

GBP–USD	HARCH			EMA–HARCH		
coefficient	Estimate	Standard error	t-statistics	Estimate	Standard error	t-statistics
c_0	1.489×10^{-7}	0.03430×10^{-7}	43.42	0.876×10^{-7}	0.03198×10^{-7}	27.38
I_1	0.1455	0.007284	19.98	0.1672	0.008498	19.67
I_2	0.1809	0.009423	19.19	0.1621	0.011263	14.39
I_3	0.1469	0.008744	16.80	0.1609	0.011251	14.30
I_4	0.0732	0.007307	10.02	0.0491	0.009415	5.22
I_5	0.1077	0.007099	15.18	0.1420	0.010769	13.18
I_6	0.0655	0.006114	10.71	0.0823	0.011088	7.42
I_7	0.0502	0.004026	12.46	0.0759	0.007694	9.87
Log-likelihood		5.856335			5.864520	

Table 8.5 Comparison between the coefficients and impacts of the two HARCH processes, fitting a half-hourly USD–CHF series which is equally spaced in ϑ-time over 10 years. Instead of the coefficients C_i, the impacts I_i are given. These provide a direct measure of the impacts of the market components on the HARCH variance. The market components are those defined in Müller et al. (1997) for HARCH and as in equations (4) and (6) for EMA–HARCH. The distribution of the random variable $\varepsilon(t)$ is normal with zero mean and unit variance

USD–CHF	HARCH			EMA–HARCH		
coefficient	Estimate	Standard error	t-statistics	Estimate	Standard error	t-statistics
c_0	2.156×10^{-7}	0.05376×10^{-7}	40.10	1.000×10^{-7}	0.06646×10^{-7}	15.05
I_1	0.1342	0.006670	20.13	0.1530	0.007736	19.78
I_2	0.1822	0.009068	20.09	0.1659	0.011189	14.83
I_3	0.1436	0.008065	17.81	0.1781	0.011465	15.53
I_4	0.0556	0.006661	8.35	0.0446	0.009663	4.62
I_5	0.0905	0.006312	14.34	0.1293	0.010249	12.61
I_6	0.0968	0.007037	13.75	0.1350	0.011312	11.93
I_7	0.0761	0.005717	13.30	0.0915	0.010395	8.79
Log-likelihood		5.662343			5.668801	

Table 8.6 Comparison between the coefficients and impacts of the two HARCH processes, fitting a half-hourly DEM–JPY series which is equally spaced in ϑ-time over 10 years. Instead of the coefficients C_i, the impacts I_i are given. These provide a direct measure of the impacts of the market components on the HARCH variance. The market components are those defined in Müller et al. (1997) for HARCH and as in equations (4) and (6) for EMA–HARCH. The distribution of the random variable $\varepsilon(t)$ is normal with zero mean and unit variance

DEM–JPY	HARCH			EMA–HARCH		
coefficient	Estimate	Standard error	t-statistics	Estimate	Standard error	t-statistics
c_0	1.110×10^{-7}	0.02466×10^{-7}	45.01	0.607×10^{-7}	0.02504×10^{-7}	24.23
I_1	0.1554	0.006465	24.04	0.1697	0.007544	22.49
I_2	0.1627	0.008697	18.67	0.1485	0.010434	14.24
I_3	0.1411	0.008057	17.52	0.1767	0.011027	16.03
I_4	0.0856	0.007121	12.02	0.0765	0.010345	7.40
I_5	0.0940	0.006382	14.73	0.1470	0.011048	13.30
I_6	0.0752	0.005814	12.85	0.1013	0.010310	9.82
I_7	0.0781	0.004442	17.60	0.0704	0.007451	9.44
Log-likelihood		5.958331			5.968624	

APPENDIX B   TABLES OF FORECASTING PERFORMANCE

We present here forecasting performance results for four other FX rates. They are computed on the same sample as the results in Table 8.2. Because of slight variations in the ϑ-time, the number of observations can also vary slightly. This number is reported in each table.

Table 8.7 Forecasting accuracy of various models in predicting short-term market volatility. The performance is measured every hour over 5 years which means 43040 independent observations. In parentheses, the accuracy of rescaled forecasts is shown

USD–JPY	Q_d	Q_r	Q_f
Static optimization			
Benchmark	67.9% (67.4%)	49.0% (50.5%)	0.000
GARCH(1,1)	68.6% (67.9%)	53.1% (54.3%)	0.065 (0.070)
HARCH(7c)	69.8% (69.5%)	53.8% (54.9%)	0.123 (0.139)
EMA–HARCH(7c)	70.2% (69.7%)	54.5% (55.8%)	0.140 (0.148)
Dynamic optimization			
Benchmark	67.9% (67.2%)	49.0% (50.9%)	0.000
GARCH(1,1)	68.6% (67.5%)	53.0% (54.8%)	0.070 (0.073)
HARCH(7c)	69.5% (68.4%)	56.1% (56.4%)	0.105 (0.115)
EMA–HARCH(7c)	69.9% (68.6%)	55.5% (57.1%)	0.126 (0.129)

Table 8.8 Forecasting accuracy of various models in predicting short-term market volatility. The performance is measured every hour over 5 years which means 43 215 independent observations. In parentheses, the accuracy of rescaled forecasts is shown

GBP–USD	Q_d	Q_r	Q_f
Static optimization			
Benchmark	67.7% (67.8%)	52.7% (52.4%)	0.000
GARCH(1,1)	66.8% (66.6%)	58.3% (58.5%)	0.090 (0.069)
HARCH(7c)	68.1% (68.1%)	59.0% (59.1%)	0.120 (0.105)
EMA–HARCH(7c)	69.4% (69.2%)	59.0% (59.4%)	0.134 (0.113)
Dynamic optimization			
Benchmark	67.7% (67.9%)	52.7% (52.4%)	0.000
GARCH(1,1)	67.4% (67.3%)	58.5% (58.7%)	0.089 (0.071)
HARCH(7c)	67.7% (68.0%)	58.9% (59.0%)	0.108 (0.099)
EMA–HARCH(7c)	68.8% (68.8%)	59.3% (59.5%)	0.125 (0.108)

Table 8.9 Forecasting accuracy of various models in predicting short-term market volatility. The performance is measured every hour over 5 years which means 43 261 independent observations. In parentheses, the accuracy of rescaled forecasts is shown

USD–CHF	Q_d	Q_r	Q_f
Static optimization			
Benchmark	67.7% (67.6%)	53.7% (54.1%)	0.000
GARCH(1,1)	68.9% (68.5%)	58.9% (59.5%)	0.099 (0.090)
HARCH(7c)	69.2% (68.6%)	55.9% (55.9%)	0.115 (0.112)
EMA–HARCH(7c)	69.3% (68.7%)	57.9% (58.3%)	0.117 (0.107)
Dynamic optimization			
Benchmark	67.7% (67.6%)	53.7% (54.3%)	0.000
GARCH(1,1)	68.3% (67.5%)	59.1% (59.5%)	0.088 (0.076)
HARCH(7c)	68.4% (67.8%)	57.1% (57.6%)	0.102 (0.097)
EMA–HARCH(7c)	68.9% (68.2%)	58.5% (59.1%)	0.112 (0.103)

Table 8.10 Forecasting accuracy of various models in predicting short-term market volatility. The performance is measured every hour over 5 years which means 43 292 independent observations. In parentheses, the accuracy of rescaled forecasts is shown

JPY–DEM	Q_d	Q_r	Q_f
Static optimization			
Benchmark	66.2% (64.2%)	58.4% (58.3%)	0.000
GARCH(1,1)	66.2% (63.4%)	60.0% (60.4%)	0.063 (0.061)
HARCH(7c)	65.3% (62.7%)	59.1% (56.8%)	0.072 (0.092)
EMA–HARCH(7c)	65.3% (62.3%)	61.6% (58.6%)	0.072 (0.075)
Dynamic optimization			
Benchmark	66.2% (65.7%)	58.4% (58.6%)	0.000
GARCH(1,1)	65.4% (64.5%)	59.8% (59.6%)	0.050 (0.045)
HARCH(7c)	64.2% (63.3%)	59.3% (58.8%)	0.044 (0.050)
EMA–HARCH(7c)	65.0% (63.9%)	62.1% (61.3%)	0.074 (0.064)

High Frequency Switching Regimes: A Continuous-time Threshold Process

ROBERTO DACCO' and STEVE SATCHELL

1 INTRODUCTION

In this chapter we investigate the modelling of high frequency exchange rates (FX) for the dollar/Deutschmark exchange rate. A great deal of research has been carried out on high frequency FX data. We refer to Müller et al. (1990), Goodhart and Figliuoli (1991), Goodhart et al. (1993), Bollerslev and Domowitz (1993), LeBaron (1994), Dacorogna et al. (1993) for a general discussion.

High frequency data arrive in irregular time intervals so that an analysis of such data cannot rely on standard econometric techniques which are based on fixed time interval analysis. The process under investigation evolves as transactions occur rather than as calendar time. This time deformation problem has been discussed by Clark (1973), Tauchen and Pitts (1983), Stock (1988), Müller et al. (1990), Ghysels et al. (1995) and Engle and Russel (1995).

Issues of temporal aggregation play a key feature in high frequency data analysis. For example, if we aggregate transactions data into some fixed short time interval, then there will be some intervals with no new information and conditional heteroscedasticity of a particular form will be introduced into the data. On the other hand, if a long interval is chosen, then some interesting features of the data will be lost. For currency markets, where there are clear periods of high and low activity as markets around the world open and close, the choice of a suitable interval is extremely difficult. More difficulties are present if the frequency of transactions is typically low, but may suddenly become very high.

Nonlinear Modelling of High Frequency Financial Time Series.
Edited by Christian Dunis and Bin Zhou. © 1998 John Wiley Sons Ltd

Different approaches have been proposed. Goodhart *et al.* (1993) relate such bursts with some observable news release, Engle and Russel (1995) link such events to an unobservable stochastic process, Stock (1988) applies a Kalman filter to estimate the parameters of a continuous time system subject to time deformation, Dacorogna *et al.* (1993) propose a heterogeneous market hypothesis where volatilities are measured over different interval sizes. Guillaume *et al.* (1994) propose a new time scale transformation to model the intra-daily deterministic seasonal patterns of the volatility caused by the geographical dispersion of market agents. This last approach leads to the modelling of instantaneous volatility instead of time average volatility.

Two themes recur in this chapter. Firstly, we propose an alternative to fixed interval analysis and secondly, we stress the link between the time deformation literature and switching regime models. As pointed out by Stock (1988), time deformation models have important similarities to autoregressive conditional heteroscedasticity (ARCH) models and to switching regression models, the similarity depending on the form chosen for the time scale transformation.

In what follows we shall suppose that irregularly observed data have been sampled from a continuous time threshold process. Continuous time threshold models were introduced by Tong and Yeung (1991) and by Brockwell, Hyndman and Grunwald (1991). Further developments are presented in Brockwell (1992), Brockwell (1994) and Hyndman (1994). We make some original contributions by analysing the steady-state properties of our model and developing new procedures to model observations which have changed regime between transactions. These procedures seem preferable to the procedures originally suggested by Tong and Yeung (1991), since they allow for more asymmetry in returns: the time spent in the two regimes is not equally allocated, for example, our model suggests that more time is spent in the negative return regime than for the linear interpolation method proposed by Tong and Yeung (1991).

The remainder of the chapter proceeds as follows. Section 2 reviews threshold modelling in the case where the observations are equally spaced. Section 3 presents the continuous time model and discusses the stationary distribution and boundary conditions. We then present empirical results in section 4, conclusions follow in section 5.

2 SETAR AND TAR MODELLING

Threshold models were introduced by Tong and Lin (1980) and are extensively discussed by Tong (1983, 1990). The basic idea may be explained as follows. We start with a linear model for a series x_t and then allow the parameters of the model to vary according to the values of a finite number of past values of an associated series z_t (TAR). In most applications the associated series coincides with the series under investigation, in such case we have a self-exiting threshold autoregressive model (SETAR). A time series x_t is a SETAR process if it satisfies the model

$$x_t = \alpha_0^i + \alpha_1^i x_{t-1} + \ldots + \alpha_d^i x_{t-d} + \ldots + \alpha_p^i x_{t-p} + \varepsilon_t^i \tag{1}$$

if

$$x_{t-d} \in R^i \quad i = 1, 2, \ldots k \quad \text{and} \quad \varepsilon_t^i \sim \text{i.i.d. } N(0, \sigma^i)$$

where R^i form a non-overlapping partition of the real line, k is the number of threshold regimes, d is the delay parameter or threshold lag and p is the autoregressive order. We can allow for more general rules as to which regime R^i the system attains.

2.1 Parameter Identification

We next discuss the identification of the SETAR model given by equation (1). For expositional purposes, we consider the case where $K = 2$ and the regime regions consist of $R_1 = x_{t-d} \leq r$ and $R_2 = x_{t-d} > r$. Then equation (1) becomes

$$x_t = \alpha_0^1 + \sum_{j=1}^{p} \alpha_j^1 x_{t-j} + \sigma^1 \varepsilon_t \quad \text{if } x_{t-d} \leq r \tag{2}$$

$$= \alpha_0^2 + \sum_{j=1}^{p} \alpha_j^2 x_{t-j} + \sigma^2 \varepsilon_t \quad \text{if } x_{t-d} > r \tag{3}$$

where $\varepsilon_t \sim$ i.i.d. $N(0, 1)$.

Tong (1983) proposed a grid-searching algorithm based on the use of the Akaike (1973) criterion. We fit n different models for n possible values of r and we choose the model, i.e. a particular value for r, with the minimum Akaike criterion. The algorithm proceeds in three different steps as follows. For the case of a single threshold model we have:

- *Step 1.* For given values of d and r, fit separate AR models to the appropriate subsets of the data. Let AIC(p_1), AIC(p_2), denote the Akaike criterion for the individual models where AIC(p_i) is defined as in the Akaike (1973) paper, and let $\hat{p}_1$, $\hat{p}_2$ denote these values which minimize AIC(p_1), AIC(p_2), respectively. Write

$$\text{AIC}(d, r) = \text{AIC}(\hat{p}_1) + \text{AIC}(\hat{p}_2)$$

- *Step 2.* Consider a set of n possible values for r. Repeat step 1 for $r = r_i$, $i = 1 \ldots n$, with d remaining fixed. Choose that value $\hat{r}$ for which AIC(d, r) attains its minimum value, and write

$$\text{AIC}(d) = \text{AIC}(d, \hat{r})$$

- *Step 3*. Now search for the best value of d over a range of possible values and repeat both steps 1 and 2 for $d = d_i, i = 1 \ldots q$. Select that value of d for which AIC(d) attains its minimum value.

Tong argues that in determining the final choice of model one need not adhere strictly to the values of the structural parameters selected by the Akaike criterion. Rather, the Akaike criterion is used as a guide to select a relatively small subclass of plausible models which may then be examined by an extensive set of diagnostic checks aimed at assessing whether a fitted model shares the main characteristics of the data.

2.2 Model Estimation, Testing and Forecasting

A SETAR model may be estimated by fitting each of the two components separately to the appropriate subset of the observations and using standard least squares exactly as in the case of the linear AR model. Tong (1990) showed that for an ergodic SETAR model the set of estimated coefficients has an asymptotic multivariate normal distribution. This result does not take into account the sampling properties of the estimate of the threshold parameter, but assumes that it is known a priori. In the case of Gaussian errors, the log-likelihood function is equivalent to the conditional sum of squares. We shall minimize the following expression:

$$L_N(\Theta) = \sum_{t=1}^{N} (x_t - E_\Theta(x_t | \Omega_{t-1}))^2 \tag{4}$$

Where Ω_{t-1} is the σ-algebra generated by $x_0, x_1, \ldots x_{t-1}$ and $E_\Theta(.|.)$ is the conditional expectation assuming that Θ is the true parameter vector. The estimation of the coefficients thus presents little difficulty. However, the evaluation of the results is a more difficult problem.

We can test the model against the null linear model. This test, however, does not have a standard null distribution. Two reasons are relevant. Let us consider equations (2) and (3); if we set $\sigma^1 = \sigma^2 = \sigma$ and define $I(r)$ as the indicator variable $I(r) = 0$ if $x_{t-d} \leq r$ and $I(r) = 1$ otherwise, we can write equations (2) and (3) as

$$x_t = \left(\alpha_0^1 + \sum_{j=1}^{p} \alpha_j^1 x_{t-j} \right) (1 - I(r)) + \left(\alpha_0^2 + \sum_{j=1}^{p} \alpha_j^2 x_{t-j} \right) (I(r)) + \sigma \varepsilon_t$$

Under the null hypothesis $\alpha_j^1 = \alpha_j^2, j = 0, 1 \ldots p$ the parameter r is not identified. This means that the large sample likelihood surface is flat, under the null, with respect to the threshold parameter. The asymptotic likelihood has no unique maximum and is not locally quadratic. Second, the score with respect to r is identically zero when evaluated at the null hypothesis. Either of the conditions is sufficient to render standard asymptotic theory inapplicable.

Chan and Tong (1990) and Chan (1990) addressed the null distribution of the likelihood ratio statistic for threshold autoregression with normally distributed noise. It is also shown that, in some specific cases, the asymptotic null distribution of the test statistic depends only on the degree of freedom and not on the exact null joint distribution of the time series. The authors develop an approximation for the test distribution using a chi-square random variable with three degrees of freedom in this special case. Chan (1991) extended this analysis, tabulating the approximate upper percentage points for the general case. The problem is that Chan and Tong (1990) and Chan (1990, 1991) consider a single regression with indicator functions given by the single index multiplying the lags of the time series. Thus, the residual variance is restricted to be constant across regimes. Alternatively, we could consider Hansen's (1992) testing approach, where the likelihood is viewed as an empirical process over different values of the nuisance parameters r; see for example Pesaran and Potter (1994), Potter (1995) and Hansen (1996). For our data set the computation time of such procedures is hopelessly costly, thus we shall not investigate these extensions in this chapter.

2.3 Time Deformation and TAR Modelling

As discussed in Stock (1988) there is a close link between time deformation models and switching models. Here we have a time deformation model that relates a latent process $\psi(s)$, evolving in operational time s, to the observable process y_t, evolving in observational time t. The process $\psi(s)$ is observed in calendar time t, which is related to the operational time scale by a continuous transformation $s = g(t)$. Thus when observed at discrete points in calendar time, y_t and the latent operational time process $\psi(s)$ are related by

$$y_t = \psi(g(t)) \tag{5}$$

Specification of the time deformation model consists of two parts: the choice of $g(t)$ and the specification of the latent process. Stock (1988) assumes that the n-dimensional $\psi(s)$ is Gaussian with increments having zero mean and diagonal covariance matrix. The increments of the time scale transformation are allowed to depend on a vector of variables z_{t-1} through an exponential parametric form, i.e.

$$\partial g(t)/\partial t = g'(\tau, z_{t-1}) = \exp(\beta z_{t-1})/T^{-1} \sum_{t=1}^{T} \exp(\beta z_{t-1})$$

Let us consider the special case where the increments of the time scale transformation $g'(\tau, z_{t-1})$ take on only two values, depending on whether in the previous fixed time period the number of transactions was above or below a given threshold r. Letting z_{t-1} be equal to the number of transactions between time $t - 2$ and $t - 1$, and y_t equal to the logarithmic return between time t and time $t - 1$, we have

$$y_t = a_1 + b_1 y_{t-1} + \sigma_1 \varepsilon_t \quad \text{if } z_{t-1} \leq r \tag{6}$$

$$= a_2 + b_2 y_{t-1} + \sigma_2 \varepsilon_t \quad \text{if } z_{t-1} > r \tag{7}$$

where $\varepsilon_t \sim$ i.i.d. $N(0, 1)$.

As discussed in the introduction, the results will depend on the chosen time interval. This model can be extended in several ways. For example, the switching criterion could be based on the number of transactions over several previous periods, and on the sign and size of previous returns. Alternatively, several regimes could be included rather than just two. We might also consider different regimes in overlapping subregions, instead of the usual disjoint ones.

3 CONTINUOUS TIME THRESHOLD AUTOREGRESSIVE MODEL

We propose to model returns by a continuous process, this is analogous to the modelling of the spot rate in the term structure literature. Given we have 6000 daily prices quotes we will interpret $X(t)$ as the instantaneous change in FX at time t. Between time t and s we calculate

$$X(t, s) = \frac{\ln(FX(t)) - \ln(FX(s))}{t - s} \quad s < t \tag{8}$$

where $FX(t)$ is the exchange rate at time t. In what follows we omit a representation using two subscripts to avoid excessive notation. We simply write

$$X(t) = \lim_{s \to t} \frac{\ln(FX(t)) - \ln(FX(s))}{t - s} \quad s < t \tag{9}$$

Before we present our continuous time models, we digress briefly to describe a model familiar to readers, the Ornstein–Uhlenbeck (OU) model. This is given by

$$d(X)(t) = (\alpha X(t) + \beta)\, dt + \sigma\, dW(t) \tag{10}$$

where $W(t)$ denotes standard Brownian motion (BM).

This model is equivalent to a continuous time AR(1) process. It can be solved by integration to find a solution. Multiplying both sides by $e^{-\alpha t}$ we have

$$d(e^{-\alpha t} X(t)) = \beta e^{-\alpha t} dt + \sigma e^{-\alpha t} dW(t)$$

Noting that

$$\int_0^t e^{-\alpha s} ds = \frac{e^{-\alpha t} - 1}{-\alpha}$$

$$X(t) = e^{\alpha t} X(0) + \beta e^{\alpha t} \frac{e^{-\alpha t} - 1}{-\alpha} + \sigma e^{\alpha t} \int_0^t e^{-\alpha s} dW(s) \tag{10a}$$

Finally, since

$$\text{Var}\left[e^{\alpha t}\int_0^t e^{-\alpha s}dW(s)\right] = e^{2\alpha t}\int_0^t e^{-2\alpha s}ds$$

$$= e^{2\alpha t}\left(\frac{e^{-2\alpha t}-1}{-2\alpha}\right)$$

$$= \frac{1-e^{2\alpha t}}{-2\alpha}$$

we end up with

$$X(t)|X(0) \sim N\left(e^{\alpha t}X(0) - \frac{\beta}{\alpha}(1-e^{\alpha t}), \sigma^2\frac{1-e^{2\alpha t}}{-2\alpha}\right) \tag{11}$$

This process is Gaussian, and, if $\alpha < 0$, has a stationary distribution which is

$$N\left(\frac{-\beta}{\alpha}, \frac{\sigma^2}{-2\alpha}\right),$$

in which case it is autocorrelated and, if it was observed at equi-spaced intervals, it would have an exact discrete-time representation as an AR(1) model. One could solve the above equation for $FX(t)$ and by integrating equation (10a) we have

$$\ln(FX(t))-\ln(FX(0)) = \frac{\left(\frac{\beta}{\alpha}+X(0)\right)[e^{\alpha t}-1]}{\alpha} - \left(\frac{\beta}{\alpha}\right)t + \sigma\int_0^t e^{\alpha s}\int_0^s e^{-\alpha v}dW(v)$$

The error term is an integral of a diffusion. It is known that such processes are inappropriate for prices, the no-arbitrage condition fails to hold; however, our prices are not prices of trades. Furthermore, our model can be seen, if we let the time interval, t, equal 1 so that we have equally spaced data, as a model with an AR(2) component with a unit root and a second root equal to $(e^\alpha - 1)/\alpha$. The error term is white noise over discrete intervals due to the independent non-overlapping increment property of BM.

3.1 CTAR(1)

The continuous time analogue to a SETAR model is described next. This is the first-order continuous time threshold process, denoted by CTAR(1), and is defined to be a stationary solution of the piecewise linear stochastic differential equation

$$dX(t) = \alpha(X(t))X(t)dt + \beta(X(t))dt + \sigma(X(t))dW(t) \tag{12}$$

where $W(t)$ denotes standard BM,

$$\alpha(x) = \alpha_i \qquad \beta(x) = \beta_i \quad \text{and}$$

$$\sigma(x) = \sigma_i \quad \text{for } r_1 < \ldots r_{i-1} < x < r_i < \ldots r_{K-1}$$

and the threshold values r_i are partitions of the real line. The above process is a process with drift coefficient

$$\mu(x) = \alpha(x)x + \beta(x) = \sum_{i=1}^{K}(\alpha_i x + \beta_i)I_{r_{i-1},r_i}(x)$$

and diffusion coefficient

$$\Sigma(x) = \sum_{i=1}^{K}\frac{\sigma_i^2(x)}{2}I_{r_{i-1},r_i}(x)$$

where I_{r_{i-1},r_i} is defined as the indicator variable $I_{r_{i-1},r_i} = 1$ if $r_{i-1} < x < r_i$ and $I(r) = 0$ otherwise.

The CTAR(1) process defined by equation (12) has a stationary distribution if and only if (see Brockwell, Hyndman and Grunwald 1991 for details of the proof)

$$\lim_{x\to\pm\infty}(\alpha(x)x^2 - 2\beta(x)x) > 0$$

and, the stationary distribution, if this condition is satisfied, has probability density

$$\pi(x) = \sum_{i=1}^{K} c_i \text{p.d.f.}_i(x)I_{r_{i-1},r_i}(x) \tag{13}$$

Table 9.1 CTAR estimates

	Coefficient	Standard deviation	
Model 1: Tong crossing time			
α_1	−12.531279	2.2866382	***
β_1	−0.0411252	0.0075340	***
σ_1^2	0.0004283	7.859E-05	***
α_2	−11.003708	1.4179584	***
β_2	0.0354101	0.0046273	***
σ_2^2	0.0006239	8.104E-05	***
−LL	−42899.2		
Model 2: Expected crossing time			
α_1	−18.810476	1.5142497	***
β_1	−0.0630600	0.0184103	***
σ_1^2	0.0006121	0.0001559	***
α_2	−19.369322	3.4904004	***
β_2	0.0644716	0.0120011	***
σ_2^2	0.0011030	0.0002010	***
−LL	−42815.9		

***Means significant at the 5% level. Parameters defined in equations (19) and (20).

where $i = 1, 2 \ldots K$ and

$$\text{p.d.f.}_{.i}(x) \sim N\left(\frac{-\beta_i}{\alpha_i}, \frac{\sigma_i^2}{-2\alpha_i}\right) / \text{prob}(x \in I_{r_{i-1}, r_i}(x))$$

as discussed after equation (11) and $\sum_i c_i = 1$, $c_i \geq 0$.

However, the process is not uniquely defined until the behaviour of the process at the thresholds is specified. The constants c_i are uniquely determined by the condition $\int \pi(x)\,dx = 1$ and by the boundary conditions at the thresholds $r_1 \ldots r_{K-1}$. Hyndman (1994) considers three possible boundary conditions each of which has some useful properties.

We list them below; we can impose $\pi(x)$ to be continuous at $x = r_i$, condition A, or we can alternatively consider $\sigma_i \pi(x)$, condition B, or $\sigma_i^2 \pi(x)$, condition C, to be continuous at $x = r_i$.

Brockwell, Hyndman and Grunwald (1991) consider boundary condition B, while Brockwell (1994) considered a CTAR process with boundary condition A. Clearly, if $\sigma(x)$ is continuous, there is no distinction between the three boundary conditions. In general, i.e. when $\sigma(x)$ is not continuous, CTAR(1) processes with identical parameters, but different boundary conditions, have quite different stationary distributions.

Following through the mathematics we see that if $\sigma_i^j \pi(x)$, $j = 0, 1, 2$ is continuous at $x = r$, then in the two-regime case given by equation (13), when $l = 2$, it must be the case that

$$1 = c_1 + c_2$$

We note that $\text{prob}(x \in I_{\infty, r}(x)) = \Phi_1$ and $\text{prob}(x \in I_{r, \infty}(x)) = 1 - \Phi_2$, where

$$\Phi_i = \Phi\left(\frac{r + \beta_i/\alpha_i}{\sigma_i/\sqrt{-2\alpha_i}}\right)$$

and Φ is the standard normal distribution function. Using conditions (A), (B) and (C)

$$\sigma_1^j c_1 \text{p.d.f.}_{.1}(r)(1 - \Phi_2) = \sigma_2^j c_2 \text{p.d.f.}_{.2}(r)\Phi_1$$

solving we see that

$$c_1 = \frac{\sigma_2^j \text{p.d.f.}_{.2}(r)\Phi_1}{\sigma_2^j \text{p.d.f.}_{.2}(r)\Phi_1 + \sigma_1^j \text{p.d.f.}_{.1}(r)(1 - \Phi_2)} \qquad (14)$$

$$c_2 = \frac{\sigma_1^j \text{p.d.f.}_{.1}(r)(1 - \Phi_2)}{\sigma_2^j \text{p.d.f.}_{.2}(r)\Phi_1 + \sigma_1^j \text{p.d.f.}_{.1}(r)(1 - \Phi_2)}$$

for $j = 0, 1, 2$ depending on conditions (A), (B) and (C).

This shows that the steady-state p.d.f. of the process is a mixture of two autoregressive processes, the weights c_1 and c_2 varying depending upon the boundary conditions used.

3.2 Moments and Correlation

We now turn to an investigation of the properties of the stationary stochastic process given by equation (14).

Lemma 1 *If $x \sim N(\mu, \sigma^2)$ are truncated at r, then the moment-generating function (m.g.f.) of the truncated variable x, such that $x < r$ is given by $M(s)$, where*

$$M(s) = \exp\left(s\mu + \frac{s^2\sigma^2}{2}\right) \Phi\left(\frac{r-\mu}{\sigma} - s\sigma\right) \bigg/ \Phi\left(\frac{r-\mu}{\sigma}\right) \qquad (15)$$

and

$$E(x|x < r) = \mu - \sigma\phi\left(\frac{r-\mu}{\sigma}\right) \bigg/ \Phi\left(\frac{r-\mu}{\sigma}\right)$$

$$V(x|x < r) = \sigma^2 \left(1 - \left(\frac{r-\mu}{\sigma}\frac{\phi(r-\mu)/\sigma}{\Phi(r-\mu)/\sigma}\right) - \left(\frac{\phi(r-\mu)/\sigma}{\Phi(r-\mu)/\sigma}\right)^2\right)$$

We see also that

$$E(x^2) = E(x^2|x < r)c_1 + E(x^2|x > r)c_2$$
$$= (V(x|x < r) + E^2(x|x < r))c_1 + (V(x|x > r) + E^2(x|x > r))c_2$$

and $V(x) = E(x^2) - E^2(x)$. Hence using Lemma 1 we can compute the steady-state first and second moments.

For the m.g.f. in Lemma 1 we denote this by $M_1(s)$, where μ and σ are replaced by μ_1 and σ_1. Now to compute $M_2(s)$, the m.g.f. of x given $x > r$, we note that for $\mu_1 = \mu_2$ and $\sigma_1 = \sigma_2$

$$M^*(s) = M_1(s)\Phi_1 + M_2(s)(1 - \Phi_2) \qquad (15a)$$

where

$$\Phi_1 = \Phi\left(\frac{r-\mu_1}{\sigma_1}\right) \quad \text{and} \quad \Phi_2 = \Phi\left(\frac{r-\mu_2}{\sigma_2}\right)$$

and

$$M^*(s) = \exp(\mu s + \tfrac{1}{2}\sigma^2 s^2)$$

so that, for μ_2 and σ_2,

$$M_2(s) = \exp\left(s\mu_2 + \frac{s^2\sigma_2^2}{2}\right)$$

$$\times \left(1 - \Phi\left(\frac{r-\mu_2}{\sigma_2} - s\sigma_2\right)\right) \bigg/ \left(1 - \Phi\left(\frac{r-\mu_2}{\sigma_2}\right)\right) \qquad (15b)$$

It follows from equations (15), (15a) and (15b) that $M(s)$, the m.g.f. of the steady-state distribution, can be written as

$$M(s) = c_1 M_1(s) + c_2 M_2(s)$$

Now

$$\mu^+ = E(x|x > r) = \mu_2 + \sigma_2\phi_2/(1 - \Phi_2)$$

$$\sigma^{2+} = V(x|x > r) = \sigma_2^2\left(1 + \left(\frac{r - \mu_2}{\sigma_2}\right)\frac{\phi_2}{1 - \Phi_2} - \left(\frac{\Phi_2}{1 - \Phi_2}\right)^2\right)$$

where

$$\phi_1 = \phi\left(\frac{r - \mu_1}{\sigma_1}\right) \quad \text{and} \quad \phi_2 = \phi\left(\frac{r - \mu_2}{\sigma_2}\right)$$

and μ^- and σ^{2-} are defined analogously. From the above, we can easily construct

$$E(x^2) = E(x^2|x > r)c_1 + E(x^2|x < r)c_2$$
$$= (\sigma^{2+} + \mu^{2+})c_1 + (\sigma^{2-} + \mu^{2-})c_2$$

We now ask the question, what is the correlation between $X(t)$ and $X(s)$ when the process follows the steady-state distribution?

In the normal (OU) single regime case given by equation (10), we can write

$$\text{cov}(X(t), X(s)) = \text{cov}(X(t) - X(s), X(s)) + \text{cov}(X(s), X(s))$$

$$= \text{cov}(X(s)(\exp(\alpha(t - s)) - 1) + y, X(s)) + \text{cov}(X(s), X(s))$$

where

$$y = \frac{\beta}{\alpha}(\exp(\alpha(t - s)) - 1) + \sigma \exp(\alpha(t - s))\int_s^t \exp(-\alpha v)\,dW(v)$$

and $\text{cov}(X(s), y) = 0$. It follows that

$$\text{cov}(X(t), X(s)) = \text{cov}(X(s), X(s))(\exp(\alpha(t - s)) - 1 + 1)$$
$$= \exp(\alpha(t - s))\,\text{cov}(X(s), X(s)) \qquad (16)$$

and

$$\text{corr}(X(t), X(s)) = \exp(\alpha(t - s))$$

which is always positive.

We now move on to consider the two-regime case. There we need to calculate, for $\Delta = t - s$,

$$\text{cov}(X(t) - X(s), X(s)) = E(X(s + \Delta)X(s)) - E(X(s + \Delta))E(X(s)) \qquad (17)$$

as previously discussed, the steady-state p.d.f. of the two-regime process is a mixture of two autoregressive processes, with weights c_1 and c_2 varying depending upon the boundary conditions in question. We have

$$E(X(s + \Delta)|X(s)) = X(s)(c_1\exp(\alpha_1\Delta) + c_2\exp(\alpha_2\Delta))$$

$$+ c_1\frac{\beta_1}{\alpha_1}(\exp(\alpha_1\Delta) - 1) + c_2\frac{\beta_2}{\alpha_2}(\exp(\alpha_2\Delta) - 1)$$

The above expectation has been taken conditional on $X(s)$ as in equation (11), but over the steady-state distribution. The result is not exact since what we are considering are only those sample paths that stay in their regimes from which they originate. We assume that the proportion of such paths is proportional to their steady-state probabilities. We ignore paths that cross the regions at least once over the time period Δ. Such an approximation may not be accurate, but an exact calculation seems remarkably difficult. Hence, using equation (17), we end up with

$$
\begin{aligned}
\operatorname{cov}(X(s + \Delta), X(s)) = {} & E(X^2(s))(c_1 \exp(\alpha_1 \Delta) + c_2 \exp(\alpha_2 \Delta)) \\
& + \left[c_1 \left(\frac{\beta_1}{\alpha_1} (\exp(\alpha_1 \Delta) - 1) \right) \right. \\
& \left. + c_2 \left(\frac{\beta_2}{\alpha_2} (\exp(\alpha_2 \Delta) - 1) \right) \right] E(X(s)) - E^2(X(s)) \quad (18)
\end{aligned}
$$

Note that if $c_1 = 1$ and $c_2 = 0$, then $E(X(s)) = -\beta/\alpha$ and equation (18) reduces to equation (16), where $\alpha = \alpha_1$ and $\beta = \beta_1$.

$$
\begin{aligned}
\operatorname{cov}(X(s + \Delta), X(s)) &= E(X^2(s)) \exp(\alpha_1 \Delta) - \frac{\beta_1}{\alpha_1} \left(\frac{\beta_1}{\alpha_1} (\exp(\alpha_1 \Delta) - 1) \right) - \frac{\beta_1^2}{\alpha_1^2} \\
&= \operatorname{cov}(X(s), X(s)) \exp(\alpha_1 \Delta)
\end{aligned}
$$

In general, substituting,

$$
E(X^2(s)) = \operatorname{Var}(X(s)) + E^2(X(s))
$$

and dividing by $\operatorname{Var}(X(s))$ we have

$$
\begin{aligned}
\operatorname{corr}(X(s + \Delta), X(s)) = {} & c_1 \exp(\alpha_1 \Delta) + c_2 \exp(\alpha_2 \Delta) \\
& + c_1 \left(\frac{\beta_1}{\alpha_1} (\exp(\alpha_1 \Delta) - 1) \right) \frac{E(X(s))}{\operatorname{Var}(X(s))} \\
& + c_2 \left(\frac{\beta_2}{\alpha_2} (\exp(\alpha_2 \Delta) - 1) \right) \frac{E(X(s))}{\operatorname{Var}(X(s))} \\
& + (c_1 \exp(\alpha_1 \Delta) + c_2 \exp(\alpha_2 \Delta) - 1) \frac{E^2(X(s))}{\operatorname{Var}(X(s))}
\end{aligned}
$$

We note in passing that one of the serious restrictions in using the OU process is that it will always have positive autocorrelation; Lo and Wang (1995) have proposed extensions of OU models to allow for arbitrary correlation. However, the continuous CTAR model is not so restricted and it is possible, using our approximation, to obtain more complex patterns of autocorrelation without requiring any extensions to our process; in particular, as we will show, we can explain negative correlation.

3.3 Behaviour between Observations

As a prelude to maximum likelihood methods we need to consider what the likelihood of our data might be. This requires thinking about how the process behaves between observations. All previous empirical work that we are aware of assumes that the process, if it moves across regimes between observations, moves only once; we shall also make this assumption. Three possible approaches are discussed. The first we consider is the first passage time of the process $X(t)$ to the point r. The second approach, used by Tong and Yeung (1991), approximates the time of crossing by a linear interpolation between the observation times. The third one considers the expected occupation time in the current state.

We shall investigate the following model:

$$dX(t) = (\alpha_1 X(t) + \beta_1)\,dt + \sigma_1 dW(t) \quad \text{if } X(t) \leq r \tag{19}$$

$$dX(t) = (\alpha_2 X(t) + \beta_2)\,dt + \sigma_2 dW(t) \quad \text{if } X(t) > r \tag{20}$$

The first passage time T of $X(t)$ to the point $r > x_0$ is defined by $X(0) = x_0$, $X(t) < r$ and $X(T) = r$. Cox and Miller (1965) have shown that the use of an absorbing barrier is a convenient means of studying passage times. We suppose, therefore, that there is an absorbing barrier at r and we let $p(x, x_0; t)$ be the probability density that $X(t) = x$ and that the process does not reach the barrier in the interval $(0,t)$. The function $p(x, x_0; t)$ satisfies the forward and backward equation for a general time homogeneous diffusion process. The backward equation is the appropriate one to use for the passage times since we want the passage time distribution as a function of the initial state x_0 for a fixed final state r. We proceed from the following equation where $\sigma(x_0)$ is the volatility and $\mu(x_0)$ is the mean term:

$$\frac{1}{2}\sigma(x_0)^2 \frac{\partial^2}{\partial x_0^2} p(x_0, x; t) + \mu(x_0)\frac{\partial}{\partial x_0} p(x_0, x; t) = \frac{\partial}{\partial t} p(x_0, x; t)$$

Let r be an absorbing barrier and let $T = T(r, x_0)$ be the time at which absorption at r occurs when $X(0) = x_0$, $(x_0 < r)$. Thus T is the first passage time out of the interval $(-\infty, r)$ for an unrestricted process starting at the point x_0 inside the interval. We now define $p(x_0, x; t)$ as the transition probability density of the process $X(t)$ restricted by the two absorbing barriers. Hence

$$1 - G(t) = \text{prob}(T > t) = \int_{-\infty}^{r} p(x_0, x; t)\,dx$$

where $G'(t) = g(t) = g(t|x_0)$ is the p.d.f. of T. As discussed in Cox and Miller (1965), we can show that the m.g.f.

$$\gamma(x_0) = g^*(s|x_0) = \int_0^{\infty} e^{-st} g(t|x_0)\,dt$$

satisfies the differential equation

$$\frac{1}{2}\sigma(x_0)^2\frac{d^2\gamma}{\partial x_0^2} + \mu(x_0)\frac{d\gamma}{dx_0} = s\gamma$$

for $x_0 < r$.

In the case of an OU process with volatility σ and drift $\alpha x + \beta$, the above equation becomes

$$\sigma^2\frac{d^2\gamma}{\partial x_0^2} - 2(\alpha x_0 + \beta)\frac{d\gamma}{dx_0} = 2s\gamma$$

Appropriate boundary conditions and a discussion on the general solutions can be found in Gardiner (1994). Closed-form solutions are generally not available unless we have special boundary conditions, see for example Daniels (1969) and Buonocore, Nobile and Ricciradi (1987). These techniques can be solved when there is a closed-form solution for a pure BM boundary case and we can transform the BM boundary to an OU boundary by a suitable time transformation. This is a promising avenue to explore; linear BM boundaries for which there are closed forms become parabolic OU boundaries. The economic meaning of a parabolic OU boundary in terms of market microstructure or agent behaviour or institutional structure seems difficult to rationalize, and we do not pursue this here.

We now discuss the second procedure of modelling between observations behaviour. Tong and Yeung (1991) make the assumption that if $x(t_i)$ and $x(t_{i+1})$ lie in the same regime, then there is no switching between the regimes during the period (t_i, t_{i+1}). But if $x(t_i)$ and $x(t_{i+1})$ lie in different regimes, then they assume that the integral path of $x(t_i)$ crosses the threshold once and only once over the time interval. The time of crossing t^* is approximated by a linear interpolation between the observation times as

$$t^* = \frac{\delta_i[r - x(t_i)]}{x(t_{i+1}) - x(t_i)} + t_i \tag{21}$$

where $\delta_i = t_{i+1} - t_i$. Unfortunately this procedure requires $x(t_{i+1})$ to be in our information set at time t_i which seems inappropriate for financial data.

To avoid these difficulties, we could instead consider a small noise solution to the problem. In this way the first passage time becomes a nonlinear deterministic function of parameters. Let us consider the case where we are in the first regime, i.e. $X(0) \leq r$, then the time t^* needed to switch from regime 1 to regime 2 is, considering equation (12) and setting $\sigma = 0$ and solving for t^*,

$$t^* = \frac{1}{\alpha_1}\log\left(\frac{r + \beta_1/\alpha_1}{X(0) + \beta_1/\alpha_1}\right) \tag{22}$$

If $X(0) = r, t^* = 0$, i.e. the time needed to switch is zero when we are on the threshold. Note that if $t^* > \delta_i$, we need to make some assumptions. We assume that $t^* = \delta_i$. In general we should impose some restrictions on the parameters α and β such that $(r + \beta/\alpha)/(X(0) + \beta/\alpha)$ be always greater than one. Such conditions can be considered a generalization to those imposed by a simple random walk, namely that when there is a drift towards the barrier the probability of ultimate absorption is unity, while when the drift is away from the barrier there is a non-zero probability of never reaching the barrier.

We now discuss a third procedure which is the procedure we shall adopt. We can derive the expected occupation time as discussed in Karlin and Taylor (1981, p. 252). For any given subset A, in our case $(-\infty, r]$ and (r, ∞), contained in the state space $(-\infty, \infty)$ let

$$I_A(X_t) = 1 \quad \text{for } X_t \in A$$
$$= 0 \quad \text{otherwise}$$

be the indicator function of the set A. The random variable, occupation time, $L_A(t)$, of the set A up to time t is defined by

$$L_A(t) = \int_0^t I_A(X(\tau))\, d\tau$$

We can calculate its successive moments. Specifically, for an initial state $X(0)$, we have

$$\Pr(X(\tau) \in A \mid X(0)) = \int_A p(\tau, x)\, dx$$

Where $p(\tau, x)$ is the transition density of the process. Then we obtain

$$E_x[L_A(t)] = E_x\left[\int_0^t I_A(X(\tau))\, d\tau\right]$$

$$= \int_0^t E_x[I_A(X(\tau))]\, d\tau$$

$$= \int_0^t \left[\int_A p(\tau, x)\, dx\right] d\tau \qquad (23)$$

In our case we have for $p(\tau, x)$,

    p.d.f. $(X(\tau)|X(0))$

$$\sim N\left(\exp(\alpha\tau)X(\tau) + \frac{\beta}{\alpha}(\exp(\alpha\tau) - 1),\ \sigma^2\left(\frac{\exp(2\alpha\tau) - 1}{2\alpha}\right)\right) \qquad (24)$$

where we have suppressed the subscript j. In general we should have $\alpha_j, \beta_j, \sigma_j$ for $j = 1, 2$ if $X(0) \le r$ or $X(0) > r$ respectively. Finally if $A = (-\infty, r)$ and we denote, as before, with Φ the c.d.f. of a standard normal p.d.f., we have

$$\Pr(X(\tau) \in A|X(0)) = \int_A p(\tau, x)\, dx$$

$$= \Phi\left(\frac{r - \exp(\alpha\tau)X(0) - (\beta/\alpha)(\exp(\alpha\tau) - 1)}{\sigma\sqrt{((\exp(2\alpha\tau) - 1)/(2\alpha))}}\right)$$

and

$$t^* = E_x[L_A(t)] = \int_o^t [\Phi(\cdot)]d\tau \tag{25}$$

Similar results follow for the second regime, i.e when $B = (r, \infty)$, where we end up with

$$t^{**} = E_x[L_B(t)] = \int_0^t [1 - \Phi(\cdot)]d\tau \tag{26}$$

where $t^* + t^{**} = t$. We assume that the value t^* is our solution for the unique switch time, which will be correct on average.

3.4 Maximum Likelihood Estimation

In this section we take as given any of the switching-time rules discussed in section 3.3; our results will hold for an arbitrary switching-time rule.

Our aim is to maximize the likelihood of the data given by equations (19) and (20). In general we have four different cases. Two adjacent observations can either lie in regime 1, lie in regime 2, or the t_ith observation is in regime 1 and the t_{i+1}th observation is in regime 2 and vice versa. In each of the four cases, the solution of $dX(t)$ over a finite time step δ_i can be written as

$$X(t_{i+1}) = \beta_j + \alpha_j X(t_i) + \sigma(t_i) \quad \text{for } j - 1, 2, 3, 4 \quad \text{and} \quad i = 1, 2, \ldots n \tag{27}$$

where n is the number of observations. Defining $\mu_j = \beta_j + \alpha_j X(t_i)$, we have for cases 1 and 2

$$\mu_j(\delta_i) = \exp(\alpha_j \delta_i) X(t_i) + \frac{\beta_j}{\alpha_j}(\exp(\alpha_j \delta_i) - 1) \tag{28}$$

$$\Psi_j(\delta_i) = \int_0^{\delta_i} \exp(\alpha_j(\delta_i - t))\sigma_j w(t) \, dt \tag{29}$$

where $j = 1, 2$ and $w(t)$ is the random input at time t. For the third and fourth cases we define $\delta_{1i} = t^* - t_i$ and $\delta_{2i} = t_{i+1} - t^*$, where t^* is given by equation (21) or (25). We have for case 3

$$\mu(\delta_i) = \exp(\alpha_i \delta_{1i}) X(t_i) + \left(\frac{\beta_1}{\alpha_1}\right)(\exp(\alpha_1 \delta_{1i}) - 1)$$
$$+ \exp(\alpha_2 \delta_{2i}) X(t_i) + \left(\frac{\beta_2}{\alpha_2}\right)(\exp(\alpha_2 \delta_{2i}) - 1) \tag{30}$$

$$\Psi(\delta_i) = \exp(\alpha_2 \delta_{2i}) \int_0^{\delta_{1i}} \exp(\alpha_1(\delta_{1i} - t))\sigma_1 w(t) \, dt$$
$$+ \int_0^{\delta_{2i}} \exp(\alpha_2(\delta_{2i} - t))\sigma_2 w(t) \, dt \tag{31}$$

and for case 4

$$\mu(\delta_i) = \exp(\alpha_2\delta_{1i})X(t_i) + \left(\frac{\beta_2}{\alpha_2}\right)(\exp(\alpha_2\delta_{1i}) - 1)$$

$$+ \exp(\alpha_1\delta_{2i})X(t_i) + \left(\frac{\beta_1}{\alpha_1}\right)(\exp(\alpha_1\delta_{2i}) - 1) \qquad (32)$$

$$\Psi(\delta_i) = \exp(\alpha_1\delta_{2i})\int_0^{\delta_{1i}} \exp(\alpha_2(\delta_{1i} - t))\sigma_2 w(t)\,dt$$

$$+ \int_0^{\delta_{2i}} \exp(\alpha_1(\delta_{2i} - t))\sigma_1 w(t)\,dt \qquad (33)$$

Cases 1 and 2 are obvious; for cases 3 and 4 we note that the process is in the first regime for δ_{1i} and consequently this contributes to $\mu(\delta_i)$ and $\Psi(\delta_i)$, the second terms follow from the time in the other regime δ_{2i}. From these we can derive the likelihood and find the maximum likelihood estimates of the parameters. Defining $\Sigma(\delta_i) = E(\Psi^2(\delta_i))$ our likelihood can be written as

$$L_N(\theta) = \prod_{x \in R_i} N(\mu(\delta_i), \Sigma(\delta_i)) \quad \text{if } i = 1, 2, 3, 4$$

where $x \in R_1$ means that $x(t_i)$ and $x(t_{i+1})$ lie in regime 1 and as before the other three cases, and where the variance term in the normal distribution is taken for the $\Sigma(\cdot)$ processes described in the appropriate equation given by equation (29), (31) or (33).

As for the discrete time case, the likelihood is not differentiable in the threshold parameter value r. Tong and Yeung (1991) adopt an identification procedure similar to that for the discrete time case. We could grid search over a preselected set of threshold values and choose $\hat{r}$ which gives the minimum normalized Akaike criterion (NAIC). In what follows we shall consider only the $r = 0$ case, while for the switching time between observations we shall look at the method proposed by Tong and Yeung (1991) and at the expected waiting method we proposed in section 3.3.

4 RESULTS

4.1 A Brief Survey of the Markets and the Empirical Literature

A number of recent papers have explored the behaviour of the FX markets using tick-by-tick data. Before discussing our results, in the next section we shall briefly present some well-known issues of the data under investigation.

It is well known that there are three basic patterns of activity across the three main regional areas. Market activity in the Far East is bimodally distributed around the lunch hour, i.e. the decrease in lunchtime activity is marked in these centres. European markets also show a bimodal distribution, but the falls are less marked and more gradual. Activity picks up near the open and the close of the market, with moderate trading in between. New York has instead a unimodal distribution of activity, peaking at the lunch hour, which roughly coincides with closing time in London and Frankfurt.

Most authors focus on the second conditional moment of the logarithmic returns and many special factors come into play. For example, we can allow for intra-day seasonalities, i.e. Andersen and Bollerslev (1995), deal with heterogeneous market participants, i.e. Müller *et al.* (1990) or incorporate news announcement effects as in Goodhart *et al.* (1993).

Less attention has been addressed to the conditional mean. Here Goodhart (1990) and Goodhart and Figliuoli (1991) first reported the existence of negative first-order autocorrelation of the price changes at the highest frequencies. They also showed that this negative autocorrelation is not affected by the presence of major news announcements nor caused by bouncing prices between different geographical areas with different information sets. The bid–ask bounce cannot be blamed for such an effect, see Roll (1984) and Bollerslev and Domowitz (1993) who reported significant negative autocorrelation for the bid and ask price changes. A possible explanation of this fact put forward by Guillaume *et al.* (1994) is that traders have diverging opinions about the impact of news on the direction of prices. Zhou (1996), instead, attributed the negative autocorrelation to the high level of noise in the price series. The implied return thus contains a moving average component with a coefficient of -1, which leads to a negative autocorrelation which would be -0.5 if the process were stationary.

4.2 CTAR Results

We shall consider 5 July as estimation sample. Between time t and s we calculate

$$X(t, s) = \frac{\ln(FX(t)) - \ln(FX(s))}{t - s} \qquad s < t$$

where $FX(t)$ is the logarithmic average of bid and ask price at time t.

We are not considering the zero returns observations. We end up with 4881 observations. We have fixed the threshold to be equal to zero. Hence the first regime contains observations with negative returns, while in the second past returns were positive. In most of the observations, i.e. 3364 over 4881, we switch from regime 1 to regime 2 or vice versa. We remain in the first regime and second regime 718 and 799 times, respectively. That means that for more than one-third of the observations we have positive autocorrelation.

The time between two consecutive ticks is measured in seconds. The minimum time is 1 second, while the maximum is 335 seconds, recorded early in the morning.

We compare the results obtained using the crossing time suggested by Tong and Yeung (1991), equation (21), and using the expected occupation time as described in equation (25). We should stress that the two models are not properly nested since Tong's version incorporates the return at time $t+1$ in the information set at time t.

The two models describe very similar processes (see Table 9.4), and we note scale differences in the estimated parameters. Considering the forecast mean and variance in the four different regimes, the model that uses the linear interpolation as crossing time does a better job forecasting the variance. Both models perform badly with the mean. In particular, see Table 9.2, the expected crossing time model is not able to forecast positive returns in regime 3, i.e. when we switch from negative to positive returns. As an explanation, we should look at the time spent in each regime for the two models. The time spent in the negative regime differs significantly. Over a mean of roughly 11 seconds, the linear interpolation assigns half the time in the positive and half in the negative regime, see Table 9.2. However, the expected occupation time suggests that most of the time is spent in the negative regime, i.e. 9 seconds.

This suggests the possibility of asymmetric behaviour. The log ratio test, $2(\log L_{\text{unrestricted}} - \log L_{\text{restricted}})$, follows asymptotically under the symmetric hypothesis a chi-squared variable with three degrees of freedom, the 95% critical value is 7.81. We reject the null hypothesis for both models, LR $= 752$ and LR $= 713$, respectively. This suggests a statistically significant asymmetry in the upside downside process. This is a new stylized fact that cannot be explained by the leverage effect, but it could be caused by some microstructure effects related to the pivotal role of the US dollar.

Another issue is to see how the two models can replicate the observed moments. In Table 9.3 we report the moments and in particular the correlation for the raw data and for the steady state of the two models considered. The parameters c_1 and c_2 are not free parameters, but depend on the boundary conditions and on the other parameters of the models. Unless we impose some economic interpretation for the boundary conditions, the parameters c_1 and c_2

Table 9.2 CTAR mean and variances

	Tong	Expected time	Raw data
μ_1	−0.0032819	−0.0033517	−0.0004845
μ_2	0.0032173	0.0033278	0.0005569
μ_3	−0.0001314	−3.016E-05	0.0016243
μ_4	4.374E-05	−1.671E-05	−0.0017280
Σ_1	0.004338	0.0042377	0.0021478
Σ_2	0.005528	0.0055400	0.0028363
Σ_3	0.006583	0.0095727	0.0045689
Σ_4	0.006594	0.0095728	0.0048855
t_-	5.8438430	8.978525	
t_+	5.9387009	2.761282	

The four states are defined in equation (27); μ is the expected mean, Σ the expected volatility, t_- is the time in the negative regime and t_+ is the time in the positive regime.

Table 9.3 Moments and correlation

		Sample moments		
	$E(X(s))$	$E(X(s)^2)$	$V(X(s))$	$CORR(X(t), X(s))$
	$-3.133448e{-}05$	$6.355975e{-}05$	$6.357179e{-}05$	-0.2895478

Tong's model: estimated moments for different values of c_1

c_1	$E(X(s))$	$E(X(s)^2)$	$V(X(s))$	$CORR(X(t), X(s))$
0.10	0.0046051240	3.5319064e-05	1.4111897e-05	-0.66476404
0.20	0.0035586728	2.6288898e-05	1.3624746e-05	-0.42854145
0.30	0.0025122217	1.9448853e-05	1.3137595e-05	-0.23794465
0.40	0.0014657705	1.4798928e-05	1.2650445e-05	-0.09824524
0.50	0.0004193193	1.2339123e-05	1.2163294e-05	-0.01555940
0.60	-0.0006271318	1.2069438e-05	1.1676144e-05	0.002097599
0.70	-0.0016735830	1.3989873e-05	1.1188993e-05	-0.05101882
0.80	-0.0010734776	1.2620712e-05	1.1468358e-05	-0.01064646
0.90	-0.0001302435	1.1924422e-05	1.1907458e-05	0.00267240

Expected occupation model: estimated moments for different values of c_1

c_1	$E(X(s))$	$E(X(s)^2)$	$V(X(s))$	$CORR(X(t), X(s))$
0.10	0.0046554289	3.5913034e-05	1.4240016e-05	-0.65221212
0.20	0.0036034060	2.6708911e-05	1.3724376e-05	-0.42299090
0.30	0.0025513830	1.9718293e-05	1.3208737e-05	-0.23703005
0.40	0.0014993601	1.4941179e-05	1.2693098e-05	-0.09960172
0.50	0.0004473371	1.2377569e-05	1.2177459e-05	-0.01687107
0.60	-0.0006046857	1.2027464e-05	1.1661819e-05	0.00390634
0.70	-0.0016567087	1.3890864e-05	1.1146180e-05	-0.04586759
0.80	-0.0021827201	1.5652628e-05	1.0888361e-05	-0.10034361
0.90	-0.0008473510	1.2260883e-05	1.1542879e-05	-0.00097064

Parameters are defined in section 3.2.

are not identified. We report the results for a different range of c_1 and c_2. We can match both the first and second moments and the negative autocorrelation present in the data.

Finally we estimated the model without rescaling the returns by the time interval. The results are very similar and thus are not reported. We note two differences. Firstly, as expected, the mean and variance of the unscaled process in the two regimes are higher in absolute value, i.e. the parameters α and σ, secondly, the process seems to be less asymmetric: we reject the symmetric

Table 9.4 $\dfrac{-\beta}{\alpha}$, $\dfrac{\sigma}{\sqrt{-2\alpha}}$, ϕ and Φ

Model	$\dfrac{-\beta_1}{\alpha_1}$	$\dfrac{-\beta_2}{\alpha_2}$	$\dfrac{\sigma_1}{\sqrt{-2\alpha_1}}$	$\dfrac{\sigma_2}{\sqrt{-2\alpha_2}}$	Φ_1	ϕ_1	Φ_2	ϕ_2
Tong	-0.0032	0.0032	0.0041	0.0053	0.7863	0.2910	0.2728	0.3323
Expected time	-0.0033	0.0033	0.0040	0.0053	0.7970	0.2824	0.2663	0.3284

Parameters defined in section 3.2.

hypothesis only for the expected occupation model, this is because some large falls occur over long intervals.

5 CONCLUSIONS

High frequency FX data arrive in irregular time intervals so that an analysis of such data cannot rely on standard econometric techniques which are based on fixed interval analysis. The choice of a suitable interval is extremely difficult. There are clear periods of low and high market activity as markets around the world open and close. Sometimes the frequency of transactions is low and suddenly becomes very high.

We have USD–DM tick-by-tick quotes. From these we derive the return series that is a marked process of the original one. Zero returns are excluded from the analysis. The sample under investigation contains 4881 quotes for 5 July 1995.

Thus 5-minute analysis is easier, but we lose information on market activity. We model irregularly observed data as being sampled from a continuous time process. The family of continuous time processes we examine are the OU processes. A serious restriction in using the OU process is that they will always have positive autocorrelation, while a strong negative autocorrelation is a stylized fact of FX tick-by-tick data. We have extended the basic OU process by considering a threshold continuous time process, where it is possible to obtain more complex patterns of autocorrelation. We examine in detail ways of modelling the unobserved behaviour between observations and ways of allocating observations to our two regimes. We propose the expected occupation time to model the behaviour between observations.

Our model describes some interesting features of the return process. Returns follow an asymmetric process for negative and positive values; correlation, defined over the steady-state distribution, is negative both in the data and in the estimated model. Our model complements the work of Zhou (1996) who has provided explanations of negative correlation. The high level of noise in intraday data causes our model to switch regimes as well. We manage, however, to retain the OU structure.

Finally, does this asymmetry in returns mean anything? One might argue that if we were trading DM–USD we would expect the opposite and certainly averaged monthly data look remarkably symmetric. We conjecture that this reflects two aspects: (i) the pre-eminent role of the dollar as the international currency, and (ii) the prevailing conditions of demand and supply on the day (5 July). Further work could investigate other currencies and other dates to see how ubiquitous this asymmetry actually is.

ACKNOWLEDGEMENTS

We would like to thank John Knight for correcting several earlier errors in our Lemma 1 and in the consequent arguments. We would also like to thank Alan Brown (State Street

Global Advisors) and William Perraudin for helpful suggestions. The usual disclaimer applies. The first author is funded by Kleinwort Benson Investment Management and the Newton Trust, the second author is funded by INQUIRE.

REFERENCES

Akaike, H. (1973), 'Information Theory and an Extension of the Maximum Likelihood Principle,' in B.N. Petrov (ed.), *2nd Int. Symp. on Inf. Th.*, pp. 267–283.
Andersen, T.G. and Bollerslev, T. (1995), 'Intraday Seasonality and Volatility Persistence in Financial Markets', forthcoming *Journal of Empirical Finance*.
Bollerslev, T. and Domowitz, I. (1993), 'Trading Patterns and Prices in the Interbank Foreign Exchange Market', *Journal of Finance*, **48**, 1421–1443.
Brock, W.A., Hsieh, D.A. and LeBaron, B. (1991), *Nonlinear Dynamics, Chaos and Instability: Statistical Theory and Economic Evidence*, MIT Press, Cambridge, Mass.
Brockwell, P.J. (1992), 'On Continuous Time Threshold Autoregression', *International Journal of Forecasting*, **8**, 157–173.
Brockwell, P.J. (1994), 'On Continuous Time Threshold ARMA Process', *Journal of Statistical Planning and Inference*, **39**, 291–303.
Brockwell, P.J., Hyndman, R.J. and Grunwald, G.K. (1991), 'Continuous Time Threshold Autoregressive Models', *Statistica Sinica*, **1**, 401–410.
Buonacore, A., Nobile, A.G. and Ricciradi, L.M. (1987), 'A New Integral Equation for the Evaluation of First Passage Time Probability Density', *Advances in Applied Probability*, **19**, 784–800.
Chan, K.S. (1988), 'Consistency and Limiting Distribution of Least Squares Estimates of a Threshold Autoregressive Model', *Tech. Rep. 245*, Department of Statistics, University of Chicago.
Chan, K.S. (1990), 'Testing for Threshold Autoregression', *Annals of Statistics*, **18**, 1886–1894.
Chan, K.S. (1991), 'Percentage Points of Likelihood Ratio Tests for Threshold Autoregression', *Journal of the Royal Statistical Society*, **B53**, 691–696.
Chan, K.S. (1993), 'Consistency and Limiting Distribution of the Least Squares Estimator of a Threshold Autoregressive Model', *The Annals of Statistics*, **21**, 520–533.
Chan, K.S. and Tong, H. (1990), 'On Likelihood Ratio Test for Threshold Autoregression', *Journal of the Royal Statistical Society*, **B52**, 469–476.
Chen, R. (1995), 'Threshold Variable Selection in Open Loop Threshold Autoregressive Models', *Journal of Time Series Analysis*, **16**, 461–481.
Clark, P.K. (1973), 'A Subordinated Stochastic Process with Finite Variance for Speculative Prices', *Econometrica*, **41**, 135–156.
Cox, D.R. and Miller, H.D. (1965), *The Theory of Stochastic Processes*, Methuen, London.
Dacco', R. and Satchell, S. (1995), 'Why Do Regime Switching Models Forecast So Badly?' Working Paper in Financial Economics, Birkbeck College.
Dacorogna, M.M., Muller, U.A., Nagler, R.J., Olsen, R.B. and Pichet, O.V. (1993), 'A Geographical Model for the Daily and Weekly Seasonal Volatility in the Foreign Exchange Market', *Journal of International Money and Finance*, **12**, 413–438.
Daniels, H.E. (1969), 'The Minimum of a Stationary Markov Process Superimposed on a U-shaped Trend', *Journal of Applied Probability*, **6**, 399–408.
De Goojer, J.G. and Kumar, K. (1992), 'Some Recent Developments in Nonlinear Time Series Modeling, Testing and Forecasting', *International Journal of Forecasting*, **8**, 101–123.
Engle, R.F. and Russell, J.R. (1994), 'Autoregressive Conditional Duration: A New Model for Irregularly Spaced Transaction Data', mimeo, University of California at San Diego.

Engle, R.F. and Russell, J.R. (1995), 'Forecasting the Frequency of Changes in Quoted Foreign Exchange Prices with the ACD Model', *First International Conference on High Frequency Data in Finance*, Olsen & Associates, Zurich.

Gardiner, C.W. (1994), *Handbook of Stochastic Methods for Physics, Chemistry and the Natural Sciences*, 3rd printing, Springer-Verlag, Berlin.

Geweke, J. and Terui, N. (1993), 'Bayesian Threshold Autoregressive Models for Nonlinear Time Series', *Journal of Time Series Analysis*, **14**, 441–454.

Ghysels, E., Jasiak, J. and Gouriéroux, C. (1995), 'Trading Patterns, Time Deformation and Stochastic Volatility in Foreign Exchange Markets', *First International Conference on High Frequency Data in Finance*, Olsen & Associates, Zurich.

Goodhart, C.A.E. (1990), 'News and the Foreign Exchange Markets', LSE Financial Market Group Discussion Paper, 71.

Goodhart, C.A.E. and Figliuoli, L. (1991), 'Every Minute Counts in Financial Market,' *Journal of International Money and Finance*, **10**, 23–52.

Goodhart, C.A.E., Hall, S.G., Henry, S.G.B. and Pesaran, B. (1993), 'News Effects in a High Frequency Model of the Sterling Dollar Exchange Rate', *Journal of Applied Econometrics*, **8**, 1–13.

Guillaume, D., Dacorogna, M.M. and Pichet, O.V. (1994), 'From the Bird's Eye to the Microscope: A Survey of New Stylized Facts of the Intra-Daily Foreign Exchange Markets', Discussion Paper DMG 1994-04-06, Olsen & Associates, Zurich.

Hansen, B.E. (1992), 'The Likelihood Ratio Test under Non-standard Conditions: Testing the Markov Trend Model of GNP', *Journal of Applied Econometrics*, **7**, 61–82.

Hansen, B.E. (1996), 'Inference when a Nuisance Parameter is not Identified under the Null Hypothesis', *Econometrica*, **64**, 413–430.

Hyndman, R.J. (1994), 'Approximations and Boundary Conditions for Continuous Time Threshold Autoregressive Processes', *Journal of Applied Probability*, **31**, 1103–1109.

Jarque, C.M. and Bera, A.K. (1980), 'Efficient Tests for Normality, Homoscedasticity and Serial Independence of Regression Residuals', *Economics Letters*, **6**, 255–259.

Karlin, S. and Taylor, H.M. (1981), *A Second Course in Stochastic Processes*, Academic Press, London.

LeBaron, B. (1994), 'Nonlinear Diagnostics and Simple Trading Rules for High Frequency Foreign Exchange Rates', in A.S. Weigend, and N.A. Gershenfeld (eds), *Time Series Prediction: Forecasting the Future and Understanding the Past*, Santa Fe Institute, pp. 457–474.

Lewis, P.A.W., Ray, B.K. and Stevens, J.G. (1994), 'Modelling Time Series by Using Multivariate Adaptive Regression Splines', in A.S. Weigend and N.A. Gershenfeld (eds), *Time Series Prediction: Forecasting the Future and Understanding the Past*, Santa Fe Institute, pp. 297–319.

Lizieri, C., Satchell, S. and Dacco', R. (1996), 'Property Company Performance and Real Interest Rate: A Regime Switching Approach', paper presented at the 12th Annual American Real Estate Meeting.

Lo, A.W. and Wang, J. (1995), 'Implementing Option Pricing Models When Asset Returns Are Predictable,' *Journal of Finance*, **50**, 87–129.

Müller, U.A., Dacorogna, M.M., Olsen, R.B., Pichet, O.V., Schwarz, M. and Morgenegg, C. (1990), 'Statistical Study of Foreign Exchange Rates, Empirical Evidence of a Price Change Scaling Law, and Intraday Analysis', *Journal of Banking and Finance*, **14**, 1189–1208.

Pesaran, M.H. and Potter, S.M. (1994), 'A Floor and Ceiling Model of U.S. Output,' DAE Working Paper, University of Cambridge.

Petrucelli, J. and Davies, N. (1986), 'A Portmanteau Test for Self Exciting Threshold Autoregressive Type Nonlinearity', *Biometrika*, **73**, 687–694.

Potter, S. (1995), 'A Nonlinear Approach to US GNP', *Journal of Applied Econometrics*, **10**, 109–125.

Roll, R. (1984), 'A Simple Implicit Measure of the Effective Bid–Ask Spread in an Efficient Market', *Journal of Finance*, **39**, 1127–1159.

Stock, J. (1988), 'Estimating Continuous Time Processes Subject to Time Deformation: An Application to Post War US GNP', *Journal of the American Statistical Association*, **83**, 77–85.

Stramer, O. (1996), 'On the Approximation of Moments for Continuous Time Threshold ARMA Process', *Journal of Time Series Analysis*, **17**, 189–202.

Tauchen, G. and Pitts, M. (1983), 'The Price Variability Volume Relationship on Speculative Markets', *Econometrica*, **51**, 485–505.

Tong, H. (1983), *Threshold Models in Nonlinear Time Series Analysis*, Lecture Notes in Statistics, Vol. 21. Springer-Verlag, New York, Heidelberg, Berlin.

Tong, H. (1990), *Nonlinear Time Series. A Dynamical System Approach*, Oxford Science Publications.

Tong, H. and Lin, K.S. (1980), 'Threshold Autoregression, Limit Cycles and Cyclical Data (with discussion)', *Journal of the Royal Statistical Society*, **B42**, 245–292.

Tong, H. and Moeanaddin, R. (1988), 'On Multi-Step Nonlinear Least Squares Prediction', *The Statistician*, **37**, 101–110.

Tong, H. and Yeung, I. (1991), 'Threshold Autoregressive Modelling in Continuous Time', *Statistica Sinica*, **1**, 411–430.

Tsay, R.S. (1986), 'Nonlinearity Tests for Time Series', *Biometrika*, **73**, 461–466.

Tsay, R.S. (1989), 'Testing and Modeling Threshold Autoregressive Processes', *Journal of the American Statistical Association*, **84**, 461–489.

Yadav, P., Pope, P. and Paudyal, K. (1994), 'Threshold Autoregressive Modeling in Finance: the Price Differences of Equivalent Assets', *Mathematical Finance*, **4**, 205–221.

Zhou, B. (1996), 'High Frequency Data and Volatility in Foreign Exchange Rates', *Journal of Business and Economic Statistics*, **14**, 45–52.

10

Modelling Burst Phenomena: Bilinear and Autoregressive Exponential Models

JÉRÔME DRUNAT, GILLES DUFRÉNOT
and LAURENT MATHIEU

1 INTRODUCTION

The purpose of this chapter is to show how bilinear and exponential autoregressive (EXPAR) models can be used to study intradaily exchange rate dynamics. The reasons for using such specifications are twofold.

On one hand, many authors have emphasised nonlinearities as one essential feature of exchange rates (see Hsieh 1988, 1989; Higgins and Bera 1991; Dechert and Gencay 1992). A variety of nonlinear models may be suggested as explanations for the underlying dynamics of exchange rates, each with different implications.

On the other hand, it is now widely recognised that exchange rates tend to exhibit clusters of outliers, implying that volatility evolves over time in a nonlinear fashion (see Bollerslev, Chou and Kroner 1992 for a survey). However, even though ARCH-type models are found to be useful in capturing certain nonlinearities of exchange rates, other nonlinear processes can be explored. It is known, for example, that bilinear models approximate adequately any Volterra series expansion over a finite interval. Thus, they may be regarded as natural nonlinear extensions of ARMA models. Moreover, it seems interesting to discriminate between ARCH and bilinear models. Indeed, the former make it possible to forecast the conditional variance without any gain

Nonlinear Modelling of High Frequency Financial Time Series.
Edited by Christian Dunis and Bin Zhou. © 1998 John Wiley Sons Ltd

in point forecasting ability. Conversely, the latter lead to improvements in point forecasting over ARMA modelling. From a financial economist's point of view, it is important to understand the differences between ARCH-type and bilinear processes, since investment decisions depend heavily on both assessment of future returns and risks of assets portfolios. There is another reason why the use of bilinear models seems appropriate. Exchange rate returns seem to exhibit periods of burst excursions followed by time intervals within which fluctuations are dormant. This type of behaviour is clearly indicative of a nonlinear structure and suggests the introduction of suitable models for their representation.

However, bilinear models do not capture phenomena such as amplitude-dependent frequency, jump behaviour or limit cycles, which also seem to characterise high frequency exchange rate fluctuations (see Haggan and Ozaki 1981 for a theoretical discussion and Drunat *et al.* 1996 for an application). Using exponential autoregressive models may then be more appropriate. Their specification is sufficiently general to include ARMA models and their dynamics can be readily extended to those of other nonlinear models (for instance, threshold autoregressive models, or exponential smooth transition autoregressive models). Such models describe exchange rates that evolve from periods of important variations to situations of more 'normal' changes, in much the same way as they increase from small changes to the 'middle ground'. This causes exchange rate returns to fluctuate rapidly over time.

This chapter is organised as follows. In section 2, we study the basic characteristics of our data. We observe that the underlying processes of our exchange rate returns are non-normal. In section 3, we analyse univariate EXPAR models. A Lagrange multiplier linearity test is applied to test for linearity in the conditional mean. Some evidence against linearity is shown, so the next step is devoted to the estimation of EXPAR models and forecasting. In section 4, we evaluate the performance of bilinear models both by estimating and forecasting the dynamics of our exchange rates. Next, we apply a linearity test against the alternative of bilinearity processes in order to see whether such kinds of processes emerge.

2 DATA DESCRIPTION

The series used in this chapter are the same as those presented in Chapter 4. However, we limit our attention to a few series for which the hypothesis of linearity had been rejected (using both bispectral approaches of Subba Rao and Gabr 1984 and Hinich 1982). The data concern two months, January and April respectively, for the 30-minute and 60-minute frequencies. Descriptive statistics and sample autocorrelations are displayed in Tables 10.1–10.4.

Taken as a whole, the dynamics of our exchange rates seem to be inconsistent with the hypothesis of normal distribution. The high kurtosis coefficients are indeed indicative of fat tails in the distribution and there is an obvious sign of

Table 10.1 Summary statistics (January)

Statistics	DEM/FRF(30)	USD/DEM(30)	USD/FRF(30)
Mean	4.2e − 4 (0.40)	−2.2e − 3 (0.28)	−1.8e − 3 (0.32)
Variance	2.8e − 4	4.9e − 3	3.9e − 3
Skewness	0.17 (0.024)	−1.0 (0.0)	−0.97 (0.0)
Kurtosis	9.59 (0.0)	9.25 (0.0)	9.23 (0.0)

Note: Marginal significance levels are given between brackets.

Table 10.2 Summary statistics (April)

Statistics	DEM/FRF(60)	USD/DEM(60)	USD/FRF(60)
Mean	1.9e − 3 (0.55)	6.7e − 5 (0.99)	1.4e − 3 (0.82)
Variance	5.6e − 3	3.0e − 2	2.1e − 2
Skewness	−0.22 (0.04)	0.35 (0.0)	1.12 (0.0)
Kurtosis	6.19 (0.0)	4.17 (0.0)	9.53 (0.0)

Note: Marginal significance levels are given between brackets.

Table 10.3 Autocorrelation coefficients (January)

ACF	DEM/FRF(30)	USD/DEM(30)	USD/FRF(30)
ρ_1	−0.109 (0.044)	−0.046 (0.069)	−0.011 (0.071)
ρ_2	−0.012 (0.051)	0.12 (0.065)	0.067 (0.053)
ρ_3	−0.013 (0.046)	0.005 (0.044)	0.027 (0.043)
ρ_4	0.063 (0.049)	0.045 (0.043)	0.046 (0.038)
ρ_5	−0.016 (0.041)	0.018 (0.031)	0.011 (0.038)
ρ_6	0.027 (0.045)	0.009 (0.030)	0.010 (0.036)
ρ_7	−0.064 (0.043)	−0.030 (0.028)	−0.020 (0.038)
ρ_8	−0.032 (0.045)	−0.036 (0.033)	−0.006 (0.042)
ρ_9	−0.006 (0.043)	0.022 (0.033)	0.037 (0.028)
ρ_{10}	0.015 (0.040)	0.032 (0.030)	0.016 (0.030)
ρ_{20}	−0.038 (0.028)	−0.001 (0.030)	−0.0005 (0.026)
ρ_{30}	−0.027 (0.034)	−0.030 (0.033)	−0.027 (0.030)
ρ_{40}	0.017 (0.031)	0.016 (0.026)	0.017 (0.028)
ρ_{50}	0.026 (0.037)	−0.049 (0.040)	0.06 (0.043)
$BP_\rho(50)$	88.41 (0.0)	71.42 (0.02)	42.77 (0.76)
$BP_{\rho^2}(50)$	330.77 (0.0)	366.21 (0.0)	374.30 (0.0)
$BPA_\rho(50)$	54.13 (0.32)	49.70 (0.48)	46.58 (0.61)

asymmetry, in so far as the marginal significance level of the test statistic for zero skewness and kurtosis lies under 5%.

The fact that high frequency exchange rates are too leptokurtotic to be consistent with Gaussian distributions is now well documented (see, for example, Hsieh 1989; Müller et al. 1990; Low and Muthuswamy 1995). So, this result is truly

Table 10.4 Autocorrelation coefficients (April)

ACF	DEM/FRF(60)	USD/DEM(60)	USD/FRF(60)
ρ_1	0.032 (0.072)	0.072 (0.046)	0.048 (0.043)
ρ_2	−0.081 (0.077)	−0.087 (0.061)	0.080 (0.038)
ρ_3	0.001 (0.071)	−0.052 (0.051)	−0.019 (0.042)
ρ_4	0.037 (0.060)	−0.012 (0.046)	−0.059 (0.045)
ρ_5	0.012 (0.066)	0.020 (0.042)	−0.007 (0.041)
ρ_6	−0.067 (0.060)	−0.018 (0.049)	0.0005 (0.041)
ρ_7	0.007 (0.061)	0.023 (0.049)	−0.055 (0.037)
ρ_8	0.014 (0.049)	0.022 (0.055)	−0.028 (0.036)
ρ_9	0.028 (0.053)	−0.007 (0.042)	0.040 (0.038)
ρ_{10}	−0.007 (0.058)	−0.041 (0.048)	−0.033 (0.035)
ρ_{20}	−0.002 (0.061)	0.008 (0.044)	0.038 (0.033)
ρ_{30}	−0.006 (0.046)	0.051 (0.042)	0.10 (0.029)
ρ_{40}	0.024 (0.040)	−0.11 (0.043)	−0.049 (0.031)
ρ_{50}	0.025 (0.040)	0.038 (0.038)	−0.043 (0.034)
$BP_\rho(50)$	47.46 (0.58)	52.65 (0.37)	63.44 (0.09)
$BP_{\rho^2}(50)$	237.71 (0.0)	157.79 (0.02)	22.0 (0.99)
$BPA_\rho(50)$	34.52 (0.95)	47.14 (0.59)	—

Note: ρ_k is the kth order autocorrelation coefficient. Standard errors (corrected for heteroscedasticity) are reported between brackets for each autocorrelation coefficient, except for USD/FRF (60-minute) for which there is no heteroscedasticity. $BP_\rho(\cdot)$ and $BP_{\rho^2}(\cdot)$ are Box–Pierce statistics corresponding respectively to the return and squared return series. $BPA_\rho(\cdot)$ is the adjusted Box–Pierce corresponding to the return series, in order to take into account the presence of heteroscedasticity. For these three statistics, marginal levels of significance are given between brackets.

not surprising. Associated with the concept of fat tail distributions is the fact that exchange rate returns may demonstrate sharp bursts in volatility.

Although exchange rates are indeed relative prices, the observation that our distributions are skewed illustrates the possibility that the decreases of returns on exchange rate markets are brief and more severe than increases (this conclusion holds especially when the series are negatively skewed). Moreover, when the role of asymmetries is combined with the effects of leptokurtosis, this may reflect a relation between errors and volatility which is asymmetric: unexpected losses may lead to greater volatility and unexpected profits to lower volatility.

If we now examine the correlations between the observations of our series, there seems to exist a significant lag structure for three series: DEM/FRF and USD/DEM (30-minute), and USD/FRF (60-minute). This conclusion comes from the fact that the marginal significance level of the joint test of independence between the first 50 autocorrelation coefficients using a Box–Pierce statistic is less than 5%.

It is also interesting to look at the autocorrelations of the squared returns. As noted by McLeod and Li (1983), this serves as an indication of heteroscedasticity. The corresponding Box–Pierce statistic is distributed as a chi-square with

k degrees of freedom, where k is the number of autocorrelation coefficients. As one can see, squared returns are strongly correlated except in the case of the USD/FRF (60-minute), thus suggesting the presence of heteroscedasticity in the other series. In this case, the lag structure revealed by the autocorrelation function may be misleading. Indeed, Diebold (1988) has shown that time-varying variances cause the standard errors of the autocorrelation coefficient to be underestimated. Therefore, a test for independence cannot be conducted until the heteroscedasticity nettles have been grasped. As suggested by Diebold, one needs to compute a heteroscedasticity-consistent estimate of the standard error for each autocorrelation coefficient. He further shows that the adjusted Box–Pierce statistic is asymptotically distributed as a chi-square variable with k degrees of freedom. Applying this procedure leads us to conclude that the hypothesis of no serial correlation for all the series cannot be rejected.

The finding that returns in high frequency exchange rates are uncorrelated while squared returns exhibit strong autocorrelations has been documented in other studies (see, for example, Low and Muthuswamy 1995). These authors conclude that this observation denotes the presence of nonlinear patterns in data. A commonly used approach would lead us to argue that an explanation of leptokurtotic distributions can be found in the framework of ARCH-type models. However, it seems that in practice the use of these models leads to significant unexplained kurtosis. This conclusion is true for daily foreign exchange rates (Hsieh 1989), and also holds for intradaily exchange rate returns (Drunat *et al.* 1996). There are other classes of models that can explain the bunching characteristic of exchange rate returns and which can be extended to explain skewness. Accordingly, the next section provides a new insight into exponential autoregressive models.

3 EXPONENTIAL AUTOREGRESSIVE MODELS: LINEARITY TESTING, SPECIFICATION AND FORECASTING

The approach involved in linearity tests without specific nonlinear alternatives (as is the case in the bispectral approach) is rather different from the procedures adopted when nonlinear models, against which the null hypothesis of linearity is tested, are defined. It is worth pointing out that in this second case, linearity tests are divided into two categories. If the estimation of nonlinear models is required under the alternative hypothesis, then the relevant approach is to use parametric tests such as likelihood or Wald tests. If the estimation is not required, one uses non-parametric Lagrange-multiplier (or LM) tests. The detailed format of these tests for EXPAR models is now discussed.

Exponential autoregressive models (EXPAR) were introduced by Jones (1978) and were subsequently investigated by Haggan and Ozaki (1981) and Ozaki

(1982). Let us consider the general nonlinear model:

$$x_t = \alpha_0 + \sum_{i=1}^{P} \alpha_i x_{t-i} + \sum_{i=1}^{P} \beta_i x_{t-i} F(x_{t-\delta}) + \varepsilon_t \qquad \varepsilon_t \approx \text{i.i.d.}(0, \sigma_\varepsilon)^2 \qquad (1)$$

where F is a polynomial function. An EXPAR model is a particular form of equation (1), where a specific polynomial function including exponential terms is introduced:

$$x_t = \alpha_0 + \sum_{i=1}^{p} \alpha_i x_{t-i} + \left[\sum_{i=1}^{p} \beta_i x_{t-i} \right] [1 + \exp(-d(x_{i-\delta} - \mu)^2)] + \varepsilon_t \qquad (2)$$

where μ is the sample mean of the series (x_t), $t = 1, \ldots, T$, $d > 0$ is a transition parameter and δ is a delay parameter which varies between 1 and p.

This formulation is used to describe the transition aspect of exchange rate fluctuations from periods of high returns to low returns and vice versa. By 'high' we mean situations where returns at given periods are increasing above their 'normal' level (here their mean) and conversely they are considered to be low when decreasing under their normal 'value'. We therefore define $(x_{t-\delta} - \mu)$ as a benchmark variable of the 'excess' return within the period $(t - \delta)$.

By specifying equation (1), we thus assume that excess returns at given periods have an effect on returns δ periods later. Since we are dealing with high frequency data, our a priori expectation is that exchange rate returns exhibit short memory, in the sense that a modification in the excess return at a given period will not have an influence on returns in the distant future. We accordingly consider the case where $\delta = 1$. The exponential form of the function F is useful, not only to account for a nonlinear dependence between $(x_{t-\delta} - \mu)$ and x_t, but also to take into account some types of behaviour that are known to characterise financial time series: jumping dynamics, amplitude-dependent frequency, limit cycles and chaotic dynamics. All these phenomena have been extensively discussed in the literature (see Priestley 1988 for illustrations). Let us now see how the linearity hypothesis is tested against EXPAR models.

3.1 Linearity Testing against the EXPAR Alternative

Theoretical Considerations

The linearity test is carried out as follows:

1. Fit a linear AR(p) model using a Box–Jenkins procedure and select that model for which Akaike's AIC criterion attains its minimum. A Ljung–Box or Box–Pierce statistic is further needed as a checking diagnostic that the residuals from the estimated models are not serially correlated. The selection of p needs careful attention because an overestimate of the maximum lag reduces the power of the test, whereas in the case of an underestimation the test is biased towards the rejection of the null hypothesis.

2. The procedure is then continued by constructing the test statistic. The conditional log likelihood of the model is written:

$$L = -(T/2)\ln 2\pi = (T/2)\ln \sigma_\varepsilon^2 - (1/\sigma_\varepsilon^2)\sum_{t=1}^{T}\varepsilon_1^2 \qquad (3)$$

or

$$L = -(T/2)\ln 2\pi - (T/2)\ln \sigma_\varepsilon^2$$

$$- (1/\sigma_\varepsilon^2)\sum_{t=1}^{T}[x_t - \alpha_0 - \alpha'w_t - (\beta'w_t)(1 + \exp(-d(x_{t-1} - \mu)^2))]^2 \quad (4)$$

where

$$\alpha = (\alpha_1, \alpha_2, \ldots, \alpha_p)' \quad \beta = (\beta_1, \beta_2, \ldots, \beta_p)' \quad w_t = (x_{t-1}, x_{t-2}, \ldots, x_{t-p}) \qquad (5)$$

The derivation of the test statistic requires the computation of the first derivatives of the log likelihood with respect to α_0, α' and d, under the null hypothesis H_0: $d = 0$:

$$L'_{\alpha_0} = (1/\sigma_\varepsilon^2)\sum_t \varepsilon_t \qquad (6)$$

$$L'_{\alpha'} = (1/\sigma_\varepsilon^2)\sum_t \varepsilon_t w_t \qquad (7)$$

$$L'_d = (-1/\sigma_\varepsilon^2)\sum_t \varepsilon_t[(\beta_0 + \beta'w_t)(x_{t-1} - \mu)^2 \exp(-d(x_{t-1} - \mu)^2)] \quad (8)$$

The exponential term can be approximated by its first-order Taylor expansion in the neighbourhood of $x_{t-1} = \mu$. Under H_0, equation (8) is therefore replaced by

$$L'_d = (1/\sigma_\varepsilon^2)\sum_t [-\beta_0 - \beta'w_t][x_{t-1} - \mu]^2 \qquad (9)$$

3. Computation of the second-order derivatives leads to the information matrix I_0, and the test statistic is written:

$$LM = (1/T)L'_d \times I_0^{-1} \times L'_d \qquad (10)$$

In practice, the procedure above is carried out as an auxiliary regression type test:

1′. Fit a linear AR(p) model by the regression of x_t on $(1, w_t)$. Compute the residuals $(\hat{\varepsilon}_t)$, $t = 1, 2, \ldots, T$, and the sum of squared residuals SCR_0.

2′. Use least-squares regression analysis of $\hat{\varepsilon}_t$ on $z_{1t} = -(1, w_t)$ and $z_{2t} = (\beta_0 + \beta' w_t)(x_{t-1} - \mu)^2$. An extended expression of z_{2t} is

$$z_{2t} = (\beta_0 + \beta' w_t)x_{t-1}^2 + (-2\beta_0\mu - 2\beta'\mu w_t)x_{t-1} + \mu^2\beta' w_t + \mu^2\beta_0 \quad (11)$$

Define:

$$\begin{cases} \gamma_3 = \beta \\ \gamma_2 = -2\beta\mu + \beta_0 e_d \\ \tau_0 = \alpha_0 + \mu^2\beta_0 \\ \tilde{\tau}_1 = (\tau_0, \tau_1) \\ \tau_1 = (\mu^2\beta + \alpha - 2\mu\beta e_d) \end{cases} \quad (12)$$

where e_d is a vector with 1 as the dth components and 0 elsewhere. One then estimates the coefficients of the following equation:

$$\hat{\varepsilon}_t = \tilde{\tau}_1' z_{1t} + \gamma_2' w_t x_{t-1} + \gamma_3 w_t x_{t-1}^2 + \upsilon_t \qquad \upsilon_t \approx N(0, \sigma_\upsilon) \quad (13)$$

3′. Compute the statistic

$$LM = T[(SCR_0 - SCR_1)/(SCR_1)] \quad (14)$$

where SCR_1 is the residual sum of squares of equation (13). LM has an asymptotic χ^2 distribution with $2p$ degrees of freedom.

Application to Exchange Rates

The results of the linearity test are reported in Table 10.5. The marginal significance level of the test is given between brackets. The null hypothesis of linearity H_0 is rejected if the values reported between brackets are less than 5%. It is noteworthy that in all the cases the order of the linear AR(p) models is low. This observation is in accordance with the fact that the autocorrelation coefficients in the preceding section were not significant at all, once heteroscedasticity had been removed. However, it appears that the null hypothesis is always rejected against the EXPAR alternative except for USD/DEM (60-minute). This may be due to an underestimation of the lag structure, which causes the test to be biased towards the rejection of the hypothesis of linearity. Indeed, as suggested above, we have used the AIC criterion to guide the search for the maximum lags. But looking at

Table 10.5 *p*-values of the linear AR(p) model and *LM* statistic

p/LM	DEM/FRF		USD/DEM		USD/FRF	
	30	60	30	60	30	60
p	1	1	1	1	1	1
LM	90.84 (0.0)	190.94 (0.0)	17.50 (0.0)	2.63 (0.27)	109.75 (0.0)	54.40 (0.0)

Note: Marginal significance levels are given between brackets.

the properties of the estimated residuals might also be another important part of the search process. No autocorrelation structures were detected in the residuals by the usual diagnostics based on Ljung–Box or Box–Pierce statistics. Meanwhile, evidence against normality was provided by looking at higher-order moments than order two: the residuals showed significant leptokurtosis and skewed distributions. This might explain why the null hypothesis of linearity is so often rejected.

3.2 Specification of EXPAR Models

Theoretical Considerations

We are mainly concerned here with the construction of a model that relates a return series observed at a given period t to its own lags and to 'excess' returns one period before. A practical problem that appears in the estimation of equation (2) is that of the determination of the parameters d and p. The approach that we use combines Haggan and Ozaki's (1981) procedure and a nonlinear least-squares method.

1. For a predetermined value of d, the other coefficients are estimated by the regression of x_t on $(1, w_t)$ and $w_t(1+\exp(-d(x_{t-1}-\mu)^2))$, with the order of p corresponding to the minimum value of the AIC criterion. The optimal value of d is sought over a relevant range such that the exponential term varies between 0 and 1. Let $\hat{\alpha}_0, \hat{\alpha}_i, \hat{\beta}_i$ be the estimates of $\alpha_0, \alpha_i, \beta_i, i = 1, \ldots, p$.

2. The second step requires the use of a nonlinear least-squares regression analysis to estimate the new values $\tilde{\alpha}_0, \tilde{\alpha}_i, \tilde{\beta}_i$ of $\alpha_0, \alpha_i, \beta_i$, with $\hat{\alpha}_0, \hat{\alpha}_i, \hat{\beta}_i$ as initial values. This approach is equivalent to the maximisation of the log-likelihood function and the regression is carried out by using a Gauss–Newton algorithm. It is worth while noting that the use of nonlinear optimisation often leads to unsatisfactory situations. Indeed, the updating algorithms that are usually used to revise the estimates of the parameter d do not always have good convergence properties. Not only may the values of d change over time but the parameters might also exhibit explosive behaviour. Alternatively, rather than appearing far from 'smooth' the estimates of all the parameters sometimes remain equivalent to their initial values. This poses a problem which to our knowledge has not received any answer in the literature. Many authors therefore restrict their analysis to the first stage, but for forecasting purposes we suggest combining both the first and second steps.

Once the parameters have been estimated, one may ask whether the model is well specified. A usual method consists of checking that no autocorrelation structure has been left in the residual term. One way to proceed is to use the standard tests (for example, a Ljung–Box test). Another approach based on the examination of the presence of skewed and leptokurtotic distributions in the residuals can also give some explanations of the possible rejection of normality for the error term.

As mentioned above, the estimation of EXPAR models gives some insights into the study of their dynamics. To evaluate the long-run properties of our models, we restrict our attention here to the existence of limit cycles. A sufficient condition for the existence of self-sustaining periodic fluctuations is (see Ozaki 1978)

$$V = \left[\left(1 - \sum_i \alpha_i \right) \Big/ \left(\sum_i \beta_i \right) \right] > 1 \quad \text{or} \quad < 0 \qquad (15)$$

Application to Exchange Rates

The specifications of EXPAR models are now discussed to illustrate the procedures discussed above.

For all our estimates, the parameter d has been scaled by dividing it by the variance of the series. This eliminates convergence problems in the algorithm. We found that the values of d were sometimes very large (especially for 30-minute intervals). This could be interpreted as an indication of the fact that the corresponding EXPAR models behave like linear AR models. Indeed, for large values of $-d(x_{t-1} - \mu)^2$, the exponential terms in equation (2) tend to zero. But on the other hand, the differences $(x_{t-1} - \mu)$ were very small so that it could also be natural to think that the models behave like threshold autoregressive models with abrupt transition from periods of increasing returns to periods of decreasing ones. All one can say is that the result is indeterminate, because it is not possible to know which effect is predominant over the other. However, the dominating feature of the long-run dynamics is the presence of limit cycles as indicated by the values of V (see Tables 10.6 and 10.7).

The models seemed successfully estimated. We computed static forecasts based upon the regressions. These were used for computing the Durbin–Watson and

Table 10.6 Maximum p-lag, initial values and nonlinear least-squares estimations (30-minute series)

DEM/FRF — January — EXPAR(3)

$\hat{\alpha}_1$	$\hat{\alpha}_2$	$\hat{\alpha}_3$	$\hat{\beta}_1$	$\hat{\beta}_2$	$\hat{\beta}_3$	
0.0048	−0.004	−0.0099	0.0144	0.1256	1.0015	
$\tilde{\alpha}_1$	$\tilde{\alpha}_2$	$\tilde{\alpha}_3$	$\tilde{\beta}_1$	$\tilde{\beta}_2$	$\tilde{\beta}_3$	Maximum likelihood
−0.2588	0.1487	−0.0099	0.3481	−0.1174	0.1158	1244.0380
$\tilde{d}$	DW	AIC	Skewness	Kurtosis	V	
1122.87	1.980	−13035	−0.2752	5.9578	3.2315	

USD/FRF — January — EXPAR(1)

$\hat{\alpha}_1$	$\hat{\beta}_1$	$\tilde{\alpha}_1$	$\tilde{\beta}_1$	$\tilde{d}$	DW	
−0.3082	0.0146	−0.3105	0.0077	2.8224	1.985	Maximum likelihood
AIC	Skewness	Kurtosis	V			349.289
−4933.35	−1.8771	13.4258	169.7271			

Table 10.7 Maximum p-lag, initial values and nonlinear least-squares estimations (60-minute series)

DEM/FRF — April — EXPAR(2)

$\hat{\alpha}_1$	$\hat{\alpha}_2$	$\hat{\beta}_1$	$\hat{\beta}_2$	$\tilde{\alpha}_1$	$\tilde{\alpha}_2$	$\tilde{\beta}_1$	$\tilde{\beta}_2$
−0.2948	−0.1368	−0.01407	1.8430	−1.077	−1.0751	1.3277	1.0404

$\tilde{d}$	DW	AIC	Skewness	Kurtosis	V	Maximum likelihood
1.2476	1.9979	−2174.23	7.187	105.477	1.3312	397.7871

USD/DEM — April — EXPAR(2)

$\hat{\alpha}_1$	$\hat{\alpha}_2$	$\hat{\beta}_1$	$\hat{\beta}_2$	$\tilde{\alpha}_1$	$\tilde{\alpha}_2$	$\tilde{\beta}_1$	$\tilde{\beta}_2$
0.0754	−0.0886	0.0279	3.0206	0.0786	−0.085	−7.001	0.0861

$\tilde{d}$	DW	AIC	Skewness	Kurtosis	V	Maximum likelihood
2840.22	2.009	−1702.05	0.1285	3.5737	−0.1455	121.976

USD/FRF — April — EXPAR(1)

$\hat{\alpha}_1$	$\hat{\beta}_1$	$\tilde{\alpha}_1$	$\tilde{\beta}_1$	$\tilde{d}$	DW	
−0.0383	−0.00174	−0.03123	−0.314966	95.68	1.995	Maximum likelihood
AIC	Skewness	Kurtosis	V			105.9922
−1669.17	0.64904	25.838	−3.2741			

other diagnostic tests which did not indicate any serial autocorrelation in the residuals. However, as one can see, the skewness and excess kurtosis are still in contradiction with the hypothesis of normality. As noted by Teräsvirta and Anderson (1992), this may denote the presence of shocks (in our case, the effects of news) which are not explained by the models because they are exogenous. This is a serious worry when univariate EXPAR models are used to explain exchange rate dynamics. Indeed, it seems difficult to ignore the fact that factors such as interest rates or monetary policies and foreign currencies are interrelated. But at the same time, it is worth noting that there does not exist a framework that fully covers dynamics operating on different time scales: changes occurring in fundamental variables are expected to hold over several months; conversely, high frequency exchange rates are defined on an intradaily time scale.

3.3 Forecasting with EXPAR Models

One way to evaluate the performance of EXPAR models in describing time series is to produce forecasts and compare them with that of linear and random processes. Several methods are available in the literature (the numerical method, the normal forecasting error method and the linearisation method proposed by Jones 1978 or A1-Qassam and Lane 1989). We use here an extrapolation method which is the least computationally expensive and our concern is to study static and dynamic in-sample and out-of-sample forecasts to predict the values of x_{t+h} from x_t for lead times $h = 1, \ldots, 10$. We restrict our attention to EXPAR(1) processes, because forecasting of EXPAR(p) with $p \geq 2$ for several steps ahead is much more complicated.

Forecasts are computed recursively from equation (2). For an EXPAR model, the multi-step ahead forecasts are given by the following equation:

$$
\begin{aligned}
\tilde{x}_{t+h} = {} & [\tilde{\alpha}_1 + \tilde{\beta}_1 \exp(-d(x_{t-1} - \mu)^2)]^h x_{t-1+h} \\
& + \sum_{i=0}^{h-1} [\tilde{\alpha}_1 + \tilde{\beta}_1 \exp(-d(x_{t-1} - \mu)^2)]^i \varepsilon_{t-i+h}
\end{aligned}
\tag{16}
$$

The forecast performance is summarised by considering the root mean square error:

$$
\text{RMSE} = \left[(1/T) \sum_{i=1}^{T} (\tilde{x}_i - x_i)^2 \right]^{1/2}
\tag{17}
$$

where T is the number of realisations that are generated from equation (16). The EXPAR forecasts are compared with those of linear and random walk processes. The comparison with linear models is straightforward because they can be viewed as 'sub-models' of EXPAR specifications (this is the case when d tends to infinity, or when $\tilde{\beta}_1$ converges towards zero). The comparison with random walk processes is justified by the fact that in some of our estimations the coefficients are not significantly different from zero.

Table 10.8 reports the results of 1–10 period ahead forecasts of EXPAR(1) by using in-sample and out-of-sample dynamic forecasts. Only one exchange rate has been chosen for illustrative purpose. The numbers shown are the RMSEs for EXPAR, AR and random walk models. The fitted values are based upon the regression analysis shown in Table 10.6. For the in-sample RMSEs, all values of x_{t-1} and x_{t-h} in the right-hand part of formula (16) are taken from the sample

Table 10.8 In-sample RMSEs and out-of-sample forecasts for the USD/FRF 60-min (April). Comparison with AR(1) and random walk

Lead time	In-sample RMSEs			Out-of-sample forecasts		
	EXPAR	AR	Random walk	EXPAR	AR	Random walk
1	1.3719	1.0117	1.5106	1.0716	1.0574	5.7771
2	1.6282	1.0122	1.8117	1.0585	1.0274	7.7790
3	1.8789	1.0125	2.1008	1.0408	1.0290	5.8677
4	2.1178	1.0119	2.3448	1.1182	1.0232	9.2270
5	2.3985	1.0130	2.5270	1.0567	1.0181	9.6286
6	2.6259	1.0140	2.7024	1.1779	1.0049	11.2926
7	3.0158	1.0114	2.8578	1.1222	1.0008	10.7850
8	3.3224	1.0116	3.0356	1.3147	1.0041	13.3755
9	3.6457	1.0122	3.2101	1.1817	0.9971	13.8005
10	4.1173	1.0120	3.3886	1.1067	1.0073	15.3444

returns at all steps. In contrast, in the dynamic out-of-sample forecasts, the values of x_{t-1} and x_{t-h} are computed by feeding forward forecasts of the early periods for use in the latter periods.

From Table 10.5, one observes that while EXPAR models provide useful information about the dynamics of the USD/FRF exchange rates, they are, however, outperformed by the AR(1) model. The unfavourable performance of our model for the USD/FRF exchange rate might be explained by the presence of skewed and leptokurtotic residuals which induce a forecasting 'bias'. It is, however, seen that the EXPAR models are slightly better than the random walk for short-term forecasts. The conclusions are very much the same for out-of-sample dynamic forecasts with the exception that the random walk never produces forecasts superior to the EXPAR models.

4 ESTIMATION OF BILINEAR MODELS

Bilinear models in the exchange rate literature were first used by Maraval (1983). The author's interest was centred on models describing bursts of large-amplitude fluctuations in foreign exchange markets, which regularly interrupt periods of more normal activity. Whereas Maraval's attention focused on the Spanish currency, this phenomenon is common to many exchange rates. More generally, it is known that several factors affect financial series in jump-like fashion. Merton (1976) reports that the interventions of monetary authorities yield bursts of information which are depicted in option prices behaviour as jumps. Moreno and Peña (1996) have recently constructed a model which copes with different factors that cause jumping behaviour in interest rates (supply and demand shocks or economic and political news). It is likely that traders on exchange rate markets who forecast over very short horizons, employing overbought and oversold indicators, tend to trigger burst phenomena in exchange rate returns.

Bilinear models provide a suitable empirical framework for reproducing such evolutions. Their theoretical properties have been investigated in many papers to which the reader is referred (for instance, Granger and Andersen 1978; Subba Rao and Gabr 1984; Guégan 1994; Subba Rao 1992).

4.1 Specification of Bilinear Models

Bilinear models can be viewed as extensions of linear ARMA models, that is, a Taylor expansion series of a nonlinear function where terms of a higher order than one are included. Suppose, for example, that the behaviour of a stationary process with zero mean is given by the following function:

$$x_t = f(x_{t-1}, x_{t-2}, \ldots, x_{t-p}, \varepsilon_t, \varepsilon_{t-1}, \ldots, \varepsilon_{t-q}) \qquad (18)$$

where $\varepsilon_t \approx$ i.i.d.$(0, \sigma_\varepsilon^2)$ and p and q are respectively the orders of the autoregressive and moving average parts of f. The second-order Taylor expansion of f around $x = \varepsilon = 0$ is written:

$$x_t = \sum_{k=1}^{P} f'_{x_{t-i}} x_{t-i} + \sum_{k=0}^{q} f'_{\varepsilon_{t-i}} \varepsilon_{t-i} + (1/2) \sum_{k=1}^{P} \sum_{i=1}^{P} f''_{x_{t-k} x_{t-i}} x_{t-k} x_{t-i}$$

$$+ (1/2) \sum_{k=1}^{P} \sum_{i=1}^{Q} f''_{x_{t-k} \varepsilon_{t-i}} x_{t-k} \varepsilon_{t-i} + (1/2) \sum_{k=1}^{Q} \sum_{i=1}^{Q} f''_{\varepsilon_{t-k} \varepsilon_{t-i}} \varepsilon_{t-i} \varepsilon_{t-k} \qquad (19)$$

Note that P is not necessarily equal to p and that Q is not necessarily equal to q either. Structural forms of bilinear models are given by equation (19) with the restrictions:

$$f''_{x_{t-k} x_{t-i}} x_{t-k} x_{t-i} = f''_{\varepsilon_{t-k} \varepsilon_{t-i}} \varepsilon_{t-i} \varepsilon_{t-k} = 0 \qquad \forall(k, i) \qquad (20)$$

One weakness of the EXPAR models estimated above is that they are unable to explain the excess kurtosis which has been found to characterise the distributions of our series. Bilinear models provide an interesting rationale for their presence. This is not very surprising since they can be interpreted as particular ARCH models. To illustrate this, consider the following BL(0, 0, 2, 1) model:

$$x_t = \gamma_{21} x_{t-2} \varepsilon_{t-1} + \varepsilon_t \qquad \varepsilon_t \approx \text{i.i.d.}(0, \sigma_\varepsilon^2) \qquad (21)$$

This process has unconditional moments similar to those of an ARCH process:

$$E(x_t) = 0 \qquad \text{cov}(\varepsilon_t^2 \varepsilon_{t-2}^2) = \gamma_{21}^2 \sigma_\varepsilon^2 \qquad (22)$$

From this expression, one can see that the process described by equation (21) will exhibit temporal clustering of large and small deviations, just like an ARCH process, because it is autocorrelated in squares. This has led a number of authors to test the joint presence of bilinearity and ARCH effects in exchange rates (see for illustration Higgins and Bera 1991) even though the results are mixed. We restrict our attention here to bilinear models, to see whether the fat tails observed for our series can be revealed in the returns conditional mean. Note that if we had to deal with a bilinear–ARCH mixed approach, some attention should be paid to model both the mean and the conditional variance.

A relevant procedure needed for the estimation of bilinear models has been proposed by Subba Rao and Gabr (1984):

1. The first step consists of specifying a linear AR model using the classical approach (minimising the sum of squared residuals). The maximal number of terms is selected according to the AIC criterion.
2. One continues by fitting the best full bilinear model. The approach which is adopted, combines both a Newton–Raphson method and the repeated residuals technique suggested by Subba Rao (1977) and Hannan and Rissanen (1982).

Considering the model (19) with $q = 0$, the repeated residual method is first used to obtain initial estimates of the parameters. Suppose that the regression in the first step yields a vector of residuals $(\hat{\varepsilon}_t)$, $t = p+1, \ldots, T$. For given values of P and Q, one uses a least-squares approach to estimate the parameters of the following model:

$$x_t = \alpha_0 + \sum_{k=1}^{P} \alpha_k x_{t-k} + \sum_{k=1}^{P} \sum_{i=1}^{Q} \gamma_{ki} x_{t-k} \hat{\varepsilon}_{t-i} \qquad t = p+1, \ldots, T \qquad (23)$$

The $\hat{\varepsilon}_t$ are then replaced by the residuals from the fitted model above, and the procedure is repeated until the parameter estimates converge to stable values.

Once those values are obtained, a Newton–Raphson technique is used via the Marquardt algorithm. Note that the residual method works well if the parameters are not near the invertibility region. Invertibility conditions have been derived analytically for some bilinear models. If the model is nearly non-invertible, the procedure may be in trouble. Invertibility conditions are, however, hard to obtain analytically for models with a complicated structure. As suggested by Granger and Teräsvirta (1993), these may be checked numerically on the basis

Table 10.9 Estimation of bilinear models, DEM/FRF (January/30-min)

BL(2, 0, 4, 3)

a_1	a_2	$b_{1,1}$	$b_{1,2}$	$b_{1,3}$	$b_{2,2}$
0.086	−0.014	−1.27	−1.65	9.62	0.28
$b_{2,3}$	$b_{3,1}$	$b_{3,2}$	$b_{4,1}$	AIC	σ_ε
−1.90	−11.20	10.25	−5.23	−9036	2.2e − 4
RMSE					
4.7e − 4					

Table 10.10 Estimation of bilinear models, USD/DEM (January/30-min)

BL(2, 0, 4, 3)

a_1	a_2	$b_{1,3}$	$b_{2,1}$	$b_{3,1}$	$b_{4,2}$
0.057	−0.11	2.14	−1.62	−1.9	−0.93
$b_{4,3}$	AIC	σ_ε	RMSE		
−0.374	−8306	4.4e − 3	9.2e − 3		

Table 10.11 Estimation of bilinear models, USD/FRF (January/30-min)

BL(0, 0, 4, 6)

a_1	$b_{1,1}$	$b_{1,2}$	$b_{2,1}$	$b_{2,2}$	$b_{3,1}$
0.087	−0.81	−1.28	−0.61	0.02	0.26
$b_{3,2}$	AIC	σ_ε	RMSE		
0.73	−6170	3.5e − 3	3.2e − 2		

Table 10.12 Estimation of bilinear models, USD/DEM (April/60-min)

BL(2, 0, 1, 4)

a_1	a_2	$b_{1,1}$	$b_{1,2}$	$b_{1,3}$	$b_{1,4}$
−0.098	0.97	0.035	0.31	−0.4	−0.41

AIC	σ_ε	RMSE
−1936	2.8e − 2	5.6e − 2

Table 10.13 Estimation of bilinear models, USD/FRF (April/60-min)

BL(4, 0, 1, 6)

a_1	a_2	a_3	a_4	$b_{1,1}$	$b_{1,2}$
−0.03	−0.11	0.036	0.07	0.17	−0.38

$b_{1,6}$	AIC	σ_ε	RMSE
−0.69	−2102	2.0e − 2	5.4e − 2

of forecasting evaluation (only invertible models are used for forecasting). The results for our series are given in Tables 10.9–10.13 (the results for the DEM/FRF 60-minute series are not reported as we could not estimate a good bilinear model).

4.2 Test of Linearity against Bilinear Alternatives

Two procedures have received a lot of attention in the econometric literature as diagnostic tests of linear models against bilinear alternatives: Keenan's (1985) linearity test and Saikkonen and Lüükkonen's (1991) test.

When all the cross-derivatives are null, equation (19) implies linearity. Therefore, the test of linearity against bilinear alternatives leads to a choice between the two hypotheses:

$$H_0 : x_t = \sum_{k=1}^{p} \alpha_k x_{t-k} + \sum_{k=0}^{q} \beta_k e_{t-k} \qquad \beta_0 = 1 \qquad (24)$$

against

$$H_1 : x_t = \sum_{k=1}^{p} \alpha_k x_{t-k} + \sum_{k=0}^{q} \beta_k \varepsilon_{t-k} + \sum_{k=1}^{P} \sum_{i=1}^{Q} \gamma_{ki} x_{t-k} \varepsilon_{t-i} \qquad \beta_0 = 1 \qquad (25)$$

where

$$\alpha_k = f''_{x_{t-k}} \qquad \beta_k = f''_{\varepsilon_{t-k}} \qquad \gamma_{ki} = f''_{x_{t-k}\varepsilon_{t-i}} \qquad (26)$$

Equation (25) gives the expression of a bilinear model BL(p, q, P, Q). As before, Keenan's (1985) linearity test is carried out following three stages:

1. One first estimates an ARMA model using a Box–Jenkins procedure. The appropriate values of p and q are determined using again the AIC criterion.

Compute the fitted values $\hat{x}_t$ (the forecasts are used inside the regression range) and call the sum of squared residuals $SCR(\hat{\varepsilon}_t)$. Note that t varies from $M+1$ to T, where $M = \max(p, q)$.

2.   The in-sample forecasts are used to estimate the coefficients of the regression of $\hat{x}_t$ on 1 and the past values of the series x_t up to the period $t - M$. The vector of residuals corresponding to this new regression is denoted $(\hat{\zeta}_t)$, $t = M+1, \ldots, T$.

3.   One then constructs the vector of residuals $(\hat{\eta}_t)$ corresponding to the regression of $(\hat{\varepsilon}_t)$ on $(\hat{\zeta}_t)$ and computes the corresponding Fisher statistic (denoted $\hat{F}$). Under H_0, this statistic has a Fisher distribution $F(1, T-2M-2)$.

Tsay (1986) has suggested an extension of the preceding approach by adding quadratic components in the regression (2). One thereby estimates the coefficients of the regression of $\hat{x}_t$ on (x_{t-i}) and x_{t-i}^2, $i = M, \ldots, T$. The new statistic then has a distribution with, respectively, $M(M+1)/2$ and $T-m(M+3)/2-1$ degrees of freedom. This approach has proven to have good power for bilinear models whose component sums are quadratic. However, a serious loss of power is caused whenever quadratic terms in the models under study do not exist. Tsay (1989) therefore considers a new extension of the preceding test, for which higher-order terms are included.

The procedures considered above might, however, have mediocre power properties against certain classes of bilinear specifications, for instance continuous bilinear models. In this context, score tests have been found to be superior to the Keenan family of tests. The modified tests fit into the same framework as LM tests (for an extensive discussion, see Saikkonen and Lüükkonen 1991). The approach consists of three distinct stages, namely:

1.   Estimate a linear AR(p) model and compute SSO, the sum of squared residuals.

2.   Carry out a regression taking $(\hat{\varepsilon}_t)$ the vector of residuals of the AR(p) models as the endogenous variable and the different vectors of cross-product terms $x_{t-k}\hat{\varepsilon}_{t-i}$ as the independent variables, $k = 1, \ldots, P$ and $i = 1, \ldots, Q$. Let $SS4$ be the sum of squared residuals of this second regression.

3.   Compute the statistic $BLT1 = T(SSO - SS4)/(SSO)$, where T is the number of observations used in the regression (2). Under the null hypothesis of linearity $BLT1$ has a χ^2 distribution with PQ degrees of freedom.

The results for our series are reported below.

4.3   Forecasting

Next, we investigate the predictive properties of the bilinear models. The forecasts are one-step-ahead predictions, conditional on parameter estimates based on the 1100 first data (30-minute) or the 550 first data (60-minute). The minimum mean-square error predictor is given by

$$\hat{X}_{t+k} = E[X_{t+k}|X_s; s \le t] \tag{27}$$

We consider now the bilinear model of the form $BL(p, 0, P, Q)$

$$X_t = \sum_{k=1}^{p} \alpha_k X_{t-k} + \sum_{k=1}^{P} \sum_{i=1}^{Q} \gamma_{ki} X_{t-k} \varepsilon_{t-i} \tag{28}$$

If we suppose that this model is invertible and using the fact that X_{t+r} and ε_{t+s} are independent for $s > r$, then we can write the one-step predictor as

$$\hat{X}_{t+1} = \sum_{k=1}^{p} \alpha_k X_{t-k+1} + \sum_{k=1}^{P} \sum_{i=1}^{Q} \gamma_{ki} X_{t-k+1} \varepsilon_{t-i+1} \tag{29}$$

For the application to our series the reader may refer to Tables 10.9–10.13, where the RMSEs concern the out-of-sample one-step-ahead dynamic forecasts for the last 100 data points of the series.

As seen from Table 10.14, linearity is rejected in 77% of the cases for the DEM/FRF, 66% for the USD/DEM and again 77% for the USD/FRF. Bilinearity is therefore a striking feature of our exchange rate dynamics. This result is in accordance with the conclusions found some 14 years ago by Maraval (1983) for the Spanish peseta but, since then, there has not been, to our knowledge, any application to high frequency exchange rates.

Using residual variance, the fitted models initially contained many coefficients corresponding to the bilinear cross terms (the order of Q was often equal to 4, at least). This means that in order to substantially reduce the residual variance, we needed to include many coefficients. However, Tables 10.9–10.13 contain only bilinear terms for which the AIC value is the smallest.

The final USD/FRF model retained demonstrates that, at a one-step horizon, its RMSE is much lower than those obtained from an AR(1) or a random walk

Table 10.14 Tests of linearity against bilinearity

	DEM/FRF (30-min)	DEM/FRF (60-min)	USD/DEM (30-min)	USD/DEM (60-min)	USD/FRF (30-min)	USD/FRF (60-min)
January	Bilinear	Bilinear	Bilinear	Bilinear	Bilinear	Bilinear
February	Bilinear	Bilinear	Linear	Linear	Bilinear	Bilinear
March	Bilinear	Linear	Linear	Bilinear	Linear	Bilinear
April	Bilinear	Linear	Linear	Linear	Bilinear	Bilinear
May	Bilinear	Bilinear	Bilinear	Bilinear	Linear	Bilinear
June	Linear	Linear	Bilinear	Bilinear	Bilinear	Bilinear
July	Bilinear	Bilinear	Bilinear	Linear	Bilinear	Bilinear
August	Bilinear	Bilinear	Bilinear	Bilinear	Linear	Linear
September	Bilinear	Bilinear	Bilinear	Bilinear	Bilinear	Bilinear

process, not to mention our fitted EXPAR model: this is shown by looking at the out-of-sample RMSE of Table 10.13 and comparing it with those of the out-of-sample one-step-ahead forecasts of Table 10.8.

5 CONCLUDING REMARKS

This chapter concentrates on the technical aspects of bilinear and EXPAR models, because these models are quite new to financial economists. They thus require an extensive presentation of their potential application to exchange rate modelling. In this respect, it was important to restrict our attention mainly to the logical steps involved when fitting the data with these models. The stages of the analysis can be summarised as being:

1. The application of linearity tests based on LM approaches.
2. The building of EXPAR and bilinear models as specific types of nonlinear processes.
3. The evaluation of the estimated models.
4. The predictive performance of both types of models was evaluated by studying in-sample and out-of-sample forecasts.

A first concern is whether linear models fare better than exponential autoregressive and bilinear processes when forecasting over several time steps. Another question is whether nonlinear models, which are based on a representation of the conditional mean of the series, lead to a gain in forecasting when compared with ARCH-type models. In this chapter, an answer has been given to the first question and our results show the importance of building EXPAR–ARCH and bilinear–ARCH models, which account for nonlinearities in the mean and the variance of exchange rates.

REFERENCES

Al-Qassam, M.S. and Lane, J.A. (1989), 'Forecasting Exponential Autoregressive Models of Order 1', *Journal of Time Series Analysis*, **2**, 95–113.

Bollerslev, T., Chou, R.Y. and Kroner, K.F. (1992), 'ARCH Modelling in Finance: A Review of the Theory and Empirical Evidence', *Journal of Econometrics*, **52**, 5–59.

Dechert, W.D. and Gencay, R. (1992), 'Lyapunov Exponents as a Nonparametric Diagnostic for Stability Analysis', *Journal of Applied Econometrics*, **7**, 41–61.

Diebold, F. (1988), *Empirical Modelling of Exchange Rates Dynamics*, Springer-Verlag, Berlin, p. 303.

Drunat, J., Dufrénot, G. and Mathieu, L. (1995), 'Nonlinear and Chaotic Dynamics in High Frequency Exchange Rates', *International Conference on Forecasting Financial Markets*, London, March.

Drunat, J., Dufrénot, G., Dunis, C. and Mathieu, L. (1996), 'Stochastic or Chaotic Dynamics in High Frequency Exchange Rates?', in C. Dunis (ed.), *Forecasting*

Financial Markets: Exchange Rates, Interest Rates and Asset Management, Wiley, London, pp. 33–49.

Granger, C.W.J. and Andersen, A.P. (1978), *An Introduction to Bilinear Time Series Models*, Vandenhoeck & Ruprecht, Göttingen.

Granger, C.W.J. and Teräsvirta, T. (1993), *Modelling Nonlinear Economic Relationships*, Advanced Texts in Econometrics, Oxford University Press.

Guégan, D. (1994) *Séries Chronologiques Non Linéaires*, Economica, Paris.

Haggan, V. and Ozaki, T. (1981) 'Modelling Nonlinear Vibrations Using an Amplitude-dependent Autoregressive Time Series Model', *Biometrika*, **68**, 189–196.

Hannan, E.J. and Rissanen, J. (1982), 'Recursive Estimation of Mixed Autoregressive-Moving Average Order', *Biometrika*, **69**, 91–96.

Higgins, M.L. and Bera, A.K. (1991), 'ARCH and Bilinearity as Competing Models for Nonlinear Dependence', mimeo, University of Wisconsin.

Hinich, M.J. (1982), 'Testing for Gaussianity and Linearity of a Stationary Time Series', *Journal of Time Series Analysis*, **3**(1), 169–176.

Hsieh, D. (1988), 'The Statistical Properties of Daily Exchange Rates: 1974–1983', *Journal of International Economics*, **24**, 129–145.

Hsieh, D. (1989), 'Testing for Nonlinear Dependence in Foreign Exchange Rates', *Journal of Business*, **62**, 339–368.

Ignacio, J. (1995), 'Empirical Evidence on the Term Structure of Interbank Interest Rates: Jump-Diffusion Processes', *International Conference on Forecasting Financial Markets*, London, March.

Jones, D.A. (1978), 'Nonlinear Autoregressive Processes', *Proceedings of the Royal Society of London*, Series A, **360**, 71–95.

Keenan, D.M. (1985), 'A Tukey Non-additivity-type Test for Time Series Nonlinearity', *Biometrika*, **72**, 39–44.

Low, A. and Muthuswamy, J. (1995), 'Information Flows in High Frequency Exchange Rates', *International Conference on Forecasting Financial Markets*, London, March.

McLeod, A.I. and Li, W.K. (1983), 'Diagnostic Checking ARMA Time Series Models Using Squared Residual Autocorrelations', *Journal of Time Series Analysis*, **4**, 269–273.

Maraval, A. (1983), 'An Application of Nonlinear Time Series Forecasting', *Journal of Business and Economic Statistics*, **3**, 350–355.

Merton, R.C. (1976), 'Option Pricing When Underlying Stock Returns Are Discontinuous', *Journal of Financial Economics*, **3**, 125–144.

Moreno, M. and Ignacio Peña, J. (1996), 'On the Term Structure of Interbank Interest Rates, Jump-Diffusion Processes and Option Pricing', in C. Dunis (ed.), *Forecasting Financial Markets, Exchange Rates, Interest Rates and Asset Management*, Wiley, London.

Müller, U.A., Dacorogna, M.M., Olsen, R.B., Pictet, O.V., Schwarz, M. and Morgenneg, C. (1990), 'Statistical Study of Foreign Exchange Rates, Empirical Evidence of a Price Change Scaling Law, and Intra-daily Analysis', *Journal of Banking and Finance*, **14**, 1189–1208.

Ozaki, T. (1978), *Non-linear Models for Non-linear Vibrations*, Technical Report No. 92, University of Manchester.

Ozaki, T. (1982), 'The Statistical Analysis of Pertubated Limit-cycles: Processes Using Non-linear Time Series Models', *Journal of Time Series Analysis*, **3**, 29–41.

Priestley, M.B. (1988), *Non-linear and Non-stationary Time Series Analysis*, Academic Press, London.

Saikkonen, P. and Lüükkonen, R. (1991), 'Power Properties of a Time Series Linearity Test against Some Simple Bilinear Alternatives', *Statistica Sinica*, **1**, 453–464.

Subba Rao, T. (1977) 'On the Estimation of Bilinear Time Series Models', paper presented at the 41st session of the International Statistics Institute, New Delhi.

Subba Rao, T. (1992), 'Analysis of Nonlinear Time Series (and Chaos) by Bispectral Methods', in M. Castagli and S. Eubank (eds), *Nonlinear Modelling and Forecasting*, Addison-Wesley, pp. 199-226.

Subba Rao, T. and Gabr, M.M. (1984), *An Introduction to Bispectral Analysis and Bilinear Time Series Models*, Springer-Verlag, Berlin.

Teräsvirta, T. and Anderson, H.M. (1992), 'Characterizing Nonlinearities in Business Cycles Using Smooth Transition Autoregressive Models', *Journal of Applied Econometrics*, **7**, 119-139.

Tsay, R.S. (1986), 'Non-linearity Tests for Time Series', *Biometrika*, **73**, 461-466.

Tsay, R.S. (1989), 'Testing and Modelling Threshold Autoregressive Processes', *Journal of the American Statistical Association*, **84**, 231-240.

PART IV
Non-parametric Models for Nonlinear Financial Time Series

—————— 11 ——————
Application of Neural Networks to Forecast High Frequency Data: Foreign Exchange

PETER J. BOLLAND, JEROME T. CONNOR
and A-PAUL N. REFENES

1 INTRODUCTION

In the financial markets of the 1990s, financial news (prices, news events, opinion) is disseminated across the globe almost instantaneously, requiring competitive institutions to analyse and react to market events at even higher speeds. With the increasing computerisation of the markets each individual transaction can be recorded and analysed. Transactions data and quotations are readily available from many data vendors and are a valuable source of information on the future price movements (both the volatility and expected value). The availability of data has spawned the interest of researchers from a number of different disciplines and stimulated model development for data analysis, predictive modelling and trading.

The statistical characteristics of high frequency financial data present many problems to traditional modelling methodologies. Standard time series methodologies cannot cope with erratic data arrival, distributions with unusually heavy tails and most importantly, with non-synchronicity of information arrival across different markets. Research into high frequency financial data has so far been confined to the investigation of market dynamics in isolation. This is a major drawback since most markets do not operate or evolve independently from each other. In practice, there is a high degree of interdependence, particularly

Nonlinear Modelling of High Frequency Financial Time Series.
Edited by Christian Dunis and Bin Zhou. © 1998 John Wiley Sons Ltd

between markets in which no arbitrage relationships are assumed to determine asset pricing.

The statistical model that we propose uses a state-space representation of the time series data in 'real time'. The model is not limited to univariate data and can utilise information from several time series. The Kalman filter (Kalman 1961) lies at the heart of state-space modelling and can be easily augmented to cope with missing observations and data aggregation. The methodology provides an ideal framework to model observation noise which is clearly evident in financial tick data (which other methodologies simply ignore). The methodology can also be made robust to the corrupting influence of outliers often observed in tick data (cf. section 2.2). We also show how the state dynamics of the tick data can be modelled using a non-parametric, nonlinear model.

The analysis of irregular times series presents a serious challenge to conventional modelling methodologies. Standard time series methodologies assume that data arrive at regular intervals. One approach for modelling irregular data is to choose some fixed time interval ('binning' the data) and treat the gaps in the time series as missing observations. Alternatively, a time deformation method can be used to produce a homogeneous time series. The time deformation methods proposed by several authors alleviate some of the problems associated with modelling erratic time series; however, their nature has some inherent drawbacks, i.e. only univariate (see Engle and Russell 1994 for review). Using fixed intervals of 'real time' for data analysis also presents some problems, requiring a time series methodology that can cope with missing observations and data aggregation. The choice of time interval can have serious implications on the quality of the final model produced.

The two methods for analysing irregular data assume different underlying mechanics of price evolution, namely:

- 'Time deformation' assumes the price evolves along a new (univariate) time index, the time index relating to dynamics of price observations.
- 'Real time' assumes that the prices evolve on the time scale of the chosen interval (i.e. seconds, minutes, etc.).

Time deformation was originally proposed by Clarke (1973) and suggests that prices are a subordinate stochastic process to another random variable, the arrival rate. The approach of time deformation was developed by Tauchen and Pitts (1983) and has been more recently discussed by Müller *et al.* (1990), who suggest methods of linear interpolation between erratic observations to obtain a regular homogeneous time series. Ghysels and Jasiak (1995) assume a different cause of time deformation, favouring nonlinear time deformation to 'business time' or 'tick time'. The ACD (autoregressive conditional duration) model of Engle and Russell (1994) directly models the time flow ('deformation') via an autoregressive process, similar in form to a GARCH model. The ACD approach to time deformation allows for the incorporation of exogenous variables but is still limited to univariate time series. These methods focus on understanding the stochastic dynamics of price arrival and do not estimate the dynamics of the actual price movements.

Moody and Wu (1996) use a linear state-space representation to model price movements but abandon real time and produce a homogeneous time series from the ordered data. This methodology, however, has no simple equivalent for multivariate time series, and the predictions of future prices cannot be related back to real time.

The methodology we present describes the underlying dynamics of the tick data as the states of a space model (Bolland and Connor 1995). These underlying states ('true price') are always evolving (every second) according to their stochastic dynamics, but they are only observed at random intervals via a noisy observation of a quotation or price (somebody's opinion of the true price). The states of the system can represent several time series so the model can take advantage of the asynchronous arrival of information from several intimately related assets. The state-space models observation equation expands or contracts depending on the quotes observed from the different assets (cf. section 2.1). The underlying states are updated even though this movement is not observed in the market data until the next tick occurs. The model is estimated by applying an augmented Kalman filter using a missing data framework. The state-space model and Kalman filter described are discrete, as the data are only provided in quantised time steps (i.e. seconds); however, the methodology can be extended to continuous time problems with the Kalman–Bucy filter (Meditch 1969). Our state-space representation allows us to model the system at the maximum resolution of the available data.

The filtering methodology is ideal to capture and model the observation noise of the time series. There are several causes of observation noise in high frequency financial data. In practice, the true price is bounded by a bid and ask price which are the actual traded prices. The difference between the true price and the bid and ask prices can be viewed as observation noise about the true price. Each of the indicative prices observed is simply a market participant's opinion of the 'true' price. There is always a distribution of opinion within the markets, which can be clearly seen when several quotes are observed simultaneously. In practice, prices are quoted to certain level of accuracy (3 or 4 decimal places). This rounding or quantisation induces noise in the observed quotations. Both the observation noise in the system and the data aggregation are easily represented in the state-space framework.

The state-space framework is very general and many stochastic models such as random walk, linear, auto-regressive integrated moving average (ARIMA), and non-parametric nonlinear models can be embedded within the extended Kalman filter. In section 2.3, we describe the extended Kalman filter which allows the state dynamics to be nonlinear. In our analysis, the state dynamics are estimated by a neural network model which does not impose a parametric assumption on the relationships and allows the dynamics to evolve in nonlinear ways.

Conventional modelling methodologies are inappropriate for modelling tick data as the distribution is often heavy tailed (Dacorogna 1995). Financial data, especially quotations, are prone to data corruption and outliers. Chung (1991) discovered that 0.25% of the major market index (MMI) futures quotes were outside of the daily high and low and therefore the data were seriously corrupted. Section 2.1 details our robust methodology which is similar to that described by Masreliez (1975) and Martin et al. (1983). Classical parametric statistics (frequentist or Bayesian) derive optimal procedures under exact parametric models; however, they give no measure of the behaviour of the models when the assumptions are only approximately valid. With only slight aberrations of the assumptions, many procedures break down, thus the estimated models, parameters and tests become meaningless (cf. Tukey 1960). Procedures that behave almost optimally when the assumptions are violated are termed robust. Robustly estimated models and parameters are not overly influenced by any minority of the data and are capable of estimating the structure which fits the bulk of the data.

Procedures can be made robust to various violations of the assumptions (non-Gaussian residuals, outliers, heteroscedasticity, level shifts, etc.). There is a large body of literature on methodologies that are robust when the residual distribution is non-Gaussian or outlier contaminated (output space outliers). There are several ways to achieve robustness to heavy tailed residuals: generalised maximum likelihood estimators (M-estimators) assume heavy tailed residual distributions (Huber 1964); R-estimators which use rank of the absolute values to trim heavy tails (Lehmann 1975); L-estimators achieve robustness using weighted linear combination of order statistics. It is not generally necessary to know the exact distribution of the residuals in order to obtain robust estimates, as any non-Gaussian model will usually do much better than the classical Gaussian model. In this chapter, we focus on robustness of multivariate nonlinear time series models to additive outliers in the observation equation.

Additive outliers in time series are particularly troublesome as each outlier will occur both as inputs to the model and as a target. Robust procedures for heavy tailed residuals will not necessarily be robust to input space outliers (Huber 1977). One way of rendering time series models robust is to filter outliers from the time series. The estimation methodology presented in this chapter is based on non-Gaussian filtering and is robust to both input and output space outliers (cf. Masreliez 1975; Kitagawa 1987; Connor et al. 1994).

Identifying outliers in multivariate data sets is a challenging and difficult problem. In this chapter, a robust estimator is implemented which treats each dimension of the multivariate residual independently. If an outlier occurs on just one dimension then a standard robust estimator filters all the dimensions. The estimator developed here retains the valuable information from the uncorrupted dimensions while limiting the influence of the contaminated series.

The modelling methodology outlined is employed in foreign exchange modelling. In section 3, we use the multivariate state-space framework to model triangular arbitrage relationships in the foreign exchange markets (GBP/USD, USD/DEM, GBP/DEM).

Arbitrage is a fundamental mechanism for achieving efficiency in the financial markets (Ross 1976). An arbitrage opportunity arises when a price discrepancy exists between two or more highly related assets. The opportunity can be exploited by buying the underpriced asset and selling the overpriced asset, producing a profit without incurring any risk. Mispricing is rapidly corrected in highly competitive markets (Frenkel and Levich 1975, 1977), therefore arbitrage traders need rapid identification, fast transactions and low transaction costs. Many arbitrage relationships have been identified in the financial markets. Our methodology can be applied to any system of linear arbitrage pricing relationships. The following section describes the triangular foreign exchange arbitrage we use to demonstrate the methodology. Previous studies of arbitrage pricing relationships have mainly been limited to examining daily data. Studies that have examined intraday data (Rhee and Chang 1992) have been limited to examining only a minute fraction of the data because of the need for simultaneous observations. The methodology we present allows the arbitrage price to be estimated in irregular (non-simultaneous) time series, increasing the speed and accuracy of arbitrage identification.

2 METHODOLOGY

2.1 State-space Modelling with the Kalman Filter

Multivariate time series in this chapter are modelled with the following state-space model, defined by the state update equation (1) and the observation equation (2):

$$\mathbf{x}_t = \mathbf{f}(\mathbf{x}_{t-1}) + \mathbf{e}_t \tag{1}$$

$$\mathbf{z}_t = \mathbf{H}_t \mathbf{x}_t + \mathbf{v}_t \tag{2}$$

where $\mathbf{x}_t$ represents the $(1 \times m)$ state vector of the underlying system, $\mathbf{f}(\ )$ describes the state dynamics and $\mathbf{z}_t = (z_t^{(1)}, z_t^{(2)}, \ldots, z_t^{(n)})^T$ represents the vector of observed time series. State-space models often simplify the description of data in which the observations are either time-varying or nonlinear functions of the underlying states. The observations, $\mathbf{z}_t$, can often be described in terms of states, $\mathbf{x}_t$, which have a lower dimension than the observation vector, which will often result in simplifying and reducing the dynamics which have to be estimated. State-space models allow the noise process $\mathbf{e}_t$ associated with the dynamics of the states to be separated from the noise $\mathbf{v}_t$ affecting the observations. In financial data, observation noise often occurs in the recording and transfer of market price quotations. In any modelling methodology where this is ignored, observation noise is by definition misspecified.

There are many possibilities for the state dynamics $\mathbf{f}(\ )$ in (1) (ranging from parametric or non-parametric to linear or nonlinear). This chapter focuses on estimating the dynamics and predicting the m principal states. The state-space framework is capable of representing many common time series models (regression, ARIMA, etc.). For vector autoregression lagged values of the principal states must be kept in order to be used as basis for predictions. The state dynamics, $\mathbf{f}(\mathbf{x}_t)$, represent the underlying functional forms of each of the states, which could be anything from random walks to linear or nonlinear functions:

$$\mathbf{f}(\mathbf{x}_t) = \mathbf{f}_1(\mathbf{x}_t), \mathbf{f}_2(\mathbf{x}_t), \ldots, \mathbf{f}_m(\mathbf{x}_t))^T \qquad (3)$$

$$\mathbf{f}_i(\mathbf{x}_t) = (f_i(\mathbf{x}_t)x_t^{(i)} \ldots x_{t-p+1}^{(i)})^T \qquad (4)$$

where $f_i(\mathbf{x}_t)$ denotes the deterministic component of the next state $\mathbf{x}_t$ and $x_t^{(i)}$ denote the autoregressive lags of the system.

The states, $\mathbf{x}_t$, of model given by (1) and (2) must be inferred from the observed data $\mathbf{z}_t$. For the case of a linear model, $\mathbf{f}(\mathbf{x}_{t-1}) = \Phi_t \mathbf{x}_{t-1}$ (where Φ_t is the linear state update matrix), there exists an exact Bayesian solution for estimating $\mathbf{x}_t$, the Kalman filter (Kalman and Bucy 1961). For nonlinear state dynamics, the extended Kalman filter (EKF) yields estimates of the underlying states. The EKF is not strictly Bayesian, but is a reasonable approximation which is widely used and well understood.

The model given by (1) and (2) often assumes $\mathbf{v}_t$ is generated by a multivariate Gaussian distribution with constant variance. The additive noise process is often heavy tailed in practice, which means that the number of large negative and positive noise terms is more than would be accountable by a Gaussian model.

The modelling of time series in state-space form has advantages over other techniques both in interpretability and estimation. The Kalman filter lies at the heart of state-space analysis and provides the basis for likelihood estimation. The Kalman filter is a recursive procedure for computing optimal estimates of the state vector at time t, based on all information available at time t. The Kalman filter enables the estimate of the state vector to be continually updated as new observations become available. For linear systems with Gaussian disturbance terms, the Kalman filter produces the maximum likelihood estimate of the state $\mathbf{x}_t$.

The recursive Kalman filter equations as described by Masreliez (1975) and Martin et al. (1983) are detailed below. The one-step-ahead predicted state vector $\hat{\mathbf{x}}_t$ and the predicted observation vector $\hat{\mathbf{z}}_t$ are given by

$$\hat{\mathbf{x}}_t = \mathbf{f}(\tilde{\mathbf{x}}_{t-1}) \qquad (5)$$

$$\hat{\mathbf{z}}_t = \mathbf{H}_t \hat{\mathbf{x}}_t \qquad (6)$$

where $\tilde{\mathbf{x}}_{t-1}$ is the estimated filtered state vector using all information up to and including time $t - 1$. For the Masreliez formulation of the Kalman filter the distribution terms $\mathbf{e}_t$ and $\mathbf{v}_t$ in (1) and (2) are assumed to be zero mean, serially independent and mutually independent; however, no assumptions about their distributions are made. The covariance matrices of $\mathbf{e}_t$ and $\mathbf{v}_t$ are denoted by $\mathbf{Q}_t = E(\mathbf{e}_t \cdot \mathbf{e}'_t)$ and $\mathbf{R}_t = E(\mathbf{v}_t \cdot \mathbf{v}'_t)$, respectively. The modelling methodology we employ assumes that the noise covariance matrices remain constant over time. The filtered estimate of the state vector $\tilde{\mathbf{x}}_{t|t}$ is defined by the following relationship:

$$\tilde{\mathbf{x}}_{t|t} = \hat{\mathbf{x}}_{t|t-1} + \mathbf{M}_{t|t-1}\mathbf{H}'_t\mathbf{g}_t(\bar{\mathbf{z}}_t) \tag{7}$$

where $\bar{\mathbf{z}}_t = \mathbf{z}_t - \hat{\mathbf{z}}_{t|t-1}$ is the innovations vector (the observed prediction error) and $\mathbf{g}_t(\bar{\mathbf{z}}_t)$ is the score function of the innovations and $\mathbf{M}_t$ is the prediction error covariance matrix. So the estimate of the state t is produced from the prediction based on information available at time $t-1$ ($\hat{\mathbf{x}}_{t|t-1}$), and a correction term based on the observed prediction error at time t ($\mathbf{M}_{t|t-1}\mathbf{H}'_t\mathbf{g}_t(\bar{\mathbf{z}}_t)$). The prediction error covariance matrix, $\mathbf{M}_t$, is specified by the set of relations:

$$\mathbf{M}_{t+1|t} = \Phi_{t+1|t}\mathbf{P}_{t|t}\Phi'_{t+1|t} + \mathbf{Q}_t \tag{8}$$

$$\mathbf{P}_{t|t} = \mathbf{M}_{t|t-1} - \mathbf{M}_{t|t-1}\mathbf{H}'_t\mathbf{G}_t(\bar{\mathbf{z}}_t)\mathbf{H}_t\mathbf{M}_{t|t-1} \tag{9}$$

where $\Phi_{t+1|t}$ is the state update matrix or a linearised approximation in the case of the EKF, $\mathbf{P}_{t|t}$ is the prediction error covariance and $\mathbf{G}_t$ is the differential of the score function of the innovations. Given the initial conditions, $\mathbf{P}_{0|0}$ and $\hat{\mathbf{x}}_{0|0}$, the Kalman filter gives the optimal estimator of the state vector as each new observation becomes available. The score function of the innovations process has components

$$\{\mathbf{g}_t(\bar{\mathbf{z}}_t)\}_i = -\left[\frac{\partial p\{\bar{\mathbf{z}}_t|Z_{t-1}\}}{\partial(\bar{\mathbf{z}}_t)_i}\right] \cdot [p\{\bar{\mathbf{z}}_t|Z_{t-1}\}]^{-1} \tag{10}$$

and $\mathbf{G}_t(\bar{\mathbf{z}}_t)$, the differential of the score function, has elements

$$\{G_t(\bar{\mathbf{z}}_t)\}_{ij} = \frac{\partial\{\mathbf{g}_t(\bar{\mathbf{z}}_t)\}_i}{\partial(\bar{\mathbf{z}}_t)_j} \tag{11}$$

where $p\{\bar{\mathbf{z}}_t|Z_{t-1}\}$ is the probability distribution of the innovation. If the distribution of the innovations is known then the recursive update equations can be defined. In the standard Kalman filter the density function for the innovations is assumed to be Gaussian. The score function $\mathbf{g}_t(\bar{\mathbf{z}}_t)$ for a Gaussian innovation process is linear. For heavy-tailed density functions, $\mathbf{g}_t(\bar{\mathbf{z}}_t)$ is given by a nonlinear gain function that downweights the influence of large innovations.

Section 2.2 gives the score function for several robust filters. For the case of Gaussian innovations the score function $\mathbf{g}_t(\bar{\mathbf{z}}_t)$ is given by

$$\mathbf{g}_t(\bar{\mathbf{z}}_t) = (\mathbf{H}_t\mathbf{M}_t\mathbf{H}'_t + \mathbf{R}_t)^{-1} \cdot \bar{\mathbf{z}}_t \tag{12}$$

For evenly spaced time series all the rates would be observed on every time step. Tick data observations occur on an irregular basis. For univariate time series analysis time can be deformed to 'tick time' or 'market time' to allow conventional modelling methodologies to be applied. For multivariate systems no such transformation is possible. The Kalman filter can be simply modified to deal with observations that are either missing or subject to contemporaneous aggregation. On any given second only currencies for which a quote (tick) has occurred enter the observation vector and only the rows of the observation matrix which correspond to an actual observation are used to update the filtering equations. So the dimensions of the observation vector $\mathbf{z}_t$ and the observation errors $\mathbf{v}_t$ vary at each time step $(n_t \times 1)$. The observation equation dimensions now vary with time, so

$$\mathbf{z}_t = \mathbf{W}_t \mathbf{H}_t \mathbf{x}_t + \mathbf{v}_t \quad t = 1, \ldots, N \tag{13}$$

where $\mathbf{W}_t$ is an $n_t \times n$ matrix of fixed weights. This gives rise to several possible situations.

- Contemporaneous aggregation of the first component of the observation vector, in addition to the other components. So the weight matrix is $((n+1) \times n)$ and has a row augment for the first component to give rise to the two values $z_{t,1}^1$ and $z_{t,2}^1$:

$$\mathbf{z}_t = \begin{bmatrix} z_{t,1}^1 \\ z_{t,2}^1 \\ \vdots \\ z_t^n \end{bmatrix}_{n+1} \qquad \mathbf{W}_t = \begin{bmatrix} 1 & 0 & 0 & \cdots & 0 \\ 1 & 0 & 0 & \cdots & 0 \\ 0 & 1 & 0 & \cdots & 0 \\ 0 & 0 & 1 & & 0 \\ \vdots & \vdots & & \ddots & \\ 0 & 0 & 0 & & 1 \end{bmatrix}_{(n+1)\times n} \tag{14}$$

- All components of the observations vector occur, where the weight matrix is square $(n \times n)$ and an identity:

$$\mathbf{z}_t = \begin{bmatrix} z_t^1 \\ \vdots \\ z_t^n \end{bmatrix}_n \qquad \mathbf{W}_t = \begin{bmatrix} 1 & \cdots & 0 \\ \vdots & 1 & \vdots \\ 0 & \cdots & 1 \end{bmatrix}_{n\times n} \tag{15}$$

- The ith component of the observation vector is unobserved, so n_t is $(n-1)$ and the weight matrix $(n \times (n-1))$ has a single row removed:

$$\mathbf{z}_t = \begin{bmatrix} z_t^1 \\ \vdots \\ z_t^{i-1} \\ z_t^{i+1} \\ \vdots \\ z_t^n \end{bmatrix}_{n-1} \qquad \mathbf{W}_t = \begin{bmatrix} & & 0 & & \\ \mathbf{I}_{i-1} & \vdots & \mathbf{0} \\ & \vdots & \\ & \vdots & \\ \mathbf{0} & \vdots & \mathbf{I}_{n-i} \\ & 0 & \end{bmatrix}_{(n-1)\times n} \tag{16}$$

- All components of the observations vector are unobserved, n_t is zero and the weight matrix is undefined:

$$\mathbf{z}_t = [NULL] \qquad \mathbf{w}_t = [NULL] \tag{17}$$

Expanding and contracting the observation equation in this way allows the state-space model to cope with the erratic arrival of data and immediately incorporate all new information to update its state estimates. The dimensions of the innovations $\bar{z}_{t|t-1_\psi}$ and their covariance $\Sigma_{t|t-1_\psi}$ also vary with n_t. Equation (13) is undefined when n_t is zero. When there are no observations, the Kalman filter updating equations can simply be skipped. The resulting predictions for the state and filtering error covariance are $\hat{x}_t = \hat{x}_{t|t-1}$ and $P_t = P_{t|t-1}$. For consecutive missing observations ($n_t = 0, \ldots, n_{t+1} = 0$) then we require multiple step prediction, which is achieved by repeated substitution into the transition equation. The estimates for multiple step predictions of $\hat{z}_{t+l|t}$ and $\hat{x}_{t+l|t}$ can be shown to be the minimum mean square linear estimators $E_t(y_{t+l})$.

For a Kalman filter to work on the state-space model (1) and (2), the system must be both observable and controllable; sufficient conditions for this are given in Bolland and Connor (1996a).

2.2 Robust Modelling

The Kalman filter can be adapted to filter processes where disturbance terms are non-Gaussian. The Kalman filter update equations are dependent on the score function of the disturbance terms and its derivative (Mazreliez 1975), so for a known distribution the optimal minimum mean variance estimator can be produced. In the situation where the distribution is unknown, *piecewise* linear methods can be employed to approximate it (Kitagawa 1987). As the filtering equations depend on the derivative of the distribution, such methods can be inaccurate. Other methods could be employed which take advantage of higher moments of the density functions and require no assumptions about the shape of the probability densities (Hilands and Thomopoulos 1994).

To optimally filter a data set corrupted by outliers, the distribution of the residuals must be defined. The exact form of the distribution is rarely known; however, it is generally the case that any reasonably heavy-tailed non-Gaussian procedure will have a superior performance to a Gaussian-based procedure.

There are many candidates for robust score functions, and this chapter concentrates on those related to work by Huber (1964, 1981) and Hampel et al. (1986). The class of 'M-estimators' presented in Huber (1964) minimises the maximum asymptotic variance of the estimator. Huber's least favourable distribution g_0 can be shown to be the minimax estimator for the following ε-contamination distribution:

$$P_\varepsilon = (1 - \varepsilon)F + \varepsilon E \tag{18}$$

where P_ε is the distribution of the observed data, F describes the distribution of the uncorrupted data generated by the underlying process and E represents the distribution of outliers which corrupt the data. For spherically ε-contaminated normal distributions in R^3 the score function g_0 for the Huber function is given by (ignoring constants)

$$g_0(r) = \begin{cases} r & \text{for } r \le r_0 \\ r_0 & \text{for } r > r_0 \end{cases} \tag{19}$$

which behaves as a Gaussian distribution within r_0 (i.e. linear), but underweights the influence of more extreme data to a constant. The constant r_0 is determined by the level of ε-contamination (which in most cases must be guessed) and the requirement that f_0 integrates to 1. The size of the innovations is the critical value which determines whether the observation is an outlier. The magnitude of the outlier is defined by $r_t^2 = (\mathbf{z}_t - \hat{\mathbf{z}}_t)'\Sigma^{-1}(\mathbf{z}_t - \hat{\mathbf{z}}_t)$ where Σ is the covariance of the innovations.

Hampel *et al.* (1986) suggests an alternative score function based on the influence function (the first derivative of a estimator at an underlying distribution F). The Hampel redescending estimators have good influence statistics and high breakdown points and in R^3 are given by

$$g_0(r) = \begin{cases} r & \text{for } 0 < |r| \le r_0 \\ r_0 \left(\dfrac{r_1 - |r|}{r_1 - r_0} \right) \text{sign}(r) & \text{for } r_0 < |r| \le r_1 \\ 0 & \text{for } r_1 < |r| \end{cases} \tag{20}$$

The primary advantage of the Hampel score function relative to the Huber score function is the increase in robustness to extreme data points beyond r_1. The Gaussian, Huber and redescending Hampel score functions are shown in Figure 11.1 for the one-dimensional case, the corresponding multivariate score functions have similar forms.

The score functions (19) and (20) can be given geometric interpretations. The Huber function can be viewed as projecting outlying innovations on to the surface of a hypersphere while maintaining the vector direction. The projections represent

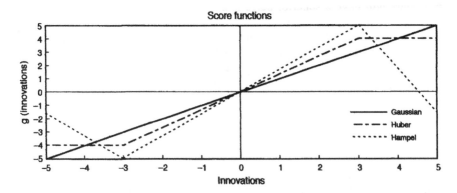

Figure 11.1 Score functions: Gaussian, Huber, Hampel

the filtered values of the innovations. All axes are filtered when a data point is outside the hypersphere.

For the Huber function it is assumed that the entire data point comes from either the true data distribution with probability $(1 - \varepsilon)$ or the contamination distribution with probability ε. It is also assumed that the level of contamination is the same for all dimensions of the innovation vector. It is often found that outliers occur independently on each axis and at different frequencies and that the underlying generating process of the outliers is different. The multivariate Huber function is clearly undesirable in this situation as filtering all axes will remove and distort valid information for the uncontaminated observations. In vector autoregressive models the filtered values form the basis for several predictions for all the time series, so incorrectly filtered values form the basis of several predictions, and incorrect filtering can degrade the performance of the model.

The contamination noise model that we assume treats the contamination of each axis independently with different contamination levels on each:

$$P_\varepsilon = (1 - \varepsilon_0)F + \sum_{i=1}^{n} \varepsilon_i E_i \qquad \text{for } i = 1, \ldots, n \qquad (21)$$

where E_i represents an additive outlier distribution for the ith dimension of the multivariate innovation vector and $\varepsilon_0 = \Sigma_{i=1}^{n} \varepsilon_i$ denotes the total proportion of additive outliers. This noise contamination model leads to a robust Kalman gain function, with components given by

$$\mathbf{g}_t(\bar{\mathbf{z}}_t)_i = s_{ti} \psi \left(\frac{\bar{z}_{ti}}{s_{ti}} \right) \qquad (22)$$

where $s_{ti} = \sqrt{(\mathbf{H}_t \mathbf{M}_t \mathbf{H}_t + \mathbf{R}_t)_i}$ is the scale associated with a given observation i. Note that equation (22) is in contrast to other robust gain functions such as equations (19) and (20) which are determined across all axes and hence a function of r.

2.3 Extended Kalman Filter

Even for strictly efficient markets there can be predictable dynamics of high frequency price movements caused by market artefacts, see for example Roll (1984). The functional form of these artefacts and other predictive dynamics is unknown. It is therefore desirable to allow the methodology to estimate the functional relationships non-parametrically. Enforcing a linear parameterisation on to the state update function may severely bias and degrade the modelling methodology.

The Kalman filter can be extended (EKF) to filter nonlinear state-space models. These models are not generally conditionally Gaussian and thus an approximate filter is used. The state-space model's observation function $h_t(\mathbf{x}_t)$ and the state update function $f_t(\mathbf{x}_{t-1})$ are no longer linear functions of the state vector. For a nonlinear state-space model the state transition matrix Φ_t in equation (8) is estimated by a pointwise linearisation of the nonlinear model. The elements of Φ_t, the state update matrix, are the partial derivatives of $\mathbf{f}$ evaluated about the robustly filtered estimates of the state vector $\tilde{\mathbf{x}}_t$:

$$\Phi_{i,j} = \frac{\partial f(\mathbf{x}_t)_i}{\partial x_j}\bigg|_{\mathbf{x}_t = \tilde{\mathbf{x}}_t} \tag{23}$$

i.e. a linearisation of the function at $\tilde{\mathbf{x}}_t$. The quality of the approximation depends on the smoothness of the nonlinearity as the EKF is only a first-order approximation of $\mathbf{E}\{\mathbf{x}_t | \mathbf{Y}_{t-1}\}$.

The individual nonlinear functions are modelled with simple feedforward neural networks with h_i hidden units and sigmoidal transfer functions (S):

$$f_i(\mathbf{x}_t) = \sum_{j=1}^{h_i} W_{i,j} S\left(\sum_{k=1}^{p_i} w_{i,j,k} x_{t-k}^{(1)} + \ldots + \sum_{k=1}^{p_i} w_{i,j,k+(m-1)p} x_{t-k}^{(m)} + \theta_{i,j}\right) + \theta_i \tag{24}$$

which is a function of the entire state, not just the lagged values of a single principal state $x_t^{(i)}$. Where the parameter vector λ consists of the neural networks weights:

$$\lambda_i = \{W_{i,1}, \ldots, W_{i,h_i}, w_{i,1,1}, \ldots, w_{i,h_i,mp}, \theta_{i,1}, \ldots, \theta_{i,h_i}, \theta_{i_i}\} \tag{25}$$

3 FX ARBITRAGE MODEL

Several FX arbitrage pricing relationships have been identified (triangular arbitrage, covered interest rate arbitrage, one way arbitrage, etc.), each placing constraints on the exchange rates. This chapter focuses on the simple FX triangular arbitrage relationships, the properties and formulation of which are described below. Our methodology, however, can be applied to any linear set of pricing relationships. In the absence of transactions costs and bid–ask spread, the following equilibrium relationships must hold for currency rates:

$$EX(0, 1)\, EX(1, 2)\, EX(2, 0) = 1$$

$$EX(0, 1)\, EX(1, 2)\, EX(2, 3)\, EX(3, 0) = 1$$

$$\vdots \qquad\qquad \vdots \qquad \vdots \qquad\quad \vdots \tag{26}$$

$$EX(0, 1)\, EX(1, 2)\, EX(2, 3) \ldots \ldots \ldots EX(m, 0) = 1$$

where $EX(i, j)$ represents the spot rate for currency j when expressed in units of currency i. If the equilibrium relationships in equations (26) hold, then a single country's m exchange rates can be used to produce estimates of all the cross rates, $EX(i, j) = EX(0, j)/EX(0, i)$; in this analysis the US dollar is used as the base currency. Taking logarithms of the triangular relationships, allows the cross rates to be expressed as

$$\log(EX(1, 2)) = \log(EX(0, 2)) - \log(EX(0, 1))$$
$$\vdots \qquad\qquad \vdots \qquad\qquad \vdots$$
$$\log(EX(i, j)) = \log(EX(0, j)) - \log(EX(0, i)) \qquad (27)$$
$$\vdots \qquad\qquad \vdots \qquad\qquad \vdots$$
$$\log(EX(m - 1, m)) = \log(EX(0, m)) - \log(EX(0, m - 1))$$

With the inclusion of bid–ask spreads, the relationships expressed in equations (27) only hold approximately. Conducting a transaction to exploit a pricing discrepancy incurs a series of additional transaction costs. These factors (transaction costs, bid–ask spread) mean that currency values are free to fluctuate within bounds where arbitrage is unable to set the currency value to the true price. The unprofitable bounds depend on the individual market. The free fluctuation of price within the unprofitable bounds can be thought of as additive observation noise around the true arbitrage price.

In addition to introducing noise into the pricing relationships, the bid–ask spread influences the dynamics of the time series. Roll (1984) showed that bid–ask bounce induced strong negative autocorrelation into financial data, an empirical effect observed in many studies (see Fama 1965). Time series of market prices contain both bid and ask prices so if no new information arrives the true value remains constant; any observed variation is caused by the difference in bid and ask price. Bouncing between bid and ask prices gives rise to a strong negative autocorrelation shown in Figure 11.2.

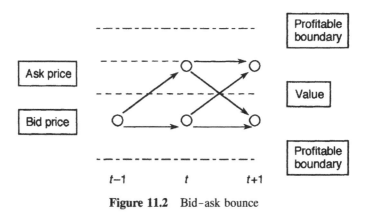

Figure 11.2 Bid–ask bounce

In addition to the bid–ask bounce effect, the pricing relationships may well have other artefacts that induce mean reversion around the true arbitrage price (price quantisation, market maker bid–ask preference, inventory effect, etc.).

The additive relationships of equations (27) are violated when mispricing anomalies occur in the market. Violations of the triangular relationships are analogous to an outlier in the data set, the larger the mispricing the larger the outlier. If the value actually moves outside the profitable bounds (and it is not a data corruption) then an arbitrage opportunity exists where riskless profitable transactions can occur. In the following section, the triangular currency relationships are encoded within a state-space form and a multivariate Kalman filter is used to filter the market noise and identify any significant violations of equations (27). Our methodology allows the arbitrage pricing relationships to be analysed as each new tick arrives, increasing the speed and accuracy of the identification of profitable trades.

3.1 Arbitrage Model Specification

The observation vector $\mathbf{z}_t$ in the FX state-space model represents the logarithm of each exchange rate observed. Expressing the exchange rates in terms of logarithms enables the construction of an additive state-space model. The additive noise models considered in this chapter are more appropriate for a state-space model based on the log of price changes, because the log of a price change can be negative and prices cannot. If all possible exchange rates (ticks) are observed at a given time step then, $\mathbf{z}_t$ is given by

$$\mathbf{z}_t = (z_t^{(0,1)}, z_t^{(0,2)}, \ldots, z_t^{(0,m)}, z_t^{(1,2)}, \ldots, z_t^{(1,m)}, \ldots, Z_t^{(m-1,m)}) \qquad (28)$$

where $z_t^{(i,j)} = \log(\mathrm{EX}(i,j))$. Usually only a subset of equation (28) is observed. The elements of $\mathbf{z}_t$ come in two principal groups:

- The log of the m exchange rates for the base currency $(0, j)$:

$$z_t^{(0,1)}, z_t^{(0,2)}, \ldots, z_t^{(0,m)} = \log(\text{base rates}) \qquad (29)$$

- The log of the corresponding cross rates (i, j):

$$z_t^{(1,2)}, \ldots, z_t^{(1,m)}, z_t^{(2,3)}, \ldots, z_t^{(m-1,m)} = \log(\text{cross rates}) \qquad (30)$$

The logs of the cross rates given in equation (30) can be expressed in terms of the base rates of equation (29) through $z^{(i,j)} = z^{(0,j)} - z^{(0,i)}$. The base rates are therefore ideal candidates for the underlying states. For the predictors of fundamental exchange rates considered in this section, the last p lags of each base rate will need to be included in the state. This leads to the choice of state $\mathbf{x}_t$ given by

$$\mathbf{x}_t = \{x_t^1, \ldots, x_{t-p}^1, \ldots, x_t^m, \ldots, x_{t-p}^m\}^T$$

where x_t^i represents the logs of the 'true' dollar exchange rate of currency i at time t which is not to be confused with the observed noisy dollar exchange rates, $z_t^{(0,i)}$. The choice of p lags for each time series was partly motivated by notational simplicity; in practice a varying number of lags for each time series should be considered.

As shown in equation (2), the observation, z_t, is linked to the observations, x_t, through the observation matrix

$$H_t = [h_t^{(0,1)T}, \ldots, h_t^{(0,m)T}, h_t^{(1,2)T}, \ldots, h_t^{(1,m)T}, \ldots, h_t^{(m-1,m)T}] \qquad (31)$$

which extracts the current base rates and the cross rates, at time t, from the state vector x_t. Each of the rows of H_t relate to a specific exchange rate, either a base rate or cross rate. The rows are defined as follows:

• For *base currency exchange rate* $(0, j)$

$$h_t^{(0,j)} = [0 \ 0_{1 \times p^{(1)}} \ 0 \ \ldots \ 0_{1 \times p^{(j-1)}} \ 1 \quad 0_{1 \times p^{(j)}} \ 0 \ \ldots \ 0_{1 \times p^{(m)}}] \qquad (32)$$

so each $h_t^{(0,j)}$ only extracts the base currency rate at time t, x_t^j, from x_t.
• For *cross currency exchange rates* (i, j)

$$h_t^{(i,j)} = [0 \ 0_{1 \times p^{(1)}} \ 0 \ \ldots \ 0_{1 \times p^{(i)}} \ -1 \ 0_{1 \times p^{(j)}} \ 1 \ \ldots \ 0 \ 0_{1 \times p^{(m)}}] \qquad (33)$$

so each $h_t^{(i,j)}$ estimates the cross rate (i, j) at time t, using the additive log relationships between the base currency exchange rates x_t^i and x_t^j, i.e. $h_t^{(i,j)} \cdot x_t = x_t^j - x_t^i$.

The arbitrage conditions in this simple currency example give rise to a state-space model in which the state update function needs only model the dynamics of the base exchange rates. Embedding the arbitrage relationships within the observation matrix H_t simplifies the representation and the model estimation.

The actual predictor of the base rate only predicts the change in the exchange rate. Predicting state changes rather than levels requires a slight reformulation of the $f_t^i(x_{t-1})$'s in equation (4). The state transitions $f( )$ are formed by two components, a random walk component $x_{t-1}^{(i)}$ (the previous state) and the state changes $d^{(i)}(x_{t-1} - x_{t-2})$, namely,

$$f(x_{t-1}) = (x_{t-1}^{(1)} + d^{(1)}(x_{t-1} - x_{t-2}), x_{t-1}^{(1)}, \ldots, x_{t-p^{(1)}+1}^{(1)},$$

$$x_{t-1}^{(2)} + d^{(2)}(x_{t-1} - x_{t-2}), x_{t-1}^{(2)}, \ldots, x_{t-p^{(2)}+1}^{(2)}, \ldots, \qquad (34)$$

$$\ldots, x_{t-1}^{(m)} + d^{(m)}(x_{t-1} - x_{t-2}), x_{t-1}^{(m)}, \ldots, x_{t-p^{(m)}+1}^{(m)})^T$$

where $d^{(i)}(x_{t-1} - x_{t-2})$ represents the predictive structure to be modelled.

Tick data for three currencies USD/DEM, GBP/USD, GBP/DEM (1993–95) were used to demonstrate the methodology. The states of our model are therefore the arbitrage values of USD/DEM, GBP/USD, so $x_t \ =$

(log(USD/DEM),
log(GBP/USD)). The dynamics of the change in states ($d^{(i)}(\mathbf{x}_{t-1} - \mathbf{x}_{t-2})$), were estimated by the following models:

- A naïve random walk model (no filter):

$$\hat{d}^{(i)}(\mathbf{x}_{t-1} - \mathbf{x}_{t-2}) = 0 \qquad (35)$$

- A neural network NVAR(n, n):

$$\hat{\mathbf{d}}(\mathbf{x}_{t-1} - \mathbf{x}_{t-2}) = \begin{bmatrix} \sum_{j=1}^{h_1} W_{1,j} S \left(\sum_{k=1}^{p_1} w_{1,j,k}(x_{t-k}^{(1)} - x_{t-k-1}^{(1)}) \right. \\ \left. + \sum_{k=1}^{p_1} w_{1,j,k}(x_{t-k}^{(2)} - x_{t-k-1}^{(2)}) + \theta_{1,j} \right) + \theta_1 \\ \sum_{j=1}^{h_2} W_{2,j} S \left(\sum_{k=1}^{p_2} w_{2,j,k}(x_{t-k}^{(1)} - x_{t-k-1}^{(1)}) \right. \\ \left. + \sum_{k=1}^{p_2} w_{2,j,k}(x_{t-k}^{(2)} - x_{t-k-1}^{(2)}) + \theta_{2,j} \right) + \theta_2 \end{bmatrix} \qquad (36)$$

The random walk model of equation (35) was included for comparison purposes.

3.2 Results

The tick data were obtained from Reuters, April 1993 to April 1995. The data used were taken from a database of Reuters' FXFX pages (USD exchange rates) and WXWX pages (major cross rates). The information shown on these screens is provided by Reuters' contributors (mainly large banks and brokers) and represents an indication of the current trading price of the market participant. Using Reuters' data, as opposed to brokers' trading data, introduces several additional sources of noise. The values are only an indication and are not tradable, as a result the arbitrage relationships are not enforceable and the bid–ask spread tends to be much larger in reality. These indications are often used as advertisements or as expressions of opinion on market movements. Reuters' data also have some pre-filtering before the indication appears on the pages. First, an automated procedure is used to remove any extreme indications. This system is not adaptive and targeted at removing gross data errors. Second, the pages are 'throttled' so that the prices are not updated at such a rate that the prices are unreadable. These additional sources of noise offer no severe problem to the methodology presented and only further highlight the presence of observation noise.

An estimation maximisation (EM) algorithm is employed at the centre of a robust estimation procedure based on filtered data (for full details see Bolland and Connor 1996a). The EM algorithm, see Dempster, Laird and Rubin (1977), is the standard approach when estimating model parameters with missing data. The EM algorithm has been used in the neural network community before, see for example Connor et al. (1994). During the estimation step, the missing data, namely the $\mathbf{x}_t$, $\boldsymbol{\varepsilon}_t$ and $\mathbf{v}_t$ of sections (1) and (2), must be estimated. This amounts to estimating parameters of the state update function f and the noise variance matrices $\mathbf{Q}_t$ and $\mathbf{R}_t$, respectively. With the estimated missing data assumed to be true, the parameters are then chosen by way of maximising the likelihood. This procedure is iterative, with new parameter estimates giving rise to new estimates of missing data which in turn give rise to newer parameter estimates. The iterative estimation procedure was initialised by constructing a contiguous data set (no arrival noise) and estimating a linear autoregressive model, VAR(1,1) to approximate the transitions matrix:

$$\hat{\mathbf{f}}(\mathbf{x}_{t-1}) = \begin{bmatrix} x_t^{(1)} \\ x_t^{(2)} \end{bmatrix} + \begin{bmatrix} -0.5065 & 0.0358 \\ -0.0564 & -0.4361 \end{bmatrix} \cdot \begin{bmatrix} x_{t-1}^{(1)} - x_{t-2}^{(1)} \\ x_{t-1}^{(2)} - x_{t-2}^{(2)} \end{bmatrix} \tag{37}$$

The strength of the negative diagonal terms demonstrates mean reversion. This model was used in the Kalman filter to produce a filtered data set without missing observations from which subsequent models were produced. The variances of the disturbance terms are non-stationary. To remove some of this non-stationarity the intraday seasonal pattern of the variances were estimated (Bolland and Connor 1996b). The parameters of the state update function were assumed to be stationary across the length of the data set.

Table 11.1 shows the filtering results for the neural network Kalman filter and the naïve random walk hypothesis. The Kalman filter produces superior results as indicated by the mean squared error (MSE) and the robust median absolute deviations (MAD).

Figures 11.3 and 11.4 demonstrate the Kalman filter identifying outliers. In Figure 11.3 the filtered estimated states for the USD/DEM exchange rate are represented by the solid line, the actual observed trades by circles, and trades occurring on the other exchange rates by vertical lines. The filtered states represent estimates of the log of the true arbitrage prices (not the bid or ask values). The effect of market frictions has been incorporated into the estimate $\mathbf{R}_t$, so filtered states are always within the actual bid and ask values observed. The Kalman filter identifies an outlier and uses pure prediction for the estimate of the USD/DEM rate at time 15:07:41 and does not follow the spurious price movement. The mispricing is filtered and classified as an outlier ($r_t = 4.65$) by the robust algorithm presented here.

Figure 11.3 also demonstrates how new information occurring on any of the exchange rates is immediately incorporated in the robust estimates of all the

Table 11.1 Model comparison

Model	MSE	MAD
RW model (no filter)	2.169 (10^{-4})	0.0084
Neural network Kalman filter	1.511 (10^{-4})	0.0075

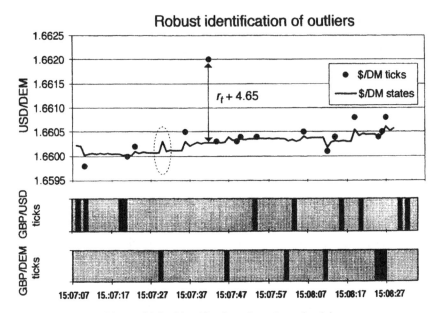

Figure 11.3 Identification of market mispricing

Table 11.2 Tick data (bold) and estimated rates (normal)

USD/DEM Ticks	GBP/USD Ticks	GBP/DEM Ticks	USD/DEM Estimate	GBP/USD Estimate	GBP/DEM Estimate	USD/DEM Standard deviation	GBP/USD Standard deviation
1.6601		**2.4351**	**1.66018**	1.46637	**2.43444**	**4.33**	8.38
			1.66021	1.46624	2.43439	4.21	7.9
1.6604			**1.66031**	1.46627	2.43447	**4.35**	8.18
			1.66030	1.46626	2.43443	4.21	7.71
	1.4662		1.66031	**1.46622**	2.43439	4.65	**8.38**
			1.66031	1.46624	2.43440	4.34	7.7
			1.66031	1.46623	2.43440	4.57	7.9
1.6608			**1.66055**	1.46617	2.43464	**4.6**	8.4
			1.66042	1.46619	2.43449	4.21	8.31
	1.4665	**2.4356**	1.66047	**1.46638**	**2.43488**	4.65	**8.38**

states. At time 15:07:27, the vertical dotted line indicates the observation of a GBP/DEM trade, the estimate of the USD/DEM state is instantly updated to incorporate the effect of the rise in the GBP/DEM.

Table 11.2 demonstrates the ability of the Kalman filter to deal with the erratic arrival of tick data. Bold font exchange rates represent seconds when ticks are observed, and normal font represents the Kalman filter estimates. When

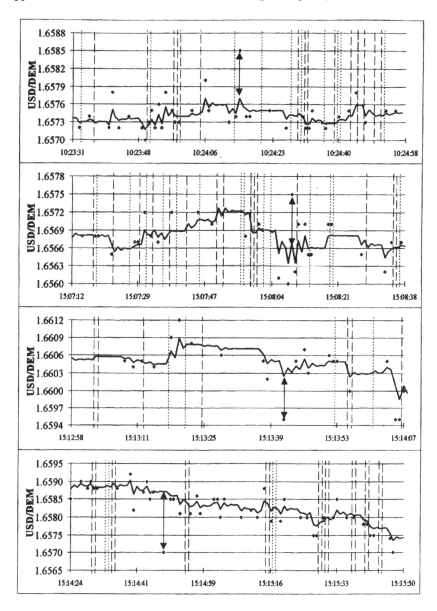

Figure 11.4 Identification of market mispricing

incomplete observation vectors are observed, the Kalman filter uses the multi-variate autoregressive structure to estimate the unseen rates. In seconds where no observations are observed the filter uses pure prediction to estimate the missing currency rates. The last two columns in Table 11.2 show the estimated prediction standard deviations for the log of the states. Again, bold font indicates the seconds where ticks were observed and normal font indicates the recursive estimates of the Kalman filter. The prediction error standard deviations grows steadily in periods where no ticks are observed, and collapses to the one second state prediction error standard deviation for the prediction based on new information (ticks).

4 CONCLUSIONS

We have presented a methodology to model high frequency financial tick data. This methodology was composed of three distinct parts: arbitrage relationships, dynamics of fundamental prices and robust methods. This methodology was placed within the unifying framework of state-space models. The methodology was demonstrated on tick data for the problem of FX arbitrage.

By placing arbitrage relationships within a state-space model a great reduction in the number of statistical models is obtained. Only models of the fundamental prices are needed. The Kalman filter, the estimation technique used to estimate states within state-space models, is ideal for tracking tick data with highly erratic arrival rates. We were able to track unobserved price moves on less frequently traded assets through both arbitrage relationships and correlation between price movements.

Financial tick data are notoriously noisy. This noise is due to misleading quotes and typographical errors, both of which take place frequently. We demonstrated how a robust Kalman filter provides reliable estimates of the true price in the presence of data contamination. In addition to producing robust predictions, robust models are estimated by only using 'clean' data within the parameter estimation procedure.

In addition to outright misleading quotes, observed prices are frequently found within a narrow band surrounding the arbitrage free price. This narrow band is due to bid–ask bounds, quantisation errors and inventory effects. The use of state-space models allows the definition of a measurement error which reflects how far an observed price is expected to deviate from the true price.

Because of the cohesive nature of our methodology, it can be applied to any financial problem with the appropriate modifications. This is an important feature in a world where the number of traded quantities is growing each year.

5 REFERENCES

Bolland, P.J. and Connor, J.T. (1995), 'A Robust Non-linear Multivariate Kalman Filter for Arbitrage Identification in High Frequency Data', *Proceedings of Neural Networks in the Capital Markets*, World Scientific.

Bolland, P.J. and Connor, J.T. (1996a), 'A Constrained Kalman Filter for Price Estimation in High Frequency Financial Data', submitted to *International Journal of Neural Information Processing Systems*, January.

Bolland, P.J. and Connor, J.T. (1996b), *Estimation of Intraday Seasonal Variances*, Technical Report, London Business School.

Clarke, P.K. (1973), 'A Subordinated Stochastic Process Model with Finite Variance for Speculative Prices', *Econometrica*, **41**(1), January, 122–134.

Connor, J.T., Bolland, P.J. and Lajbcygier, P. (1996), 'Intraday Modelling of the Term Structure of Interest Rates', *Proceedings of Neural Networks in the Capital Markets*, World Scientific pp. 122–134.

Connor, J.T., Martin, R.D. and Atlas, L.E. (1994), 'Recurrent Neural Networks and Robust Time Series Prediction', *IEEE Transactions on Neural Networks*, March, 240–254.

Chung, P.Y. (1991), 'A Transactions Data Test of Stock Index Futures Market Efficiency and Index Arbitrage Profitability', *Journal of Finance*, **46**, December, 1791–1809.

Dacorogna, M.M. (1995), 'Price Behaviour and Models for High Frequency Data in Finance', Tutorial NNCM Conference, London, England, 11–13 Oct.

Dempster, A.P., Laird, N.M. and Rubin, D.B. (1977), 'Maximum Likelihood from Incomplete Data via the EM Algorithm', *Journal of the Royal Statistical Society*, **B39**, 1–38.

Engle, R.E. and Russell, J.R. (1994), 'Forecasting Transaction Rates: The Autoregressive Conditional Duration Model', National Bureau of Economic Research, Inc., Working Paper No. 4966.

Fama, E.F. (1965), 'The Behaviour of Stock Market Prices', *Journal of Business*, **38**, January, 34–105.

Frenkel, J.A. and Levich, R.M. (1975), 'Covered Interest Arbitrage: Unexploited Profits?' *Journal of Political Economy*, **83**, 325–338.

Frenkel, J.A. and Levich, R.M. (1977), 'Transaction Costs and Interest Arbitrage: Tranquil Versus Turbulent Periods', *Journal of Political Economy*, **85**, 1209–1226.

Ghysels, E. and Jasiak, J. (1995), 'Stochastic Volatility and Time Deformation: An Application of Trading Volume and Leverage Effects', *Proceedings of the HFDF-I Conference*, Zurich, Switzerland, 29–31 March, vol. 1, pp. 1–14.

Hampel, F.R., Ronchetti, E.M., Rousseeuw, P.J. and Stahel, W.J. (1986), *Robust Statistics, the Approach Based on Influence Functions*. Wiley, New York.

Hilands, T.W. and Thomoploulos, S.C. (1994), 'High-order Filters for Estimation in Non-Gaussian Noise', *Information Sciences*, **80**, 149–179.

Huber, P.J. (1964), 'Robust Estimation of Location Parameter', *Annals of Mathematical Statistics*, **35**, 73–101.

Huber, P.J. (1977), *Robust Statistical Procedures*, No. 27, Regional Conference Series in Applied Mathematics, Philadelphia: SIAM.

Huber, P.J. (1981), *Robust Statistics*, Wiley, New York.

Kalman, R.E. (1961), 'A New Approach to Linear Filtering and Prediction Problems', *Trans. ASME J. Basic Eng. Series D*, **82**, March, 35–46.

Kalman, R.E. and Bucy, R.S. (1961), 'New Results in Linear Filtering and Prediction Theory', *Trans. ASME J. Basic Eng. Series D*, **83**, 95–108.

Kitagawa, G. (1987), 'Non-Gaussian State-space Modelling of Nonstationary Time Series, *Journal of the American Statistical Association*, **82**, 1033–1063.

Lehmann, E.L. (1975), 'Nonparametric: Statistical Methods Based on Ranks', Holden-Day, San Francisco.

Martin, R.D., Samarov, A. and Vandaele W. (1983), 'Robust Methods for Time Series', in A. Zellner (ed.), *Applied Time Series Analysis of Economic Data*, US Bureau of the Census, Washington, pp. 153–169.

Masreliez, C.J. (1975), 'Approximate Non-Gaussian Filtering with Linear State and Observation Relations', *IEEE Transactions on Automatic Control*, February, 107–110.

Meditch, J.S. (1969), *Stochastic Optimal Linear Estimation and Control*, McGraw-Hill, New York.

Moody, J. and Wu, L. (1996), 'What is the "True Price"? State-space Models for High Frequency Financial Data', *Proceedings of the International Conference on Neural Information Processing*, Hong Kong, Springer-Verlag, September, pp. 346–358.

Müller, U.A., Dacorogna, M.M., Olsen, R.B., Pictet, O.V., Schwarz, M., Morgenegg, C. (1990), 'Statistical Study of Foreign Exchange Rates, Empirical Evidence of a Price Change Scaling Law, and Intraday Analysis', *Journal of Banking and Finance*, **14**, 1189–1208.

Rhee, S.G. and Chang, R.P. (1992), 'Intraday Arbitrage Opportunities in Foreign Exchange and Eurocurrency Markets', *Journal of Finance*, **47**, March, 363–379.

Roll, R. (1984), 'A Simple Implicit Measure of the Effective Bid–Ask Spread in an Efficient Market', *Journal of Finance*, **39**, September, 1127–1140.

Ross, S.A. (1976), 'The Arbitrage Theory of Capital Asset Pricing', *Journal of Economic Theory*, **13**, December, 341–360.

Tauchen, G.E. and Pitts, M. (1983), 'The Price Variability–Volume Relationship on Speculative Markets', *Econometrica*, **51**(2), March, 485–505.

Tukey, J.W. (1960), 'A Survey of Sampling from Contaminated Distributions', in I. Olkin *et al.* (eds), *Contributions to Probability and Statistics*, Stanford University Press, Stanford, Calif., pp. 448–485.

12

An Application of Genetic Algorithms to High Frequency Trading Models: A Case Study

CHRISTIAN DUNIS, MICHAEL GAVRIDIS,
ANDREW HARRIS, SWEE LEONG
and POOMJAI NACASKUL

1 INTRODUCTION

1.1 Genetic Algorithms and Evolutionary Optimisation

A *genetic algorithm* (GA) is a computer simulation-based optimisation search methodology inspired by nature's own evolutionary process of solution discovery and environmental adaptation. GA was conceived by John Holland (1975), while similarly inspired approaches, *evolutionary programming* (EP) and *evolutionary strategies* (ES), trace their roots to the 'German School' (Rechenberg 1965; Fogel *et al.* 1966; Schwefel 1981; Bäck *et al.* 1991). Meanwhile, *genetic programming* (GP) refers to John Koza's (1992) extension of the GA framework, where the genetic structures undergoing evolution themselves constitute 'mini' computer programs. The terms *evolutionary optimisation* and *evolutionary computation* have been coined to unify GA, GP, EP and ES under a common umbrella. Surveys of these different strands of research can be found in Bäck and Schwefel (1993), Fogel (1994), and Kinnear (1994). Furthermore, GA and EP have been used in conjunction with other stochastic optimisation technologies such as *simulated annealing* (SA) (Cerny 1985; Kirkpatrick *et al.* 1983); see,

Nonlinear Modelling of High Frequency Financial Time Series.
Edited by Christian Dunis and Bin Zhou. © 1998 John Wiley Sons Ltd

for example, Davis (1987) and Yip and Pao (1993). All of these approaches share a common biological inspiration but differ in the particular aspects of the natural evolutionary process they focus on, aspects which are mimicked in their respective algorithmic simulations. A comprehensive treatment of GAs proper can be found in Goldberg (1989), Davis (1991) and Jones (1995). Additionally, 'code recipe' books also provide a very readable introduction to the subject (Masters 1993; Ladd 1996).

What is relevant for our purpose is to understand how an evolutionary algorithm approaches an optimisation problem and what can be achieved within an evolutionary framework *vis-à-vis* traditional optimisation frameworks, such as mathematical programming and dynamic programming.

Deep at the heart of many traditional tools of analysis is the presumption of the existence of a set of well-defined mathematical relationships. Moreover, traditional optimisation techniques usually require that the mathematical function which captures the problem's optimisation objective is differentiable, whence the solution search is approached from a gradient-based perspective. Great care must be taken to ensure that difficulties relating to local optimalities are adequately addressed or else simply assumed away, hence the great body of literature on the optimisation of convex problems.

On the other hand, with regard to the solution performance evaluation, evolutionary optimisation may be employed in an optimisation problem where only a pointwise performance evaluation *process* is guaranteed to be well defined. It does not presume the existence of a mathematically expressible relationship in the form of an objective function, nor that such a function, should one exist, be convex, or even differentiable. In our application, for example, a GA solution to the parameterisation of a trading model is not functionally evaluated, but instead tested against a financial data stream, i.e. in terms of how the trading position signals it generates over time would lead to profit- or loss-making positions. Clearly, our live trading model execution and data-tested performance evaluation preclude the use of traditional mathematical optimisation techniques.

In terms of the solution space, a GA is highly suitable to solving *combinatorial optimisation* problems. The genetic representation of a solution structure and the genetic crossover operations make it an ideal search engine for covering a combinatorial space. Moreover, as a genetic structure can be designed to decode onto a set of real-valued variables, a GA is also capable of handling *parametric optimisation* problems. However, due to the fact that a 'classical' GA necessarily imposes a discretised representation of the solution space, it is not expected to create a good cover over continuous-valued intervals. To an extent, this particular shortcoming can be overcome by successively spanning the binary representation over smaller and smaller continuous-valued intervals, i.e. over the course of the algorithm. At any rate, for a (possibly high-dimensional) parametric problem, where the parameters take on enumerable sets of discretised values, an essentially classical GA may be used to good result.

1.2 Genetic Algorithms and Financial Time Series Trading Models

Background

We set out to employ GAs within the context of optimising a technical financial time series *trading* model. It should be stressed at this earliest moment that we are solely interested in developing a profitable model-trading system, and not in minimising data-fitting or forecasting errors. In a relatively slow moving market, good prediction models may well equate to achieving good model-trading results, but within a high frequency data environment, such as an intra-day foreign exchange (FX) spot, the connection is rather more tenuous and cannot be taken for granted (Dunis 1996). Our aim is to develop a trading model and strategy in such a way that the profitability and money management viability criteria are *measured* directly, rather than *inferred* from the extent of forecasting errors.

A typical evolutionary trading model is developed as follows: a set of technical trading predicates is first enumerated. Often, these predicates take the form of a chartist's phrases such as 'if so-and-so indicator breaks above a certain (threshold) level' or 'when a moving average of 5 lagged variables "cuts" a 20-period moving average from below'. An evolutionary algorithm is then used to combinatorially select the subset of predicates as well as evolve a conjunctive/disjunctive decision structure based on these building blocks. These predicates may be NOTed, ANDed or ORed together such that the ultimate output from these predicates generates a *buy, sell* or *square* trading 'signal'. In addition to combinatorially selecting from among the various predicates, the GA may be asked to determine the parameters, *terminals* in GP parlance (Kinnear 1994), which parameterise the predicates. The predicate 'if an m-period moving average cuts above a certain threshold h', for example, contains two parameters, m and h. Because such a syntactical construct can be best represented on a tree-like data structure and because the genetic solutions themselves constitute logical computations, it is in fact more natural to develop a GP, *vis-à-vis* GA, solution for such a system.

In essence, these GA/GP-based systems set out to discover a collection of indicators which together can identify the hidden patterns and relationships within the time series, i.e. in order to exploit them for profitable position taking. The motivation behind such a system is not unfamiliar to the pattern-discovery thinking at the heart of *artificial neural network* (ANN) (Haykin 1994) based trading models. These evolutionary rule-discovery systems vary in the genetic representation of the solution, in the functional capabilities of the rule-base and in the intended markets in which to trade. Levitt (1995) designed an FX trading system which uses a GA to evolve a set of locally predictive nearest-neighbour-based predictors. Edmonds and Kershaw's (1994) GP-based approach represents a logically operated set of fuzzy predicates on a tree-like structure. Ruggiero (1994, 1995a, b) developed a GA-based intra-day T-bond and SP500 futures trading system based on pre-processed inputs developed for his ANN trading system. And Katz and McCormick (1997) showed how an appropriately simplified rule space can be represented by a classical GA chromosome-based scheme without resorting to GP proper.

However, in a volatile, high frequency data environment where no *stable* patterns of behaviour or market dynamics are expected to persist or recur, such hidden relationships are difficult to justify on the basis of existing theoretical and/or empirical paradigms. Therefore, our operating objective becomes the *identification* of relatively strong trending behaviours *if and when* they exist, and executing the position taking in a timely manner. Note how this contrasts sharply with the traditional *forecast-then-trade* formulation, where a good prediction performance is sought *throughout* the data period, irrespective of the profitable position-taking opportunities.

It will be that the approach we pursue is similar, at least in spirit, to that of Colin (1994), who used a GA to evolve the parameters for the exponential moving average-based trading model with stop-loss and profit-taking exit points. His article, which also illustrates a GP-based strategy acquisition approach similar to those mentioned above, is a good survey on the applicability of GAs to financial model-trading in general. A good introduction to GAs and financial model-trading applications can also be found in Davis (1994).

Objectives of Study

Once again, we stress that in our application, the challenge is to design a model-trading system which can be tested against actual trading performance and money management criteria. We start with a simple moving average-based momentum trading model which, when properly *parameterised*, captures the *trending* phases of the financial time series, signalling if and when a directional trading strategy is likely to be profitable. Thus, our optimisation objective is to identify, with the help of a GA, the set of momentum model parameters which yields a trading system that is most reliably profitable over time.

The choice of a momentum trading system as our starting point has been motivated and governed by the market practitioners' technical model-trading perspective, which ultimately traces its roots to Wilder (1978). As the development of high frequency, intra-day live trading models with evolutionary optimisation technologies is a largely unexplored area, mostly investigated by in-house proprietary traders with few published results, a simple momentum trading system also serves as a benchmark against which the incremental benefit of pursuing more elaborate models can be evaluated.

Our long-term intention is to study the effectiveness of a GA-optimised momentum trading model as a foundation for our future work in engineering an evolutionary model-trading system based on *an ensemble of trading signal models*, as one way of embellishing the functionality of a simple signal model is to utilise a collection of such simple models, each one tuned to pick up trending patterns over differing time horizons, for example. There, it is possible to explore the various forms of multi-model synthesis, i.e. how to synthesise a trading signal from a multiplicity of trading signals taken from the individual signal models within the ensemble, initially taking on an approach similar to the one devised by Colin (1994). Moreover, we also set out to explore the possibility of performing the combinatorial optimisation over the *classes* of trading signal models within the ensemble *simultaneously alongside* the parametric optimisation over the individual model parameter spaces for each of the signal models within the said ensemble. A pilot study of such a combinatorial–parametric approach to an hourly FX spot model-trading system construction and optimisation is given by Nacaskul (1997) in an article which also accounts for the necessitated object-oriented generalisation of the evolutionary optimisation paradigm itself.

The objective of this case study is thus twofold: first, to experiment with the use of a GA in the parametric optimisation over the *model parameter space* for the simple financial time series trading models presently considered; second, to lay the groundwork for future exploration in the use of evolutionary optimisation within an expanded context of performing search over the *model space* as well. Such further elaboration of the model space and genetic representation of the solution space will conform to the current framework of model-trading perfor-mance evaluation and will partly rely on the computer programming groundwork which has been laid out for the current set of experiments.

The chapter is organised as follows: section 2 documents the financial time series data and the sampling methods used for this case study; section 3 describes the basic financial time series trading models to be parametrically optimised with a GA; section 4 examines the results of the benchmark exhaustive search over the momentum model's two basic parameters; section 5 describes the imple-mentation of the standard GA as well as some basic performance-enhancement heuristics; section 6 reports the core experiments where the GA is employed to evolve the sets of trading model parameters for different model specifica-tions and for different sets of data; section 7 proposes the future directions for which this case study provides the basic foundations and concludes our discussion.

2 DATA

Two intra-day FX rates have been employed in the present analysis, namely, the US dollar against the German mark, USD/DEM, and the cross rate of the German mark against the Japanese yen, DEM/JPY. Both currency pairs represent highly liquid markets, with a large number of market participants at any time zone. We cover the period from 12 January 1996 to 20 May 1996, resulting in 764 499 ticks for the USD/DEM series and 78 190 ticks for the DEM/JPY (net of weekends and/or bank holidays). Historical data were available from the Chase Manhattan Bank's tick database to evaluate models retrospectively.

2.1 Tick Data

The selected hardware platform was Sun^{TM} workstations, subscribing to real-time tick data via Teknekron^{TM} and publishing real-time trading recommendations for viewing via traders' market sheets. This permitted several models to run on one centralised machine, ensuring that all traders received consistent recommendations, and that individual traders needed no additional hardware and software resources. All programming was in C++, using the Rogue Wave^{TM} Tools.h++ class library (1994).

Pre-processing in the early stages included appropriate *cleaning* of the incoming raw tick data to remove erroneous individual outliers. While the Bank's historical rates database is retrospectively cleaned manually, only a rather rudimentary filtering of data can realistically be undertaken in real time. This is especially true when it is a requirement that there be no discernible lag between cleaned data and genuine market movement. With the primary goal of suppressing individual outliers, we consider the median of the last three ticks as the basis for our cleaning. A trader's perspective of the market might well require the 'weakest' cleaning which would still be effective at screening out outliers. We resolve to implement our tick data cleaning method as follows.

For each incoming tick, define the *tick time, t*, of the tick to be the index of that tick, with respect to an arbitrary origin. Let the last three incoming raw prices P in tick time be P_{t-2}, P_{t-1} and P_t. Define the cleaned price, p_t, by

If mid$\{P_{t-2}, P_{t-1}, P_t\} = P_{t-1}$ or mid$\{P_{t-2}, P_{t-1}, P_t\} = P_t$		then $p_t = $ mid$\{P_{t-2}, P_{t-1}, P_t\}$, i.e the median.
Otherwise,	if $P_t < P_{t-2}$	then $p_t = \max\{2P_{t-2} - P_{t-1}, P_t\}$,
	else	$p_t = \min\{2P_{t-2} - P_{t-1}, P_t\}$.

Pictorially, this is represented by Figure 12.1. In diagrams 1*a* and 1*e*, P_t is deemed a potential outlier, and the median value, $p_t = P_{t-1}$, is used instead. Similarly, in diagrams 1*c* and 1*g*. P_t is deemed a potential outlier because $|P_{t-1} - P_{t-2}| < |P_t - P_{t-2}|$, and the moderated value p_t is used.

Our empirical research indicated that, for fast and active models, i.e. models which alter their market positions frequently over time, the manner of cleaning had a sizeable effect on paper trading results, all of which turned out to be much more promising than live trading results. Therefore, the focus is moved to slower and less active models to reduce the effect of noise and to achieve a closer convergence between paper and live trading. Otherwise, the aberrant effects of 'paper trading off the noise' swamped the effects of the models' actual performance from entering the market at the beginning of a trend and exiting at the detected trend-reversal or take-profit point.

All the model-trading data were subsequently sampled from this cleaned tick data stream.

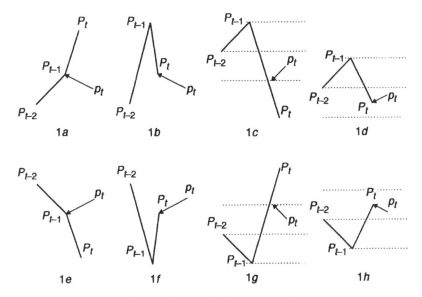

Figure 12.1 Tick filtering technique

2.2 Sampling Method

Time Series Devolatilisation

Because of the nature of the trend indicator models we work with, the tick data stream needed to be sampled in such a manner as to make realistic the assumption that the *period return* or *price change*, $p_t - p_{t-1}$, is normally distributed. High frequency, fixed interval sampling is not ideal, as it underrepresents periods of high market activity and overrepresents quiet periods. In light of this, we adopted the *devolatilisation procedure* proposed by Zhou (1996) as an alternative sampling method.

Here, sampling frequency is not based upon elapsed *physical* time, but rather on a *volatility* time, T, which advances according to

$$T(t+1) = T(t) + \left| \frac{p_{t+1} - p_t}{p_t} \right|^r \quad r \geq 1 \tag{1}$$

In our case, r was chosen to be unity, largely to minimise the effects of spurious outliers, though any value between 1 and 2 would have been reasonable. Just as a non-devolatilised series is sampled from the cleaned tick data stream at constant physical-time intervals, a devolatilised series is sampled from the cleaned tick data stream at *constant increments* of T.[1] The chosen constants, which vary from series to series, depending on the inherent volatility of the tick time series itself, typically yield *sampling intervals* which correspond, *on average*, to about 30–45 minutes of physical time.

Normality Test Statistics

To test for the normality of return assumption (and detect outlying data points), the following monthly statistics were produced daily for each currency pair:

1. The number of observations.
2. The minimum and maximum prices.
3. The minimum and maximum price changes.
4. The standard deviation, σ, skewness, S, and kurtosis K of the price changes.
5. The Jarque–Bera normality test of the price changes, i.e.

$$\frac{n}{6} \left(S^2 + \frac{(K-3)^2}{4} \right)$$

6. The first 10 autocorrelations and Ljung–Box Q-statistics.

We observed occasional spurious data points which occurred at night-time. These rates, if not filtered out, can have an adverse effect on the above statistics, especially for the devolatilised series, since its sampling method tends to pick up these very points.

Statistical results for the DEM/JPY and USD/DEM currency pairs are as follows. Table 12.1 presents the descriptive statistics of the entire sampling period for varying physical- and volatility-clock sampling intervals (which, for volatility clock, refer to units of volatility time T). The improvement from devolatilisation is clear except where the sampling interval is small. As the sampling interval decreases (sampling frequency increases), both the physical- and volatility-clock sampling methods yield a denser and denser sampled stream, approaching the entire underlying tick data stream itself. Descriptive statistics of the tick data will be non-normal (Zhou 1996), as mirrored in the limiting case of small sampling intervals (in both physical and volatility time). Comparing physical- and volatility-clock data sets with roughly the same number of points (e.g. USD/DEM sampled at every 60 minutes vs. USD/DEM sampled at every 0.03 units of volatility time, about 2000 data points each), we note that the kurtosis and Jarque–Bera statistics exhibit better evidence of normality for price changes in the devolatilised series. And the return distribution approaches near-normality at lower sampling frequencies. The same can also be said of the physical-clock sampling (Schnidrig and Würtz 1995).

Table 12.2 presents the monthly subsample descriptive statistics of selected sampling frequencies (every 30 minutes and every 0.0018 units of volatility time). For most months, the improvement from devolatilisation is clear, especially with regards to the kurtosis and the Jarque–Bera statistics. The notable exceptions are seen in March for DEM/JPY and February for USD/DEM. Both of these were caused by occasional large night-time market movements, when insufficient ticks of data were arriving for the volatility clock to advance gradually with physical time.

Table 12.1 Normality test/descriptive statistics at different sampling intervals

DEM/JPY physical clock (February–May 1996)

Sampling interval	10 minutes	30 minutes	60 minutes	120 minutes
No. of observations	7670	3187	1757	944
Std. deviation	0.00043	0.00069	0.00096	0.00013
Skewness	0.19	0.25	0.14	0.18
Kurtosis	7.2	7.9	6.5	7.6
Jarque–Bera	5748	3182	875	838

DEM/JPY volatility clock (February–May 1996)

Sampling interval	0.0006	0.0012	0.0018	0.003
No. of observations	6115	3535	2462	1536
Std. deviation	0.00050	0.00067	0.00083	0.00103
Skewness	0.19	0.21	0.09	0.13
Kurtosis	10.7	6.7	6.5	5.0
Jarque–Bera	15252	2091	1279	265.7

USD/DEM physical clock (February–May 1996)

Sampling interval	10 minutes	30 minutes	60 minutes	120 minutes
No. of observations	10512	3746	1925	963
Std. deviation	0.00044	0.00066	0.00088	0.0012
Skewness	−0.27	−0.12	0.02	−0.06
Kurtosis	20.7	8.0	9.7	5.1
Jarque–Bera	137171	3913	3648	185

USD/DEM volatility clock (February–May 1996)

Sampling interval	0.005	0.01	0.015	0.03
No. of observations	10532	5342	3583	1808
Std. deviation	0.00050	0.00061	0.00071	0.00091
Skewness	0.11	−0.07	0.11	0.06
Kurtosis	22.0	9.2	6.3	6.9
Jarque–Bera	161611	8485	1652	1168

The time series devolatilisation procedure enables the sampling process to be tuned to provide a series with as near-normal price changes as practicable. It is inappropriate, we note, to use very low sampling frequencies for these models, as the terms of reference of the project were to explore *high frequency*, real-time models. Ultimately, we decided upon 0.0018 and 0.015 units of volatility time as the sampling intervals, respectively, for the devolatilised DEM/JPY and USD/DEM series.

2.3 Trading Hours

The experiments conducted were based on two 'trading hours' categories, as follows.

Trading Hours A

This consists of trading from 9:00 a.m. to the first sampled point after 4:00 p.m., London time, with no overnight positions, i.e. hold a *square* position overnight.

Table 12.2 Normality test/descriptive statistics, monthly frequency

	Month (1996)				
	February	March	April	May	Feb.–May
DEM/JPY physical clock (30 min.)					
No. of observations	781	826	784	793	3187
Std. deviation	0.00077	0.00053	0.00070	0.00073	0.00069
Kurtosis	8.6	5.3	6.7	7.0	7.9
Jarque–Bera	1084	175	495	578	3182
DEM/JPY volatility clock (0.0018)					
No. of observations	645	559	625	630	2462
Std. deviation	0.00089	0.00083	0.00078	0.00079	0.00083
Kurtosis	5.0	14.8	3.3	2.9	6.5
Jarque–Bera	118	3245	3.1	1.2	1279
USD/DEM physical clock (30 min.)					
No. of observations	952	955	906	930	3746
Std. deviation	0.00076	0.00063	0.00064	0.00061	0.00066
Kurtosis	5.9	10.1	10.6	6.1	8.0
Jarque–Bera	337	2000	2183	389	3913
USD/DEM volatility clock (0.015)					
No. of observations	1026	877	815	862	3583
Std. deviation	0.00074	0.00069	0.00072	0.00066	0.00071
Kurtosis	7.9	6.5	5.8	3.8	6.3
Jarque–Bera	1064	452	263	23	1652

Two additional constraints which were imposed, à la expert-system priors, and which led to improved trading performance, were:

(i)   Not executing a 'stale' model position at the start of the trading day. (Only initiate a trade at the first model change of position for that day.)

(ii) Not entering a new position within 30 minutes of the end of the trading day.

Constraint (i) occasionally proved detrimental in a strongly trending market, where a prevailing *model* position could continue all day, in which case our actual *market* position would remain divergent from the model recommendation throughout. Constraint (ii) was just a pragmatic attempt to avoid incurring spread costs on very short-term positions.

Trading Hours B

This consists of 24-hour trading from 3:00 a.m. on the first business day after Sunday, applying the above constraint (i) for that day, until the first sampled point after 5:00 p.m. on the last business day before Saturday, applying the above constraint (ii) for that day. Weekend and/or bank holiday positions were

Table 12.3 Summary of trading model executions

No.	Currency pair	Clock (interval)	Hours
1	DEM/JPY	Volatility (0.0018)	A
2	DEM/JPY	Volatility (0.0018)	B
3	DEM/JPY	Physical (30 min.)	A
4	DEM/JPY	Physical (30 min.)	B
5	USD/DEM	Volatility (0.015)	A
6	USD/DEM	Volatility (0.015)	B
7	USD/DEM	Physical (30 min.)	A
8	USD/DEM	Physical (30 min.)	B

not taken due to the excessive exposure risk. Table 12.3 summarises the various trading model executions for both DEM/JPY and USD/DEM series.

3 FINANCIAL TIME SERIES TRADING MODELS

3.1 Model Architecture

According to our model-trading framework, a financial time series *trading model* is considered to be comprised of two parts: the *signal model(s)* and the *position model*. In the traditional predict-then-trade formulation, the signal model comprises the prediction engine, while the position model compares the predicted price with the current price and generates an appropriate trading instruction, given the current market position held. In this initial exploration into the GA-evolved trading system, each solution consists of one signal model and one position model, the signal model being based on the momentum trend indicator, the position model being a market entry/exit rule, to be described schematically below. But looking forward to future development and elaboration of our model-trading system, it would be possible to incorporate a multiplicity of signal models as simultaneous inputs to be integrated within and used by a single position model.

As our first use of the GA is in the parametric optimisation over the model parameter space, and not in the construction of the optimisation over the model space itself, the model-trading results of this case study will naturally depend on the types of trading models implemented for the experiments. We now describe them.

3.2 Basic Model Types

The Momentum Model

This simple 'vanilla' momentum trading model (see Figure 12.2) is based on the momentum *signal* or *oscillator* (Wilder 1978; Colin 1994), *M*, defined here as the difference between a short-term and a long-term moving average. Using

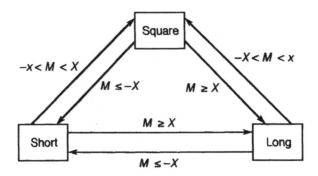

Figure 12.2 Position diagram, the momentum model

simple linear moving averages, this signal model is parameterised by only two parameters: the short-term moving average window size, s, and the long-term moving average window size, ℓ. As for the position model, a *long* position is entered and maintained if and when M is above a certain threshold, X, and is exited when M goes below another threshold, x. Hence X and x are the two position model parameters. Short positions are taken in a symmetrical fashion. This is shown schematically in Figure 12.2.

A fully active model, i.e. one which continually switches from a *long* and a *short* position and only *squares* out at the end of the trading period, is equivalent to setting the two threshold parameters, $X \geq 0$ and $x \geq 0$, both to zero. The rationale behind setting a positive value for either or both of these parameters is that, in the event of the momentum oscillating very close to zero, large *slippage costs*, i.e. model-trading transaction costs associated with the bid–ask spread, could be incurred as the model frequently switched from *long* to *short* and vice versa.

The Momentum–RSI Model

The RSI position switching model was only ever used as a *trigger* superimposed onto the momentum model, and never as a signal/position model in its own right. In other words, the use of the RSI indicator is an elaboration of the above momentum model.

To first describe the RSI indicator trigger, we define the *relative strength index* with index $n \geq 2$ at time t, denoted $\mathrm{RSI}_t^{(n)}$, of a sequence of prices $\{p_i\}_{i \geq 1}$ by

$$\mathrm{RSI}_t^{(n)} = 100 - 100 \left(1 + \frac{\sum_{i=t-n+2}^{t} \max(0, p_i - p_{i-1})}{\sum_{i=t-n+2}^{t} \max(0, p_{i-1} - p_i)} \right)^{-1} \tag{2}$$

Thus, for a strictly monotone increasing price sequence, $\mathrm{RSI}_t^{(n)} = 100$, whereas for a strictly decreasing one, $\mathrm{RSI}_t^{(n)} = 0$.

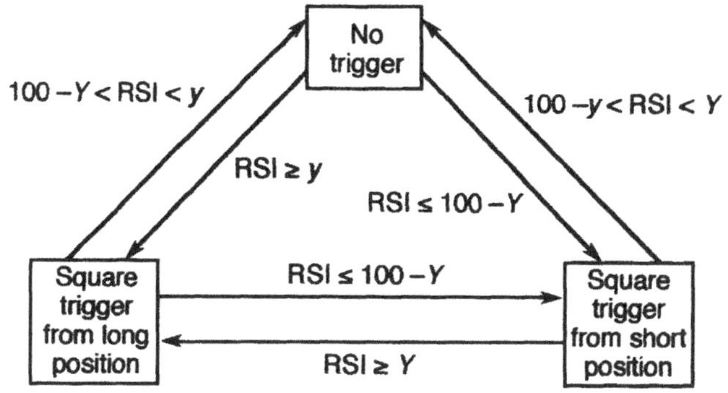

Figure 12.3 The RSI trigger

Given thresholds y and Y where $50 < y \leq Y < 100$, the RSI indicator triggers according to Figure 12.3. Typically, $y = Y = 80$, i.e. an RSI of at least 80 indicates a trigger from a *long* position, and an RSI of at most 20 indicates a trigger from a *short* position.

The RSI indicator just described was used to facilitate a type of take profit strategy with the momentum model: a *long* momentum-based position is exited if the RSI trigger moved away from the '*square* trigger from *long* position' state, i.e. if, while *long*, the RSI rose above the Y threshold, then subsequently decays below it. A *short* momentum-based position is exited in a symmetrical manner.

3.3 Performance Criteria

Initially, for simplicity and ease of development, gain (profit from netting out all the market positions taken during the trading period, minus the slippage penalty accrued for each *round-trip* market entry/exit) was taken as the sole criterion on which to evaluate models' performances. Once the initial difficulties mentioned earlier had been overcome, a composite index was constructed to give some weight to other desirable factors of the models' behaviour. The composite index is the linear combination of models' performance and risk management measures. The selected statistics were:

(i) The fraction of positions which were profitable, i.e.

$$\frac{\text{No. of winning positions}}{\text{No. of positions}}$$

(ii) The pessimistic return ratio,[2] i.e.

$$\left(\frac{\text{No. of winning positions} - \sqrt{\text{No. of winning position}}}{\text{No. of losing positions} - \sqrt{\text{No. of losing positions}}} \right) \times \text{gain/loss ratio}$$

(iii) The Sharpe ratio.

(iv) The annualised cumulative gain (ACG).
(v) The 5% probability of ruin (Vince 1990).

These supplementary performance criteria are reported in our experiments regardless of whether the trading model is being optimised on the gain number or on the performance index.

The coefficients of the linear combination used in the calculation of the performance index were initially taken, somewhat arbitrarily, as 10, 1, 2, 0.2 and −0.1, respectively, though there is scope for work to refine these within a multi-criteria decision model (MCDM) (Chankong and Haimes 1983) framework proper. Moreover, it may be possible to use canonical variance analysis (CVA) or principal component analysis (PCA) to derive this linear combination (Mardia *et al.* 1994). This is achieved by treating the individual assets as observations and measures as variables of the observations. The weights of this linear combination will be the first component of the CVA or PCA that maximises the variance ratio or the variance, respectively.

In view of the degree of subjectivity in finding a suitable composite index, the results reported below are generally based on the maximisation of the gain number. For comparison, experiments using this composite index are presented in 'Optimisation over a Composite Index' in section 6.1.

4 EXHAUSTIVE SEARCH/BENCHMARKS

Four months' worth of data were used from mid-January 1996 to mid-May 1996, with a 50 : 50 in-sample : out-of-sample split. Two time frames were adopted, namely the physical clock with a 30-minute sampling interval and a volatility clock with sampling intervals 0.0018 and 0.015, respectively, for DEM/JPY and USD/DEM. Slippage penalties were taken to be 0.0007 and 0.03, respectively. We take gain as the optimisation criterion for the exhaustive searches. Bear in mind that, given the same parameter space and data set, an exhaustively searched momentum trading model represents the upper performance ceiling for the GA-optimised solution.

4.1 Exhaustive Search over Momentum Model Parameters

Here, the short- and long-term moving average window sizes, s and ℓ, were the only parameters to be searched. X and x were simply set to give a very small interval for which a momentum model would generate a *square* position signal:

$$X = X(p_t) = 0.0001 \times p_t$$

$$x = 0.0$$

The s and ℓ parameters were exhaustively searched over the ranges $2 \leq s \leq 40$ and $s + 1 \leq \ell \leq 80$, respectively. The results were tabulated into an array. A surface contour plot over this array was created to help identify parameter pairings which were profitable, a graphical-quantitative approach which improves on the procedure described in Kaufman (1987). This was possible strictly because our parametric search space is two-dimensional. In fact, it was the desire to be able to search parametrically over higher dimensional space with respect to real trading performance which prompted the original motivation for our exploratory application of a GA technology.

The exhaustively optimised vanilla momentum models are presented in Tables 12.4 and 12.5. As a cautionary note, one would be ill-advised to implement any momentum model where s and ℓ are very close to each other, as such

Table 12.4 Momentum model parameters and performances, exhaustive search, DEM/JPY

Currency	DEM/JPY							
Clock (interval)	Volatility clock (0.0018)				Physical clock (30 min.)			
Trading hours	A		B		A		B	
Parameter	Value		Value		Value		Value	
$s(2 \leq s \leq 40)$	9		34		13		38	
$l(s+1 \leq l \leq 80)$	49		55		59		45	
Performance statistics	In-sample 15/1-14/3	Out-of-sample 19/3-20/5	In-sample 16/1-14/3	Out-of-sample 20/3-20/5	In-sample 16/1-14/3	Out-of-sample 20/3-20/5	In-sample 16/1-14/3	Out-of-sample 20/3-20/5
Gain	0.72	1.02	2.16	−0.09	0.46	0.78	2.00	0.86
No. of positive sig/total	9/9	8/13	13/22	10/21	7/11	5/11	23/39	19/36
ACG	5.9%	8.6%	17.6%	−0.7%	3.7%	6.5%	16.1%	7.1%
Sharpe ratio	0.80	1.18	2.4	−0.099	0.52	0.95	2.25	1.04
Gain/loss ratio	11.3	6.68	1.92	1.01	2.28	3.17	1.72	1.42
Max. drawdown	0.07	0.16	0.89	0.55	0.21	0.17	0.83	0.45

Table 12.5 Momentum model parameters and performances, exhaustive search, USD/DEM

Currency	USD/DEM							
Clock (interval)	Volatility clock (0.015)				Physical clock (30 min.)			
Trading hours	A		B		A		B	
Parameter	Value		Value		Value		Value	
$s(2 \leq s \leq 40)$	25		32		33		2	
$l(s+1 \leq l \leq 80)$	35 ·		37		43		55	
Performance statistics	In-sample 12/1-14/3	Out-of-sample 15/3-20/5	In-sample 12/1-14/3	Out-of-sample 15/3-20/5	In-sample 15/1-14/3	Out-of-sample 15/3-20/5	In-sample 15/1-14/3	Out-of-sample 15/3-20/5
Gain	−0.0006	−0.0474	0.0083	−0.0448	0.0079	0.004	−0.0013	−0.0459
No. of positive sig/total	11/28	7/34	19/48	19/49	8/13	7/16	16/65	17/70
ACG	−0.2%	−18.7%	3.3%	−17.6%	3.15%	1.5%	−0.5%	−18.5%
Sharpe ratio	−0.0286	−0.187	0.395	−1.459	0.381	0.244	−0.065	−2.828
Gain/loss ratio	0.977	0.0034	1.09	0.463	1.85	1.347	0.985	0.569
Max. drawdown	0.0091	0.0171	0.0253	0.0218	0.0032	0.0069	0.0194	0.0196

a model would lead to an excessively active model, entering and exiting the market too frequently, suffering the spread each way, to realise any real gain per position taken.

Note how on the basis of the in-sample trading alone, neither the best momentum model which traded the devolatilised USD/DEM series during hours A, nor the best momentum model which traded the non-devolatilised USD/DEM series during hours B even managed a positive gain (-0.0006 gain, -0.2% ACG and -0.0013 gain, -0.5% ACG, respectively). The best results were obtained with model-trading DEM/JPY during hours B, where the model optimised for the devolatilised series yielded a 2.16 gain (17.6% ACG) while the one optimised for the non-devolatilised series yielded a 2.00 gain (16.1% ACG). But in-sample results can be misleading. For instance, the best exhaustively searched momentum model which traded devolatilised USD/DEM during hours B achieved a positive in-sample figure (0.0083 gain, 3.3% ACG), but also a very negative out-of-sample result (-0.0448 gain, -17.6% ACG). All of this serves to underline the need to develop more sophisticated trading signal models, ones which will likely require more than two model parameters, whence further underlining the need to be able to algorithmically explore a higher dimensional search space. Finally, note that, on the basis of in-sample result alone, optimised model-trading DEM/JPY on its devolatilised series yielded better results than on its non-devolatilised series, but not by great margins. Greater differences, in fact, existed between the two trading hours categories, with hours-B trading models outperforming their hours-A counterparts by about three to one on the basis of the in-sample data.

4.2 Exhaustive Search over Momentum-RSI Model Parameters

From our detailed examination of the positional printouts, it was noticed that momentum-based models appeared to be rather slow to exit positions once the underlying rate moved in an unfavourable direction. In an attempt to overcome this, once a momentum model had been selected, an RSI trigger (initially with a threshold of 80) was employed to facilitate a take-profit strategy. We picked two previously optimised momentum models from above, one for each currency pair, and performed an exhaustive search on the RSI parameter in the range 2–50 to produce the results which follow. Note that this is *not* an exhaustive search over the three-parameter search space.

As presented in Table 12.5, the optimal vanilla momentum model which traded devolatilised USD/DEM during hours B optimally specified $s = 32, \ell = 37$. Overlaying the $RSI^{(n)}$ model for a take-profit achieved the following results (see Table 12.6).

For $n \geq 19$, the RSI model was never activated as a take-profit in the in-sample case. Table 12.6 clearly shows there to be no benefit in using the RSI trigger in this way. For all intents and purposes, it is useless to optimise one parameter *after* the other two parameters had been optimised *independently*. We have to be able to search over the RSI parameter together with the momentum parameters,

Table 12.6 Overlaying momentum model with RSI trigger, in- and out-of-sample gain on USD/DEM

n	2	3	4	5	6	7	8	
In-sample gain	−0.0344	0.0000	−0.0005	−0.0303	−0.0017	−0.0149	−0.0218	
Out-of-sample	−0.0529	−0.0440	−0.0474	−0.0519	−0.0400	−0.0468	−0.0525	
n	9	10	11	12	13	14	15	
In-sample gain	−0.0166	−0.0237	−0.0337	−0.0109	−0.0035	0.0021	0.0047	
Out-of-sample	−0.0529	−0.0512	−0.0396	−0.0467	−0.0572	−0.0569	−0.0478	
n	16	17	18	19	20	21	22	No RSI
In-sample gain	−0.0020	0.0013	0.0018	0.0083	0.0083	0.0083	0.0083	0.0083
Out-of-sample	−0.0488	−0.0509	−0.0499	−0.0505	−0.0505	−0.0499	−0.0494	−0.0448

Table 12.7 Overlaying momentum model with RSI trigger, in- and out-of-sample gain on DEM/JPY

n	2	3	4	5	6	7	8	9	10	11	12
In-sample gain	−0.04	0.74	1.30	1.72	1.14	0.92	1.52	0.89	1.24	0.92	0.60
Out-of-sample	−0.09	−0.45	0.46	0.24	−0.28	−0.73	−0.89	−0.83	−0.87	−0.68	−0.82
n	13	14	15	16	17	18	19	20	21	22	23
In-sample gain	0.98	0.94	1.68	1.09	1.65	1.68	2.01	2.01	2.16	2.16	2.16
Out-of-sample	−0.80	−1.37	−0.83	−1.12	−1.57	−1.57	−1.15	−1.35	−0.78	−1.33	−0.69

the multi-dimensional task left for the GA in the upcoming sections. Our general experience was that the application of an RSI trigger in this *ad hoc* manner was only beneficial in making a very poor momentum model slightly less poor.

The results for appending an RSI trigger onto a momentum model exhaustively optimised (at $s = 34$, $\ell = 55$) for trading devolatilised DEM/JPY during hours B are given in Table 12.7. As with USD/DEM, none of these led to improvement on the in-sample gain. Those that managed to match the in-sample performance figures (i.e. by not being RSI-triggered) ended up with poorer out-of-sample numbers.

From the above, it becomes clear how the application of a GA can assist in performing parametric optimisation search over higher dimensional spaces while ensuring that the same model-trading performance evaluation process can still be used in the same consistent manner.

5. GENETIC ALGORITHM METHODOLOGY

5.1 Standard GA Implementation

Evolutionary Population Manager Template

GA computer programming codes need to address the following two questions, one relating to *data representation* and the other to *algorithmic implementation*.

First, how can the solution to a particular optimisation problem be represented as a genetic object undergoing evolution; and second, how can the evolutionary algorithm implement the storage and evolution of these genetic solutions? The first concerns the design and implementation of the *genetic/evolutionary objects/solutions*; the latter concerns the design and implementation of an *evolutionary population manager*.

In order that our GA program can readily incorporate future advancement in the trading models themselves, the population manager is programmed independently of the internal operations of the genetic solutions. In *object-oriented programming* (Stroustrup 1991), it is the responsibility of the evolutionary trading model *class* to create and maintain the genetic representation of the trading model parameters, to implement the genetic operations (reproduction, crossover and mutation) on the encoded *genotype*, and to furnish the model-trading functionality which defines a genetic solution's behavioural *phenotype* (which, in turn, determines the performance evaluation). Our population manager is thus implemented as a C++ *template* (Stroustrup 1991) of genetic evolutionary objects. This separation of duties at the code level reflects the distinction between the GA optimisation methodology in general and the application-specific solution requirements in particular.

In our GA, at each generation, an entire 'child population' (equal in size to the parent population) is created, appended to the parent population, and sorted according to evaluated performance (raw fitness), from whence the top performing half of this enlarged solution set is kept as the next parent population, from which the reproductive fitness numbers are calculated, and so on. For the genetic crossover operation, the first partner parent is chosen on basis of fitness, the second randomly over the rest of the parent population.

Model Configuration File

Each GA-optimised model parameter has an associated entry in a configuration file of the form '$m/M/\Delta/c$', where:

(i) m is the parameter's minimum search value.
(ii) M is the parameter's maximum search value.
(iii) Δ is the granularity of the increment between the minimum and the maximum.
(iv) c is the amount of clustering (described in 'Clustering' in section 5.3), set to zero for the moment.

Each model parameter is assigned enough binary addresses to cover its search space, i.e. $(2^b-1)\Delta \geq M-m$, where b is the number of assigned binary addresses. It is straightforward to decode the parameter value from the genetic sequence, letting $000\ldots0$ represent the minimum, m, and $000\ldots1$ to represent $m+\Delta$, and so on. Clearly, unless $M-m = (2^b-1)\Delta$, some valid binary strings would decode to an invalid parameter, i.e. where the value exceeds M. These are detected at run-time, and an invalid trading model, i.e. one with invalid parameter(s), is assigned a performance number of zero. To avoid a plethora of invalid models in the population, it remains the user's responsibility to choose the configuration file parameters with care. The presence of this type of invalid solution impedes the effectiveness of a GA by diluting the evolutionary population.

A complete chromosome, or solution genotype, is a concatenation of all the binary addresses assigned to all the model parameters. The trading model, with all its parameters decoded, constitutes the behavioural phenotype from a GA perspective. In our experiments, we enumerated each model parameter's search interval such that all valid chromosomes decode to valid trading models.

5.2 Modification to Standard GA

Gray Coding

Gray encoding is applied to the binary chromosome to help improve the GA search process (Masters 1993). Gray encoding is a way of transforming binary numbers so that a unit numerical change corresponds to a change of a single bit in the binary representation. Table 12.8 illustrates the first few four-bit Gray coded numbers. Note that, although the binary representations of 7 and 8 differ in all four bits, their Gray codes only differ in one. This maintenance of topological closeness in genetic encoding has important implications concerning such issues as the preservation of genetic schema and the perturbation effect of the genetic mutation operator.

Over-initialisation

We initialise the GA population with twice as many randomised genetic solutions as specified by the population size, then prune out the poorer performing half. This helps 'jump start' the genetic population with a higher quality gene pool,

Table 12.8 Binary vs. Gray coding scheme

Decimal	Binary	Gray
0	0000	0000
1	0001	0001
2	0010	0011
3	0011	0010
4	0100	0110
5	0101	0111
6	0110	0101
7	0111	0100
8	1000	1100

and also prevents poorly performing solutions from staying in the population, but with very little chance of being selected for reproduction (Masters 1993).

One- and Two-point Crossover

The original GA used a one-point crossover. It has since been pointed out that a two-point crossover helps preserve genetic schema represented by bits separated by a long distance along the chromosome. Following Masters (1993), we implemented a random call between a one-point and a two-point crossover method to help preserve spatially localised as well as spatially distributed schema.

Object Storage

It turned out that model-trading performance evaluations of individual models suffered quite a high computational cost, typically several seconds of CPU time for a month's worth of high frequency data. This is because the program was initially designed for executing real-time trading, coupled with simple overnight evaluations on selected models for next-day inspection, so computational run-time performance had not been critical up to now. We left this issue until rather late in the project.

As the GA population may contain many genotypically identical solutions, especially towards convergence in the latter stages of the algorithm, the time-consuming performance evaluation routine may be repeated needlessly over and over, with identical results. Given that the *genotype space* is discrete, defined by the binary chromosome representation scheme, we devised a binary tree archive of evaluated genetic solutions, indexed by the *gene values* or *alleles* themselves. The Rogue Wave™ Tools.h++ class library contains a 'RWBTreeOnDisk' class which rendered this easy to implement. A further advantage of this approach was that the GA program itself could be safely interrupted and restarted at any time. The restarted algorithm would then evolve entirely and speedily off the stored evaluations up to the point of interruption. We did not, however, provide a means of synchronising the pseudo-random number generator seeds between GA runs with different points of interruption.

Fitness Bias and Entropy of GA Population

In the initialisation of the genetic population, every randomly initialised genetic solution is assigned an equal fitness number, i.e. $1/N$ for a population of N genetic solutions. Thereafter, each fitness number is determined in relative terms against the other genetic solutions' performance (raw fitness) numbers. It often happens that in the first few generations, one or a very few superior genetic solutions appear to dominate the gene pool, threatening the genetic diversity of the population (Masters 1993). At any rate, we wish to be able to 'anneal' the variability in the relative fitness numbers in a more gradual manner. For this, we devised a heuristic based on 'contaminating' these fitness numbers with the initial fitness numbers.

Let the original vector of fitness numbers be denoted by f^r and the constant vector of initialising fitness number, i.e. the vector of $1/N$'s be denoted by f^o, then the treated fitness, f, will be simply the renormalised linear combination of the two:

$$f = \frac{\lambda f^o + (1 - \lambda)f^r}{\|\lambda f^o + (1 - \lambda)f^r\|} \quad 0 \le \lambda \le 1 \tag{3}$$

where we continuously reduce the value of λ, the contaminant *control parameter*, from 0.5 in the first generation gradually towards 0.0.

If we were to consider the fitness numbers as the reproductive selection probabilities, and in the classical 'roulette-wheel' parent selection method, they certainly are, then one can measure the extent of variability in fitness numbers/selection probabilities by the entropy measure (Jaynes 1983):

$$E(f) = -\sum_{i=1}^{N} f_i \ln(f_i) \tag{4}$$

This number is maximised with the initialising fitness numbers and minimised when one genetic solution is assigned a fitness value of 1 (all the fitness) while the rest are assigned 0. Thus, it is expected that this entropy number, which starts at its maximum value of $\ln(N)$ at initialisation, becomes reduced throughout the course of the algorithm, reverting to maximum when all the genetic solutions within the population converge to a common solution, with identical fitness numbers. The above fitness reassignment procedure is intended to make this entropy reduction process a gradual one.

5.3 In-sample vs. Out-of-sample Performance Evaluation

In-sample Search, Out-of-sample Succession

Our GA also provides a facility where each generation's best performing solution is evaluated against a second criterion, i.e. the model-trading performance measured against the out-of-sample data set. Additionally, we also store the best out-of-sample performing solution. At the end of each generation, the current out-of-sample best solution is compared against, and possibly *succeeded* by, the new *in-sample* best solution on the basis of the *out-of-sample* performance number. The best out-of-sample solutions found in this manner are not reported here, but do conform to our expectation: outperforming the GA-optimised (in-sample) solutions with respect to the out-of-sample data sets, but generally not performing as well with respect to the in-sample measures.

Clustering

Successive runs of the GA illustrated another problem, especially when evaluating on relatively small data sets, namely that a particular trading model can be fortuitously good, while its 'neighbours', i.e. models obtained by slight parametric perturbations, can be quite poor.

Table 12.9 Clustering momentum signal model parameter

		30	31	32	33	34
		Short-term average window size				
Long-	35	−0.0073	−0.0107	−0.0201	−0.0446	−0.0341
term	36	−0.0007	−0.0034	−0.0090	−0.0256	−0.0386
average	37	−0.0072	−0.0116	0.0083	−0.0179	−0.0418
window	38	−0.0165	−0.0195	0.0012	−0.0205	−0.0293
size	39	−0.0128	−0.0091	−0.0138	−0.0175	−0.0208

Recall, for example, that the best exhaustively searched momentum model for trading devolatilised USD/DEM on trading hours B (see Table 12.5) was parameterised by (32, 37). There, although the particular model itself was profitable, it was surrounded by unprofitable ones. To wit, gains for a selection of surrounding models are shown in Table 12.9. Clearly, it would have been unwise to implement this particular pair of parameters.

As a partial solution to this, albeit a computationally rather onerous one, it was decided that the performance measure for each specific trading model should also reflect the trading performance of its parametric neighbours. For instance, instead of using the number 0.0083 for the (32,37) momentum model, we should incorporate the numbers −0.0090, −0.0179, 0.0012 and −0.0116 as well. Thus the *in-sample* trading performance of a particular set of trading model parameters (the genetic solution's raw fitness number) was evaluated in terms of a (weighted) average of its own model-trading performance and the model-trading performances of its *cluster* of parametric neighbours. In our experiments, we used equal weighting. Note that although the GA is set to optimise on this mean measurement, the tabulated result of each GA optimisation run reports the individual performance number itself. Taking account of the parametric neighbours in two-dimensional space, within the context of manually optimising a moving average-based model-trading system, is described in Kaufman (1987).

In general terms, where appropriate, each parameter was assigned a cluster parameter c, typically 0, 1 or 2. This is used to indicate by how many increments or decrements that parameter could be perturbed when undertaking in-sample evaluations. Thus, a raw fitness or performance evaluation of a genetic solution with parameters $y_1, y_2, \ldots, y_n$, and cluster parameter $c_1, c_2, \ldots, c_n$, respectively, entails evaluating the solution parameterised by $y_1, y_2, \ldots, y_n$ and also its clustered neighbours:

$$y_1 - c_1, y_2, \ldots, y_n \quad \cdots \quad y_1 - 1, y_2, \ldots, y_n$$
$$\vdots \qquad\qquad \vdots \qquad\qquad \vdots$$
$$y_1, y_2, \ldots, y_n - c_n \quad \cdots \quad y_1, y_2, \ldots, y_n - 1$$
$$y_1 + 1, y_2, \ldots, y_n \quad \cdots \quad y_1 + c_1, y_2, \ldots, y_n$$
$$\vdots \qquad\qquad \vdots \qquad\qquad \vdots$$
$$y_1, y_2, \ldots, y_n + 1 \quad \cdots \quad y_1, y_2, \ldots, y_n + c_n$$

In case the clustering procedure were to consider one or more clustered neighbour(s) with parameter value(s) beyond the valid bound(s), the mean performance is taken from only the valid trading models within the cluster. Consider, for example, in the case of the momentum model, when the search range for s is $s_{min} \leq s \leq s_{max}$, with cluster parameter c. Here, the clustered performance measure of a trading model with $s = s_{min}$ would only encompass the evaluations of the clustered models with s falling within the range $s_{min} \leq s \leq s_{min} + c$.

6 GENETIC ALGORITHM EXPERIMENTS

6.1 GA Search over Momentum Model Parameters

Optimisation over Gain

In this series of experiments, a GA is used to optimise all four momentum model parameters: s and ℓ (previously exhaustively searched) as well as x and X. But here we modify the search parameters slightly. Firstly, we work s and $\ell - s$, the latter being the window size of the long-term moving average *over and above* s. This simplifies our enforcing the $\ell > s$ constraint within the genetic encoding scheme.

Secondly, in order to lay the groundwork for our developing a model-trading system where several different signal models are to be used together, we have to 'normalise' the output of each signal model so that we work instead with a momentum signal value strictly between -1 and $+1$, where a number approaching -1 signifies a strong downward trend signal and a number approaching $+1$ signifies a strong upward trend signal. This would give us a range space which is essentially uniform across all signal models. We used a hyperbolic sigmoid function to achieve this normalisation. Hence, the following transformation was adopted.

Let $\alpha \in (0, 1)$ and $\beta > 0.0$. Define the thresholds x', X' and the transformed momentum M' by

$$M' = \tanh \left(\frac{M}{\beta} \tanh^{-1} 0.5 \right)$$

$$X' = 0.5$$

$$x' = \alpha X'$$

In this way, we are guaranteed that $-1 < M' < 1$, while the original position-taking schematic (Figure 12.2) remains valid.

The two parameters introduced, α and β, replace x and X as the model parameters to be GA-optimised, respectively, within $\alpha \in \{0.6, 0.7, 0.8, 0.9\}$ and $\beta \in \{0.0001, 0.0002, \ldots, 0.0016\}$. The search intervals for s and $\ell - s$ are given by $2 \leq s \leq 65$ and $1 \leq \ell - s \leq 64$. Note how the number of possibilities for each

Table 12.10   Default GA parameters

Population size	20
(Minimum) number of generations	20
Long-term moving average clustering	2
Short-term moving average clustering	1
α and β clustering	0

of these is equal to a power of two. This conveniently avoids genetic solutions with invalid model parameters altogether.

To ensure fair comparison, in all the experiments reported below, the parameters listed in Table 12.10 pertinent to the GA search were used throughout. The population size and the (minimum) number of generations used in an actual trading system optimisation would need to be considerably more than those used here, which are kept small in order to facilitate fairly speedy experiments and replications. Bear in mind that each reported result is taken from a single GA run, notwithstanding the fact that, in reality, a GA is itself a stochastic process, whose single-run results can properly be interpreted as the point estimates of some random variables.

One small approximation made in the preparation of the results presented here was the following. Different moving average-base signal models require different amounts of warm-up data, that is, historical data needed in order to 'prime' the moving averages. A momentum model based on relatively long moving average(s), i.e. large value(s) for ℓ (and s), requires more warm-up data than a model with a small ℓ parameter (whence also a small s), and so on. For consistency in the GA search, a constant amount of warm-up data was used in all models. The warm-up data were specified to be just large enough to accommodate those models within the search space that required the most. Once the GA had selected a model for closer scrutiny, it was then re-evaluated by another, more detailed evaluation software, which had been implemented independently as part of a live trading system, and which assumed a warm-up period appropriate to the selected model. The effect of all this is to alter the reported gain slightly.

For brevity, we restrict our attention to the devolatilised series models, which we noted to be marginally more promising than the non-devolatilised results. The results are presented in Table 12.11.

Let us discuss these results using ACG, as it is equivalent to gain, but can be interpreted uniformly across different currency pairs. With regards to the DEM/JPY data, the GA-optimised model, with four search parameters, trading on hours A managed a 5.9% ACG (6.4% out-of-sample), compared with the exhaustive benchmark (Table 12.4), with two search parameters, which yielded 5.9% ACG (8.6% out-of-sample). During hours B, the GA-optimised model achieved a slightly less good performance in-sample (14.3% vs. 17.6%), but achieved a relatively high out-of-sample (9.3% ACG), whereas the benchmark model was slightly negative (-0.7% ACG) on the same data. Perhaps this was

Table 12.11 Momentum model parameters and performances, GA optimisation over gain

Currency	DEM/JPY				USD/DEM			
Clock (interval)	Volatility clock (0.0018)				Volatility clock (0.015)			
Trading hours	A		B		A		B	
Parameter	Value		Value		Value		Value	
s	8		20		53		63	
ℓ	51		80		61		76	
α	0.6		0.7		0.7		0.8	
β	0.0011		0.0007		0.0013		0.0015	
Performance statistics	In-sample 15/1-14/3	Out-of-sample 19/3-20/5	In-sample 17/1-14/3	Out-of-sample 19/3-20/5	In-sample 16/1-14/3	Out-of-sample 19/3-20/5	In-sample 16/1-14/3	Out-of-sample 19/3-20/5
Gain	0.73	0.75	1.72	1.06	0.0068	−0.0013	0.0105	−0.0187
No. of positive sig/total	8/9	9/14	7/15	8/14	2/2	1/2	4/5	2/8
ACG	5.9%	6.4%	14.3%	9.3%	2.7%	−0.5%	4.2%	−7.5%
Sharpe ratio	0.82	0.87	1.95	1.26	0.327	−0.07	0.51	−1.04
Gain/loss ratio	5.9	3.27	2.29	1.55	∞	0.071	6.25	0.134
Max. drawdown	0.08	0.21	0.74	0.72	0.0000	0.0014	0.0017	0.112

due to our clustering heuristic, which aimed at preventing over-specialisation on the in-sample basis. More critically, we were able to obtain positive in-sample performance on the USD/DEM for both trading hours A and B (2.7 and 4.2% ACG respectively), against the benchmark, which was negative (−0.2% ACG) on hours A, and gave a slightly less, but still positive, figure (3.3% ACG) on hours B. The out-of-sample results for the GA-optimised models on hours A and B were negative (−0.5 and −7.5% ACG), but nowhere near as bad as the benchmark numbers (−18.7 and −17.6% ACG), the latter corresponding to the model cited as a prime example of the need for the clustering procedure (see 'Clustering' in section 5.3).

Optimisation over a Composite Index

Recall that it was suggested (see section 3.3) that a composite index might be an appropriate measure of performance. The results are presented in Table 12.12. For purpose of comparisons, the constituent criteria, rather than the composite index itself, are reported in the table.

It is interesting to observe that these models (GA-optimised on the composite index) are very close parametrically to those GA-optimised on the basis of gain alone. And in fact their gain (and hence ACG) numbers are quite comparable. This is clearly due to that fact that the composite index's constituent criteria have a tendency to follow each other, i.e. a perturbation of a trading model which increases its gain also tends to increase its Sharpe ratio and decrease the probability of ruin, etc. In other words, these model-trading performance multi-criteria form a basket of correlated measures.

Table 12.12 Momentum model parameters and performance, GA optimisation over composite index

Currency	DEM/JPY				USD/DEM			
Clock (interval)	Volatility clock (0.0018)				Volatility clock (0.015)			
Trading hours	A		B		A		B	
Parameter	Value		Value		Value		Value	
s	8		22		51		62	
ℓ	52		80		60		77	
α	0.6		0.6		0.7		0.8	
β	0.0013		0.0011		0.0013		0.0015	
Performance statistics	In-sample 15/1-14/3	Out-of-sample 19/3-20/5	In-sample 17/1-14/3	Out-of-sample 19/3-20/5	In-sample 16/1-14/3	Out-of-sample 19/3-20/5	In-sample 16/1-14/3	Out-of-sample 19/3-20/5
Gain	0.66	0.85	1.74	1.18	0.004	−0.007	0.01	−0.0187
No. of positive sig/total	8/9	9/13	8/15	7/13	3/6	0/5	5/9	4/11
ACG	5.4%	7.2%	14.4%	8.8%	1.6%	−2.8%	4.1%	−7.0%
Sharpe ratio	0.74	0.99	1.97	1.18	0.19	−0.39	0.48	−0.07
Gain/loss ratio	5.40	3.58	2.16	1.52	1.83	0.00	2.00	0.23
Max. drawdown	0.08	0.16	0.89	0.92	0.0048	0.007	0.0055	0.017
Prob. ruin (at 5%)	0.00	0.00	0.0001	0.015	0.00	~Certain	0.00	~Certain

6.2 GA Search over Momentum-RSI Model Parameters

We observed earlier that the use of an RSI take-profit trigger superimposed on an exhaustively optimised momentum model had a detrimental effect on model performance. Recall also that the applied procedure was *ad hoc*, necessitated by the need to restrict the exhaustive search process to at most two dimensions.

We take advantage of the GA's ability to search multi-dimensionally by embellishing the RSI take-profit strategy further. Firstly, an RSI trigger now works on two thresholds, i.e. in the case of a prevailing *long* position, the RSI trigger effects a take-profit if the RSI index rises above one threshold, denoted the *flag threshold*, then subsequently decays below yet another threshold, denoted the *decay threshold*. Obviously, if the decay threshold is higher than the flag threshold, and the RSI index rose to some value between the two thresholds, then the RSI trigger would have been *triggered* and immediately *fired*, i.e. to effect a take-profit on the prevailing *long* position.

Secondly, we made a provision for *up to* three RSI triggers to be used in conjunction, instead of one, as was the case with the exhaustive procedure. With a set of RSI triggers, the overall trigger rule is the conjunctive (ANDing) among the trigger states of the RSI triggers within the *flag set*, i.e. *when all* individual RSI triggers within the flag set are triggered. The overall firing rule is the disjunctive (ORing) among the firing states of the RSI triggers within the *decay set*, i.e. *if any* individual RSI trigger within the decay set has been fired. The flag set is determined by three 'set-membership' Boolean variables assigned to three RSI triggers 'on stand-by'. Three more Boolean variables define the decay set, using the same three RSI triggers. Note that if either the flag set or the decay set were empty, then no RSI take-profit strategy is ever actuated (either the overall trigger cannot be set, or the overall trigger cannot be fired).

To summarise the new RSI take-profit strategy's model parameters, there are three RSI indices, n_1, n_2, $n_3 \geq 2$, for the three RSI triggers, denoted $RSI^{(n_1)}$, $RSI^{(n_2)}$ and $RSI^{(n_3)}$, three flag thresholds, Y_1, Y_2 and $Y_3 \in (50, 100)$, three decay thresholds, y_1, y_2 and $y_3 \in (50, 100)$, and finally six Boolean variables to define the flag and decay sets.

To define the RSI take-profit strategy formally, let $S_{\text{flag}}, S_{\text{decay}} \subseteq \{1, 2, 3\}$, where 1 denotes the first RSI trigger, and so on, and define Boolean flags $f_t^{(\text{long})}$ and $f_t^{(\text{short})}$ at time t as follows:

$$f_t^{(\text{long})} = \text{TRUE} \quad \text{if } S_{\text{flag}} \neq \varnothing \quad \text{and} \quad RSI_t^{(n_i)} > Y_i \; \forall i \in S_{\text{flag}}$$

$$f_t^{(\text{short})} = \text{TRUE} \quad \text{if } S_{\text{flag}} \neq \varnothing \quad \text{and} \quad RSI_t^{(n_i)} < 100 - Y_i \; \forall i \in S_{\text{flag}}$$

Now define Boolean decays $d_t^{(\text{long})}$ and $d_t^{(\text{short})}$ at time t by

$$d_t^{(\text{long})} = \text{TRUE} \quad \text{if} f_t^{(\text{long})} = \text{TRUE} \quad \text{and} \quad \exists i \in S_{\text{decay}} \text{ such that } RSI_t^{(n_i)} \leq y_i$$

$$d_t^{(\text{short})} = \text{TRUE} \quad \text{if} f_t^{(\text{short})} = \text{TRUE} \quad \text{and} \quad \exists i \in S_{\text{decay}} \text{ such that } RSI_t^{(n_i)} \geq 100 - y_i$$

In the event of the momentum model being *long*, the *long* momentum-based position is exited when $d_t^{(\text{long})} = \text{TRUE}$. Once again, the *short* situation is symmetrical, a *short* momentum-based position being exited when $d_t^{(\text{short})} = \text{TRUE}$. The 'old' single RSI trigger system is equivalent to our restricting that $S_{\text{flag}} = S_{\text{decay}} = \{1\}$ and that $y_1 = Y_1$.

We enumerate the GA search intervals for these RSI take-profit strategy's model parameters as: n_1, n_2, $n_3 \in \{10, 12, \ldots, 40\}$, y_1, y_2, y_3, Y_1, Y_2, $Y_3 \in \{60, 70, 80, 90\}$, as well as six more binary addresses for $S_{\text{flag}}, S_{\text{decay}} \subseteq \{1, 2, 3\}$.

We briefly remark that in this GA search, there is an element of genotype redundancy, in the sense that two different valid chromosomes can give rise to functionally identical models. In GA parlance, the genotype-phenotype map is many-to-one: different genotypes decoding to a common behavioural phenotype. An instance of this is when two momentum–RSI models hold identical RSI triggers and the flag/decay set definitions in permuted orders. This is not a problem from the perspective of the GA search, and could even be construed as beneficial to the extent that the optimal solution (phenotype) may be reached by means of any one of several different chromosomes (genotypes), giving the GA search process some inherent robustness.

Our optimisation criterion was gain. The results are presented in Table 12.13, where we let (n) denote an unused RSI trigger's flag/decay threshold.

Comparing the momentum–RSI results in Table 12.13 with our earlier results from the vanilla momentum trading models (also GA-optimised over gain) in Table 12.11, the results were quite mixed and rather unstable. In particular, the

Table 12.13 Momentum–RSI model parameters and performances, GA optimisation over gain

Currency	DEM/JPY		USD/DEM	
Clock (interval)	Volatility clock (0.0018)		Volatility clock (0.015)	
Trading hours	A	B	A	B
Parameter	Value	Value	Value	Value
s	11	23	52	X
ℓ	64	81	59	X
α	0.6	0.8	0.6	X
β	0.0001	0.0013	0.0013	X
n_1, n_2, n_3	34, 36, 14	12, 10, 24	14, 24, 12	X
S_{flag}	{3}	{2}	{1, 3}	X
S_{decay}	{1}	{1, 2}	{2}	X
Y_1, Y_2, Y_3	$(n), (n), 80$	$(n), 90, 80$	$70, (n), 70$	X
y_1, y_2, y_3	$70, (n), (n)$	$70, 60, 80$	$(n), 70, (n)$	X

Performance statistics	In-sample 16/1–14/3	Out-of-sample 19/3–20/5	In-sample 17/1–14/3	Out-of-sample 19/3–20/5	In-sample 16/1–14/3	Out-of-sample 19/3–20/5	In-sample 16/1–14/3	Out-of-sample 19/3–20/5
Gain	0.06	1.15	2.34	−0.76	0.0097	−0.0013	X	X
No. of positive sig/total	5/8	7/10	11/17	5/11	2/2	1/2	X	X
ACG	0.5%	9.9%	19.6%	−6.7%	4.0%	−0.5%	X	X
Sharpe ratio	0.0647	1.35	2.67	−0.91	0.47	−0.07	X	X
Gain/loss ratio	1.17	5.6	2.84	0.63	∞	0.13	X	X
Max. drawdown	0.33	0.20	0.43	0.99	0.0	0.0015	X	X

model optimised for trading DEM/JPY on hours B achieved a remarkable 19.6% ACG in-sample, but at the expense of a negative (−6.7% ACG) performance out-of-sample. Moreover, we were disappointed by the weak in-sample performance on the hours-A DEM/JPY data, especially since the GA-optimised vanilla momentum model previously yielded a higher positive number (5.9% ACG). The worst result came with the USD/DEM data under trading hours B, where the GA selected models which never actually traded, because those that did gave negative performance (hence the column entries marked with 'X'). This, despite the fact that the GA-optimised vanilla momentum models did achieve positive returns in our previous analysis. In a situation such as this, where we were better off with the vanilla momentum model, we had rather hoped that the GA would 'prune out' any detrimental RSI take-profit strategy and end up with an equally matched vanilla momentum model. That this did not happen was a cause for concern.

We suspect this was due to the fact that while the same default GA parameters (see Table 12.10) had been used throughout all our experiments, this particular set of experiments entailed a much larger search space for the GA, which perhaps warranted increased population size, etc. In our future work, we also need to devise a GA convergence procedure which would reflect the search complexity and dimensionality associated with a particular optimisation problem.

It is interesting to compare the momentum parameters obtained here, as part of the GA-optimised set of momentum–RSI model parameters, with those obtained in the vanilla momentum experiments, where they alone comprised the entire set of model parameters. Note the results for the hours-A USD/DEM data. Here, the four momentum parameter values (52, 59, 0.6, 0.0013) are quite similar to the GA-optimised vanilla momentum model's (53, 61, 0.7, 0.0013). To a lesser extent, the same is also true in the case of the hours-B DEM/JPY data (23, 81, 0.8, 0.0013 vs. 20, 80, 0.7, 0.0007). This seems to suggest a degree of *separability* between the optimisation search over the momentum parameters themselves and over the RSI take-profit strategy's model parameters, somewhat surprising in light of, but not contradicted by, our experience with the *ad hoc* application of the RSI trigger (which yielded no performance improvement whatsoever). For the hours-A USD/DEM series, the GA-optimised momentum–RSI model also executed a total of two traded positions, both of which were positive, as did the GA-optimised vanilla momentum model on the same data. From a GA perspective, this could be loosely construed as similarity in phenotype behaviours. At any rate, we suspect the slight increase in performance (4.0 vs. 2.7% ACG in-sample) to be attributable to the RSI profit-taking system arbitrating better exit points. But overall, the introduction of this new RSI take-profit strategy did not seem to produce reliable performance improvement over the vanilla momentum model.

7 CONCLUSIONS

Within the context of this case study, a GA has been used as a parametric optimiser. That is, it searches over the specified model parameter space in order to optimise a real-time trading performance measure. As the GA is not yet entrusted with the task of model building, the performance of a GA-optimised trading model is still bounded by the functionality of the model class whose parameters it optimises. As we have started with simple moving average-based trend indicator models, the next natural step is to investigate more sophisticated trading models, i.e. more information-rich *signal* models as well as more robust *position* models.

What has been achieved thus far in this case study can be best thought of as a foundation for future exploration in the area. Here, we have shown that a GA is capable of searching over a given trading model's parameter space and optimising the trading performance criteria with respect to the in-sample data period. However, despite our initial hope that simple momentum-based trend indicator models, while they may achieve moderate in-sample gains, would remain stable with regards to the out-of-sample performance evaluation and robust with respect to shifting market dynamics, our results have demonstrated that some optimised models, while clearly showing in-sample profits, failed to make positive returns on the out-of-sample runs.

This cannot be emphasised enough. The single most important lesson which our experience with the GA methodology has borne out concerns the out-of-sample performance evaluation. Keep in mind that the basic materials we work with, the financial time series trading signal models, are not endowed with machine-learning capability. As the models are optimised with respect to the in-sample measures, it is of no surprise that the GA would optimise the in-sample performance to the detriment of the out-of-sample measure. Our experimentation with larger population sizes has revealed greater disparity between the in-sample and the out-of-sample performance numbers. And one cannot simply incorporate out-of-sample performance evaluation as a second criterion, as per bi-criteria optimisation, for that would effectively merge the two previously independent data sets, thereby compromising the integrity of the out-of-sample testing procedure. As a remedial measure, perhaps our 'best so far' out-of-sample solution should be updated, not just with every new generation's best in-sample, but with a few 'top solutions'. We put forward that this and the surrounding issues are perhaps less than adequately addressed in the GA literature. This is no doubt due to the fact that a GA is an optimisation algorithm, while out-of-sample performance testing is commonly dealt with within the statistical estimation and/or machine-learning paradigms. As evolutionary optimisation has been employed within the context of artificial neural learning, we are optimistic that these issues will soon be resolved, both theoretically as well as empirically.

Our present task is twofold: implement signal and position models of greater sophistication and greater consistency in term of in-sample vs. out-of-sample performance measures, and develop a coherent ensemble system consisting of a multiplicity of signal models in the hope that the diverse market information they capture as individual signal models will make possible a more profitable and more stable trading system when they are used in conjunction. Ultimately, our aim is towards a globally optimised system where an evolutionary algorithm is employed to search combinatorially over the signal models' combination space as well as parametrically search over the parameter spaces of the individual signal models within the ensemble. This will no doubt require greater sophistication in terms of the genetic representation of the solution structure and the algorithmic representation of a search over a combinatorial–parametric space.

From this case study, we have been encouraged by the results, but equally made aware of the many more thorough analyses and empirical investigations that need to be carried out before these issues can be resolved and difficulties overcome.

ENDNOTES

1. A note should be made at this stage, namely that each sampling is activated only by the arrival of a *new* price. Thus, a 10-minute sampling period actually denotes waiting 10 minutes, then sampling the next incoming price, then waiting another 10 minutes, then sampling the next incoming price, and so on, similarly for the devolatilised series sampling. For the non-devolatilised series, this also means that the number of observations is not exactly equal to the reciprocal of the sampling interval multiplied by the total time span of the series.

2. See Vince (1990), where the gain/loss ratio is defined as

$$\frac{\text{total gain of winning positions}}{\text{total loss of losing positions}}$$

REFERENCES

Bäck, T., Hoffmeister, F. and Schwefel, H-P. (1991), 'A Survey of Evolution Strategies', in R.K. Belew and L.B. Bookers (eds), *Proceedings of the Fourth International Conference on Genetic Algorithms*, Morgan Kaufmann, San Mateo, Calif.

Bäck, T. and Schwefel, H-P. (1993), 'An Overview of Evolutionary Algorithms for Parameter Optimisation', *Evolutionary Computation*, 1(1), 1–23.

Cerny, V. (1985), 'Thermodynamical Approach to the Travelling Salesman Problem: an Efficient Simulation Algorithm', *Journal of Optimisation Theory and Applications*, 45, 41–51.

Chankong, V. and Haimes, Y. (1983), *Multiobjective Decision Making: Theory and Methodology*, North-Holland, New York.

Colin, A. (1994), 'Genetic Algorithms for Financial Modeling', in G. Deboeck (ed.), *Trading on the Edge: Neural, Genetic and Fuzzy Systems for Chaotic Financial Markets*, Wiley, New York, Ch. 9, pp. 148–173.

Davis, L. (1987), *Genetic Algorithms and Simulated Annealing*, Morgan Kaufmann, Los Altos, Calif.

Davis, L. (1991), *Handbook of Genetic Algorithms*, Van Nostrand Reinhold, New York.

Davis, L. (1994), 'Genetic Algorithms and Financial Applications', in G. Deboeck (ed.), *Trading on the Edge: Neural, Genetic and Fuzzy Systems for Chaotic Financial Markets*, Wiley, New York, Ch. 8, pp. 133–147.

Dunis, C. (1996), 'The Economic Value of Neural Network Systems for Exchange Rate Forecasting', *Neural Network World*, 6, 43–55.

Edmonds, A.N. and Kershaw, P.S. (1994), 'Genetic Programming of Fuzzy Logic Production Rules with Application to Financial Trading', *IEEE World Conference on Computational Intelligence*, Orlando, Fla.

Fogel, D.B. (1994), 'An Introduction to Simulated Evolutionary Optimisation', *IEEE Transactions on Neural Networks*, 5(1), 3–14.

Fogel, L.J., Owens, A.J. and Walsh, M.J. (1966), *Artificial Intelligence through Simulated Evolution*, Wiley, New York.

Goldberg, D.E. (1989), *Genetic Algorithms in Search, Optimisation and Machine Learning*, Addison-Wesley Reading, Mass.

Haykin, S. (1994), *Neural Networks: A Comprehensive Foundation*, McMillan College Publishing Company, New York.

Holland, J.H. (1975), *Adaptation in Natural and Artificial Systems*, U. of Michigan Press, Ann Arbor, Mich.

Jaynes, E. (1983), *Papers on Probability, Statistics, and Statistical Physics*, R.D. Rosenkrantz (ed.), Dordrecht, Holland.

Jones, A.J. (1995), *Model of Living Systems: Evolution and Neurology*, Lecture Notes, Imperial College of Science, Technology & Medicine, London.

Katz, J.O. and McCormick, D. (1997), 'Genetic Algorithm and Rule-based Systems', *Technical Analysis of Stocks & Commodities*, February issue, 46–60.

Kaufman, P. (1987), *The New Commodity Trading Systems and Methods*, Wiley, New York.

Kinnear, K.E. Jr. (1994), *Advances in Genetic Programming*, MIT Press, Cambridge, Mass.

Kirkpatrick, S., Gelatt, C.D. and Vecchi, M.P. (1983), 'Optimisation by Simulated Annealing', *Science*, **220**, 671–680.

Koza, J.R. (1992), *Genetic Programming: On the Programming of Computers by Means of Natural Selection*, MIT Press, Cambridge, Mass.

Ladd, S.R. (1996), *Genetic Algorithms in C + +*, M&T Books, New York.

Levitt, M. (1995), 'Machine Learning for Foreign Exchange Trading', in A-P. Referes (ed.), *Neural Networks in the Capital Markets*, Wiley, Chichester Ch. 16, pp. 233–243.

Mardia, K.V., Kent, J.T. and Biddy, J.M. (1994), *Multivariate Analysis*, Academic Press, London.

Masters, T. (1993), *Practical Neural Network Recipes in C + +*, Academic Press, London.

Nacaskul, P. (1997), 'Phenotype–Object Programming, Phenotype–Array Datatype, and an Evolutionary Combinatorial–Parametric Optimisation of a Financial Time-series Model-trading System', paper presented at the Fourth Forecasting Financial Markets Conference (FFM'97), London.

Rechenberg, I. (1965), 'Cybernetic Solution Path of an Experimental Problem', *Royal Aircraft Establishment Translation No. 1122*, Royal Aircraft Establishment, Ministry of Aviation, Farnborough, Hants.

Rogue Wave™ Software (1994), Tools.h++, Class Library, Version 6, Rogue Wave Software Inc., Oregon.

Ruggiero, M.A. (1994), 'How to build an artificial trader', *Futures: The Magazine of Commodities & Options [CMM]*, **23**(10), 56–58.

Ruggiero, M.A. (1995a), 'Taking Evolution into Warp Speed', *Futures-Cedar Falls [CMM]*, **24**(9), 42–44.

Ruggiero, M.A. (1995b), 'Building a Real Day-trading System', *Futures-Cedar Falls [CMM]*, **24**(14), 50–52.

Schnidrig, R. and Würtz, D. (1995), 'Investigation of the Volatility and Autocorrelation Function of the USD/DEM Exchange Rate on Operational Time Scales', paper presented at the High Frequency Data in Finance Conference, Zurich.

Schwefel, H-P. (1981), *Numerical Optimisation of Computer Models*, Wiley, Chichester.

Stroustrup, B. (1991), *The C++ Programming Language, 2nd edn*, Addison-Wesley, Reading, Mass.

Vince, R. (1990), *Portfolio Management Formulas*, Wiley Finance Editions, Wiley, New York.

Wilder, J.W. Jr. (1978), *New Concept in Technical Trading Systems*, Trend Research, Greensboro, NC.

Yip, P. and Pao, Y-H. (1993), 'A Fast Universal Training Algorithm for Neural Networks', *Proceedings of the 1993 World Congress on Neural Networks*, No. 3, pp. 614–621, International Neural Network Society.

Zhou, B. (1996), 'Forecasting Foreign Exchange Rates Subject to Devolatilization', in C. Dunis (ed.), *Forecasting Financial Markets*, Wiley, Chichester, pp. 51–68.

——— 13 ———
High Frequency Exchange Rate Forecasting by the Nearest Neighbours Method

HERVÉ ALEXANDRE, ISABELLE GIRERD-POTIN
and OLLIVIER TARAMASCO

1 INTRODUCTION

Financiers in the early 1990s showed intense interest in a new theory derived from physics and mathematics, namely that of deterministic chaos. Although many researchers attempted to verify the chaotic character of prices or profitability of financial series, no clear and irrefutable response was forthcoming. However, the deterministic nature of chaotic processes related to the complexity of attractors opened up the way for a new forecasting method based on the nearest neighbours methodology.

Over the same period of time, advances in data processing techniques made it possible to store and use 'high frequency' financial time series. Empirical studies can now be made of financial series with frequencies of well under 1 hour. Some databases, such as the one used herein, contain quote-by-quote data. Increasing the series' frequency over the same period does not improve the measurement of chaos, but the use of high frequency series does lead to a change of scale that may enhance the detection of chaos.

The aim of this chapter is to apply the nearest neighbours forecasting method, a non-parametric method, to three series of high frequency exchange rates (DEM/FRF, USD/FRF and USD/DEM) after verifying the chaotic nature of the series by appropriate methods. This nearest neighbours method is based on the

Nonlinear Modelling of High Frequency Financial Time Series.
Edited by Christian Dunis and Bin Zhou. © 1998 John Wiley Sons Ltd

existence of a strange attractor for the series and on the fact that, despite the sensitivity to initial conditions that characterises such series, very short-term forecasting is still possible. To this end, section 2 sets out the forecasting method based on nearest neighbours after a brief presentation of the characteristics of a chaotic series. Section 3 reviews the value of high frequency data and the specific features of such data. Finally, section 4 tests the forecasting method on three series of high frequency exchange rates after testing the chaotic character of each series by calculating their highest Lyapunov exponent.

2 CHAOS AND NEAREST NEIGHBOURS FORECASTING

Chaos is a deterministic process the trajectories of which look like those of stochastic processes. Such a phenomenon is only possible if the relation that links the system variables over time is nonlinear.

A deterministic dynamic system is described perfectly if we know its state vector x_t (of dimension n, equal to the number of variables in the system) at each instant and the differential equations governing it. But sometimes the observer only has at any instant a partial measure of the process state: these are observations a_t (dimension 1). Generally, the time series of real numbers a_t can be explained deterministically if there is a system (h, F, x_0) such that

$$h : R^n \to R \qquad F : R^n \to R^n \quad h \text{ and } F \text{ are deterministic functions}$$

$$\begin{cases} a_t = h(\mathbf{x}_t) \\ \mathbf{x}_t = F(\mathbf{x}_{t-1}) \quad \text{for } t \geq 1 \end{cases} \quad \text{for a discrete system}$$

$$\begin{cases} a_t = h(\mathbf{x}_t) \\ \dfrac{d\mathbf{x}_t}{dt} = F(\mathbf{x}_{t-1}) \quad \text{for } t \geq 0 \end{cases} \quad \text{for a continuous system}$$

x_0 is the initial condition ($t = 0$).

F and x_t are known to nature but not to the observer. The observer collects observations $a_t = h(\mathbf{x}_t)$ where h is a measuring instrument. With respect to the applications in this chapter, observations a_t are relative variations in the exchange rates connected by an unknown factor h to the unknown state vector x_t of dimension n, which is also unknown. (In the present case, the components of vectors x_t may be the actual exchange rates and other economic variables likely to influence these exchange rates.)

Such a definition of the deterministic process is not enough to produce a chaotic dynamic system. Deterministic chaotic systems possess two other characteristic properties: their attractor and their sensitivity to initial conditions.

2.1 Attractor

If by definition x_t the state vector defined in R^n is the set of coordinates representing the state of a dynamic system at a given moment t, system evolution can be pointed out by the trajectory of x_t in the state space R^n. As they evolve, dynamic systems may retain the state-space volume (conservative systems) or on the contrary reduce it (dissipative systems): either x_t extends to all of R^n, or x_t ends up occupying only part of R^n. In the latter case, the trajectory leads to and remains in a part X of R^n termed the attractor.

There are several types of attractors defined in this way. The simplest is the point. All trajectories converge upon a fixed point. There may be several points of attraction for the same system. Each then has its attraction manifold. These manifolds may have highly complex structures that are fractal in Mandelbrot's sense (i.e. they are scale-invariant, having the same ordered structure when examined under increasing magnification). The second category of attractors is periodical. An ellipse is such an attractor. Finally, the last category and the one that interests us more especially is that of chaotic or strange attractors (notice that quasi-periodicity is one of the transient phases towards chaos). They may take on various shapes (e.g. Lorenz's butterfly with dimension between 2 and 3). They are termed 'strange' not because of their geometrical aspect but because of divergence or sensitivity to initial conditions.

Chaos and fractals are very often associated, but the two concepts are only superficially related. Fractals are static objects and the order of appearance of points on the figure is not a matter for study. By contrast, chaos is about dynamic processes and trajectories. Fractals are part of geometry, chaos is part of process dynamics. Eckmann and Ruelle (1985) explain that chaotic (or strange) attractors and fractal attractors are unrelated concepts. Even if strange attractors are usually fractals (as with the most famous example, Lorenz's attractor), there are such things as strange non-fractal attractors.

2.2 Sensitivity to Initial Conditions

In a chaotic process, two state vectors on the attractor however close in R^n will have divergent trajectories. The system evolves by contracting in some directions and diverging in others. In practice, this means that a very small measurement error in the initial conditions entails large forecasting errors beyond the very short term. Now there is always some uncertainty in knowing the initial condition. Laskar (1992, p. 202) provides an example concerning the chaotic behaviour of the trajectories of planets of the inner solar system (Mercury, Venus, Earth and Mars): 'A 0.000 000 01% error in the initial conditions leads to an error of only 0.000 000 1% after 10 million years but the error reaches 100% after 100 million years.'

For financial applications, sensitivity to initial conditions makes a chaotic process consistent with the occurrence of risk. If a financial series is chaotically deterministic, the price over the coming period (not too short) may be anywhere (on) the attractor. For an investor, it is as though the price were (fixed by) observation of a random variable. The values observed have the statistical properties of a sample of values drawn at random on the attractor in keeping with ergodic probability.[1]

In order to specify a chaotic process two characteristics must be ascertained: the dimension of the attractor measured by the correlation dimension and sensitivity to initial conditions measured by the first Lyapunov exponent.

2.3 Forecasting

If the process that generates exchange rates is non-chaotically deterministic, forecasting of the future rate is immediate: to determine future rates exactly, one need simply apply the evolution function to past rates. The forecasting error on the future rate is equal to the measurement error on the current rate. If the process generating exchange rates is chaotically deterministic, this property becomes false. Because trajectories diverge, an error of one-tenth of a per cent on the current rate can rapidly evolve into an error of several percentage points, thus prohibiting any long-term forecasting.

However, provided that the Lyapunov exponents are not too high, it is possible to obtain a correct short-term forecast. There remains one problem to overcome though: it is not state vector x_t that is observed directly but a transformation of that vector (observations a_t) via the measuring instrument h. Takens's theory (1981) can be used to ascertain the properties of the entire system from incomplete data.

From a time series of dimension 1, comprising T observations $\{a_1, \ldots, a_T\}$ we can construct $T - m + 1$ vectors with m dimensions $(a_t)_t = 1, T - m + 1$, termed historical-m values, whose components are consecutive values of the observed series:

$$\mathbf{a}_t^m = \begin{pmatrix} a_t \\ a_{t+1} \\ a_{t+m-1} \end{pmatrix} \quad t = 1, T - m + 1$$

Construction of the historical-m values is a reconstruction operation. Takens's theory states that provided a sufficiently large value of m is chosen, the behaviour of the historical-m values imitates that of the unknown underlying system. In particular, if the system is based on chaotic dynamics, the historical-m values also behave chaotically. In practice, m is large enough if m is greater than or equal to $2n + 1$ where n is the unknown dimension of the state vector, the dimension we are trying to estimate. In this case, m is termed the embedding dimension.

For an embedding dimension m and for a discrete system, there is a function $\psi^m : R^m \to R^m$ such that $\mathbf{a}_t^m = \Psi^m(\mathbf{a}_{t-1}^m)$ for $t \geq 1$. To predict the next exchange rate (a_{t+1}), one need simply estimate the function ψ^m from the trajectory $(a_s, s \geq t)$ and apply the estimate to vector $\mathbf{a}_t^m$. This produces a vector $\hat{\mathbf{a}}_{t+1}$ whose last component is the estimate of the next exchange rate.

2.4 The Nearest Neighbours Method

The nearest neighbours method consists of estimating the vector $\mathbf{a}_{t+1}^m$ from the evolution of one or more points $(\mathbf{a}_s^m, s < t)$ close to $\mathbf{a}_t^m$. The simplest method consists of:

- Finding the nearest neighbour to $\mathbf{a}_t^m$ in the past, i.e. finding an index $s < t$, such that $\|\mathbf{a}_t^m - \mathbf{a}_s^m\|$ is minimum.
- Estimating $\mathbf{a}_{t+1}^m$ by $\hat{\mathbf{a}}_{t+1}^m = \mathbf{a}_{s+1}^m$.

A more sophisticated method consists of establishing a linear interpolation of the evolution of a set of points close to $\mathbf{a}_t^m$ and applying the function to $\mathbf{a}_t^m$. More precisely, the following calculation is made. Let $p_1, p_2, \ldots, p_n$ be the n nearest neighbours to $\mathbf{a}_t^m$ and let $q_1, q_2, \ldots, q_n$ be their evolution after one iteration of the system. A linear approximation of the evolution of these n points can be written using a matrix U of dimensions $m \times m$ and a vector b of dimension m, by the relation

$$U p_i + b = q_i \quad i = 1, \ldots, n$$

Note P is the $(m + 1) \times n$ matrix defined by

$$P = \begin{bmatrix} P_{1,1} & P_{1,2} & \cdots & P_{1,n} \\ P_{2,1} & P_{2,2} & \cdots & P_{2,n} \\ \cdots & \cdots & \cdots & \cdots \\ P_{m,1} & P_{m,21} & \cdots & P_{m,n} \\ 1 & 1 & \cdots & 1 \end{bmatrix} \qquad \text{where } p_{i,j} \text{ is the } i\text{th coordinate of point } p_j$$

B is the $m \times (m + 1)$ matrix defined by

$$B = \begin{bmatrix} u_{1,1} & u_{1,2} & \cdots & u_{1,n} & b_1 \\ u_{2,1} & u_{2,2} & \cdots & u_{2,n} & b_2 \\ \cdots & \cdots & \cdots & \cdots & \cdots \\ u_{m,1} & u_{m,21} & \cdots & u_{m,n} & b_m \end{bmatrix}$$

where $U = (u_{i,j})_{i,j=1,\ldots,m}$ and $b = (b_i)_{i=1,\ldots,m}$, and Q is the $m \times n$ matrix defined by

$$Q = \begin{bmatrix} q_{1,1} & q_{1,2} & \cdots & q_{1,n} \\ q_{2,1} & q_{2,2} & \cdots & q_{2,n} \\ \cdots & \cdots & \cdots & \cdots \\ q_{m,1} & q_{m,2} & \cdots & q_{m,n} \end{bmatrix} \qquad \text{where } q_{i,j} \text{ is the } i\text{th coordinate of point } q_j$$

giving

$$BP = Q$$

Breaking down the transpose P' of matrix P singular values gives

$$P' = WDV'$$

where:

- W is an $n \times (m + 1)$ matrix such that $W'W = I_{m+1}$, unitary matrix of order $m + 1$.
- V is an $(m + 1) \times (m + 1)$ matrix, orthogonal $(V' = V^{-1})$ whose columns are the eigenvectors of PP'.
- D is the $(m + 1) \times (m + 1)$ matrix, diagonal of singular values.

We obtain

$$B = QWD^{-1}V'$$

which can be used to estimate matrix U and vector b.

If certain singular values are close to 0 (which amounts to saying that matrix D is non-invertible, or close to being non-invertible), they may be eliminated in D together with the corresponding rows and columns in the W and V matrices.

The estimated value of $\hat{a}_{t+1}^m$ is then obtained by writing

$$\hat{a}_{t+1}^m = U a_t^m + b$$

3 HIGH FREQUENCY DATA IN FINANCE

Technological advances in data processing enabled intraday data to be used in finance. For the FX market, tick-by-tick data can now be studied. Guillaume et al. (1994) explain that Olsen & Associates have, for example, 8 238 532 quotations for the USD against the DEM for the period from 1 January 1987 to 31 December 1993, i.e. an average of 4500 quotations per day.

A serious drawback with tick-by-tick data is that they are not evenly spaced over time and are not amenable to classical time series processing. We may also ask whether it is time that defines information or information that creates the time unit. In other words, do we have to confine investigations to regularly spaced data (say every 3 minutes) even if this means using linear interpolation for the weekend when quotations are fewer and more widely spaced, or can we consider that each new quotation introduces a new unit of time with new information.

Müller et al. (1993) resolve the problem by defining the time unit as the interval between two quotations (theta time). Hence time is no longer defined ex ante but corresponds to the arrival of new information. This definition of time series lends more importance to periods with high activity levels while giving less weight to weekends and holidays.

Analysis of autocorrelations of price variations with a frequency of 20 minutes indicates an absence of memory (Guillaume et al. 1994). Furthermore, the analysis of absolute price variations generates richer information and exhibits considerable seasonality (physical time) which is scarcely reduced by the use of theta time. This last representation shows an autocorrelation function that decreases hyperbolically and non-exponentially, indicating an extensive and substantial memory in the series.

4 EMPIRICAL STUDY

The data are tick-by-tick observations but we wish to work with data with an average of 20-minute spacing for purposes of comparison with other studies.

For the empirical study we chose to work in tick time, i.e. one period for one quotation. For example, a financial series of 155 000 observations for 1 year runs to approximately $155\,000/360 = 430$ observations on average per day. By contrast, a 20-minute interval provides $3 \times 24 = 72$ observations per day. To achieve this frequency, we take only one observation out of $430/72 = 6$ observations made. Our sample has an average data spacing of 20 minutes. The use of tick time means our study is not biased by any significant seasonal variation as with Guillaume *et al.* (1994). Prices are market maker bid prices because market makers decide on the bid prices and then choose the spread to cover their risk. Returns are calculated by $r_{t,t+T} = p_{t+T} - p_t$ where p_t is the bid price.

4.1 Measuring the Fractal Dimension

The topological dimension is always integral and can in no way be used to measure objects whose characteristic feature is precisely that they are of non-integral dimensions. For this reason, we must resort to dimensions that can cope with the existence of measurements of objects with unusual dimensions (unless it is an integral dimension which is an unusual case).

Consider an object located in p-dimensional space. To cover this object will require $N(\varepsilon)$ hypercubes of side ε. (A hypercube is to n dimensions what a cube is to three dimensions.) The fractal dimension of the object, also termed the Hausdorff–Besicovitch dimension, is

$$D = \lim_{\varepsilon \to 0} \frac{\ln[N(\varepsilon)]}{\ln(1/\varepsilon)}$$

In many instances, though, this means of calculating the dimension of a fractal object has proved inadequate. The method works for fractals constructed on a recursive basis such as *Cantor dust* or *Koch flakes*. Otherwise we must resort to another means of rapidly evaluating a fractal dimension v. This dimension is less than but close to D. The value D is based on the attractor's geometric constitution and provides a maximum measurement of the attractor's dimension, whereas v depends on the density of points on the attractor.

Suppose there is a set of points uniformly distributed in a plane. $N(r)$ is the number of points of this set contained in a circle of radius r. Dimension v is determined by the actual definition of the fractal dimension. The fractal dimension describes the way in which an object fills the space where it is located. Therefore

v is calculated depending on the variation of $N(r)$ with r. For example, if the points lie on a curve (dimension 1) then

$$N(r) \sim r \quad \text{or} \quad N(r) \sim r^v \quad \text{with } v = 1$$

If the points are uniformly distributed on a plane (dimension 2) then

$$N(r) \sim r^2 \qquad v = 2$$

Let us consider a chaotic process $\{Xt\}$. There is no significant correlation between this variable at time t and at time $t - \tau$. However, all the points are located on the same attractor and there is some spatial correlation taken into account in the following way:

$$C(r) \lim_{m \to \infty} \frac{1}{m^2} \sum_{t,s=1}^{m} H(r - |\vec{x}_t - \vec{x}_s|)$$

where H is the Heaviside function giving

$$\begin{array}{ll} 1 & \text{if } |\mathbf{x}_t - \mathbf{x}_s| < r \\ 0 & \text{elsewhere} \end{array}$$

$C(r)$ is also $N(r)$ counted in the hyperspheres centred on all points of the attractor, which makes the calculation longer but more accurate. $C(r)$ is consequently proportional to $N(r)$ and therefore

$$C(r) \sim r^v$$

Grassberger and Procaccia (1983) define the attractor's dimension on this basis as

$$v = \frac{\log C(r)}{\log r}$$

The result depends on the value ascribed to r. If r is too large then almost all the points are covered and $C(r)$ approaches 1. Conversely, if r is too small then few points are covered and the calculation of $C(r)$ is also poor as it is too weak in this case. Ramsey and Yuan (1987) show that the value found for v may be biased in samples of 2000 observations.

One solution suggested is to calculate the dimension for different values of r. Then the different values of n found can be represented in a Cartesian mapping with $\log(r)$ on the x-axis and $\log(C(r))$ on the y-axis. The slope of the straight line obtained with the different points provides an estimate of the covering dimension. However, there is no indication a priori as to the dimension of the phase space in which the system operates, as the only information available is a one-dimensional series of values xt.

Vectors $\mathbf{x}_1^p = (x_1, \dots, x_p)$ must be constructed on the basis of this series and $C(r)$ calculated for increasing vector sizes. Each time around, the slope is calculated from the linear part of points found in the previously defined Cartesian map.

In the case of white noise, for example, the slope will increase indefinitely with the size attributed to the vector. That reflects the fact that white noise is random and a phase space of infinite dimension is required to represent it (an infinity of initial conditions). In the case of a system with a fractal attractor of finite size, dimension v is independent of p which is the 'embedding dimension'. Slope v remains constant even when p increases. This constant slope is the attractor dimension. If v is a non-integral value, then the attractor is fractal and therefore the series is chaotic.

In the following graphs (Figures 13.1(a), 13.2(a) 13.3(a)), we plot $\log(C(r))$ versus $\log(r)$ for different values of m. For each value of m, different points are calculated depending on the value of r. Then we calculate the slopes of the line plotted for a given value of m. In the other graphs (Figures 13.1(b), 13.2(b) and 13.3(b)), we plot the slopes versus m. If the slope converges to a finite value, this last is the calculated dimension of the attractor. If it is non-integer then the series possesses a fractal attractor, and we need to estimate the largest Lyapunov exponent.

The slope increases with m. It means that there is no attractor and the series cannot be said to be chaotic. So we do not apply the nearest neighbours method to it.

The results, here, are surprising because the value of the slope reaches a maximum for m equal to 5 and then decreases when m increases. We shall calculate the Lyapunov exponent of this series before applying the nearest neighbours method.

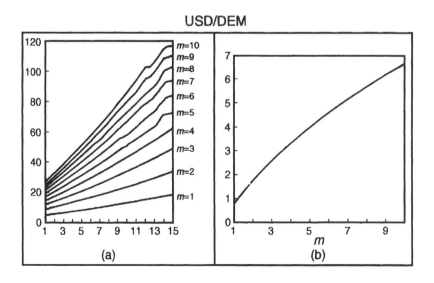

Figure 13.1   USD/DEM

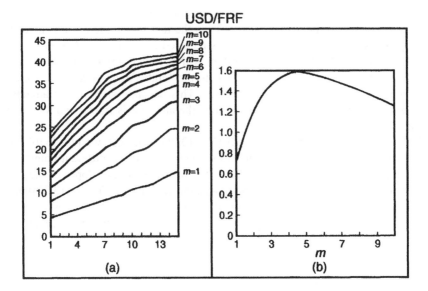

Figure 13.2 USD/FRF

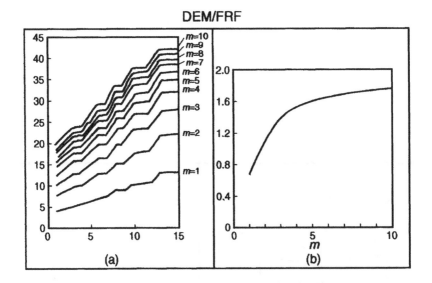

Figure 13.3 . DEM/FRF

In Figure 13.3(b) (slope versus m) we can clearly see that the slope converges to a value near to 1.75 which can be seen like the fractal dimension of the attractor of the series.

But measuring this fractal dimension is not enough to characterize chaos and then we calculate the Lyapunov exponent which is the only way to 'test' for chaos.

4.2 The Largest Lyapunov exponent

The geometrical analysis of systems developed by Poincaré (1890) can be used to investigate the stability of a set of trajectories of a system. Hyperbolic dynamic systems are of special interest to us as they display the properties defined as sensitivity to initial conditions and correspond to certain properties of the chaotic process. Thus in unstable systems, the number of separate trajectories increases exponentially with the size of observations. The exponent depends directly on the entropy of the system (Sinaï 1992).

Expressed differently, this means that a difference between two trajectories increases over time as e^{λ}. The value λ is Lyapunov's exponent which also measures the system's entropy. More strictly, there are as many Lyapunov exponents as dimensions to the system; each measures the force of contraction or extension exerted upon the system by one dimension. With a fixed point, for example, all the Lyapunov exponents are negative. For a limit cycle or torus, the greatest Lyapunov exponent is zero because any shift along the trajectory is neither amplified nor diminished over time. Conversely, the highest exponent in a deterministic chaotic system is positive, reflecting entropy, i.e. the creation of information. The problem now is to introduce a method of calculating this exponent for trajectories whose underlying structural form is unknown.

To do this, let us assume $\mathbf{x}_{t+1} = F(\mathbf{x}_t)$ is a system of dimension N. Let us set $\mathbf{x}_0$ as the initial condition. We shall now study the behaviour of the trajectory for an initial condition y_0 close to x_0. In order to express the comparative evolution of the two trajectories, we need merely express the order 1 Taylor development in the neighbourhood of $\mathbf{x}_t$:

$$F(\mathbf{y}_t) = F(\mathbf{x}_t) + D_x F(\mathbf{x}_t)(\mathbf{y}_t - \mathbf{x}_t) + \text{remainder}$$

where $D_x F(\mathbf{x}_t)$ is the square matrix of order N of the first derivatives at time t.

Linear approximation allows us to write

$$F(\mathbf{y}_t) - F(\mathbf{x}_t) = D_x F(\mathbf{x}_t)(\mathbf{y}_t - \mathbf{x}_t)$$

By writing $\mathbf{y}_t - \mathbf{x}_t = \mathbf{u}_t$ and therefore $F(\mathbf{y}_t) - F(\mathbf{x}_t) = \mathbf{u}_{t+1}$, the previous equation becomes

$$\mathbf{u}_{t+1} = D_x F(\mathbf{x}_t)\mathbf{u}_t$$

Where the first derivative matrix is not time-dependent, the properties of system stability can be deduced from the eigenvalues of the matrix. But here the matrix is time-dependent. Hence, we must use mean values to be able to draw any conclusions. Standardising the previous equation gives

$$\|\mathbf{u}_{t+1}\| = \|D_x F(\mathbf{x}_t)\mathbf{u}_t\|$$

By rewriting the equation we can bring out the local expansion rate:

$$\|\mathbf{u}_{t+1}\| = \frac{\|D_x F(\mathbf{x}_t)\mathbf{u}_t\|}{\|\mathbf{u}_t\|}\|\mathbf{u}_t\| = L(t)\|\mathbf{u}_t\|$$

$L(t)$ is the local expansion rate, it measures the rate of expansion along the trajectory at time t in direction $\mathbf{u}_t$. This magnitude can be used to obtain a value characterising the deviation at time t of two trajectories that were initially close to one another. The mean expansion rate which is the Lyapunov exponent must then be calculated:

$$\lambda(t) = \frac{1}{T}\sum_{t=1}^{T}\ln\frac{\|D_x F(\mathbf{x}_{t-1})u_t\|}{\|\mathbf{u}_{t-1}\|}\|\mathbf{u}_{t-1}\|$$

with

$$\mathbf{u}_{t+1} = D_x F(\mathbf{x}_t)\mathbf{u}_t \quad \text{and} \quad \|\mathbf{u}_0\| = 1$$

The point is that usually only the time series of the study variable is available, F is unknown. We need then to be able to calculate the first derivatives of a function without knowing the structural form. Wolf, Swift, Swinney and Vastano were the first to attempt to solve this dilemma in 1985.

Wolf et al. (1985) use an interactive procedure based on the comparison between the behaviour of the series and that of a series with a very close initial condition after reconstructing the series in a dimension calculated from the estimated fractal dimension.

Using this algorithm, the calculated largest Lyapunov exponent of each series is positive depending on the value of the parameter of the algorithm. This largest exponent is positive, even small, and we can conclude that the series is a chaotic series.[2]

4.3 Forecasting

A forecast was made for the series DEM/FRF and USD/FRF with an embedding dimension value of 5 or 7 and above all two different values of the number of

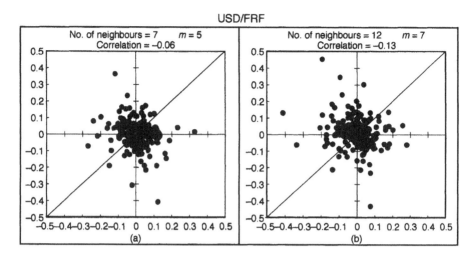

Figure 13.4   USD/FRF

near neighbours considered. In the first case, we consider 12 nearest neighbours and a dimension of 7 and in the second 7 nearest neighbours and a dimension of 5 (Figure 13.4).

Results tend to be poor (correlation between forecast and real value is negative) and the method appears to be inefficient.

Then, we applied the same method to the series DEM/FRF and we find more interesting results. Indeed, the correlation between forecast and real value is 0.094 (12 nearest neighbours and embedding dimension equal to 7) and 0.1273 (7 nearest neighbours and embedding dimension equal to 5) which is weak but somewhat less so than before.

These mixed results do not allow any conclusions to be made in favour of the nearest neighbour method for establishing forecasts on the series of high frequency exchange rates examined.

5 CONCLUSION

In this chapter, we examined the forecasting properties of the nearest neighbour method. Evidence from two series of high frequency exchange rates tends to indicate that the nearest neighbour forecasting method proves inconclusive. The correlation between the value forecast by the method and the actual value is low and does not allow us, at this stage, to confirm the occurrence of chaos in the series and the possibility of making use of such deterministic chaos to establish high frequency forecasts. However, the method should be applied to other high frequency series before drawing any definite conclusions.

Index

Index complied by Geoffrey Jones

Printed and bound by CPI Group (UK) Ltd, Croydon, CR0 4YY

23/04/2025

14660955-0001